MEN IN GROUPS

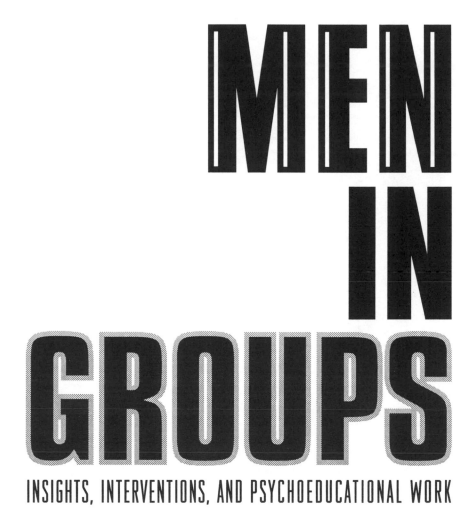

MEN IN GROUPS

INSIGHTS, INTERVENTIONS, AND PSYCHOEDUCATIONAL WORK

EDITED BY **MICHAEL P. ANDRONICO**

American Psychological Association, Washington, DC

Published by
American Psychological Association
750 First Street, NE
Washington, DC 20002

Copies may be ordered from
APA Order Department
P.O. Box 2710
Hyattsville, MD 20784

In the UK and Europe, copies may be ordered from
American Psychological Association
3 Henrietta Street
Covent Garden, London
WC2E 8LU England

Typeset in Goudy by PRO-IMAGE Corporation, Techna-Type Division, York, PA

Printer: Data Reproductions Corp., Rochester Hills, MI
Cover Designer: Supon Design Group, Washington, DC
Technical/Production Editor: Molly R. Flickinger

Library of Congress Cataloging-in-Publication Data
Men in groups : insights, interventions, and psychoeducational work /
    edited by Michael P. Andronico.
        p.   cm.
    Includes bibliographical references and index.
    ISBN 1-55798-326-7 (acid-free paper)
    1. Men (Psychology).   2. Group counseling.   3. Group psychotherapy.
I. Andronico, Michael P.
BF692.5.M45   1995
155.3'32—dc20   95-20968
                                                                                      CIP

British Library Cataloguing-in-Publication Data
A CIP record is available from the British Library

Printed in the United States of America
First edition

I dedicate this book to the men in my family:
my father, Paul Andronico; my brother, John Andronico;
my son, Steven Andronico; my brother-in-law, Peter Vaselekos;
and my son-in-law, Michael Flores.

CONTENTS

CONTRIBUTORS

Michael P. Andronico, University of Medicine and Dentistry of New Jersey, Robert Wood Johnson Medical School

Jose M. Arcaya, John Jay College of Criminal Justice

Robert L. Barret, University of North Carolina

Judith V. Becker, University of Arizona

Frances Bonds-White, Philadelphia, Pennsylvania

Gary Brooks, Olin E. Teague Veterans Center, Temple, Texas

John E. Calamari, Finch University of Health Sciences and the Chicago Medical School

Don R. Catherall, Phoenix Institute, Chicago, Illinois

W. Miles Cox, University of Wales, Bangor, Wales

Gregg A. Eichenfield, Family Services, Stillwater, Minnesota

Kendal Evans, California Family Study Center, Phillips Graduate Institute, North Hollywood

Joel C. Frost, Boston, Massachusetts

Barry G. Ginsberg, Center of Relationship Enhancement and Ginsberg Associates, Doylestown, Pennsylvania

Alex S. Hall, Saint Joseph's College

Jeffrey B. Harrison, Richard Hall Mental Health Center, Bridgewater, New Jersey

Michele Harway, California Family Study Center, Phillips Graduate Institute, North Hollywood

Arthur M. Horne, University of Georgia

David L. Jolliff, Phoenix Associates, Fort Wayne, Indiana

Kevin R. Kelly, Purdue University

Mark S. Kiselica, Trenton State College

Richard F. Lazur, Alaska Pacific University and University of Alaska

Ronald F. Levant, Cambridge Hospital and Harvard Medical School

David M. McPhee, River City Mental Health Center, St. Paul, Minnesota

Larry A. Morris, Tucson, Arizona

James M. O'Neil, University of Connecticut

Eric W. Roth, Colmery-O'Neil Veteran's Affairs Medical Center, Topeka, Kansas

Jeffrey D. Roth, Chicago, Illinois

Robert B. Shelton, Phoenix Institute, Chicago, Illinois

Jack Sternbach, Hay Associates, Cambridge, Massachusetts

David Sue, Western Washington University

Alexander Sutton, Sutton and Associates, Plainfield, New Jersey

Sam Tsemberis, Pathways to Housing and New York University Medical Center

Glenn W. Wissocki, Somerset Institute for Psychotherapy, Education, and Research, Somerset, New Jersey

PREFACE

Throughout my life and my professional career, I have been acutely aware of the phenomenon of the pressure that the traditional male role has placed on men in U.S. society. During my last 2 years of graduate school, I participated in a leaderless all-male student group. This group experience forever impressed on me the value of a group for personal growth and the need for men to gather together in groups to discuss their issues among themselves. Within a year of graduation, I was leading an all-male religious leaders' group (which continued for several years), and I have led various men's groups in the more than 35 years since the start of that group.

I readily embraced the beginnings of the women's movement as an opportunity for men, myself included, to be able to share the huge burden of responsibilities and pressures placed on men in American society. It is not by chance that I selected a career that is designed to help others empower themselves. Equality has true advantages for both genders.

As I continued my professional involvement with groups and group psychotherapy, I maintained an interest in all-male groups. A few years ago, I started to recognize the need for a wider dissemination of knowledge of group psychotherapy—in particular, knowledge of men's groups—in a variety of forms. I began to moderate panels on working with men in groups at the annual convention of the American Psychological Association (APA). After the first few panels, I decided that the positive response was indicative of the need for a compilation of the burgeoning work, both complete and in progress, regarding men in group settings. In fact, for many situations, if not most, therapy for men is best done in groups; it could even be said that therapy for men might be minimally effective if not undertaken in a group setting. The combination of these two factors—the growth in men's studies and the obvious value of work being done in a group setting with men—led to the conception of a book that would combine these areas.

In the past few years, an increasing number of books on men and men's issues have been published and well received. Following the popular books of the mythopoetic branch of the men's movement, mental health professionals began to get involved. This book is designed to fill a huge void of information concerning much of the new work with men and men's issues that is being done in the mental health field.

The main purpose of this book is therefore to compile an extensive overview of work that is currently being done concerning men's issues in the field of mental health. I hope that this book serves to both enlighten readers and stimulate their desire to pursue their own particular interests in helping men alleviate the disproportionate burdens of responsibilities, real or imagined, to allow them to attain a fuller expression of their potential and, in so doing, facilitate women in pursuing their own potential. I encourage readers to "follow their bliss" and hope that they experience the fun, caring, and fulfillment from their work with men that I have encountered in mine.

It is impossible to list all of the people who have contributed in one form or another to this book. I would like to first acknowledge my close colleague, Barbara Dazzo, for her encouragement, support, and caring as well as for her scholarly assistance. I also thank all of my colleagues at the Somerset Institute of Psychotherapy, Education, and Research. I would especially like to thank Glenn W. Wissocki and Bill Bishop, who have helped develop and lead the men's weekends and the men's programs at the institute.

I thank Jay Fidler for sparking my initial interest in group therapy and Bob Goulding for role modeling a spirit of innovation and excitement in his work. Thanks are also due to my many friends and colleagues at the American Group Psychotherapy Association and the New Jersey Group Psychotherapy Association for their contributions to my growth and development as a group psychotherapist. Likewise, I am grateful to friends and colleagues of Division 49 (Group Psychology and Psychotherapy) of the APA for the opportunity to widen my horizons in the field I love so much.

The many authors who have participated in writing this book have earned my gratitude for contributing their support and encouragement during the many stages of the book's development. Thanks also to Ron Wilder, Peggy Schlegel, Beth Beisel, and Molly Flickinger at the APA books department for suggestions and continuing encouragement. Thanks are due to my secretaries: Pat Cohen, who helped bring organization to chaos, and Jaya Bhambhwani, who stepped in and helped put the final pieces in place. Also, thanks to Norah McCormick for her editorial comments.

I give special thanks to my wife, Joan Cassano, whose quiet, steady love and support is greatly appreciated and has been invaluable in this project.

Finally, and perhaps most important, I would like to acknowledge the many, many men (and women) who have participated in workshops and various groups with me and thank them for teaching me so much.

MICHAEL P. ANDRONICO

INTRODUCTION

Since the 1960s, there has been a monumental change in Western society's outlook on gender roles. The contemporary women's movement has caused many to question the stereotypical thinking that has limited women's opportunities for achievement and well-being in the workplace, in the family, and in society as a whole. Women have been encouraged to empower themselves to counter these stereotypes, to claim their rights, and to exercise their responsibilities as participants who are fully equal (although, perhaps, different in some ways) to men in most spheres.

That gender stereotypes have also had deleterious effects on men has, however, only come into focus over the past 2 or 3 decades. Several studies have highlighted the fact that rigid gender role stereotyping may be as harmful to men as to women. Men in U.S. society are more likely to suffer heart disease than are woman before the age of 50, by a margin of 4 times (U.S. Department of Health and Human Services, 1990). Men's life expectancy also averages 8 years less than that of women (U.S. Bureau of the Census, 1990). But, as they enter the twenty-first century, many men are unaware of the negative influence of society's expectations of their gender. These expectations may contain overt and covert conflict, and they certainly involve stress. For example, men are expected to spend time being nurturing to their partners and children and sharing household chores while still climbing the ever-steeper corporate ladder, often at an accelerated pace. Although corporations no longer provide a safety net of job security for loyal employees, most men still feel that the primary responsibility of providing a financial safety net for their families belongs to them.

xvii

Some men feel expected to be Renaissance men on the weekend and skilled specialists during the work week. In the workplace, the land mines of sexual harassment charges may seem about to explode if their gender socialization results in an unseemly comment, however regretted.

After years of being taught to ignore, deny, or hide feelings, men now find that they are expected to be expert in expressing their emotions and receiving emotional communications from others, particularly women. Moreover, this expertise is often expected to emerge without training. Although women have been socialized to deal with feelings and to focus on interpersonal relationships, men have traditionally been taught to "fix" things or to solve problems by doing, not by talking. In fact, in the past (and, in many settings, in the present), men who were attuned to other's feelings or expressed their emotions openly and affectionately were often faced with derision, through the awkward silences of other men or being labeled as "sissy" when boys. Although younger men raised in certain family environments may be more oriented toward the expression of feeling in the context of relationships, it is clear that other young men and middle-age and older men are still struggling with these new expectations. Thus, whereas women have felt that they have been "dancing as fast as they can," some men are feeling that they no longer know the steps to the dance at all.

THE VALUE OF MEN'S GROUPS

In these times, men are privy to anxieties that their forefathers never faced. As they struggle to share responsibilities and power with women, they are faced with many unanswered questions, both person and societal. In what ways are men different from and the same as women? Is men's reduced longevity the price they must pay for "success" in their work roles? How can men prepare themselves for different gender roles? Can they afford to leave the definitions of these roles up to women? Where can they find role models to look up to?

This book argues that groups—based in therapy, education, and support—are ideal forums in which to raise and consider these and many other issues pertinent to men in the twenty-first century. Groups are facilitative during times of transition, and men are more familiar with them than with any other type of format that is currently used for interpersonal growth and change (e.g., individual or family therapy).

Men have participated in groups for centuries. They have gathered together in armies, monasteries, universities, Alcoholics Anonymous fellowships, and industrial groups. Younger men have found satisfaction in Boy Scouts, athletic teams, and fraternities. This orientation toward banding together for a common purpose and a shared group identity makes groups ideal settings in which men can explore and learn new gender roles and responsibilities.

However, many questions remain to be answered when considering groups as vehicles of growth for men. If group psychotherapy is considered the treatment of choice for today's male, for example, then one must ask what the special challenges and opportunities are for males involved in this form of treatment (Krugman & Osherson, 1993). Therapists have historically had difficulty engaging men in psychotherapy, particularly in group settings. Many men fear that therapy will be an environment in which they will be shamed and humiliated for displaying their vulnerabilities. How, then, can therapists hope to attract men to this mode of treatment? If educational groups can help men with their roles, such as parenting, then what should such groups teach, and how should the material be taught so that it is both effective and cost-efficient? If support groups can help men deal with transitions, such as divorce, then how are these groups best structured? Moreover, how can all of these groups support men in addressing the issues that face them as men in today's world? Finally, how can one reach the most men who need assistance while still working within the constraints of time and financial resources? This last question gains even more importance as the nation's health care crisis continues.

Despite the number of unanswered questions, it is already known from clinical experience and data that groups can engender the kinds of changes in people that are not as easily achieved in other modalities (Alonso & Rutan, 1984). Cohesion, the strength of group norms, commitment, and self-disclosure in groups continue to be among the dynamics that Yalom (1995) described as unique and Rosenbaum, Lakin, and Roback (1992) affirmed in their chapter on psychotherapy in groups.

Particularly powerful is the contribution of the group modality in combating the alienation that men may feel today. Whether educational, supportive, or therapeutic in nature, groups help people feel more connected with each other and with themselves. The sense of community engendered by groups leads men to feel less isolated and alone in this age of family strife and divorce, economic uncertainty, mobility and rootlessness, and the information explosion. Groups can provide protection and support from compensatory behavior, such as addictions (to alcohol and other drugs, work, or gambling), and from the overemphasis on the consumption of material goods that pervades society (particularly through the media). As men observe other men coping in groups, they discover alternatives to misusing power (e.g., violence) when they are feeling powerless.

One way in which groups have been powerful has been in getting men in touch with their spiritual sides. Although women (as well as some men) have found organized religion a way to express spirituality, some men have found that they need alternative ways to approach this crucial aspect of life. A prime resource in this regard has been the men's movement.

THE MEN'S MOVEMENT AND OTHER ROOTS

The beginnings of the men's movement were in gatherings of men in large groups, led by such charismatic leaders as Robert Bly, Michael Meade, Joseph Campbell, and James Hillman. Values and other dynamics related to spirituality have been core aspects of such groups. One result of this work is a reorientation toward appreciating elders as sources of wisdom, knowledge, and experience rather than eschewing them as out-of-date models in today's world. Today it is becoming more common, particularly in urban areas, to find men meeting in smaller groups to continue their discussion of gender roles and related issues.

Other than leading discussion groups, mental health professionals have not typically taken leadership roles in such groups. In fact, it has only been fairly recently that they have made significant contributions to the area of men's studies and services designed with the special needs of men in mind. As they continue to make their way into this territory, mental health professionals bring a wealth of psychological knowledge and skills that can be honed to the advantage of the men's movement as well as the growth of individual men. As they blaze this trail, such professionals need an avenue to share what they have learned about men and about men in groups, how they have learned it, and how this knowledge can be integrated with more general psychological knowledge about human growth and development. This book was created in part to provide such an avenue. It has been expressly written to accomplish the first two of these goals, and it will be successful if it serves as a springboard and invitation to others to work toward accomplishing the third.

SCOPE AND ORGANIZATION OF THE BOOK

This book was written for all who have an interest in men's issues, particularly as they manifest themselves in group settings. Its main purpose is to provide, in one resource, an extensive overview of the work in progress in the area of men's issues in the field of mental health. This "one-stop shopping" book offers the opportunity of an overall view of the issues that men in general face in America, as well as a wide range of programs designed to address those issues. This is not an encyclopedic work, covering every conceivable topic and approach, but one that ranges far enough to give the reader a thorough idea of what is presently being done. I hope that the information it conveys stimulates others to apply some of this work in their own areas of interest and expertise. Throughout the book, chapter authors deal in detail with the group setting and how to best use this crucial modality and the various interventions associated with it.

The book will appeal to a wide range of those interested in men's issues and various group programs. Members of this audience range from undergraduate students in the various helping professions that deal with men to graduate students in these fields as well as experienced professionals who wish to gain an overview of this area of study.

In the various chapters of this book, men struggle to have better relationships with themselves, their society, their parents, their children, and their partners. Other men discover the value of mentoring, the need for new skills and knowledge, and the roadblocks that society still places in the way of full development of members of both genders. Still others grapple with alcoholism, with their abuse of women, and with their own abuse in childhood. The authors provide clinical experiences with men from a wide range of backgrounds: Middle-class men, men who are homeless, men of varied ethnic backgrounds, and gay men are all represented.

In thinking of themselves as facilitators, mental health and other professionals will learn new ways of working with men and will have at their disposal a wide range of interventions. In addition to describing verbal discussions and interactions among group members, chapter authors cover the use of didactic materials, nonverbal communication techniques, letter and journal writing, and action-oriented methods of working with men. Some chapters discuss the use of multimedia techniques, whereas others convey treatments that involve music, flowers, and other cultural and natural resources.

The book is organized into four parts. Each part typically contains chapters on therapy, support, and educational groups, some of which have overlapping aspects of other types of groups. The structure of many of the chapters is similar. First, the authors orient the reader in the cultural aspects to be examined, then they discuss how a particular group is run—what works and what to avoid.

Part I presents chapters that primarily discuss all-male, homogeneous groups. One of the benefits of having men meet in these all-male groups is that men are used to being in groups with other men, to achieve goals and solve problems. This team orientation reduces their initial anxieties and appeals to their cognitive orientation. The absence of women tends to both reduce potential competitive and shaming elements of the group and reduce sexual tensions. The supportive and cooperative aspects of male bonding tend to be more easily evoked in an all-male group.

For some men, homophobic fears may be evoked in all-male group interventions. For others who rely on the "soft shoulder" of a woman to express their feelings, the all-male group may also be initially threatening. However, the experiencing of support and encouragement for emotional expressiveness in such groups usually results in new, profound, and positive experiences for men.

Part II contains chapters in which mixed groups predominate. The members of these groups can vary in ethnic background, sexual orientation, or gender. Similar advantages and disadvantages apply here as in Part I. In addition, the chapters in this part tend to be more descriptive of how various categories of men tend to react in different types of groups. The value of these chapters is in how they (a) help the reader understand the cultural dynamics that influence men in these groups and (b) give potential group leaders specific insights and interventions to use, whether they are treating men in homogeneous groups, mixed groups, or other forms of therapy.

Because parenting is one of the most important roles for men (if not the most important), Part III is devoted to chapters on fathering and being fathered. The blurring of gender roles in U.S. society during the past few decades has been accompanied by a blurring of the role of fatherhood. The chapters in this part do not put forth any definitive answers about what a father should or could be. They do, however, give concrete examples of how men can develop fathering skills that can substantially improve their relationships with their children. These skills are particularly crucial for working with families in which parents are not together or have teenage fathers.

Part IV looks at the darker side of being a man in today's world. The hazards of alcohol problems for men and their special needs in recovering from trauma are described. Battering and sexual offenses against others are viewed from a perpetrator-treatment perspective. Men who are not abusive themselves are beginning to realize that they must hold accountable and seek to change other men who do victimize people. Apart from the moral correctness of this position, men must do this if they are to expect females and other victimized groups (e.g., gay men) to have the patience and energy to hear their struggles and participate in their growth.

Many of the groups described in Parts I–IV are therapy groups. Although others may not meet the criteria for conventional psychotherapy groups, they are nonetheless therapeutic in effect and may act to reduce the need for formal psychotherapy or its length. Support and educational groups may serve as stepping stones to psychotherapy groups, both all-male and male–female groups. Men who participate in them are gradually introduced to the values of discovery and exploration of feelings (Levant, 1990), and they may be more likely to be open to group psychotherapy in the future. Support and educational groups have high value in and of themselves, however, as they may actually help prevent problems that might have required psychotherapeutic resources, not only for the male member but also for others in his relationship network (Andronico, 1995).

It should be noted that research in the area of men's groups is still in its infancy. Although the chapters in the book draw on published material, the authors' insights and suggestions for interventions are principally based on their multiple years of clinical experience working with men in groups. There is clearly a need for empirical support of these high expectations for men's groups as well as a need for continued research into the effects of gender roles on both men and women. Until those data are in, practitioners still need usable information and guidance that will help them work with men today.

CONCLUSION

As Robert Bly (1990) suggested, when male authority is vague and devalued—as Bly feels it is in American culture today—there is an increasing need to replace the often-absent father with a male image that men can relate to and respect. Men need other men to help them prepare to take leadership in the direction in which the gender wants to grow.

As I have said elsewhere (Andronico, 1993), the twenty-first century man needs to understand the circumstances of his predecessors' actions and to help build a better world in which the orientation is toward the empowerment of oneself and others in a cooperative rather than competitive mode. At the very least, men need to trade the "win at all costs" maxim for a win–win perspective that takes into account relationships and the environment. Indeed, given the gamut of social and ecological problems that men and their partners face in the twenty-first century, the entire metaphor of winning may best be replaced by one that has cooperation as its hub.

Although such a goal may be far from universally accepted, by men or by women, practically no one will deny that overt discussion of the changing roles between and among the genders is urgently needed. In this regard, groups—based in therapy, support, or education—can and should play a primary role. This book is devoted to supporting that goal and to the empowerment of all people—male and female.

REFERENCES

Alonso, A., & Rutan, S. (1984). The experience of shame and the restoration of self-respect in group psychotherapy. *International Journal of Group Psychotherapy, 38,* 3–14.

Andronico, M. P. (1993). Whither goes man? A vision for the 21st century male. *New Jersey Psychologist, 43,* 11–14.

Andronico, M. P. (1995, April). *Whither goes group psychotherapy? The future of groups.* Keynote address presented at the Annual Convention of the New Jersey Group Psychotherapy and Psychodrama Society, Lincroft, NJ.

Bly, R. (1990). *Iron John.* New York: Addison-Wesley.

Krugman, S., & Osherson, S. (1993). Men in group therapy. In A. Alonso & H. Swiller (Eds.), *Group therapy in clinical practice* (pp. 393–420). Washington, DC: American Psychiatric Press.

Levant, R. (1990). Psychological services designed for men: A psycho-educational approach. *Psychotherapy, 27,* 309–315.

Rosenbaum, M., Lakin, M., & Roback, H. B. (1992). Psychotherapy in groups. In D. Freedheim (Ed.), *History of psychotherapy: A century of change* (pp. 695–724). Washington, DC: American Psychological Association.

U.S. Bureau of the Census. (1990). *Statistical abstracts of the United States: 1990.* Washington, DC: U.S. Government Printing Office.

U.S. Department of Health and Human Services, Centers for Disease Control. (1990). *Vital statistics of the United States* (Pt. A, Section 1, p. 44). Washington, DC: U.S. Government Printing Office.

Yalom, I. (1995). *The theory and practice of group psychotherapy* (4th ed.). New York: Basic Books.

I

HOMOGENEOUS ALL-MALE GROUPS

INTRODUCTION

HOMOGENEOUS ALL-MALE GROUPS

Mental health professionals have typically had difficulty getting men into psychotherapy groups or groups that are largely publicized as being similar to psychotherapy groups. Chapters in the first part of this book cover the various issues involved in getting men into all-male groups and the dynamics that emerge when men meet together with other men for the purposes of self-improvement. Authors of varied backgrounds discuss in turn why the group setting is crucial and how to lead these groups.

Being in all-male, homogeneous groups presents some distinct advantages for male clients that are not available in groups with mixed memberships. By the same token, there are some disadvantages to men being treated in all-male groups. Identifying these issues and determining how to deal with them is the common goal of chapters in this part, in preparation for the contrast presented in Part II on men in mixed groups.

Part I covers a wide scope of all-male groups, with memberships ranging from homeless men to those seeking psychological and spiritual renewal at a weekend retreat. In the first chapter, Brooks reveals the obvious problems of dealing with men's reluctance to enter therapeutic milieus and offers suggestions to help overcome these impediments in a group setting. He explains such options as the "hard sell" versus the "soft sell," which can be chosen to increase the motivation of resistive men, along with specific group interventions designed to encourage emotional closeness, such as by increasing communication skills.

In the next chapter, McPhee combines useful methods of working with male groups with an approach for working beyond psychotherapy. He begins by describing techniques that are helpful in ongoing men's groups. He then goes on to describe a program for men who have "graduated" from psychotherapy groups into more long-term, self-led groups that no longer require the leadership of a professional therapist.

Next, Tsemberis invites the reader into a little-known area of contemporary society—that of the homeless male. He presents the many reality-based problems that these men face in their everyday lives and reveals how the group environment can help them develop more of a sense of community and improve their feelings about themselves.

Moving back to the problem of middle-class men, Jolliff and Horne explore their work with men of mainstream America. These authors detail how the group format can be used to the most benefit with this group of men. They also show how middle-class men can be helped to cope with and express feelings, particularly their anger and their grief, without the potentially inhibiting and shaming presence of women. Specific techniques that they have found useful with these men—such as the empty chair technique, role-playing, and letter writing—are elaborated on.

A growing population of men in American society are of Asian descent. These men face severe conflicts in their male roles because American society may have a very different cultural outlook on male behavior than that in which they were acculturated. Sue reveals much about these cultural discrepancies, the specific problems involved with these discrepancies, and how the proper use of the group setting is particularly helpful for Asian and Asian American men hoping to better adjust to American society. He points out specific interventions, such as feedback methods, which are helpful in reducing some of the potential constraints of the group setting for these men.

Moving into the academic setting, Eichenfield reports on an egalitarian group program for men in transition that is based at a university. Composed of male faculty, students, staff personnel, and their dependents, the group focuses on integration issues, class and classism, relational codependency, fathering, and dealing with women. Eichenfield discusses the value of this particular group setting as well as how one should manage the sensitive dynamics and interactions of this setting.

Continuing within the university setting and the theme of men helping other men, Horne, Jolliff, and Roth describe how the male group can become an important environment for mentoring. They examine the dynamics of the process of men mentoring other men and how this process can best be facilitated.

The final chapter in this part, by Wissocki and Andronico, concerns the use of a natural environment to help stimulate and deepen men's awareness and appreciation of nature—both the marvelous external, natural environment and the panorama of men's inner sensations and natures. A departure from the typically interactive, dynamic approach to groups is revealed. The authors combine aspects of the Native American vision quest, Ericksonian hypnotic methods, initiation ceremonies, and group dynamics to help men attending retreat weekends achieve a better appreciation of their psychological and spiritual selves.

1

TREATMENT FOR THERAPY-RESISTANT MEN

GARY R. BROOKS

Although many observers have reported substantive increases in the numbers of men seeking psychotherapy (Betcher & Pollack, 1993; Bograd, 1991; Erickson, 1993; Kupers, 1993; Meth & Pasick, 1990), traditional masculinity and psychotherapy continue to be problematic companions. Men remain outnumbered by women in therapists' offices by a ratio of 2:1 (Vessey & Howard, 1993), and, even when finding themselves there, men are far less likely to behave as "ideal" therapy clients. A prominent theme in the recent men's studies literature has been this poor match between the dictates of the male gender role and the patient role (Brooks, 1990; Ipsaro, 1986; Levant, 1990; Ragle, 1993; Scher, 1990; Silverberg, 1986; Solomon, 1982).

Levant (1990) noted,

> the male role requires that men be independent, strong, self-reliant, competitive, achievement-oriented, powerful, adventurous, and emotionally restrained. These characteristics . . . make it difficult for men to seek and use psychological services. (p. 309)

Scher (1990) has observed that, because male gender roles have two foci—to be in control and to be unlike women—the man who enters the therapy room does so because he believes "there is no alternative" (p. 323). Furthermore, "the typical qualities of men . . . are contrary to the qualities necessary for therapy . . . [that is,] openness and willingness to examine oneself with the aid of another person [and] accepting one's vulnerability" (Scher, 1990, p. 323). Similarly, Osherson and Krugman (1990) cited emotional restrictiveness, ego boundedness, and emphasis on rationality in men as explanations of why "male utilization of psychotherapy lags behind that of women" (p. 327). Finally, in his 1993 review of the literature, Ragle found strong agreement that male socialization encourages men to

> be controlling of the therapy process, to compete with the therapist, to be emotionally restricted, to avoid help in subtle ways, to demand tangible outcomes, to find the intimacy of the therapeutic relationship confusing and anxiety-provoking, and to misperceive the therapeutic relationship as sexual. (p. v)

Because of this problem of men and therapy, there have been many suggestions about how to make therapy more user-friendly for men. In general, the men's literature has suggested showing greater gender sensitivity, increased attention to special content issues, and efforts to help men with special process issues, such as emotional inexpressiveness. As yet, however, this new men's studies literature has not given much attention to two issues that may have critical bearing on the capacity of men to use therapy: (a) the degree that the male client is resistant—that is, the degree to which he seeks therapy to satisfy others rather than to satisfy himself—and (b) the selection of therapy format—individual, group, couples, or family. It is on these two issues that I focus in this chapter.

RECOGNIZING AND OVERCOMING THERAPY RESISTANCE

As noted above, traditional male socialization pressures men to resist any process like psychotherapy. During the past 2 decades, however, increasing numbers of men have become dissatisfied with the restrictiveness of the male role and have used psychotherapy as one avenue for exploration and change. In the terminology of O'Neil and Egan (1992), these men have used therapy as an important step in their "gender role journeys." This is an exciting new development and likely a major reason for the upsurge of writing about psychotherapy for men. But this trend toward help seeking among some men should not lead one to the naive assumption that most men who appear in therapists' offices are there primarily because they want help or because they are seeking dramatic alterations in their traditional masculine mode of life. My principal tenet in this chapter is that, at this historic juncture, most men who encounter a mental health professional are at best highly ambivalent about change and, to a large extent, are resistant to psychotherapy. Therefore, successful outcomes depend on therapists recognizing this resistance and "selling" men on the benefits of psychotherapy. If this is not done, then initial sessions may go poorly, which will solidify the man's resistance and reinforce his belief that therapy has nothing to offer him. However, if the initial visit is conducted effectively, it may become the first step of a resistant man's psychotherapy journey.

THE PSYCHOTHERAPY JOURNEY OF RESISTANT MEN

Ideally, men should be able to enter psychotherapy for any number of reasons and should be able to benefit from a wide variety of therapy modalities that could be entered at any point along their overall journey. However, traditional male socialization has made this very difficult, because most men, to some extent, have been trained to resist psychotherapy. Some men, in fact, will be profoundly resistant, seeing psychotherapy as representing everything they fear and despise: loss of control, dependency, vulnerability, and femininity. Such clients require special handling. Because there are more potential missteps and hazards in their therapy journeys, the all-male therapy group is offered as the best treatment alternative for therapy-resistant men.

In general, the journey of resistant men comprises (a) the initial therapy contact, in which change-resistant forces are either overcome or exacerbated; (b) intense involvement in a men's group, wherein change-enhancing forces are discovered and nourished and personal growth is realized; (c) transition to marital and family therapy, in which changes are translated into higher levels of relationship functioning; and (d) social activism, through which men encourage other men to consider new role potentials. In the following sections, I describe the first two phases of this journey.

Beginning the Journey: Selling Therapy

Because they do not want to ask for help and are, at best, ambivalent about change, traditional men will usually present for therapy with their emotional distress disguised behind other symptoms or interpersonal postures. Commonly they will have attempted to cope through flight, avoidance, or emotional suppression, and presenting symptoms may include alcohol or substance abuse, an unhappy marital partner, interpersonal violence, or a combination of all three. Sometimes these clients' psychic distress will be expressed somatically, and they will come concerned about their physical health or because their physician has insisted that they seek help. If the men have had difficulty "performing"—whether physically, vocationally, or sexually—they may seek a therapist with the narrow objective of improving their performance in a given area (e.g., improving a golf swing, selling more products, or having more sexual intercourse). At times, they will frame their distress as a lack of information and will come to a therapist with specific questions and a desire for concrete advice.

Whatever form this initial presentation takes, the therapist must take full advantage of this first contact to engage the reluctant man in therapy. If the therapist takes the position that therapy cannot begin unless the client displays a well-articulated rationale or uncomplicated motives, then a workable therapeutic contract will be difficult to achieve. Resistant men are unlikely to respond favorably to vigorous scolding, moralizing, or political lecturing. Sometimes, they may not be able to provide an acceptable answer to the commonly asked question "Just what is it that you expect to get from psychotherapy?"

Given these obstacles, it is incumbent on the therapist to take full advantage of first contact with the reluctant male client to sell the virtues and potentials of therapy. The therapist must choose between two options at this point: the hard sell or the soft sell.

Hard Sell

The hard-sell approach is one that directly identifies and challenges the resistance of the male client. It includes identifying the client's self-defeating methods of suppressing or denying psychic distress and pointing out the long-term implications of these patterns. The distinction between this hard sell and scolding or moralizing is that, although it does not ignore the victims of a man's behavior, the former also focuses on the man himself as a victim of contemporary role pressures. Men can be confronted supportively about how they have been programmed to live a life that ultimately does them great physical, psychological, and spiritual harm. Therapists familiar with recent men's studies literature should have no problems enacting this complicated confrontation, because they are able to see how modern men can be both the victimizers and the victimized.

In general, the hard-sell approach works best if it is novel to the man, that is, if it is not the predominant message that he has heard from members of his family and social network. Often, a man comes into therapy after having been told repeatedly about his failings and misbehaviors, and he may expect the therapist to provide more of the same. However, if the therapist surprises the male client by recognizing the psychic suffering and his hiding behind a mask of rage or frustration, then the man will usually respond very positively. Gender-informed therapists are readily able to show resistant male clients that therapy is not just for women and children but, in fact, has a great deal to offer men as well.

Soft Sell

Some men, perhaps because significant others have been giving them an unrelenting hard sell about the need for therapy, will do better with a soft-sell approach. This approach is one that recognizes the coercive forces in the man's life and emphasizes the therapist's respect for the man's good sense. It sides with the logic of the man's resistance (e.g., therapy is costly, time-consuming, and without thorough scientific validation of effectiveness) and encourages him to set his own timetable for considering change. However, while granting respect for knowledge about the man's own needs, the therapist can simultaneously request that he respect the therapist's experiences with other men and observations about pressures of modern manhood, as well as consider the possible penalties of unwillingness or inability to change. In this manner, the therapist can suggest that many men are finding their male roles to be burdensome, their lives to be unfulfilling, and their options to be narrow. The wisdom of the client's resistance is acknowledged, but he is nevertheless encouraged to consider a return visit for further discussions about the dilemmas of modern manhood.

SELECTING A FORMAT FOR THERAPY

To date, the men's psychotherapy literature has shown no consensus about the most effective therapy format for men. Below, I highlight the advantages of the all-male group and point out some potential problems with other therapy formats.

Pitfalls of Marital and Family Therapy

Previously, I have argued against "premature" marital and family therapy for resistant traditional men (Brooks, 1990, 1991). My basis for this point of view lies in the fact that marital therapy takes place in a political context, as it often begins with heterosexual couples in a state of political disequilibrium. Therapy may promote or sabotage relationship changes and, usually, the parties most interested in new relationship patterns are women. Conversely, the parties most interested in maintaining the status quo are men. Therefore, unless men are helped to recognize the potential advantages of new relationship patterns and the adverse consequences of rigid adherence to old ones, they will enter marital therapy with a limited and regressive agenda.

Most contemporary men enter therapy with some disadvantages not typical of women, partially because they have been taught to resist seeking help. In addition, men are relative newcomers to gender role explorations, whereas most women have spent years learning about the negative impact of culture on their gender. Women may often meet to compare notes and share feelings about their experiences, but men rarely do this. Women are more accustomed to self-reflection, whereas men are relative novices.

Problems of Individual Therapy

In many ways, the basic arrangement of the individual therapy format exacerbates men's difficulties in getting therapeutic help. Men are generally uncomfortable in emotionally intense, face-to-face relationships, which form the very essence of the individual therapy format. This is because a man tends to experience shame when asking for help, often feeling that he is the only man with such "weakness" or "frailty." The secrecy and insulation of individual therapy may perpetuate the troubled man's painful sense that his failures are unique. Similarly, many men are emotionally isolated from other men, even after completing individual therapy. This may be because men tend to think in hierarchical terms, anxiously measuring themselves against other men and thinking that they are supposed to stay "one up" on women. This can be particularly problematic in individual therapy, where a man is likely to react negatively to the "one down" aspect of his position as a client.

Benefits of the All-Male Therapy Group

Obviously the drawbacks of marital and individual therapies are neither universal nor insurmountable. Nevertheless, readers should keep these issues in mind while examining the considerable benefits of the male therapy group.

Offering Familiar Terrain

Exclusionary, ritualized male groups have been present throughout history (Farr, 1986; Kimmel, 1987; Tiger, 1969; Tolson, 1977), and although there has been considerable debate about the merits of these groups, there can be little doubt that they have been central to the male experience. Farr observed that men's groups are part of a general pattern: a collective alliance designed to promote masculinity through competition, aggressiveness, and independence. The male peer group has been described by Tolson as an informal culture that interacts with, and sometimes explicitly counteracts, the formal culture of the "school." Rotundo (1993) has provided enlightened historical analysis of how "boy culture" and "male youth culture" have distinctively shaped American manhood. Berstein (1987) described the male group as the "single most powerful source of rites of passage in the psyche of man" (p. 139). Pittman (1990) expanded on this description of actual social groups to describe a more abstract group, an "invisible male chorus that haunts men's lives" (p. 41). According to him, this male chorus—made up of all of a man's comrades, rivals, buddies, bosses, male ancestors, cultural heroes, and, especially, his father—pushes a man to "sacrifice more and more of his humanity for the sake of his masculinity" (p. 42).

On examining these men's groups—either the actual groups or those of the male psyche—one finds that they all share certain essential features. Specifically, they are pervasive in men's lives, they are rule governed, and they emphasize utilitarian functions far more than interpersonal intimacy, emotional expressiveness, and emotional support. For example, Aries (1976) found that when men gather together they are intensely competitive and preoccupied with hierarchy, to the point that all the men studied were continually concerned about "how they stood in relation to each other" (p. 13).

Because these natural groups have such salience in the lives of traditional men, it follows that the psychotherapy group can be an especially useful format with which to assist reluctant, yet troubled, men. Groups can offer a powerful reexperiencing of past stresses and failures with the male chorus, as well as a chance for nostalgic rediscovery of the more positive aspects of male-bonding groups. The critical issue, it seems, would be whether the group's pervasive influence can be used for therapeutic advantage without perpetuating narrow masculine-role behaviors. The challenge is for the therapist to use the male group to attract and hold men while expanding the male group's usual norms, to allow for greater role flexibility, decreased competitiveness, and enhanced intimacy among men.

Overcoming Men's Emotional Isolation

Although men often function in the public sphere, surrounded by work associates, and often report a large number of "buddies" or casual friends, most contemporary men live lives of marked emotional isolation. Research into gender patterns of friendship has revealed that, although men and women report similar amounts of time spent in same-gender friendships, they spend this time quite differently and their friendships are not at the same level.

Brehm (1985) found that men tend to have friendships characterized by "activity sharing" (e.g., hunting, working on a car motor, or playing cards) whereas women are more likely to have friendships characterized by interpersonal intimacy and discussion of feelings. This difference has been described by Wright (1982) as resulting from men's preference for "side-by-side" relationships and women's preference for "face-to-face" relationships. Many researchers have documented that traditional role-oriented men are less likely to "open up" and discuss personal problems with other men, even those men they identify as best friends (Dosser, Balswick, & Halverson, 1986; Snell, Miller, & Belk, 1988).

Because they lead these emotionally isolated lives, many men may find therapy groups to offer immense potential for interpersonal connectedness and recognition of common struggles. Yalom (1975) argued that a major curative factor of groups is their potential to promote a "universality," that is, a sense that "we are all in the same boat" (p. 8). In an all-male group, participants commonly discover the universality of men's issues, such as the challenges of the worker and good provider role, doubts about one's ability to meet the expectations of male family leadership, insecurities about sexuality, and emotional distance from children. When group members discover that most other men share these concerns, they usually experience, to borrow Yalom's words, a "disconfirmation of their feelings of uniqueness . . . a powerful source of relief" (1975, p. 7).

Countering Overdependence on Women

Because men limit emotional expressiveness and intimacy with other men, they tend to become emotionally overdependent on women. Pleck (1980), in a careful analysis of the roots of men's psychological need to control women, implicated two types of power that men grant to women. The first is "expressive power," whereby men have learned to experience their emotions vicariously through women. The second is "masculinity-validating power," whereby women are expected to validate a man's worth through appreciation of his contributions as a protector, provider, or sexual gratifier.

Others have also reported on this pattern of male dependence on women. Lerner (1974) explained men's sexism and disparagement of women in part as an outgrowth of this overdependence. Gove and Tudor (1972) and Bernard (1972) have noted that married men (as opposed to single men) have higher indexes of mental health and happiness, supporting the idea that marriage has a "protective" function for men. Tschann (1988) found that married men are much less self-disclosing with male friends than single men, do little to keep male friendships intact, and depend on their wives for friendship and dependency needs. It is therefore not surprising that one of the most formidable challenges for divorcing men is the need to replace the multiple emotional contributions of the lost spouse (Myers, 1989). Because men have allowed themselves to become so significantly dependent on women for social facilitation, nurturance, and validation, the all-male therapy group can offer an especially valuable corrective emotional experience, as men learn to trust and value intimate male friendships.

Encouraging Participative Self-Disclosure

Self-disclosure, an essential process in psychotherapy, is anathema to traditional men. Thus, men are especially wary of personal revelations, feeling that private admissions could cause them to be seen in a negative light. Because the one-on-one encounters of individual psychotherapy initially highlight differences in power and competence between the client and therapist, they may be especially problematic, particularly when the therapist is a fellow male. Self-disclosure, viewed by the male client as further evidence of his inferiority in relation to the therapist, may be vigorously avoided, and one may then find what Scher (1990) has called the "jockeying for power" at the outset of therapy.

The all-male therapy group, however, can provide a potent environment to counter this antitherapeutic pattern so common to men in individual therapy. Self-disclosure is known to be a sequential process, whereby one person with an inclination to reveal personal information will initially make low-level disclosures, hoping to obtain affirmation, support, and reciprocal disclosures from another (Yalom, 1975). The male therapy group seems to have significant advantages for overcoming men's socialized tendencies to avoid self-revelations, allowing them to be coaxed gradually and reciprocally to reveal insecurities, disappointments, and private fears, in a process of shared self-exposure.

Instilling Hope

Yalom (1975) described the "instillation of hope"—that is, the generation of faith in therapy's potential benefits—as a powerful curative factor in group psychotherapy. His idea that group members can receive encouragement from others who are further along in the "coping-collapse continuum" is especially relevant when men's therapy issues are conceptualized from the perspective of the male gender role journey. Testimonials from enthusiastic group veterans can be a major source of incentive and demystification for men who might otherwise see therapy as a threatening or emasculating process.

Discovering Emotional Connections

Men frequently share deep and intense feelings and are capable of deep interpersonal connections, but they typically only interact intensely when fighting or competing. Leaders of the mythopoetic men's movement have been particularly concerned about this emotional estrangement among men, because they view life in contemporary culture as robbing men of their deep and timeless interconnections (Erkel, 1990). Although mythopoetic men's leaders are commonly not proponents of traditional psychotherapies, they do advocate men developing greater access to their repressed feelings and connecting through rituals and other emotionally cathartic experiences. Of course, emotional expression or catharsis by themselves have limited value in producing behavior change (Berzon, Pious, & Parson, 1963), but shared discovery of intense feelings can surely energize men in therapy and provide dramatic new perspectives to those men who have adopted emotional suppression or situational flight as coping techniques.

Because men learn to cover or avoid most emotions, the group environment may be an ideal setting in which to change. Provoking strong emotions in one group member often generates considerable affective resonance in other men, heightening the intensity of therapy. Many men are amazed to realize the strength of the feelings they suppress and, thereafter, are unlikely to question the relevance of psychotherapy.

Naturally, because many men have become fearful of emotional intensity, they will need considerable reassurance and ample opportunity to escape emotional flooding or loss of behavioral control. The men's group in which an atmosphere is created that encourages exploration of powerful suppressed emotions with adequate safeguards can become electric in its intensity. Furthermore, when group members are able to pursue an emotionally painful issue through to emotional catharsis, without resorting to flight or chemical suppression, an invaluable type of emotional reeducation can take place.

Improving Communication Skills

Several authors have identified deficient communication skills as principal features of men's interpersonal difficulties. Farrell (1987) noted a tendency for men to practice "self-listening," whereby a man "listens to a conversation, not to take in or genuinely appreciate what a person is saying, but only to be able to jump in and discuss his own experiences" (p. 143). Tannen (1990) has since argued that men have difficulty with language that emphasizes connection and intimacy, preferring language that emphasizes status and independence. She viewed men to be far more comfortable with "report talk" than with "rapport talk"—that is, with conversation that demonstrates knowledge and skill as opposed to that emphasizing the display of similarities and matching of experiences. Levant (1990) found men to be so deficient in the critical skills of empathic listening and nonverbal communication that he designed a skills-oriented program to instruct men in these areas.

The usual communication patterns of men, which are mostly adaptive for men in certain environments, create substantial problems for them in interpersonal relationships. The group, as a social microcosm, is abundant with opportunities for men to experience the consequences of their communication style, and when encouraged to experiment with alternatives, they can become far more effective in the interpersonal realm.

CONCLUSION

Because male socialization emphasizes independence, emotional stoicism, and maintaining the upper hand in relationships, men's resistance to psychotherapy should be anticipated, understood, and respected. Unfortunately, however, this has not always been the case, because many initial meetings between resistant men and therapists have frequently gone poorly. Understandably, this leaves the client reaffirmed in his distaste for therapy and the therapist disheartened about men's potential as therapy clients. As I have discussed, this does not have to be the case.

In this chapter I have argued that although many men are uncomfortable with what they imagine therapy will be like, they do not have to be uncomfortable with what therapy actually is. Historically and culturally, men have been accustomed to working and socializing in all-male groups, and many contemporary men yearn to be part of a supportive male community. Naturally, the more restrictive aspects of traditional men's groups will need to be reshaped, but this is not a significant problem for a gender-aware therapist.[1] It is my contention that, because of the male affinity for all-male environments, men's groups can overcome individuals' initial resistance to psychotherapy and can propel them into a therapy journey that will profoundly alter their lives.

REFERENCES

Aries, E. (1976). Interaction patterns and themes of male, female, and mixed groups. *Small Group Behavior, 7*, 7–18.

Bernard, J. (1972). *The future of marriage.* New York: World.

Berstein, J. (1987). The male group. In L. Mahdi, S. Foster, & M. Little (Eds.), *Betwixt and between* (pp. 135–145). LaSalle, IL: Open Court Press.

Berzon, B., Pious, C., & Parson, R. (1963). The therapeutic event in group therapy: A study of subjective reports by group members. *Journal of Individual Psychology, 19*, 204–212.

Betcher, R. W., & Pollack, W. S. (1993). *In a time of fallen heroes: The re-creation of masculinity.* New York: Atheneum.

Bograd, M. (Ed.). (1991). *Feminist approaches for men in family therapy.* New York: Harrington Park Press.

---

[1]Obviously, the issue of the therapist's gender is an important one that deserves thorough discussion. Such a discussion is not possible here, however. For present purposes it is sufficient to note my position that male and female therapists each have advantages and disadvantages as leaders of men's groups. The most critical point is that the therapist have extensive familiarity with men's gender socialization experiences.

Brehm, S. (1985). *Intimate relationships*. New York: Random House.

Brooks, G. R. (1990). Psychotherapy with traditional role oriented males. In P. A. Keller & L. G. Ritt (Eds.), *Innovations in clinical practice: A sourcebook* (pp. 61–74). Sarasota, FL: Professional Resource Exchange.

Brooks, G. R. (1991). Traditional men in marital and family therapy. In M. Bograd (Ed.), *Feminist approaches for men in family therapy* (pp. 51–74). New York: Haworth Press.

Dosser, D., Balswick, J., & Halverson, C. (1986). Male inexpressiveness and relationships. *Journal of Social and Personal Relationships, 3,* 241–258.

Erickson, B. (1993). *Helping men change: The role of the female therapist*. Newbury Park, CA: Sage.

Erkel, R. T. (1990). The birth of a movement. *Family Therapy Networker, 14,* 26–35.

Farr, K. A. (1986). Dominance bonding through the good old boys socializing group. *Sex Roles, 18,* 259–277.

Farrell, W. T. (1987). *Why men are the way they are*. New York: McGraw-Hill.

Gove, W. R., & Tudor, J. (1972). Adult sex roles and mental illness. *American Journal of Sociology, 73,* 812–835.

Ipsaro, A. (1986). Male client–male therapist: Issues in a therapeutic alliance. *Psychotherapy, 23,* 257–266.

Kimmel, M. S. (1987). The contemporary "crisis" of masculinity in historical perspective. In H. Brod (Ed.), *The making of masculinities* (pp. 121–153). Boston: Allen & Unwin.

Kupers, T. A. (1993). *Revisioning men's lives: Gender, intimacy, power*. New York: Guilford Press.

Lerner, H. G. (1974). Early origins of envy and devaluation of women: Implications for sex-role stereotypes. *Bulletin of the Menninger Clinic, 38,* 538–553.

Levant, R. F. (1990). Psychological services designed for men: A psychoeducational approach. *Psychotherapy, 27,* 309–315.

Meth, R. L., & Pasick, R. S. (1990). *Men in therapy: The challenge of change*. New York: Guilford Press.

Myers, M. F. (1989). *Men and divorce*. New York: Guilford Press.

O'Neil, J. M., & Egan, J. (1992). Men's gender role transitions over the life span: Transformation and fears of femininity. *Journal of Mental Health Counseling, 14,* 305–324.

Osherson, S., & Krugman, S. (1990). Men, shame, and psychotherapy. *Psychotherapy, 27,* 327–339.

Pittman, F. (1990). The masculine mystique. *Family Therapy Networker, 14,* 40–52.

Pleck, J. H. (1980). Men's power with women, other men, and society: A men's movement analysis. In E. Pleck & J. H. Pleck (Eds.), *The American man* (pp. 417–433). Englewood Cliffs, NJ: Prentice Hall.

Ragle, J. D. (1993). *Gender role related behavior of male psychotherapy patients*. Unpublished doctoral dissertation, University of Texas, Austin.

Rotundo, E. A. (1993). *American manhood*. New York: Basic Books.

Scher, M. (1990). Effect of gender-role incongruities on men's experience as clients in psychotherapy. *Psychotherapy, 27*, 322–326.

Silverberg, R. (1986). *Psychotherapy for men: Transcending the masculine mystique*. Springfield, IL: Charles C Thomas.

Snell, W., Jr., Miller, R., & Belk, S. (1988). Development of the Emotional Self-Disclosure Scale. *Sex Roles, 18*, 59–73.

Solomon, K. (1982). The masculine gender role: Description. In K. Solomon & N. Levy (Eds.), *Men in transition: Theory and therapy* (pp. 45–76). New York: Plenum Press.

Tannen, D. (1990). *You just don't understand: Women and men in conversation*. New York: William Morris.

Tiger, L. (1969). *Men in groups*. New York: Random House.

Tolson, A. (1977). *The limits of masculinity*. London: Tavistock.

Tschann, J. (1988). Self-disclosure in adult friendship. *Journal of Social and Personal Relationships, 5*, 65–81.

Vessey, J. T., & Howard, K. I. (1993). Who seeks psychotherapy? *Psychotherapy, 30*, 546–553.

Wright, P. (1982). Men's friendships, women's friendships, and the alleged inferiority of the latter. *Sex Roles, 8*, 1–20.

Yalom, I. D. (1975). *The theory and practice of group psychotherapy*. New York: Basic Books.

2

TECHNIQUES IN GROUP PSYCHOTHERAPY WITH MEN

DAVID M. McPHEE

In spite of a growing body of literature on the men's movement and the cultural context for gender role transitions, there has been little research on psychotherapy with male clients. There has been even less study of non-problem-specific, open-ended group psychotherapy for men.

The men's movement is well underway, and courses in men's studies are available on campuses throughout the country (Brod, 1987; Femiano, 1990). Popular expression of the movement (Bly, 1990; David & Brannon, 1976; Goldberg, 1979, 1987; Keen, 1991; Kipnis, 1991; Moore & Gillette, 1990; Pasick, 1992) has generated special issues of national magazines and become an industry for enterprising leaders of "Warrior Weekends" and the like.

Following similar time frames, professional sociologists and psychologists have described the shifting social construction of male gender roles (Clatterbaugh, 1990; Gilmore, 1990; Hearn & Morgan, 1990; Kimmel, 1990; Pleck & Pleck, 1980; Skovholt & Hansen, 1980, Solomon, 1982) and addressed the specific needs of men as counseling clients (Meth & Pasick, 1990; Moore & Leafgren, 1990; O'Neil, 1982, 1990; Scher, Stevens, Good, & Eichenfield, 1987; Skovholt, Schauble, & Davis, 1980).

Men, even if they are of the "Forty-Nine Percent Majority" (David & Brannon, 1976), are a special client population with more serious emotional and mental problems and less access to mental health services than women (Levant, 1990b). They may get off on the wrong foot in school (Chapman, 1978; Good & May, 1987; Skovholt & Hansen, 1980). They live in rapidly changing times under increasing gender role pressure and strain (Levinson, 1978; O'Neil, 1982, 1990; Pleck, 1987b; Scher, 1979, 1990). And they may have special problems with expressivity (Balswick, 1982, 1988; Lewis, 1978; May, 1990; Moore, 1990).

Men are caught in a double bind. Expressive, interdependent men, acting in ways incongruent with traditional gender roles, tend to be judged as less well adjusted (and sometimes less likable) than those who do not deviate from the norm (Costrich, Feinstein, Kidder, Marecek, & Pascale, 1975; Hayes, 1984; Polyson, 1978; Rosenwasser, Gonzales, & Adams, 1985; Shaffer & Johnson, 1980; Werrbach & Gilbert, 1987). This makes traditional therapy, with its emphasis on admission of problems and affective expression, less attractive to men.

Men have special needs in psychotherapy and counseling and so need counseling approaches tailored to their particular problems (Good, Dell, & Mintz, 1989; Levant, 1990b; Robertson & Fitzgerald, 1992). These special needs have been addressed in the area of individual psychotherapy (Meth & Pasick, 1990; O'Neil, 1990; Solomon, 1982; Solomon & Levy, 1982). There is also a growing body of literature on men in topic-specific groups, dealing with such issues as violence (Grusznski & Bankovics, 1990; Reilly & Grusznski, 1984), affective expressivity (May, 1990; Moore, 1990), or fathering (Levant, 1990a; Pleck, 1987a). Less thoroughly addressed, however, has been non-topic-specific guidance concerning mainstream men in psychotherapy groups.

In this chapter, I first suggest five reasons why the special needs of male clients may be best met in a group psychotherapy setting. I then offer a list of 20 practical techniques that have proven successful in my clinical practice. Finally, I conclude with the description of a model for posttherapy, leaderless support groups for men.

ADVANTAGES OF GROUP OVER INDIVIDUAL PSYCHOTHERAPY FOR MEN

Male groupings occur in every society, as confirmed by cultural anthropology and contemporary experience. The male therapy group offers a safe setting for men by reducing the need for competition or display, and it provides a necessary experience of the novice role. In groups, men can explore their masculine identity and experience both cooperation with and accountability to other men, while working toward insight, self-esteem, and behavioral change.

Masculine Identity

The conventional wisdom has been that, because men are socialized to be concrete and results oriented, therapists should offer them clear goals and plans for action that emphasize behavioral outcomes; but such a mechanical, nonrelational approach can perpetuate the isolation and inexpressivity that causes men problems in the first place (Dougherty, 1990). A more positive case formulation, at least for relatively high-functioning men, would be to identify concerns in terms of male self-esteem, or masculine identity.

Scher (1990) has pointed out that most men come to therapy with a restricting definition of their masculinity. Therefore, a group approach that is designed to explore, expand, and strengthen that masculine identity may serve male clients better than traditional modalities.

Every culture has traditions or rituals that mark the passage from childhood into adulthood. In some tribal cultures, boys are taken from their mothers in late latency and initiated into the mysteries of the men's hut—emerging with tattoos, broken teeth, circumcision, or some other mark of their new manhood. In preindustrial Western societies, boys gained manhood through competency in a skill, often mastering farming or a trade at their fathers' side. Today, boys in Westernized cultures may grow up in increasingly feminized societies. Female teachers and power figures may punish them for the aggression, competition, and boundary testing that mark their emerging masculinity. Boys have few adequate male role models today and so may be initiated by other immature youths like themselves. Examples of male groupings in America today may begin with Little League and scouting, be replaced later by the military, and, still later, involve sports teams, the American Legion, or the Knights of Columbus. Such modern American male groupings are often inadequate for fostering movement toward manhood, offering shallow initiations at best (Corneau, 1991; Kipnis, 1991; Osherson, 1986; Pleck, 1987c).

Psychotherapy was originally an enterprise designed by male professionals primarily for women patients. Therapy had stereotypically feminine goals (sensitivity, collaboration, and emotional expressivity), and androgyny was code for mental health practice (Wolleat & Skovholt, 1980). In what some view as an increasing feminization of the profession, most of today's new graduates in psychology tend to be women. Against this backdrop, exploring and enhancing masculine identity, especially in men's group psychotherapy, might be considered a useful approach with male clients. A simple summary of the goal shift might be this: Men do not need to become more feminine, they need to become more masculine.

Value of the Men's Group

From the earliest days of their heritage as hunters, men have regularly separated from the feminine world and retreated with other men for rest, modeling, challenge, and correction (Gilmore, 1990). This masculine need is today reflected in men's formation of fraternal clubs and participation in traditionally male activities (e.g., fishing). All-male groups offer secure retreats, a level of secrecy, and the opportunity for commitment and accountability to other men that is unavailable in everyday life.

Men's therapy groups, especially those in which members' occupations and social status are similar or unknown, dramatically decrease the need for distracting competition and male display. In addition, the group provides a setting in which a man of any age can experience both a novice and a senior role. Many male clients who are new to group work first resist but then revel in the role of beginner—not only gladly seeking guidance from other men on group rules and process, but also benefiting from the life examples of other, more advanced men. This is significant, because men today rarely permit themselves to be seen as beginners in major life areas. In a similar transformation, clients moving toward the end of their time in the group embrace their roles as experienced, senior members and offer guidance and coaching to novice members. Both the novice and senior roles enhance self-awareness and self-esteem in terms of masculine identity.

Most men have been socialized to define and measure their masculinity by their distance from femininity and from homosexuality (O'Neil & Egan, 1992; Pleck, 1987c). The men's group, especially if it includes gay male members, offers new ways for men to define masculinity, through self-comparison and emulation and by obtaining ongoing, reliable feedback about their values, behavior, and self-presentation.

The physical setting of the men's group is more male friendly than individual therapy. In one-on-one sessions—even when participants sit at the "therapy-correct," nonconfrontational angles—there can be a conflictual, even aggressive flavor because of the need for a dyadic interaction to be sustained for an extended period. Group therapy, in which men sit in a circle with 6 to 10 other men, allows an ongoing process of disengagement and engagement, of silence and speech, that is more reflective of male interaction, to say nothing of the real world.

CLINICAL TECHNIQUES

I see about 50 male clients per week for psychotherapy in a private practice. Twenty come individually, and 30 are in one of three weekly, intensive, open-ended psychotherapy groups. Each of these groups has 10 members, and I usually conduct them with a cotherapist, often an intern. Over the years, I have found a number of clinical ideas and interventions useful, and I describe some of them here. None are entirely original, and all reveal a theoretical bias. They are offered not as a manual or model for conducting men's groups, but simply as a collection of practical ideas, some of which may be useful to other clinicians.

Structure

The explicit expectation is that all the men be in place and ready to go when group is scheduled to begin. Latecomers enter as quietly as possible, and their arrivals are noted but ignored if the group has begun work. Group members usually interpret the tardiness at some time in the session, especially if it has become a pattern.

Check in is an arrival and gathering ritual in which each man takes an uninterrupted turn, lasting from 1 to 2 minutes, to describe his week, to report on commitments made previously, or to bid for time during the session. The therapist and cotherapist also check in briefly, but they maintain a fairly superficial level of personal disclosure.

Jump ball is the therapist's verbal invitation (i.e., I just say "jump ball"), after check in, to begin the group's work.

Closing statements are part of an ending ritual, announced by the therapist, in which each member has 1 or 2 minutes to summarize his experience of the session or, occasionally, to offer a behavioral commitment about the coming week. The therapists' closing statements often acknowledge and reinforce good work and set the stage for the next session.

Group Rules

Before being admitted to the group, prospective members contract with me about three group rules. These rules, described below, have enhanced group participation and stability, and average attendance in my groups has been approximately 90%.

1. Confidentiality. Considerable emphasis is placed on absolute confidentiality, not only about the content of group sessions but also with regard to the identity of members.
2. One Free Miss. Members can miss one session every 12 weeks, but they are charged for all other absences at the full rate.
3. Three Weeks Notice. All members agree to give at least 3 weeks notice before leaving the group, to allow an opportunity to discuss the timeliness of their departure, to consolidate gains made in the group, and to say goodbye.

Group Comfort

An inviting and comfortable physical setting seems to enhance participation and process. My group room contains a large leather sectional sofa, two padded rockers, and a supply of padded folding chairs. The advantages of variety are not only the comfortable selection offered to the men, but also the opportunity for the therapists to interpret members' choice of seating. It is not unusual, for example, that over several months a man will move from a relatively isolated perch on a folding chair by the door to a spot in the center of the sectional couch.

Although eating during the session is discouraged, as a distraction, therapists brew and serve coffee to members throughout the meeting. Other comforts include stuffed animals and a huge bowl of objects, including fossils, feathers, moon tubes, geodes, and foreign currency. Many men hold or play with something from the bowl during the session, and a number pick up one of the teddy bears.

Making Promises: An Accountability Model

My cotherapist and I encourage men to make promises to themselves, to the group, and to the people in their lives. We tell them that noticing, naming, and expressing feelings, while necessary, are not the ultimate goals of therapy. Instead, committed behavior is the aim, and emotions can become the "background music" for the chosen action. Men are reminded that they are not in the group simply to feel better, but to do better, which often results in their feeling better anyway. Feelings are always a secondary focus; the doing is an end in itself. An accountability model that we offer for this process consists of four questions, to be answered over time in the group: Who am I? What do I want? What am I willing to risk to get it? and What promises am I now making and keeping to achieve it?

Keeping in Touch

Although some group models discourage member contact between sessions, we promote it and sometimes prescribe it. After sessions, many of our groups reconvene, without therapists, at a restaurant or coffee shop in the neighborhood. Members also request or offer telephone contact with each other during the week, and this contact can be part of the treatment plan. We do discourage members from pairing off in exclusive dyads, and we ask that between-session contacts be reported at check in, so that the focus remains in the group.

Coaching

Many men have trouble with trust. A coaching relationship, familiar from school athletics, can create a breakthrough in self-esteem for the coach and in trust for the man receiving the coaching. We encourage coaching for men who feel stuck or confused. A man may select a willing member (not one of the therapists) and ask to be coached through a narrowly defined problem or situation outside of group time. He agrees in advance to do what the coach says. He does not negotiate or even discuss alternatives with the coach. His only option other than compliance is to end the coaching relationship.

Humor

Laughter is a critical element of the group process. Humor can caricature maladaptive behavior without ridicule, and wildly exaggerated interpretations of group process can convey a message without the threat of direct confrontation. Humor also offers needed, brief respite from the intense work that group process is.

Homework

Although members generate their own commitments and promises to the group, there are times when therapists or other members take the initiative and ask men to accept specific homework assignments. Homework tasks can range from reading a book, to phoning another member, to spending time each day with a son or daughter.

Adjunctive Individual Work

Like encouraging between-session contact, this item is somewhat controversial. My experience has been that focused, one-on-one therapy can enhance and strengthen the group experience in some cases. Men who are acutely anxious may need personal attention in developing containment and coping strategies to be able to participate in the group. Others may benefit from insight-oriented therapy, perhaps focused on family-of-origin issues that can be revealed to be replicated in the group process. Individual work should emphasize bringing material back into the group, rather than avoiding it.

Instant Replay and Slow Motion

A favorite saying in my groups is "How you are is how you are," meaning that members bring their own personalities, defenses, and coping strategies to the sessions and that problematic interpersonal behaviors will eventually show up in group interactions. In the group, however, one has the luxury of stopping the action to study the behavior.

Therapist Modeling and Self-Disclosure

Often, men resist the role of sick patient and are reluctant to view the therapist as a "doctor." The group setting offers the opportunity for members to observe cotherapists interacting with other men in positive, caring, well-boundaried ways, at a level of complexity not possible in one-on-one therapy. Limited, judicious self-disclosure by therapists is also more possible in groups, because the impact tends to be more diffused.

Role-Plays

Standard role-play and behavior-rehearsal techniques work especially well in groups because of the trust and self-recognition that the same-sex grouping allows.

Worthies: Show and Tell

We encourage men to bring objects or items that will help the group understand and know them better or that they are proud of. Members often bring photographs, but some men have shared art portfolios, played tapes of their music, or brought in a father's watch or a high school track trophy.

Touching

Touching between men is interpreted much differently in a group than when two men are alone, and I have observed that more physical contact is initiated by group members toward therapists than occurs in individual therapy. Although the therapists rarely initiate touch with members, even in the group setting, they can do so when appropriate because of the safety that the group provides.

Plan for Living

When a member gives his 3-week notice to leave the group, he also begins a summary for the group of why he came to therapy in the first place, what has happened, and how his life is different now. After completing this summary, he is expected to share a plan for living that includes some form of accountability for the specific, behavioral steps he will take to maintain the gains he has made.

Cushioned Confrontation

Confrontation is the simultaneous presentation to a client of two or more of his statements or behaviors to demonstrate inconsistency or lack of accountability. In the group, the intensity of a confrontation, whether initiated by therapist or member, is softened because of the universality of most issues raised and the support that commonality generates.

Use of the Cotherapist

Whenever possible, I work with a cotherapist, who may be a doctoral intern or a colleague. This allows a deeper and longer engagement with a member or the group, because the second therapist can remain relatively watchful and disengaged. It has also been extremely useful to debrief after sessions, share insights, and obtain criticism and feedback. In addition, interactions between cotherapists can provide useful modeling for group members.

Recognitions and Acknowledgments

Many men handle acknowledgments poorly and often withhold praise or resist compliments. In groups, men can learn not only to give detailed, specific, and honest acknowledgments to one another but also to accept this kind of recognition and even, occasionally, to ask for it. The therapists regularly model this behavior for the men, and sometimes offer guidance in how to do it.

Marathons

The limitations of time can often be frustrating with a relatively large group. Every few months we plan a session without a time limit, send out for pizza, and work until we are done. Typically, these sessions last from 3 to 4 hours.

Starting Leaderless Groups

Some graduating members' plans for life after therapy include starting a men's support group of their own. In the next section, I describe a way of doing this.

BEYOND THERAPY: THE LEADERLESS MEN'S GROUP

For the same reasons that they do so well in group psychotherapy, men can benefit from membership in regular support groups. Men are already accustomed to all sorts of groups in their everyday lives. Most of these groups, however, focus on an activity or a cause instead of on the men themselves.

So-called leaderless groups are often formed by men who have graduated from psychotherapy groups. Such groups are not topic focused. Their aim is not to provide or gain information, to develop skills, or even to foster personal growth—although all of these may occur. Instead, these groups offer support in the fellowship of other men, which is seen as an end in itself. I have been an active member of three groups of this kind at different times. All three have been life affirming and have had structures composed of four elements:

1. The Gathering. Once a month, in late afternoon (often on a Sunday), eight or nine men convene in the home of one of the members. That member has a loose leadership role, moves the group casually through its agenda, and sets the tone for the evening.

2. The Gift. When everyone has arrived, the host makes some kind of offering to the group. Over the years, offerings have included such things as reading a poem, a minicourse in flytying, a video of a favorite program, or just an invitation to talk about a particular idea. The gift is a contribution to the other men and is meant to honor them. It is also a transition point for settling in and being present to each other.

3. The Sharing. Around the circle, each man talks about his life over the past month, framing it in any way he likes and often interacting with other members about it. Check ins are as brief as 2 or 3 minutes per member or occasionally as long as 1 hour. By unwritten rule, there is no challenge or confrontation. The men simply enjoy and honor each other's stories as they unfold. This marks a striking difference from therapy groups, in which the check in is a minor ritual, followed by the real work of challenge and growth. In the support group, the check in itself is the "meat" of the evening.

4. The Meal. Under the leadership of the host, members help prepare and serve a meal, during which the discussion continues. As the meal comes to an end, the group sets the time and place for the next meeting.

Any persistent and committed man can establish a men's support group. The process may be daunting in terms of the risks entailed in making requests of other men, but the act itself is simple. A man need only make a list of others with whom he would enjoy meeting monthly, set a time and place, begin telling other men about the idea, and ask them to come. Even if only one or two others attend the first meeting, the process is well begun. Those few men can be enrolled in the task of finding and inviting others, until after a few months, a full group is established.

SUMMARY

Men need other men. Although there has been too little outcome-based research on open-ended group psychotherapy for men, new studies and proposals about individual therapy for men offer insights that can be applied to the group setting. The group therapy approach that I have presented here is consistent with male socialization and supported by the developing men's movement. Clinical experience provides a number of useful strategies specifically targeted to male clients in psychotherapy groups, and even nontherapy support groups can help men explore masculine identity.

The group approach seems intuitively right for many male clients, and clinicians increasingly report success with the technique. This may be reason enough for researchers to begin serious study of the process and outcomes of open-ended male group psychotherapy. In an ongoing collaboration with clinicians, researchers can suggest refinements for existing approaches and propose new strategies for therapy that will be increasingly responsive to the needs of male clients. At the same time, these advances will suggest models that go beyond the psychotherapy setting, making men's groups accessible to nonclient men as well.

REFERENCES

Balswick, J. O. (1982). Male inexpressiveness: Psychological and social aspects. In K. Solomon & N. B. Levy (Eds.), *Men in transition: Theory and therapy* (pp. 131–150). New York: Plenum Press.

Balswick, J. O. (1988). *The inexpressive male.* Lexington, MA: Lexington Books.

Bly, R. (1990). *Iron John: A book about men.* Reading, MA: Addison-Wesley.

Brod, H. A. (1987). A case for men's studies. In M. Kimmel (Ed.), *Changing men: New directions in research on men and masculinity* (pp. 263–277). Newbury Park, CA: Sage.

Chapman, R. B. (1978). Academic and behavioral problems of boys in elementary school. *Counseling Psychologist, 7,* 37–40.

Clatterbaugh, K. C. (1990). *Contemporary perspectives on masculinity: Men, women, and politics in modern society.* Boulder, CO: Westview.

Corneau, G. (1991). *Absent fathers, lost sons: The search for masculine identity.* Boston: Shambala.

Costrich, N., Feinstein, J., Kidder, L., Marecek, J., & Pascale, L. (1975). When stereotypes hurt: Three studies of penalties for sex-role reversals. *Journal of Experimental Social Psychology, 11,* 520–530.

David, D., & Brannon, R. (Eds.). (1976). *The forty-nine percent majority: The male sex role*. Reading, MA: Addison-Wesley.

Dougherty, P. (1990). A personal perspective on working with men in groups. In D. Moore & F. Leafgren (Eds.), *Problem-solving strategies and interventions for men in conflict* (pp. 169–182). Alexandria, VA: American Association for Counseling and Development.

Femiano, S. (1990). Developing a contemporary men's studies curriculum. In D. Moore & F. Leafgren (Eds.), *Problem-solving strategies and interventions for men in conflict* (pp. 237–248). Alexandria, VA: American Association for Counseling and Development.

Gilmore, D. D. (1990). *Manhood in the making: Cultural concepts of masculinity*. New Haven, CT: Yale University Press.

Goldberg, H. (1979). *The new male: From self-destruction to self-care*. New York: Morrow.

Goldberg, H. (1987). *The inner male: Overcoming roadblocks to intimacy*. New York: Penguin.

Good, G., Dell, D., & Mintz, L. (1989). Male roles and gender-role conflict: Relationships to help-seeking in men. *Journal of Counseling Psychology, 3*, 295–300.

Good, G., & May, R. (1987). Developmental issues, environmental influences, and the nature of therapy with college men. In M. Scher, M. Stevens, G. Good, & S. Eichenfield (Eds.), *Handbook of counseling psychotherapy with men* (pp. 150–164). Newbury Park, CA: Sage.

Grusznski, R., & Bankovics, G. (1990). Treating men who batter: A group approach. In D. Moore & F. Leafgren (Eds.), *Problem-solving strategies and interventions for men in conflict* (pp. 23–28). Alexandria, VA: American Association for Counseling and Development.

Hayes, M. (1984). Counselor sex-role values and effects on attitudes toward and treatment of non-traditional male clients (Doctoral dissertation, Ohio State University, 1984). *Dissertation Abstracts International, 45*, 3072B.

Hearn, J., & Morgan, D. H. (Eds.). (1990). *Men, masculinities, and social theory*. Boston: Unwin-Hyman.

Keen, S. (1991). *Fire in the belly: On being a man*. New York: Bantam.

Kimmel, M. (1990). After fifteen years: The impact of the sociology of masculinity on the masculinity of sociology. In J. Hearn & D. H. Morgan (Eds.), *Men, masculinities, and social theory* (pp. 93–109). Boston: Unwin-Hyman.

Kipnis, A. R. (1991). *Knights without armor: A practical guide for men in quest of masculine soul*. New York: Tarcher Perigee.

Levant, R. F. (1990a). Coping with the new father role. In D. Moore & F. Leafgren (Eds.), *Problem-solving strategies and interventions for men in conflict* (pp. 81–94). Alexandria, VA: American Association for Counseling and Development.

Levant, R. F. (1990b). Psychological services designed for men: A psychoeducational approach. *Psychotherapy, 27*, 307–315.

Levinson, D. (1978). *The seasons of man's life*. New York: Knopf.

Lewis, R. A. (1978). Emotional intimacy among men. *Journal of Social Issues, 34*, 108–121.

May, R. (1990). Finding ourselves: Self-esteem, self-disclosure, and self-acceptance. In D. Moore & F. Leafgren (Eds.), *Problem-solving strategies and interventions for men in conflict* (pp. 11–21). Alexandria, VA: American Association for Counseling and Development.

Meth, R., & Pasick, R. S. (Eds.). (1990). *Men in therapy: The challenge of change*. New York: Guilford Press.

Moore, D. (1990). Helping men become more emotionally expressive: A ten week program. In D. Moore & F. Leafgren (Eds.), *Problem-solving strategies and interventions for men in conflict* (pp. 180–200). Alexandria, VA: American Association for Counseling and Development.

Moore, D., & Leafgren, F. (Eds.). (1990). *Problem-solving strategies and interventions for men in conflict*. Alexandria, VA: American Association for Counseling and Development.

Moore, R., & Gillette, D. (1990). *King, warrior, magician, lover: Rediscovering the archetypes of the mature masculine*. San Francisco: Harper.

O'Neil, J. M. (1982). Gender role conflict and strain in men's lives: Implications for psychiatrists, psychologists, and other human services providers. In K. Solomon & N. B. Levy (Eds.), *Men in transition: Theory and therapy* (pp. 5–44). New York: Plenum Press.

O'Neil, J. M. (1990). Assessing men's gender-role conflict. In D. Moore & F. Leafgren (Eds.), *Problem-solving strategies and interventions for men in conflict* (pp. 23–38). Alexandria, VA: American Association for Counseling and Development.

O'Neil, J. M., & Egan, J. (1992). Men's gender role transitions over the life span: Transformations and fears of femininity. *Journal of Mental Health Counseling, 14*, 305–324.

Osherson, S. (1986). *Finding our fathers: The unfinished business of manhood*. New York: Free Press.

Pasick, R. (1992). *Awakening from the deep sleep: A powerful guide for courageous men*. San Francisco: Harper.

Pleck, J. (1987a). American fathering in historical perspective. In M. Kimmel (Ed.), *Changing men: New directions in research on men and masculinity* (pp. 83–97). Newbury Park, CA: Sage.

Pleck, J. (1987b). The contemporary man. In M. Scher, M. Stevens, G. Good, & S. Eichenfield (Eds.), *Handbook of counseling and psychotherapy with men* (pp. 16–27). Newbury Park, CA: Sage.

Pleck, J. (1987c). The theory of male sex-role identity: Its rise and fall, 1936 to the present. In H. Brod (Ed.), *The making of masculinities: The new men's studies* (pp. 21–38). Boston: Allen & Unwin.

Pleck, J., & Pleck, E. (Eds.). (1980). *The American man*. Englewood Cliffs, NJ: Prentice Hall.

Polyson, J. A. (1978). Sexism and sexual problems: Societal censure of the sexually troubled male. *Psychological Reports, 42*, 843–850.

Reilly, P., & Grusznski, R. (1984). A structured didactic model for men for controlling family violence. *International Journal of Offender Therapy and Comparative Criminology, 28*, 223–235.

Robertson, J., & Fitzgerald, L. (1992). Overcoming the masculine mystique: Preferences of alternative forms of assistance among men who avoid counseling. *Journal of Counseling Psychology, 39*, 240–246.

Rosenwasser, S. M., Gonzales, M. H., & Adams, V. (1985). Perceptions of a housespouse: The effects of sex, economic productivity, and subject background variables. *Psychology of Women Quarterly, 9*, 258–264.

Scher, M. (1979). On counseling men. *Personnel and Guidance Journal, 58*, 252–254.

Scher, M. (1990). Effect of gender-role incongruities on men's experience as clients in psychotherapy. *Psychotherapy, 27*, 322–325.

Scher, M., Stevens, M., Good, G., & Eichenfield, S. (1987). *Handbook of counseling psychotherapy with men*. Newbury Park, CA: Sage.

Shaffer, D. R., & Johnson, R. D. (1980). Effects of occupational choice and sex role preferences on the attractiveness of competent men and women. *Journal of Personality, 48*, 505–519.

Skovholt, T. M., & Hansen, A. (1980). Men's development: A perspective and some themes. In T. M. Skovholt, P. Schauble, & R. Davis (Eds.), *Counseling men* (pp. 1–29). Monterey, CA: Brooks/Cole.

Skovholt, T. M., Schauble, P. G., & Davis, R. (Eds.). (1980). *Counseling men*. Monterey, CA: Brooks/Cole.

Solomon, K. (1982). Individual psychotherapy and changing masculine roles: Dimensions of gender-role psychotherapy. In K. Solomon & N. B. Levy (Eds.), *Men in transition: Theory and therapy* (pp. 247–274). New York: Plenum Press.

Solomon, K., & Levy, N. B. (Eds.). (1982). *Men in transition: Theory and therapy*. New York: Plenum Press.

Werrbach, J., & Gilbert, L. A. (1987). Men, gender stereotyping, and psychotherapy: Therapists' perceptions of male clients. *Professional Psychology: Research and Practice, 18*, 562–566.

Wolleat, P., & Skovholt, T. (1980). Sculpting roles for men and women: The symmetry option. *Journal of Career Education, 2*, 78–89.

3

FROM OUTCASTS TO COMMUNITY: A SUPPORT GROUP FOR HOMELESS MEN

SAM TSEMBERIS

For homeless men, feelings of alienation and isolation are common. In this chapter, I describe a support group for homeless men held at the 44th Street Independence Support Drop-In Center (ISC) in New York City, whose purpose is to alleviate these feelings and create a sense of community. To provide a context for understanding the experiences of these homeless men, I first review the relevant literature in several areas. I briefly discuss the social, political, and economic factors that influence their lives and compare the clinical and demographic characteristics of the group members to those of the homeless population at large.

Throughout the chapter, I present clinical vignettes to supplement the descriptions of the structure and composition of the support group. These include accounts of the men's struggles with alcoholism, substance abuse, mental illness, relationships, and violence. Their personal accounts portray some of the ways that the group helps these men cope with the daily struggle of maintaining a semblance of sanity in the chaos of a lifestyle called *homelessness*.

This chapter is dedicated to the memory of two young men, Louis Henderson and Raymond Copeland, who were members of the homeless men's support group and who died as a result of drug overdoses.

SOCIAL FORCES, ECONOMIC FACTORS, AND CULTURAL VALUES

Homelessness continues to be a serious and growing urban social problem. The estimated number of people who are homeless in the United States varies from 1.5 million to 3 million (Rossi, 1989). In New York City, estimates range from 70,000 to 90,000 (Smith, 1989). Approximately 78% of all homeless adults are men (Wright, 1990).

A major factor contributing to the growth of homelessness is the lack of low-income housing to accommodate the poor (Wright & Lam, 1987). In New York City, more than 30,000 rooms in single-room-occupancy residences were lost between 1975 and 1981 because of renewal projects that marked the real estate boom of the 1980s (Hopper & Hamburg, 1984). Poor people were either evicted by unscrupulous landlords or moved on and were then no longer able to afford the higher rents.

Shinn and Gillespie (1994) have addressed the issues of housing shortages through McChesney's (1990) analogy of homelessness as a game of musical chairs. In this analogy, the players are the poor and the chairs are affordable housing units. In 1991, there were 7.98 million households in the bottom 25% income group, but only 2.76 million units of housing were available for them (Dolbeare, 1991). When a unit does become available, individuals with problems related to poor health, mental illness, or substance abuse are most likely to lose out in the competition with the more able-bodied. Consequently, the proportion of people who are homeless and have severe problems increases.

There are also sociocultural reasons for homelessness that account for the disproportionate number of men among the homeless (Marin, 1991). First, life on the streets is more dangerous for women, and better shelters and services are available for them. Second, women are more accustomed to asking for help from others. Third, the fact that young men, especially adolescents, tend to behave in more aggressive and rebellious ways means that they are more likely to end up in marginal roles. Finally, in poor families, who have difficulty providing room and board for all members, young men are more likely to leave home for the streets whereas young women, considered more vulnerable, are kept at home even under the most difficult circumstances.

Marin (1991) has argued that the welfare system also contributes to the disproportionate number of men on the streets. Welfare provides services differentially for men and women because of fundamental values and attitudes about what it means to be a man and a woman in Western culture. For example, homeless families draw advocates, public support, and sympathy more often than do single men. Until recently, Aid to Families With Dependent Children (welfare) was a program designed primarily for women and children and limited to households headed by women. As long as an adult man remained in the household as a mate, companion, or father, no aid was forthcoming. Such differences were felt even more severely in the 1980s as the Reagan administration eliminated or reduced social welfare benefits (Hopper & Hamburg, 1984). Men were forced to become "ghost lovers" and "ghost fathers," staying out of sight in case there should be an unannounced visit from the welfare worker (Marin, 1991).

The following vignette illustrates the differences in the public perception of homeless men and women.

> Imagine walking down a street and passing a group of homeless women. Do we not spontaneously see them as victims and wonder what has befallen them, how destiny has injured them? Do we not see them as unfortunate and deserving of help and want to help them?
>
> Now imagine a group of homeless men. Is our reaction the same? Is it as sympathetic? Or is it subtly different? Do we have the very same impulse to help and protect? Or do we wonder, instead of what befell them, how they have gotten themselves where they are?
>
> And remember, too, our fear. When most of us see homeless or idle men we sense or imagine danger; they make us afraid, as if, being beyond the pale, they are also beyond all social control. (Marin, 1991, p. 48)

This example is, of course, not meant to diminish the suffering of families or children. It is presented to provide the broader social context of gender biases that often tend to exacerbate the problems and the numbers of men on the streets.

A major economic factor contributing to the growing presence of homeless men is the loss of many manufacturing jobs (Wilson, 1987). The vast increase in the implementation of automated systems has significantly reduced employment opportunities for transient work and low-paying service-sector jobs. Moreover, African Americans and Latinos have been more widely affected by these socioeconomic changes, so that over 50% of the population of homeless men is African American or Latino (Koegel, Burnam, & Farr, 1988; Rossi, 1989; Tessler & Dennis, 1989). The place of men in poor families and the meaning of work in a man's life are among the most deeply held cultural prejudices or attitudes about men. In American culture, men are not supposed to be dependent (Marin, 1991). They are expected to work and to take care of others and themselves. When they cannot do this, "the built-in assumption at the heart of the culture is that they are *less than men* and therefore unworthy of help. . . . [Thus,] simply by being in need of help, men forfeit the right to it" (Marin, 1991, p. 48).

PHYSICAL HEALTH PROBLEMS AND HOMELESSNESS

Homelessness has a significant negative impact on a person's physical health. In an effort to systematically address the issue of health care, the Robert Wood Johnson Foundation and the Pew Charitable Trusts established clinics to provide services to people who are homeless in 19 U.S. cities. This 4-year, $25 million initiative was subsequently evaluated by James Wright (1990), who found that people who are homeless suffer from most of the physical health problems experienced by the general population, but at an "elevated and often exceptionally elevated rate" (p. 62). Wright reported that most common acute ailments are related to the stress of being homeless. These include upper respiratory infections (33%), traumas (25%), minor skin ailments (15%), and nutritional deficiencies (2%). The main chronic conditions among the homeless are hypertension, gastrointestinal disorders, peripheral vascular disease (the major chronic physical disorder associated with homeless existence), poor dentition, neurological symptoms and disorders, and seizure disorders (Wright, 1990).

Homelessness increases a person's exposure to infectious disorders and can be the direct cause of such diseases as tuberculosis. Other infectious diseases in this population include AIDS and sexually transmitted venereal diseases. In the homeless population, the rate of occurrence of these three diseases exceeds that of the general population by factors of 25, 10, and 2, respectively. Overall, communicable and infectious diseases occur at the rate of 5 or 6 times that of a domiciled population. Because homeless people with infection and those free of infection live in large public spaces and not in isolation, their illnesses threaten their own well-being as well as public health. Wright (1990) concluded that it is difficult to conceive of a greater risk to a person's physical well-being than the hazards one faces while homeless.

Results of physical exams on a sample of homeless clients conducted by the physician at the ISC have confirmed the findings reported in the literature. Approximately 50% of the men tested positive for tuberculosis infection. Rates were also extraordinarily high for other diagnosed conditions, including hypertension, trauma, high blood pressure, HIV, morbid obesity, poor dentition, diabetes, hepatitis B, osteoarthritis, edema, and sarcoidosis.

MENTAL ILLNESS

Homelessness is too frequently and erroneously associated with mental illness. Methodologically rigorous studies sponsored by the National Institute of Mental Health (NIMH) have reported that between one fourth and one third of homeless people are severely mentally ill (Tessler & Dennis, 1989). Other studies have found high rates of depression (Susser, Struening, & Conover, 1989) and demoralization (Rossi, 1989). Although mental illness is much more prevalent in the homeless than in the general population, it can be argued that the mentally ill and the "not mentally ill" are more similar than different when forced to cope with the stress of homelessness (Cohen & Thompson, 1992). Cohen and Thompson suggested that, unless the term *mental illness* is limited to the major psychotic and affective disorders on Axis I of the *Diagnostic and Statistical Manual of Mental Disorders* (3rd ed., revised; American Psychiatric Association, 1987), it is difficult to distinguish the degree of mental illness among the homeless.

Homelessness can closely approximate combat conditions in peacetime, so people can develop psychiatric signs and symptoms once they are homeless in response to the conditions they encounter while sleeping on the streets (Cohen & Thompson, 1992). After a couple days of rest, regular meals, and warm social contact these symptoms abate (Baxter & Hopper, 1982). Interviews that I have conducted with people who have moved into their own apartments after living on the streets for a long time have confirmed these observations. The newly housed clients reported tremendous reductions in the levels of anxiety, fear, and paranoia that they experience when they begin sleeping in their own place. Having a secure place of their own increases their sense of safety and provides people with a restful night of sleep because they can control their own schedules. Providing housing for people who are homeless quickly reduces many psychiatric signs and symptoms.

ALCOHOL AND SUBSTANCE ABUSE

Alcohol and substance abuse among the homeless is extremely high (Caton, Wyatt, Grunberg, & Felix, 1990; Tessler & Dennis, 1989). Many people become homeless because of alcohol or drug abuse, and others are very likely to begin using alcohol and drugs after they become homeless (Koegel & Burnam, 1988). Thus, alcohol and drug abuse may lead to homelessness, may be caused by homelessness, and, if the problem is severe and untreated, it may lead again to homelessness after the person finds housing. People with severe mental illness and substance abuse constitute 10%–20% of the homeless population (Drake, Osher, & Wallach, 1991). They are the most vulnerable and the most difficult to engage in services. This dually diagnosed group constitutes approximately 75% of ISC clients.

THE ISC

The ISC is funded by the Department of Homeless Services as part of the New York–New York Grand Central Initiative and is operated by Gouverneur Hospital, a member of the New York City Health and Hospitals Corporation. The Health and Hospitals Corporation operates the largest municipal hospital system in the United States, providing comprehensive medical services to all New Yorkers regardless of their ability to pay. The ISC offers services to the most vulnerable groups among the homeless street-dwelling population in the Grand Central area.

The mission of the ISC is to provide a temporary sanctuary from the streets for people who are homeless and have psychological and substance abuse problems. The center is staffed by an interdisciplinary team of case managers that includes people who were homeless or are recovering from alcoholism or drug abuse. Services include mental health, physical health, and substance abuse treatment; case management; and assistance in dealing with social service agencies. In addition, clients may be provided with food and clothing, as well as access to showers, lockers, and telephones. Some clients are provided nightly respite beds at local church and temple sites made available by the Partnership for the Homeless. One of the major goals of the program is to assist clients in obtaining transitional and permanent supported housing.

The center's philosophy is based on a low-demand, client-driven approach. There are only minimal behavioral expectations of the drop-in center users. There are three simple rules: no violence, no weapons, and no drugs. People who do not observe the rules are asked to leave for a "time out," and they can return when they are able to observe the rules again. There are a number of regularly scheduled groups, including a community meeting, a women's group, a writing group, and a meditation group. Clients are invited to participate if they wish. The men's group is held every Friday afternoon.

The Men's Group

Purpose

The purpose of the men's group is to provide a brief respite from daily pressures as well as time to reflect, share, and, perhaps, get a glimpse of life beyond homelessness. One hope for the group is to provide the men relief from their feelings of alienation through the sharing of experiences. The group becomes a place where the men belong, where they can be heard, and where their lives matter to others. The primary therapeutic ingredient is the sense of community that is fostered through ongoing participation.

The men in the group develop and participate in a series of formal and informal rituals that include celebrating birthdays, mourning the deaths of peers, and exchanging information regarding members' hospitalizations, incarcerations, or getting into housing. Even after obtaining a place to live, some of the men continue to participate in the group.

Structure and Rules

Ironically—and unwittingly mirroring the treatment of men by the welfare system—the men's group at the drop-in center was formed when the men were asked to leave the center for a time so that the women could hold a women's group. To provide a useful activity for those men, organizers located an empty classroom space and started the men's group. The men were angered by yet another in a long series of evictions, this time from the staff and the female clients who shared the drop-in center. The entire day of a homeless person is spent either waiting in line for services or being asked to move along from public spaces. They were not expecting an eviction from a program that advertised sanctuary. Their collective revolt against this injustice led to the development of common concerns and united the men in a powerful manner.

During the first five or six meetings, one of the primary themes was the anger the men felt about being thrown out. This anger and indignation was directed at the women, the program, the coordinator, and the staff members. One man was more articulate than the next in discussing the unfair treatment the men had received and how the situation should be remedied. The men were establishing themselves in the group, and spokesmen and leaders emerged.

The men's anger was in response to the manner in which the space arrangements were made and not the arrangements per se. Staff members had neglected to consult with them at the outset about what they might have wanted. Once they understood the men's feelings, the staff offered to share the use of the drop-in center space on a biweekly schedule. This eliminated the arguments about the eviction, but the process had served an important function in the formation of the group.

The structure of the men's group eventually developed to be informal, flexible, and primarily client driven. The resulting operational structure is a blend between leader-assisted and mutual support. There is a regular meeting time, but participation is voluntary, and the agenda is set by those who attend. Staff serve to facilitate participation by all members, to ask questions for clarification, and to structure the time. The staff may share personal experiences, but they do not offer interpretations. The object is to have members participate in a mutual-help model with some assistance provided by the staff. Membership is open-ended; some men attend regularly whereas others attend sporadically. The group is also ongoing. The only requirement for participation is that members agree to respect each other's confidentiality concerning the material discussed.

Contrary to popular images of homeless men as being reclusive, angry, and ill, the majority of men in the group share their stories and experiences readily once they feel comfortable. Likewise, in contrast to gender stereo-types of men as competitive and lacking compassion or cooperation, the participants express their vulnerabilities and comfort one another. Issues discussed in this group, however, are not considered a part of the ongoing case management or treatment for the members. For example, when the much-raised topic of drug use is discussed, members will share their experiences as equals, much like at an Alcoholics Anonymous or Narcotics Anonymous meeting, rather than as clients.

Group Leaders

The role of the ISC men's group leader is modeled after the leadership style used in trauma groups (Herman, 1992). The leader, like all of the participants, is male. This same-gender choice is believed to facilitate the formation of relationships that encourage and enhance men to respond to each other in such nontraditional ways as listening actively and demon-strating empathy and compassion when group members report their experiences. The male leader may also serve as a positive role model.

The leader is an active and engaged member of the group. His primary responsibility is to facilitate a climate of acceptance and safety to help the participants develop a sense of community with each other. The leader must listen and "bear witness" to the men's stories, without becoming emo-tionally overwhelmed by them. It is useful to have several staff members attend the group, especially those who have personal experience with homelessness, recovery, or psychiatric disability. Encouraging staff and members to participate develops an atmosphere of mutual support.

Demographic Characteristics

The demographic and clinical characteristics gathered for the men are based on observation and on client records. The men's group compo-sition varies somewhat, but at a typical meeting approximately 12 to 15 participants and 2 to 3 staff members are present. The men who attend the drop-in center are predominantly African American (75%), with some Latinos (15%) and a few Whites (10%). They range in age from 21 to 66 years. Primarily the men are single (80%); however, about 25% report having children. They are largely unemployed (95%), and 50% report hav-ing not held a job in over a year. One half have graduated from high school, and 10% have completed some college courses. These character-istics are virtually the same as those data collected systematically for an

NIMH clinical demonstration project that operated at another midtown drop-in center and served the same segment of the homeless population (Shern et al., in press).

Consistent with findings from a survey of drop-in center users in general, the ISC members also experienced a high rate of foster care placement when they were children (Mangine, Royse, Wiehe, & Nietzel, 1990). Also, consistent with other studies of homeless men, ISC client profiles have indicated that many members experienced disruptive childhood events, such as moving from relative to relative or having caregivers with psychiatric or substance abuse problems (Susser et al., 1989).

Clinical Characteristics

All clients are screened by the ISC staff, and only those found to have some severe psychological problems are enrolled as ISC program members. The diagnostic profiles of the men at the time this chapter was written include the following: schizophrenia, schizoaffective disorder, or other psychotic disorder (30%); affective disorder (20%); and a wide variety of personality disorders characterized by a spectrum of symptoms (50%). Symptoms of the last category include low frustration tolerance, poor impulse control, rage, disruptive or violent behavior, depression, and suicidal behavior. In addition, the men report feelings that often accompany homelessness: disconnectedness, self-blame, demoralization, and powerlessness. Approximately 85% of the men use drugs or alcohol. Consistent with findings from other samples of homeless people, a disproportionately large number have been victims of childhood physical or sexual abuse and have had much more contact with the legal system than the domiciled population (Belcher, 1988; Gelberg, Linn, & Leake, 1988; Tessler & Dennis, 1989).

Topics and Discussions of the Group

Homelessness

Homelessness can be described on a continuum that ranges from people who live with relatives or use shelters and emergency public housing to others who have temporary dwellings. The men in the ISC group are at the latter, extreme end of the poverty homeless continuum. These men are literally homeless: They sleep in cardboard boxes on the streets, in doorways, train stations, bus and ferry terminals, or sitting up on metal folding chairs provided by the drop-in center. Approximately 50% report that they had been homeless for over 3 years, and 30% have been homeless for more than 4 years.

One of the constant themes in the group is the discussion concerning the daily hardships of homelessness. The overwhelming consensus is that homelessness is about never having any privacy. For most men, homelessness involves waiting in lines for hours to do even the simplest things. For example, the day may begin at 5:30 a.m. for the men staying in the church shelter beds. At the beginning of each day many do not know where they will sleep that night. They must vacate the church before the preparation for the 7:00 a.m. service. They wait in line to use the one available toilet and, on returning to the drop-in center, wait until 9:00 a.m. for breakfast to be served. They wait in line for breakfast, lunch, and dinner; wait to see their case manager; wait for the center's banking hours; wait for someone to give them the key to their locker; and wait for the opportunity to make a free telephone call. The long lines only serve as reminders of the personal costs for obtaining even these paltry basic services.

In one discussion of what it means to be homeless, a group member, Larry, relayed the following experience:

> Homelessness is about losing everything that you ever had to your name. After I lost my job as a janitor I was evicted from the building. I was unemployed for about a year and staying with relatives or friends but after a while I felt that I may have overstayed my welcome. So, I bought a brand new duffel bag, packed my clothes, and started sleeping on trains or in Grand Central. The second day I was out there my bag was stolen while I was sleeping. I still had some money, so I bought a new one and got some new clothes from the drop-in center. Then that one was stolen. I couldn't afford to buy another bag and so I started keeping my things in a plastic garbage bag. Even that was stolen a couple of times. By that time I became suspicious of everyone around me, and I could hardly sleep at night. I was so tired and angry and desperate. I became obsessed with having something of my own, anything. I started collecting the paper towels and toilet paper from bathrooms and stuffing that in my garbage bag. One day an outreach worker stopped me and asked why I was carrying all that paper trash around. I couldn't begin to explain the whole thing.

Another man described his experience of having lived in the tunnels under Grand Central Station. He spoke about the darkness and the strands of dust that would brush against his face as he walked slowly, full of fear, hoping to find a place to lie down. One time, just as he was about to place his things on the ground, a large rat ran by—scaring him half to death. When he related this story, the members listening to him did not know whether to laugh or cry.

One of the ways that the men in the group are helped and help others is by participating in a form of self-enhancing social comparison. The men who have been homeless for shorter periods of time show compassion for those who have been homeless for years; those using church beds often express sympathy for those who have to sleep on chairs; and the street dwellers will commiserate with those people who have to go into the tunnels of Grand Central or the subways. These discussions concerning the misfortune of others allow the men to feel a positive and generous sense of themselves, an experience rarely afforded to the extremely poor.

These men cover a broad spectrum of abilities in their psychological stability, severity of addiction, degree of abuse, level of social competence, and ability to function. Despite this tremendous diversity, group members at all levels are accepting and respectful of each other.

Trauma and Abuse

A significant number of ISC members (70%) have disclosed their experiences of physical and sexual abuse. Such a history of abuse and disruptive childhood is thought to be strongly related to the development of psychiatric problems in adulthood (Herman, 1992). In general, survivors of childhood abuse display significantly more insomnia, sexual dysfunction, dissociation, anger, suicidal behavior, drug addiction, and alcoholism than other patients (Briere & Zaidi, 1989). These symptoms are exacerbated by the daily stressors of homelessness, making accurate diagnosis of homeless people difficult without long-term observation (Tsemberis, Cohen, & Jones, 1993). Consequently, when homeless clients with histories of childhood abuse seek treatment, they have "disguised presentations" (Gelinas, 1983); that is, it is unlikely that they will initially address the issue of sexual abuse directly. Typically, people who have been sexually abused seek help because of their many physical health problems, their psychiatric symptoms, or their difficulty with relationships. Over the course of treatment, as trust develops, the traumatic events are disclosed.

Male Violence Against Women

Several men in the group are in relationships with female members of the drop-in center. It is not uncommon for these men to be verbally or physically abusive to the women. The literature on male violence against women has indicated that the homeless population is at high risk for intimate violence, but as a sample it is often excluded from studies (Koss et al., 1994). Men who are not married (and have a history of abuse and violence) are more likely to have higher rates of aggression toward their partners than married men (Ellis, 1989; O'Carroll & Mercy, 1986). Many of the group members possess these characteristics.

The men's group discussions concerning male violence against women often address the cultural beliefs and values that sanction those attitudes, such as men's sense of entitlement to control women. The discussions always include effective self-help statements that can be used to relieve tension in the heat of an argument, such as "Take time out," "Stop, stay stopped!" "The threat to hit is hitting," "You can change," "You deserve help," "Control your behavior, not hers," and "Drugs and booze mean bruises" (Gondolf & Russell, 1987, pp. 42–43).

As the men share their experiences and discuss the abuse in efforts to break through their denial, they become increasingly aware that abusive behavior is a serious and dangerous problem. The mutual support of the group facilitates an open exchange, and one member can comfortably challenge another when he feels that there is denial in his colleague's account of a stormy exchange with his lover.

Alcoholism and Substance Abuse

Many of the men perennially struggle to keep drug and alcohol intake under control. For the men with serious addictions, the first of the month is anxiously awaited, because on that day Social Security Insurance checks are distributed. Typically, they will disappear for a few days—staying in a cheap hotel and partying until the money is exhausted. When they return to the drop-in center, they are usually tired, irritable, and ashamed.

One of the members, Clifford, shared the story of his struggles with alcoholism. His caseworker, Ricky, was a recovering crack addict who had also lived in Grand Central Station during the time he was homeless. Clifford related the following story:

> I was raised decently, really decently. . . . When I was younger I was shot and lost the use of my left side. I have never recovered from that. I began drinking—heavily—I was very angry. I would hurt people. Before I started coming here I was staying in Grand Central Station. In the winter I would go several levels below the trains and sleep there. When I came out in the morning I would see people going to work, and I was aware that I was dirty, still wearing the same clothes from the night before.
>
> My caseworker, Ricky, kept talking to me. At first I wasn't paying much attention, and then he began coming across to me. He said that I didn't have to live that way. He planted that idea in my head. One day I agreed to go with him to a detox. From there it was a rehabilitation program. And now? Excuse the smile, but now, I have an apartment.

Psychiatric Problems

For many people, including homeless people with psychiatric problems, alcohol and drugs serve as tranquilizers. Neuroleptics are unpopular because of their side effects, and it is not uncommon for the men to resort to experimenting with their own drugs. One group member, Louis, recalled riding the subway trains each night, being unable to get enough sleep, and feeling scared and exhausted.

Sometimes I would hear my name called out or I'd hear other familiar voices. I had no idea where they were coming from and I was very anxious. I couldn't really tell if they were coming from inside my own head or if there was someone there who knew me. I became very paranoid. I was paranoid to start with, but the voices made me even more paranoid. If I had a couple of beers, the voices would stop.

CONCLUSION

Homeless men who live on the streets of U.S. cities are painful reminders of society's unsolved economic and social problems. These men who live at the extremes of poverty are suffering the consequences of unemployment, racism, lack of a national health plan, and the failure to implement a community mental health system. It is not surprising that most politicians are advocating laws to increase involuntary commitment and remove these men from the streets.

The men who live each day in the war zone of homelessness have been ostracized by society and, in many cases, abused by their families and caregivers. They have retreated into a world where daily survival is the primary concern. One of the men in the ISC group described his life before coming to the group as follows:

> I was living on the streets, by the FDR Drive, in a box. It was cold and windy. I would show up at the center and say that I was staying with my aunt. The worse thing for me is that I didn't know who I could trust. I was taking medication and doing drugs. I felt disoriented and afraid. For me, it wasn't the program that changed things; it was the people. People I felt I could trust, like Hilary and Jan. It was a new feeling; letting down and letting somebody care for me. It was definitely a new feeling, but I began to trust that. Letting somebody care for me made me begin to care about myself.

Traumatic events, especially those occurring in childhood, and the current torment of homelessness have destroyed the bonds that sustain these men in the community. Survival and recovery depend on connection with others. Trauma isolates, whereas the group creates a sense of belonging (Herman, 1992). The success of a group for homeless men begins with solidarity. The sense of community that develops protects against terror and despair and offers the possibility of recovery and a glimmer of hope.

REFERENCES

American Psychiatric Association. (1987). *Diagnostic and statistical manual of mental disorders* (3rd ed., revised). Washington, DC: Author.

Baxter, E., & Hopper, K. (1982). The new mendicancy: Homeless in New York City. *American Journal of Orthopsychiatry, 52,* 393–408.

Belcher, J. R. (1988). Are jails replacing the mental health system for the homeless mentally ill? *Community Mental Health Journal, 24,* 185–195.

Briere, J., & Zaidi, L. Y. (1989). Sexual abuse histories and sequelae in female psychiatric emergency room patients. *American Journal of Psychiatry, 146,* 1602–1606.

Caton, C. L. M., Wyatt, R. J., Grunberg, J., & Felix, A. (1990). An evaluation of a mental health program for homeless men. *American Journal of Psychiatry, 147,* 286–289.

Cohen, C. I., & Thompson, K. S. (1992). Homeless mentally ill or mentally ill homeless? *American Journal of Psychiatry, 149,* 816–823.

Dolbeare, C. N. (1991). *Out of reach: Why everyday people can't find affordable housing* (2nd ed.). Washington, DC: Low Income Housing Information Service.

Drake, R. E., Osher, F. C., & Wallach, M. A. (1991). Homelessness and dual diagnosis. *American Psychologist, 46,* 1149–1158.

Ellis, L. (1989). *Theories of rape: Inquiries into the causes of sexual aggression.* Washington, DC: Hemisphere.

Gelberg, L., Linn, L. S., & Leake, B. D. (1988). Health, alcohol and drug use, and criminal history among homeless adults. *American Journal of Psychiatry, 145,* 191–196.

Gelinas, D. (1983). The persistent negative effects of incest. *Psychiatry, 46,* 312–332.

Gondolf, E. W., & Russell, D. M. (1987). *Man to man: A guide for men in abusive relationships.* Brandenton, FL: Human Services Institute.

Herman, J. L. (1992). *Trauma and recovery.* New York: Basic Books.

Hopper, K., & Hamburg, J. (1984). *The making of America's homeless: From skid row to new poor.* New York: Community Services Society.

Koegel, P., & Burnam, A. (1988). Alcoholism among homeless adults in the inner city of Los Angeles. *Archives of General Psychiatry, 45,* 1011–1018.

Koegel, P., Burnam, A., & Farr, R. K. (1988). The prevalence of specific psychiatric disorders among homeless individuals in the inner city of Los Angeles. *Archives of General Psychiatry, 45,* 1085–1092.

Koss, M. P., Goodman, L. A., Browne, A., Fitzgerald, L. F., Keita, G. P., & Russo, N. F. (1994). *No safe haven: Male violence against women at home, at work, and in the community.* Washington, DC: American Psychological Association.

Mangine, S. J., Royse, D., Wiehe, V. R., & Nietzel, M. T. (1990). Homelessness among adults raised as foster children: A survey of drop-in center users. *Psychological Reports, 67,* 739–745.

Marin, P. (1991). Born to lose: The prejudice against men. *The Nation, 253,* 2, 46–51.

McChesney, K. Y. (1990). Family homelessness: A systemic problem. *Journal of Social Issues, 46,* 191–205.

O'Carroll, P. W., & Mercy, J. A. (1986). Patterns and recent trends in Black homicide. In D. F. Hawkins (Ed.), *Homicide among Black Americans* (pp. 29–42). Lanham, MD: University Press of America.

Rossi, P. (1989). *Down and out in America: The origins of homelessness.* Chicago: University of Chicago Press.

Shern, D., Tsemberis, S., Winarski, J., Cope, N., Cohen, M., & Anthony, W. (in press). Implementing a psychiatric rehabilitation research demonstration for individuals who are street dwelling and who have serious disability related to mental illness. In W. Breakey & J. W. Thompson (Eds.), *Innovative programs for the homeless mentally ill.* New York: Harwood Academic.

Shinn, M., & Gillespie, C. (1994). The roles of housing and poverty in the origins of homelessness. *American Behavioral Scientist, 37,* 505–521.

Smith, P. (1989). *Moving forward: A status report on homelessness in America, a 46 city survey.* New York: Partnership for the Homeless.

Susser, E., Struening, E. L., & Conover, S. (1989). Psychiatric problems in homeless men. *Archives of General Psychiatry, 46,* 845–850.

Tessler, R. C., & Dennis, D. L. (1989). *A synthesis of NIMH-funded research concerning persons who are homeless and mentally ill.* Washington, DC: National Institute for Mental Health.

Tsemberis, S., Cohen, N. L., & Jones, R. (1993). Conducting emergency psychiatric evaluations on the street. In S. Katz, D. Nardacci, & A. Sabatini (Eds.), *Intensive treatment of the homeless mentally ill* (pp. 71–89). Washington, DC: American Psychiatric Press.

Wilson, W. J. (1987). *The truly disadvantaged: The inner city, the underclass, and public policy.* Chicago: University of Chicago Press.

Wright, J. D. (1990). Poor people, poor health: The health status of the homeless. *Journal of Social Issues, 46,* 49–64.

Wright, J. D., & Lam, J. A. (1987). Homelessness and the low income housing supply. *Social Policy, 17,* 48–53.

4

GROUP COUNSELING FOR MIDDLE-CLASS MEN

DAVID L. JOLLIFF and ARTHUR M. HORNE

THE MIDDLE-CLASS MALE EXPERIENCE

As far back as 1977, Herb Goldberg was writing about the hazards of being male (Goldberg, 1976). While acknowledging the privileges that were more accessible to men in American culture, he ventured to inform people of the huge costs that come with men's access to privilege. Examples include emotional restrictiveness, being caught in the success trap, addictions, dependencies on women, and self-denial. Not the least of these hazards is the cost to men's health. Take the destruction of the male body, for example. Why do Americans—especially adult men, who are considered the privileged group—kill themselves? Ironically, it is this supposedly privileged, successful class in American society that is also the suicide class. In fact, American men kill themselves at a rate 4 times greater than women (U.S. Department of Health and Human Services, Centers for Disease Control, 1992).

One possible answer to why such a successful class of people in America commit suicide is that the benefits of privilege come at a great, although often unrecognized, cost. Being successful in a materialistic world can be hazardous to one's health. If the pressure to succeed can be measured in terms of survival, then this may explain why after males have approximately the same suicide rates as females in childhood, 4 out of 5 suicide

51

deaths of all adults are men. In the 20- to 24-year-old age group, men are over 6 times more likely to commit suicide than women, and by the age of 85, men are 11 times more likely to take their own lives (U.S. Department of Health, 1992).

Boys are expected to become performers in American society, and adolescent boys may be pushed to perform beyond their resources. In athletics, the physically talented high school boys are expected to place their talents and their egos on the line in front of peers and adults, who may either cheer them on or boo them. These cheers are led by the prettiest girls in the school in short skirts. Both the cheers and the short skirts may be seen as promises of what is to come if, and only if, these boys become successful men. To the victor go the spoils. The victor is taught that his self-worth depends on his performance.

The victor also learns that his access to affection, love, and sex depends directly on his ability to perform in ways that are tangible, visible, and judgable against the opinions of others. Just as women have suffered great costs by being financially dependent on men, it can be said that men have suffered from being obligated to provide for women and children. Women's commodity in the dating game has been their ability to offer or withhold affection, love, and sex. Men's commodity has been their ability to offer or withhold financial security. Thus, a man's access to love has depended on his ability to provide. In earlier, agrarian culture, this was challenge enough in a world where most of the determinants of success were beyond men's control (e.g., the weather). The challenge became even greater in the nineteenth century, when the industrial revolution pulled most men from their primary sources of love and affection—their wives and children—and placed them in factories and offices. This limitation of access to love and affection has contributed to men's becoming more dependent on success as a means of compensation. The risk of losing their success becomes a form of double jeopardy: Losing success means not only losing self-esteem but losing love as well. This risk has driven several generations of men to become "success-aholics."

Striving to succeed can be a silent killer. Farrell (1993) has called this tendency in men "killing himself softly." American men are 4 times more likely than women to suffer heart disease before age 50 (U.S. Department of Health, 1990). In fact, men die sooner than women from all 15 of the leading causes of death (U.S. Department of Health, 1989). When a male infant has a projected lifespan of 7 years less than his sister (U.S. Department of Health, National Center for Health Statistics, 1991), it is reasonable to consider this a form of powerlessness. Because powerlessness is considered by society to be the opposite of manliness, there is no societal permission or context for men to conceptualize themselves as victims; thus, there is no vehicle for men's prevention or recovery.

Many successful men are doing quite well. However, some are in deep pain, grief, and denial. They have discovered that the promise of great rewards for all of their hard work has not been delivered. Their wives may divorce them, their kids may see them as the family cash register, they may be neglecting their bodies and suffering from health problems, their emotions may be deadened, and their addictions may be going strong—substance and nonsubstance (e.g., to work or sex) alike.

Lee (1987) has called the men described above "flying boys." Another appropriate name for them might be "golden boys." The sense is that these men fly off to money, status, materialism, accolades, sex, alcohol, or drugs. They often seek extremes, are addicted to risk, and get bored easily, and only the experience of ecstatic highs may give them a sense of feeling, a sense of being alive. They learn of their destiny as "flyers" during boyhood, at an age when they are unable to comprehend the magnitude of this path but are easily seduced by its promise. They experience early success with athletics, academics, or both and, consequently, may experience success with young women—who seem to be drawn to these potential "success objects," as Farrell (1986) has called them. They advance from these early successes into the expected mainstream lifestyle with a career, wife, children, house, cars, television sets, travel, and country club memberships. They seek to climb the career ladder, to gain material comforts and pleasures for their families, and to fulfill those destinies that were thrust on them by their talents and the expectations of others. They continue to climb the success ladder, believing that they are doing it all for their families and that they will be as appreciated and admired as they were on the basketball court or in the classroom.

Like the phoenix of Greek mythology, however, one day these men may have a crash-and-burn experience. Those who have depended on them may become enraged at them, blaming and criticizing them for doing exactly what they were taught to do and what they thought would bring them continued admiration, appreciation, and love. The crash-and-burn experiences come, for example, when their company downsizes and eliminates their jobs; when they suffer heart attacks; or when their wives leave them, taking half their assets and all their children. The children may begrudgingly see them every other weekend, making it clear that they would rather be with their friends. These men have failed; that is, they have failed the test of manhood. Goldberg (1993) explained that in American culture a real man is one who can satisfy the dependency needs of those he is personally involved with. Therefore, the definition of a "real man" changes over the male lifespan, from athletic heroism to meeting the dependency needs of others. Nothing in the realm of athletics teaches a young man how to mature into this provider of other's needs, but he is expected to succeed at this just as he is expected to succeed at any endeavor.

What is the solution? Like the phoenix, each man must pull himself together and once again fly high, but with a new set of values and goals—values and goals that are consistent with a life full of purpose and satisfaction.

In the struggle to satisfy the dependency needs of others, men may deny their own needs. According to Goldberg (1993), they do this through "exaggerated autonomy," which manifests itself in such behaviors as demanding personal space, minimizing intimacy and commitment, and avoiding close relationships with male friends. Such men are unable to ask for help, must maintain denial of their own desires, and are likely to disguise their dependency by appearing angry or by participating only in relationships that are hierarchical. Other symptoms of this denial include irrational outbursts of violence toward others or themselves or entering into close relationships only with those with whom they can fulfill their provider and protector roles. They become role bound, isolated, and alone, with no real friends. "Defensive autonomy" is another term used by Goldberg to describe this phenomenon. These lonely, middle-class men become attached to their work, their money, their material objects, their addictive pleasure seeking, their goals, and their achievements. This is not unprecedented, because men have traditionally found their place in the community through their work (Gilmore, 1990; Wilinsky, 1961). Without a sense of place, they feel lost. Most of all, however, they feel the betrayal and ingratitude of those for whom they have worked and sacrificed. They have climbed the ladder of success, only to find that it was leaning against the wrong wall. In other words, each has made his mark in the world as expected, only to find that the promise of reward, recognition, and love was a lie.

Work and the Struggle for Self-Determination

Can work truly be the escape into a world under control for middle-class men? Few men report feeling in control of their work lives; in fact, many may work at meaningless or dangerous jobs because they feel they have no choice. Ninety-four percent of those who die in the U.S. workplace are men (Basic Information on Workplace Safety, 1992). Keen (1992) has pointed out that very few men, certainly those in the middle class, work to supply their own needs or the needs of those they love. Mostly they work to buy the things that they and their families desire. Until recently, people identified their needs and then saved money until they could make the necessary purchase. This process gave work a sense of meaning. Men's work may not have been satisfying, but at least it had a purpose that could be identified, and it was likely to be appreciated at home, at the workplace, and in society on the whole. In this vein, Keen

(1991) asked himself the following very poignant question: "In working so much have I done violence to my being?" (p. 223).

Today, many men no longer feel those appreciations. The workplace provides one example. Mergers, buyouts, weakening labor unions, the transition from a manufacturing economy with high wages to a service economy with lower wages, and the increased emphasis on getting women and minorities into the workplace have placed in doubt the sense of job security that was once a hallmark of a middle-class working man's career. Between 1983 and 1993, the percentage of White male professionals and managers in the workforce dropped from 55% to 47%, whereas percentages of White female counterparts jumped from 37% to 42% (Galen & Palmer, 1994). It should be noted that the 47% figure for White male professionals and managers was consistent with their representation in the workforce, whereas at 42%, women were doing somewhat better than their overall representation in the workforce, which was 38% (Galen & Palmer, 1994).

Being middle class means being a member of a socioeconomic group of people, located between the upper class and lower class, that shares common social characteristics and values. It does not necessarily mean being of White or European descent. Minority, middle-class men have a double jeopardy. They have been socialized by the values of mainstream, middle-class America, but they face past and present discrimination and oppression. At the same time, they are striving to successfully establish themselves as significant, contributing members of the wider community, to adequately provide for their families, and to maintain a presence in their community.

Middle-class men who are not heterosexual may also suffer a double jeopardy. Gay and bisexual men are further discriminated against and may be beaten, harassed, stalked, and forced to hide their sexuality for fear of social and employment discrimination. Although they possess the intelligence and skills to be successful in a chosen field, they must operate fearlessly in an environment that is rife with potential dangers. Just like men from the majority culture, gay men and men of minority backgrounds are seeking a place in the wider community. This search for place is made more difficult by the fact that the very community in which they search has, for several hundred years, tried to keep them out of the mainstream. These men are also striving to adequately provide for their families, who are caught between two cultures and may not always see the benefits of attaining the hard-earned middle-class position. Minority wives are no less likely to have provider and protector expectations for their husbands than are wives of the majority culture (Farrell, 1993). Also, newly middle-class children may have little appreciation for the benefits accruing from their father's efforts because they have never suffered the oppression of poverty. All the while, the minority man subjects himself to the hazards of the upwardly striving, middle-class man, including health issues, emotional restrictiveness, addiction, and isolation.

Male Therapy Groups

When we do training seminars on running men's therapy groups, two questions of disbelief are always asked: "How do you get men to join a group?" and "How do you get the men to open up and relate to each other?" The implied statement behind these questions is that men will not voluntarily join a therapy group and share openly. A common stereotype holds that men cannot relate to each other in a nurturing, supportive manner or share their feelings with one another.

Encouraging Men to Join

The question of how to enlist men into therapy groups is certainly relevant. Getting a men's group going can be a challenge unless the overall setting is predominantly male, such as at a Veterans Administration hospital. Many clinicians in private practice or clinical settings have found that getting the word out and encouraging men in the process is not as easy as it is with women. Practicing therapists have recognized that this lower rate of participation is not unique to group work, so this phenomenon deserves examination. Goldberg (1980) has suggested that psychotherapy in general is an unmasculine process requiring traditionally unmasculine behaviors. For example, the therapy client is required to ask for help, to expose his or her weak side, to depend on someone, to acknowledge and expose emotions, to suspend any desire for action-oriented solutions, to spend money on treatment that is intangible, to experience and conquer blocks to intimacy, and to confront and suspend the urge to compete.

Interestingly, when the question is raised about low use of counseling services by minorities and those who ethnically and culturally differ from European ancestry, it is with the assumption that something is wrong with the counseling service that makes it unamenable to the needs of minorities. When it comes to working with male clients, however, the tendency has been to blame men for not being open to the counseling experience. Rather than chiding men for not using the services, it may be useful to ask how therapy can be made more relevant for men. One answer is through group work. Men spend a lot of time in all-male groups throughout their lives. However, few men have the opportunity to share a group experience with men (or women) that is safe from shame and blame, in a male-friendly environment.

The answer to getting men to join therapy groups is not clear. What does seem apparent is that clinicians must reach out to men and seek masculine forms of therapeutic intervention. In private practice, one recruiting strategy is to market oneself as a specialist in men's group work and to make sure that other clinicians and referral sources are aware of the service. Other ideas include being involved with Alcoholics Anonymous and drug and alcohol treatment communities that require follow-through services, providing employee assistance programs to business and industry, giving speeches to men's and women's service and church groups, participating in local men's movement activities, and offering weekend retreats for men. On college campuses, men are often recruited through posters and announcements offering group experiences on specific topics, such as dating, exploring a particular men's issue, or discussing a current book on the topic of men. These groups are commonly called *psychoeducational groups*.

Encouraging Men to Relate in Groups

The question of how to help group members become more nurturing and supportive is also relevant to men's work. A therapist can facilitate open, man-to-man relationships most readily by personally avoiding stereotypical or sexist attitudes toward men. Our experience with male clients in groups has demonstrated that men can be very nurturing and supportive to each other. Most men seem to open up to each other quite readily and to nurture each other adequately. They do it somewhat differently than women, but no less effectively.

Modeling is vitally important to helping men open up in a group. Reluctant members will imitate models and follow their lead. For that reason, ongoing groups work well because there are always experienced group members available to model appropriate communication of feelings and thoughts. In our groups, men have said to other, newer members, "I was really quiet when I first came into this group, then I opened up." Such words of encouragement help the new member to do the same.

The key to honest communication in men's groups is safety. When men are sure that they are not going to be shamed or blamed, they are eager to share openly. Observing such openness in a men's group is exciting to behold because the men communicate honestly, and often very directly, with each other. Feedback goes directly to the heart of the matter, honesty comes before niceness, genuine emotions such as anger and frustration are communicated openly, tears are not only accepted but encouraged, and profanity is not shamed. In a safe group, men can speak openly about issues of concern to them, such as affairs, pornography, masturbation, their own sexual or physical victimization in childhood, masculine wounds, masculine power, or anger toward women. All of these must be acceptable topics to be put on the table and dealt with shamelessly if successful men's work is to be accomplished.

Advantages of an All-Male Group

Male interaction changes when women become part of a group. Many men are tempted to flirt; they try to impress the women, they compete with others for their attention, and they direct a disproportionate amount of their attending behavior toward the women. In an all-male group, this distraction is eliminated, and men become more genuine.

When women are not present in group work, men are freer to be more expressive with each other. They touch more, laugh more, and they definitely talk more. Men in all-male groups share feelings more openly, unconstrained by the notion that women are the rightful arbiters of "true" feeling (Thompson, 1991). They are less likely to feel the need to defend themselves from shame or blame. Many men have been socialized to open up more emotionally in the presence of women than men, and these men may report feeling more comfortable talking with women. With women unavailable in the group, however, such men must turn to other men for emotional nourishment and so learn that other men can also be a source of nurturing and support. This leads men, many of whom do not have even one "close" friend, to develop emotional closeness with other men—an experience they may never have had or may not have had since boyhood. In our view, men must learn to be intimate with men before they can be intimate with women. The men's group provides an asexual learning environment that helps them distinguish between intimacy and sexual attraction. Learning intimacy only from women risks men's oversexualizing the intimacy experience because, with women, the learning may be associated with the potential for sexual attraction.

Another way in which men's therapy groups are considered safe is through the opportunity they provide for healing anger and grief. Often men suppress anger because they fear it. They are afraid that if they ever access the full experience of their pain and rage, it will consume them or harm others. An all-male group is a safe environment for rage work because even a man out of control cannot overpower a group of other men. If group members promise to not let an individual harm himself, anyone else, or any object in the room, then he is free to express his hurt and anger openly and genuinely. Almost always the outcome surprises him. He is seldom as out of control as he feared he would be, and the end result is usually a period of deep sadness and tears. He realizes he has been holding back the pain, and the pain is what surprises him, as he did not know the depth of this pain. This anger work usually leads to grief work on all of the losses the member has experienced in his life and the loss reactions that he has suppressed. Grief work is the core element in men's work, because grief is the common denominator that ties men's experiences together. Group work helps men understand this and gives them a setting in which to work through it.

Group Interventions

One of the first things to be determined in doing group work with middle-class men is the purpose of the group. As with the initiation of any group, there are a considerable number of issues that need to be addressed before forming the group (Ohlsen, Horne, & Lawe, 1988), including its purpose, the intended pool of participants, the abilities of its leader, location, fees, and related topics. One of the issues frequently dealt with by people coordinating a group for men is the extent of the structure to provide for participants. Many believe that a highly structured group is mandated because of their belief that men are unable to open up and share freely in unstructured groups. However, we have observed that a high level of structure is more frequently included to meet the needs of the counselor rather than to accommodate participants. In a recent doctoral-level group practicum, several of our students intended to conduct men's groups and believed that they needed a high level of structure to the group to facilitate discussion. They developed interesting names for their groups (e.g., Men at Work and How to Score at Work and on Dates) and highly structured activities for the members for each session. It became clear by the second session of each group, however, that the members wanted to place the structured activities aside to allow them to participate as open and sharing men (unless, of course, the counselors really needed the structure to meet an academic requirement or to help soothe their anxiety about leading a men's group).

Consideration must be given to the focus of the group: Is it therapy or is it personal growth and understanding? The groups we work with are not composed of people who are required to be there because of court orders mandating that they address some pathology. Rather, our groups have more often been for men who are interested in learning more about themselves and their roles in their families, work settings, and communities. A group may also have a specific focus, such as on mentoring (see Horne, Jolliff, & Roth, chap. 7, this book).

Group Activities

Following are a series of group activities that we use in conducting group therapy with men. Many have been taken from the literature on group therapy work with men. We have developed others from our own experiences, with many of these being suggested to us by male participants in our groups. Although the group activities may be applicable to either gender and to a wide variety of treatment groups, we have found them to be particularly useful for working with men in groups.

Storytelling

Men are good at telling stories. One of the interventions often taught in beginning counseling classes is for students to learn effective ways of cutting off storytelling. Conversely, our experience has been that allowing men to tell stories—which is different from storytelling—enables them to share their lives through metaphor and analogy. They share the depths of their being by telling their story. Instead of asking a group member to tell us what brought them to the group or what problem they want to address, we ask them to "tell us a story about you, a story that will help us understand you," and they subsequently provide far more data than would come from us posing interrogatives.

Metaphor Work

We ask men to identify a metaphor for their lives, or we provide several metaphors that we hear from our interactions with men (e.g., "What does it mean to work like a dog, to keep the shoulder to the grindstone, to have your back against the wall, to walk like a man"). We often have participants act out metaphors, explain how they may be taken to mean different things (e.g., "walk like a man" can mean "The Man" [a cop], or it can mean like a man in the western movies; or the man of the Filani Nation in Africa, where men preen and examine themselves in mirrors because they are so beautiful; and so on). Metaphor work is helpful because once men begin defining the metaphors of their lives they realize that they are able to redefine the metaphor, to develop new interpretations, and to select metaphors from others' examples. One activity with metaphors is to do rounds, in which each man provides a metaphor for each other man in the group, based on how the individual perceives the other members. This is very powerful and moving. We have also asked members to describe the metaphor of themselves as they are and as they intend to be at the end of the group (e.g., "I'm tired of running the rapids, I want to do some cool sailing"). For more information on metaphor work, see Siegelman (1990).

Talking Stick

The talking stick process is taken from Native American lodge ceremonies, during which the person with the stick or the totem has the floor to speak. The talking stick has been used in some male groups to bring a sense of order; for example, when one is running a group with delinquent adolescents who are apt to act out, use of the talking stick can lead to only one person speaking at a time, to sharing of speaking time, and to better involvement by all in the group. In most groups of men, however, particularly middle-class men, we have found that the talking stick serves to free men up to talk. When they hold the stick, they become more animated; they often talk to the stick, as though it were a microphone or a pet; and they often use the stick as a tool to demonstrate their emotions (e.g., as a hammer or a golf club, a steering wheel, or a pointer).

Empty Chair Work

Taken from gestalt work, the empty chair technique is used to help men address significant others in their lives. Ohlsen et al. (1988) wrote about the tasks of life, one of which is the issue of unfinished business, and the empty chair is useful for addressing this task. Many men have unfinished business with important people in their lives, such as fathers, brothers, coaches, and friends. By using the group to facilitate the empty chair, men are able to talk, symbolically, to the people with whom they have unfinished business. The process allows members to identify hurtful events in their lives; develop the courage, self-confidence, and interpersonal skills to confront relevant people; and then resolve the differences. For more on empty chair work, see Fagan and Shepherd (1970).

The empty chair process often works better if the client has a picture of whoever needs to be addressed, so that he can talk directly to the picture. We have found the process to be even more powerful when another group member can take on the role of the person with whom there is unfinished business, sit beside the empty chair, and respond to the client. With this setup, great progress occurs.

Early Recollections

Processing early recollections is a very powerful activity for men in groups. We discuss them not only as projective techniques to understand people's functioning, but also as clearer statements about what they remember and how it has affected their lives. In a recent group, for example, we asked men to share their early recollections of their first sexual experiences. There were six men in the group, and all six recounted how their first sexual activity occurred at the hands of an older woman, often a relative or a close neighbor. Each man remembered the event with strongly mixed feelings. On the one hand, as a man, he assumed that he should want sex and want to have the experience. On the other hand, each reported feeling violated, shamed, and guilty. Each one avoided sex for some time after the experience, and expressed anger with himself over the event. This reaction is not unlike stories that therapists hear from women who have been sexually molested.

Early recollections are particularly moving because they are encouraged to be told as stories rather than as data gathering events. As the men tell their stories, they become quite emotional, remembering events that they hold with pride, with sadness, or oftentimes with great anger. In a group conducted recently, each man was asked to identify his most positive event with his father; one member began crying and shared this:

> One time, when I had messed up again, my dad didn't beat me. It was the first time I could remember him not beating me, and I guess I deserved it, at least as much as any other time he beat me, but this time he just looked at me. That was the most he ever showed he cared. He left shortly after that and I never saw him again. I wondered, if he had beat me, if he might have stayed.

This man's pain and anger were clear, but neither may have come through from using the usual clinical interrogatives. For more on early recollections, see Ansbacher and Ansbacher (1956).

Genograms

Produced by the Menninger Clinic, *Constructing the Multigenerational Family Genogram* (Lerner, 1983) is an excellent video to share with a men's group. Although developed to demonstrate the genogram within a family context, the video, in fact, illustrates the roles and demands placed on men to carry out societal expectations. Through use of the genogram, it clearly illustrates how young males in each side of a family have carried out traditions for men specific to their family: in this case, responsibility in one family and reckless abandon of responsibility in another. Often, when men complete their genogram they begin to identify an older male in their family who has been the model for their behavior, that is, the one who helped identify for them the role they would play in life. The family genogram also makes family myths evident, and it is thus possible for men to identify and share the myths that they learned while growing up.

Family Reconstruction

Related to family sculpting, *family reconstruction* (Nerin, 1986) involves having men reconstruct, within the group setting, their own families. They use other men in the group and have each person take on a family role. By helping to reconstruct the family—identifying who was in the family and their influences on the family member who is part of the group—all group members develop a better understanding of that participant. The family genogram facilitates this process.

Anger and Rage Work

Many men fear expressing anger or rage, a fear that has developed from the lack of a safe environment in which to let it be expressed. Sharing that the group will not allow a man to hurt himself, others, or the room, but will allow him to be in touch with his anger and rage, frees the man to experience these emotions. Often, we have found that giving men permission to experience anger and rage also gives them permission to let go of the anger. They no longer have to hold it in; and in letting go, they let it leave them. We have seldom had to use any form of restraint; rather, participants feel safety in the group support and, even when full of rage, recognize that the rage is not with members of the group but with unfinished business that they carry for other people. This allows us to move, then, into doing unfinished business work within the group.

Support and Trust Work

We provide group members with trust exercises and support activities to build cohesiveness. Many of the general group-trust activities used in group work for years can be very effective in men's groups, such as the blind walk, the group lift, and the fall. These activities teach men who may have never trusted other men in their lives, as well as those who have, that men can be trusted to protect, support, and nurture. Therapists should be supportive of men's activities and want to teach them to support each other.

Feedback Exercises

Feedback exercises are particularly helpful in teaching men (a) to offer commentary instead of advice, (b) to be in touch with their own experience and the impact of others' behavior on them, and (c) to put that experience into words. In the exercise, a group member volunteers to be the subject and to receive feedback. Every other group member is given the opportunity to offer feedback to that person, explaining in "I" messages the impact of his behavior (e.g., "I feel scared when you yell, and I wonder if your family might feel the same"). When a member offers advice, he is interrupted and reminded of the feedback rules. When the rounds have been made, the subject of the exercise is encouraged to process the experience aloud.

Advice Go Around

When a group member is puzzled by a decision he is facing, he may ask the group for advice. A "go around" similar to that for the feedback experience is organized. In this case, however, each group member has the opportunity to give one piece of advice to the subject. The individual who is the subject, once again, may say nothing out loud until the go around is completed. He is then asked what he heard that may be worth trying. This format reduces the chances that the subject will argue with advice or deny its usefulness. The fact that advice comes from several different people tends to eliminate ownership of any particular piece of advice by those who gave it, thus reducing the tendency for members to compete with one another.

Role-Playing

We use role-playing in group situations to help an individual rehearse an interpersonal transaction prior to an encounter in real life. Perhaps he has a person he needs to confront and is not sure how he wants to approach it, or he may need to make a request of someone and want to prepare his approach. Rehearsing parenting messages or items that men are reluctant to face with wives or female friends are other examples of useful role-playing situations.

Letter Writing and Poetry

Creative writing can have several uses. Letter writing can be useful when a group member has a message to send and wishes to communicate it safely without danger of denial or abuse from the reader. The writing can be very therapeutic because it allows the writer to say the truth as he knows it without having to face the other individual. Whether the letter is sent or not, reading it aloud to the group can be a particularly powerful experience. Poetry and journaling are other activities that can facilitate opening up to one's self. The creative expression of writing from the heart has a way of getting one in touch with feelings and thoughts that may not have been accessible through more conscious processes. For many men, words that will not come out of the mouth flow easily from the pen.

Bibliotherapy

In recent years, the number of books written for men about men has grown tremendously. We supply members of our men's groups with a reading list, and we make available for loan books and audiotapes that may be inspiring or informative.

Drumming

In spite of the occasional dark humor in the media about men going into the woods and drumming and dancing around naked, the act of drumming together in a group can be quite moving. An example of appropriate use of drumming might be at the beginning of a group session. Drums or other percussion devices (we often use plastic buckets and wooden sticks so that everyone who wishes may have access to an instrument) are made available, and a leader begins a beat. Others join in on the beat. As more people become involved and the sounds continue, rhythm and tempo change and there is a passing of leadership and followership around the group. After a period of time, perhaps 15 minutes or so, a trancelike atmosphere develops, and the expression of emotion—through the drumming or through movement or dance—becomes contagious. Men who in day-to-day life seem expressionless can be seen emoting freely and expressing their joy openly. The sense of unity and brotherhood that develops facilitates later work in the group.

Homework

Giving homework assignments in the form of tasks to be performed outside the group is fitting for men's work because many men are task oriented and feel safe and competent when task focused. Assigning homework also demonstrates competence by the leader, who obviously must be skilled in his or her work and has a chest full of tools and techniques. Homework can be as varied as the person giving or receiving it: Reading, writing, conversations with significant others, meditation, and communication skills practice are just a few options.

Group Intervention Strategies

Beyond the specific techniques discussed above, there are other strategies for intervention that group leaders should be familiar with when working with men in groups. The following list of maxims includes many of these.

1. Do not shame group members for the use of profanity.
2. Teach and provide information when appropriate.
3. Give homework assignments and use bibliotherapy.
4. Assess for a lifestyle that has isolated the client; many men need to develop positive, supportive male relationships, and the group setting is ideal for this work.
5. Teach clients the skills of authenticity and self-disclosure and of identifying safe environments for sharing.
6. Encourage men in the group to access their rage so that they may own it, heal the source of it, and learn to communicate it in appropriate ways.
7. Ask clients to set goals and to assess their own progress during each session.
8. Focus always on empowering the client. Much of male hostility and violence comes from a feeling of powerlessness, not from a feeling of "having all the power."
9. Encourage members to mentor one another or to support one another as they seek out appropriate mentors in their lives.
10. Normalize and encourage self-care physically, mentally, spiritually, and emotionally. Be holistic in your group work.

11. Assess for addictions, including nonchemical addictions such as work and sex.
12. Model spontaneity, emotional expression, and self-disclosure. (This is especially important for male therapists.)
13. Communicate unconditional acceptance of clients when they are feeling weak or feeling like a failure.
14. Be comforting; communicate affection, warmth, and gentleness.
15. Do family-of-origin work with group members. Look for absence or abuse by the father and for emotional incest by the mother.
16. Use active group techniques in sessions and as homework, such as having clients write their stories, find pictures of themselves as children, or look at old family albums, do empty chair work, and so on. Tape the sessions, and have the clients listen to the tapes on their own during the coming week.
17. Expect to find a correlation between emotionally restricted men and men who are very sexual. Many men have sexualized their feelings in such a way that the penis becomes the main mode of accessing feelings and communicating them.
18. Help group members understand that many of their gifts come out of their wounds. This can be a powerfully helpful reframing mechanism.
19. Initiate boundary work. Most male clients benefit greatly from boundary work; they will probably either be isolating themselves or enmeshing themselves. Very often this takes the form of isolating themselves from men and enmeshing themselves with women or one woman.
20. Help men overcome the social myth that crying is unmanly. Men's grief work almost always results in a period of shedding tears. Many will have forgotten how—they will feel a deep sobbing but cannot get a wet tear—whereas others will often weep for no reason.

SUMMARY

We have presented some insights into the middle-class male experience in this chapter, along with justifications and suggestions for working with such men in group settings. So many men are experiencing isolation from supportive and nurturing male connections that the group experience would seem to be the ideal way to bring most men together in a healthy, noncompetitive, mutually encouraging environment. Helping men find their true sense of masculinity and supporting them in their search may be the most important gift a therapist can give and the most important contribution that can be made to the task of revitalizing today's culture. The subject of male roles in America needs to be readdressed, and group work is a recommended starting point for this enquiry.

REFERENCES

Ansbacher, H., & Ansbacher, R. (1956). *The individual psychology of Alfred Adler*. New York: Harper Torchbooks.

Basic information on workplace safety and health in the United States [database]. (1992). Washington, DC: U.S. Department of Health and Human Services, National Institute for Occupational Safety and Health.

Fagan, J., & Shepherd, I. (1970). *Gestalt therapy now*. New York: Harper Colophon.

Farrell, W. (1986). *Why men are the way they are*. New York: McGraw-Hill.

Farrell, W. (1993). *The myth of male power*. New York: Simon & Schuster.

Galen, M., & Palmer, A. (1994, January 31). White, male, and worried. *Business Week*, pp. 50–55.

Gilmore, D. D. (1990). *Manhood in the making: Cultural concepts of masculinity*. New Haven, CT: Yale University Press.

Goldberg, H. (1976). *The hazards of being male*. New York: New American Library.

Goldberg, H. (1980). *The new male: From self-destruction to self-care*. New York: New American Library.

Goldberg, H. (1993). Masculine process/masculine pathology: A new psychodynamic approach. *Journal of Mental Health Counseling, 15*, 298–309.

Keen, S. (1991). At what price? In K. Thompson (Ed.), *To be a man* (p. 223). Los Angeles: Tarcher.

Keen, S. (1992). *The Power of Stories Workshop*. Boulder, CO: Sounds True Recordings.

Lee, J. (1987). *The flying boy*. Deerfield Beach, FL: Health Communications.

Lerner, S. (Writer, Producer, & Ed.). (1983). *Constructing the multigenerational family genogram* [videotape]. Topeka, KS: Educational Video Production, the Menninger Foundation.

Nerin, W. (1986). *Family reconstruction: Long day's journey into light*. New York: Norton.

Ohlsen, M. M., Horne, A. M., & Lawe, C. F. (1988). *Group counseling*. New York: Holt, Rinehart and Winston.

Satir, V., & Bitter, J. R. (1991). The therapist and family therapy: Satir's human validation process model. In A. M. Horne & J. L. Passmore (Eds.), *Family counseling and therapy* (pp. 13–45). Itasca, IL: F. E. Peacock.

Siegelman, E. (1990). *Metaphor and meaning is psychotherapy*. New York: Guilford Press.

Thompson, K. (1991). A man needs a lodge. In K. Thompson (Ed.), *To be a man* (pp. 249–256). Los Angeles: Tarcher.

U.S. Department of Health and Human Services, Centers for Disease Control. (1989, September 26). *Monthly Vital Statistics Report, 38*.

U.S. Department of Health and Human Services, Centers for Disease Control. (1990). *Vital Statistics of the United States, 44* (Pt. A, Section 1). Washington, DC: U.S. Government Printing Office.

U.S. Department of Health and Human Services, Centers for Disease Control. (1992, January 7). *Monthly Vital Statistics Report, 40* (Suppl. 2).

U.S. Department of Health and Human Services, National Center for Health Statistics. (1991, August 28). *Monthly Vital Statistics Report, 39*, 13.

Wilinsky, H. (1961). Orderly careers and social participation: The impact of work on social integration in the middle class. *American Sociological Review, 26*, 521–539.

5

ASIAN MEN IN GROUPS

DAVID SUE

> Mr. V, a 23-year-old Vietnamese college student, was having an ad-
> justment reaction with anxiety and depression from a psychiatric per-
> spective, precipitated by his recent arrival in [America]. Although Mr.
> V was active and had been the most verbal member of the group, he
> suddenly became very quiet during the group session. When asked . . .
> the reason for the silences, Mr. V revealed that he had heard of
> dissatisfactions among some members of the group regarding his
> "attention-seeking" and "show-off" behaviors. It is better to be quiet
> than to speak out so frequently. Those who do speak out frequently
> are not well thought of or appreciated, according to Mr. V. (Lee, Juan,
> & Hom, 1984, p. 41)

A member of a therapy group, Mr. V. was having a conflict between Western group values that support open and free expression and Asian cultural
values of humility and modesty. For a variety of reasons, Asian American
men have such difficulties feeling comfortable with and participating in
groups.

In this chapter, I discuss worldview differences that may affect Asian
men's views of groups, by contrasting Western values and Asian values.
These differences need to be considered when one leads Asian groups or
has Asian members in a group. I suggest ways of organizing and structuring
groups for Asian men, and, finally, I discuss the importance of cross-cultural
training for group leaders.

Before I begin, I would like to make several points regarding the
Asian American population. First, Asian Americans make up the fastest
growing minority group in the United States, and it has been estimated
that this group will grow to over 20 million by the year 2020 (Ong & Hee,
1993). Most members of Asian populations in the United States are
foreign-born, and this characteristic will still be true for the next 30 years
(Hing, 1993). Because of the continuous influx of Asian populations, traditional Asian values will continue to play a role for Asian Americans.
This is especially true for Asian men, because they appear to acculturate
less quickly than Asian women in the United States. Second, Asian Amer-

icans constitute a truly diverse population comprising over 25 distinct sub-groups, each of which may differ in terms of norms and values. Within-group differences are also great in terms of degree of acculturation, educational level, generational status, and English language proficiency.

WESTERN GROUP GOALS AND CULTURAL DIVERSITY

In his well-known book on group counseling, *Theory and Practice of Group Counseling*, Corey (1995) listed some of the possible goals for group therapy participants: (a) "to become more sensitive to the needs and feelings of others"; (b) "to learn to confront others with care, concern, honesty, and directness"; (c) "to achieve self-knowledge and the development of a unique sense of identity"; (d) "to live by one's own expectations"; and (e) "to increase self-direction, autonomy, and responsibility toward oneself and others" (pp. 7–8). These suggested goals have been accepted by most psychotherapists as appropriate in helping individuals adjust. What is not clearly stated, however, is that these goals are based on the Western cultural perspective. As such, people from other cultures might not view these as appropriate goals.

In "Guidelines for Providers of Psychological Services to Ethnic, Linguistic, and Culturally Diverse Populations," the American Psychological Association (APA; 1993) recommended that counselors and psychologists recognize cultural diversity, assist clients in understanding and resolving sociocultural identification conflicts, and acknowledge the interaction of culture with clients' behavior and needs. Except in groups that are developed specifically for ethnic minorities, these factors are usually not considered. There is also often little discussion of the preexisting attitudes of the group leaders toward different ethnic groups. According to the APA guidelines, psychologists "are aware of how their cultural background/experiences, attitudes, values, and biases influence psychological processes. They make efforts to correct any prejudices and biases" (1993, p. 46). Yet, psychologists have not done a very good job of recognizing cultural diversity and its impact on goals and therapy, nor have they sufficiently incorporated cross-cultural issues into group leadership training.

WORLDVIEW DIFFERENCES

Although Asian American men are a diverse group, they do exhibit some similarities. Most show deference to authority, have more restrained modes of emotional expression, stress familial rather than individual goals, and have hierarchical communication patterns (D. W. Sue & Sue, 1990;

Tsui & Schultz, 1988). Saner-Yiu and Saner-Yiu (1985), in their cross-cultural study, compared values and behaviors of White Americans and Taiwanese–Chinese that might affect responsiveness to counseling. Differences were found in the areas of emotional expression, individualistic versus collectivistic orientation, and power distribution.

Emotional Expression

Among the Taiwanese, individual expression of emotion is devalued. Thus, there are few Taiwanese words to describe, to communicate, or to label one's own emotions. This lack of emphasis on emotional expression can also be found in other Asian cultures. In general, expressions of strong emotions are discouraged, especially outside of the family (F. L. K. Leong, 1986; D. W. Sue & Sue, 1990), and distress is often described in terms of physical complaints. White Americans, however, value the expression of emotions and have learned to label experiences from a psychological perspective. Even their illnesses may be thought to result from some type of stress or emotional distress. The individual expression of emotions is therefore thought to be an appropriate goal in Western-style groups. Yet, as White (1982) has observed, "it is, rather, the more psychological and psychosomatic mode of reasoning found in Western cultures which appear[s] unusual among the world's popular and traditional system[s] of belief" (p. 1520). As Saner-Yiu and Saner-Yiu (1985) have pointed out, "in general, Americans feel good or bad, [whereas] Taiwanese–Chinese are sick or healthy" (p. 140). Asian men are thus likely to seek physical explanations for their problems rather than to look at psychological factors.

Strong emotional expression has been discouraged in traditional Asian societies because it is seen as a threat to the order and unity of the family and community. This is not to say that Asian Americans do not show a range of emotions, only that these feelings are not to be displayed to outsiders. Emotionality and self-disclosure are considered signs of weakness in Asian men (Cerhan, 1990). A healthy individual is one who is in control of his or her emotions, and this is especially true among men. Women are allowed more latitude in expressing their emotions.

Restraint of emotions can produce problems in a group setting where one is expected to share feelings. White Americans equate emotional expressiveness with better adjustment, and because most group goals are associated with this value, Asian men in group settings might be seen as "resistive" or "repressed." As Tsui and Schultz (1988) have pointed out, it is "naive to assume that a minority group member would not react negatively—either on a conscious or subconscious level—to a majority of Caucasians who all share common values and behaviors" (p. 137).

Individualism Versus Collectivism

Of 40 countries studied by Saner-Yiu & Saner Yiu (1985), the United States was the most individualistic, whereas Taiwan ranked high among the collectivistic group. Asian men tend to have a family or group identity. Concepts such as self-awareness or self-esteem would therefore make little sense outside the context of the group. The focus on individual aspirations and goals that is often stressed in groups is difficult for them to identify with. Among White Americans, the focus tends to be on the *I* rather than the *we*. Hoare (1991) observed that the trend toward the "autonomous" individual who feels free to define the self apart from the community is increasing. In a study of the use of *self* prefixes in psychological abstracts from 1969 to 1989, she found an increase from 8 to 33 uses. This is probably the reason why self-knowledge, identity, self-acceptance, clarifying one's values, and increasing self-direction are often group goals. Other cultures place greater value on collectivism or group identity. Taiwanese, Chinese, and other Asian societies are among the most collectivistic of world cultures. The group becomes more important than individual needs. Achievement or nonachievement are believed to reflect on the family and community. Male family members are expected to have primary allegiance to their family of origin. Thus, being a father or husband is less important than being a son. Men are expected to carry on the family tradition.

Filial piety is a very strong value in Asian families and shows the collectivistic orientation of the culture. It refers to the responsibility that individuals have to their family and defines the interdependent relationship among family members. Especially important is the obligation and duty that children feel for their parents. This continues even when the children become adults and marry. Allegiance to one's parents is supposed to be stronger than that toward one's spouses or children. As Hsu (1953) has pointed out, "the most important thing to Americans is what parents should do for their children; to Chinese, what [is most important is what] children should do for their parents" (p. 75). The stress to maintain filial piety is especially strong among male members of the family because they are expected to pass on the family values. Asian American men, who are faced with conflicting values from the larger society, may experience stress and depression. In a sample of 24 Chinese American male students who sought counseling, nearly all showed distress associated with filial piety. In essence, pressure to meet parental expectations clashed with individual goals and desires (Bourne, 1975).

Power Distribution

Some cultures, such as the Taiwanese–Chinese, are based on an unequal power distribution; a hierarchical structure is an "existential given."

In these cultures, older individuals and males are granted an elevated status. In most Asian cultures, males have the dominant role. Communication flows from the top down, and there is little questioning of decisions. If questioning does occur, it may be seen as a challenge to the authority figure, usually, the father (Jung, 1984). Many older Asian American men feel a threat to their status. Because many of them may not speak English well, they may have to depend on their children to translate for them. Their wives may be more employable in the United States, which may compound their loss of status. Older men often do not have the support groups that children may have at schools or women may gain from handicraft gatherings (Cerhan, 1990). These problems may evidence themselves in family conflict, such that the father becomes more rigid in asserting his power in an attempt to maintain status. Among White Americans, on the other hand, power is often negotiable. Individuals are free to negotiate role assignments and relationships—even children and their parents. In groups, Asian men are more accustomed to a hierarchical structure with the leader in charge. White Americans are more used to egalitarian relationships and can function well in roles where they are allowed to express their views.

OTHER CHARACTERISTICS OF ASIAN GROUPS

Academic achievement is very important among many Asian American groups. The achievement is seen as a reflection on the family rather than on the individual. College enrollment among Asian Americans is higher than for any other group in the United States (U.S. Government Accounting Office, 1990). Parental expectations can produce additional stress. Recent immigrant men often attempt to compensate for their lack of proficiency with the English language by taking fewer courses and studying for longer hours. As a group they indicate feelings of isolation, unhappiness, and stress (S. Sue & Zane, 1985).

Acculturation into American society produces both changes and conflicts among Asian men. F. T. L. Leong and Tata (1990) have found that highly acculturated Asian American children are more likely to value self-actualization than those who were less acculturated. In their study, Chen and Yang (1986) found that values were affected unevenly through acculturation. Attitudes of Asian American adolescents about dating became more similar to those of White adolescents, but values of loyalty, conformity, and respect for the elders remained. Faced with conflicting values, many Asian American men may go through a process of questioning who they are. Different stages of identity, identified by D. W. Sue and Sue (1990), are listed below.

1. Conformity. This stage is characterized by wholesale acceptance of Western values and rejection of Asian values. In group therapy, the Asian American man would be very uncomfortable with the discussion of cultural differences because such a discussion would bring his Asian qualities to awareness.

2. Dissonance. The individual realizes that he is Asian or that others respond to him with this in mind. He becomes aware of prejudice and some of the positive aspects of Asian cultural values. At this point, he may be open to exploration of his Asian identity.

3. Resistance and immersion. Active rejection of the values of the dominant culture and total acceptance of Asian values are the characteristics of this stage. The Asian man may view White society as the cause for societal problems and conflicts, and he may show hostility to members of the majority culture.

4. Introspection. During this stage, the individual may realize that he has directed too much anger toward White society. He then attempts to evaluate his relationship with the majority culture. Men at this stage may be more open to discussing cultural factors.

5. Integrative awareness. In this last stage, the individual has worked out earlier conflicts and can see the strengths and weaknesses of different cultural groups, including his own. He subsequently develops a strong sense of personal identity, cultural pride, and acceptance of societal problems.

GROUP WORK WITH ASIAN MEN

It is clear that, although Asian men may be dealing with issues of what it means to be a father, husband, or son in U.S. society, traditional Western methods of group intervention and associated goals may be less effective with this population. The path to achieving group goals in traditional group psychotherapy generally involves the sharing of feelings and perceptions, as well as involvement with other members and the leader. To facilitate the process, group activities may include the use of drawings, paintings, visual imagery, and gestalt and psychodrama experiences. These exercises may be difficult for Asian men, however. They have likely been socialized to think of self-disclosure as inappropriate, to value silence and listening over speaking, to seek direction from authority, and to view self-disclosure as a sign of weakness. Some of the expectations found in traditional therapy groups may even evoke negative responses from Asian men.

Tsui and Schultz (1988) have suggested that "attempts to engage an Asian client through premature requests for personal disclosure might be experienced as demands by the powerful collective and, most certainly, as rude intrusions on personal boundaries" (p. 137). Asian men may also differ in terms of their stage of ethnic identity, which will affect how they participate in groups. These differences should not discourage one from leading a group of Asian men or even from participating in a group where Asian men are present, however, because group work can be productive with minor adjustments.

LEADING GROUPS WITH ASIAN MALE MEMBERS

Cross-cultural factors must be incorporated into group leadership training for those working with Asian men. Leaders must come to terms with their feelings and beliefs about Asian men, must understand the role of sociocultural factors in behavior, and must acknowledge that many goals and techniques used with groups are based on Western values and may be inappropriate for or of no value to Asian men. Leaders should thus develop a culturally diverse set of techniques and skills that may be used with the group. If possible, they should begin by participating in some groups in which Asian men are present. Female leaders may face special problems in working with Asian men, for two reasons. First, they must deal with their own feelings about men who value or are accustomed to a male-dominated society. Second, the Asian men may be conflicted and uncomfortable with having a woman in a leadership position. If these issues are not addressed, then interaction in the group may be inhibited.

In the following paragraphs, I describe the process of recruiting and leading a group of Asian men.

Recruitment

In general, I have found it more beneficial to run groups composed solely of Asian men, especially when they are less acculturated. This allows men to more openly share their feelings. Asian women tend to be more verbal, which makes men more reluctant to express their views. In mixed-gender groups, I have had to be more directive and structured so that both genders had their opportunity to respond. It has thus proved more helpful to have men meet and discuss their views and resolve issues before participating in a mixed-gender group. My attempts to recruit Asian men for personal growth or self-awareness groups have not been successful. Groups dealing with such topics as assertiveness training, career exploration, and interracial dating have been of greater interest. To get enough participants, I have had to recruit individuals at Asian clubs or through word of mouth.

Pregroup Screening

In selecting participants for Asian men's groups, I conduct a short 15-minute meeting with each potential participant. During this time, I explain the purpose of the group, discuss some of the techniques to be used, assess the man's expectations and stage of ethnic identity, and stress the importance of confidentiality. In addition to same-gender and mixed-gender groups of Asians, I have led groups with only one or two Asian male members. In the following discussion, I mainly describe groups made up entirely of Asian participants.

Initial Meeting

During the first group meeting, the purpose of the group and techniques to be used are presented again. The types of "loosening up" exercises or "ice breakers" used depend on the acculturation level of the participants. In general, the more unstructured the task, the higher the anxiety level displayed by Asian men. Pairing them up for introduction exercises in the larger group can successfully reduce tension. It is possible to use ice breakers if they are short in duration and the participants are asked to evaluate these techniques as warm-up exercises. As with other populations, the use of carefully chosen exercises prepares the participants to share reactions. One strategy that has been successful in getting nearly everyone to participate is having them write down their responses to exercises or answer specific questions on written surveys or questionnaires before reactions are to be shared.

Group Goals

For the Asian men in my groups, goals have generally been the same despite the group topic. Groups may first involve a discussion of Asian cultural heritage and problems of living in American society. Many feel pulled in two different directions but are unable to identify the source of their conflict. Discussion of Asian values and expectations of the majority culture often clarifies this issue for them. Because of the need to survive in both cultures, the goal of such groups is to help individuals widen their repertoire of responses within both their own culture and the majority culture. In conducting these group sessions, I subscribe to the definition that Ivey, Ivey, and Simek-Morgan (1993) have given for a well-functioning individual:

> The ability to generate a maximum number of thoughts, words, and behaviors; to communicate with self and others within a given culture;
> . . . to generate the thoughts, words, and behaviors necessary to

communicate with a variety of diverse groups and individuals; . . . to formulate plans, act on many possibilities existing in a culture, and reflect on these actions. (pp. 9–10)

In accomplishing these goals, members share their family upbringing, expectations, and reactions to being a man in the Asian culture and Western society. This discussion accomplishes several things. First, many feel supported in that the experiences shared are very similar. Men not only feel more pressure than women to carry on the family name and achieve for the family, they also feel more guilty about transgressions. Second, everyone discovers that there are different ways that men show filial piety. Some, with the help of their parents, are able to redefine their relationships so that obligations to their families can still be met. Different ways of approaching parents are also discussed. Third, also discussed are feelings about the ways that masculinity is described in American society (i.e., assertive, forceful, and dominant) and how the Asian values of gentleness, indirectness, and listening are viewed. Many men have felt that there was something wrong with them and begin to understand that some of their hesitancy to speak up might be related to cultural values.

Assertiveness-Training Groups

In the assertiveness-training groups I have led, some members have expressed the view that learning to be assertive does not fit with traditional Asian culture. The group then discusses behaviors that are necessary to survive and to get ahead in American society. In general, members agree that being assertive in American society is useful and that they could also continue to show deference to their parents or their elders.

Group Process

Because I have used structured tasks in my groups, the degree of conflict or struggle over the control of the group or challenges to the group leader have been minor. Trust is developed through the mutual sharing of background and experiences. There have been lively discussions between individuals who either seem to be more at the resistance or immersion stage (i.e., viewing problems as products of racism and oppression) or the dissonance stage (i.e., those who are gradually acknowledging identity with the majority culture) and individuals who are at the integrative awareness stage (when positive and negative aspects of both cultures are accepted). Exercises in which each individual must attempt to see other members' perspectives are useful in handling this conflict. When the discussion has an external focus (e.g., on cultural backgrounds, family expectations, or societal conflicts), "feeling" talk is more successful than discussing feeling without this context.

Homework Assignments

As group homework, members are asked to list some type of behavior that they want to try. For those who want to be more assertive, situations are described. The group discusses possible cultural roots to difficulties, role-plays, and gives feedback on ways of being more assertive. Possible consequences by others that may result from the group member's greater assertiveness are also discussed. Those individuals who wish to discuss differences in how they perceive the ethnic identity stages are given the assignment of trying to adopt other members' perspectives by viewing and observing the outside world from a different stage of ethnic identity. Homework assignments are discussed at the subsequent meeting.

Final Meeting

The final group meeting involves a discussion of the primary purpose of the group, of the impact of differing cultural and societal expectations, and of what each individual has learned from the experience. Members are asked to describe how the group has affected them individually and to evaluate the effectiveness of the techniques and structure used.

MIXED-GROUP WORK

Leading a group that may only have one or two Asian American men presents some additional challenges. Depending on his stage of ethnic identity, the Asian American man's behavior may range from attempts to deny being different in any way from the majority group members to attempts to blame them as oppressors. An individual at the conformity stage would be uncomfortable with any discussion of race or diversity issues; however, he would probably go along with the topic to "fit in" with the group. Some could be drawn in to wider discussions by being asked to share their reactions to cultural expectations of men in American society. Those at the resistance and immersion stage may be too angry to benefit from being in a group composed mostly of members from the majority culture. Such men might be drawn in by discussions focusing on the oppression of all men by societal expectations. Others, however, may remain unresponsive, indicating that they are not ready to participate in a group with majority culture individuals.

CONCLUSION

In group therapy, the reluctance that Asian American men have in sharing feelings and thoughts can be addressed by using structured exercises to ensure participation by all group members, by maintaining an external focus (e.g., on cultural and societal expectations), and by sharing early background feelings. I prefer to conduct groups comprising only Asian American men, so that bonding can occur through common experiences. Later, some of these issues can be shared in mixed-gender, though still all-Asian, groups. In general, unstructured exercises or those that require spontaneity or creativity do not bring positive results with Asian participants. Participants are able to do these, however, if they are first asked to evaluate the activities in terms of their own cultural comfort level. Some members have expressed the need to show more spontaneity and to practice this both in the group and outside the group as part of a homework assignment. Trust does develop as individuals share their backgrounds and present concerns.

In mixed-gender groups, I am more directive and use exercises to ensure more equal participation among men and women. Having them all write down responses to questions is useful in accomplishing this task. In groups in which there may be only one or two Asian men, I prescreen to assess these members' levels of comfort with different exercises that they will have to perform, assigning more structured tasks and assignments if I see that they are having difficulty responding to a more unstructured environment. The topic of being male in American society could help them find communality with the rest of the group members. Finally, as I suggested earlier, the leader must be aware of and respect ethnic differences to be able to use techniques and identify appropriate goals for working with groups of ethnically diverse populations.

REFERENCES

American Psychological Association, Office of Ethnic Minority Affairs. (1993). Guidelines for providers of psychological services to ethnic, linguistic, and culturally diverse populations. *American Psychologist, 48,* 45–48.

Bourne, P. G. (1975). The Chinese student: Acculturation and mental illness. *Psychiatry, 38,* 269–277.

Cerhan, J. U. (1990). The Hmong in the United States: An overview for mental health professionals. *Journal of Counseling and Development, 69,* 88–92.

Chen, C., & Yang, D. (1986). The self-image of Chinese American adolescents. *Pacific/Asian American Mental Health Research Center Review, 3/4,* 27–29.

Corey, G. (1995). *Theory and practice of group counseling* (4th ed.). Pacific Grove, CA: Brooks/Cole.

Hing, B. O. (1993). Making and remaking Asian Pacific America: Immigration policies. In *The state of Asian Pacific America* (pp. 127–140). Los Angeles: Leadership Education for Asian Pacifics, Asian Pacific American Public Policy

Institute and UCLA Asian American Studies Center, University of California, Los Angeles.

Hoare, C. H. (1991). Psychosocial identity development and cultural others. *Journal of Counseling and Development, 70*, 45–53.

Hsu, F. L. K. (1953). *American and Chinese: Two ways of life*. New York: Abeland-Schuman.

Ivey, A. E., Ivey, M. B., & Simek-Morgan, L. (1993). Counseling and psychotherapy (3rd ed.). Boston: Allyn & Bacon.

Jung, M. (1984). Structural family therapy: Its application to Chinese families. *Family Process, 23*, 365–374.

Lee, P. C., Juan, G., & Hom, A. B. (1984). Group work practice with Asian clients: A sociocultural approach. *Social Work, 7*, 37–48.

Leong, F. L. K. (1986). Counseling and psychotherapy with Asian Americans: Review of the literature. *Journal of Counseling Psychology, 33*, 196–206.

Leong, F. T. L., & Tata, S. P. (1990). Sex and acculturation differences in occupational values among Chinese American children. *Journal of Counseling Psychology, 37*, 208–212.

Ong, P., & Hee, S. J. (1993). The growth of the Asian Pacific American population: Twenty million in 2020. In *The state of Asian Pacific America* (pp. 11–24). Los Angeles: Leadership Education for Asian Pacifics, Asian Pacific American Public Policy Institute and Asian American Studies Center, University of California, Los Angeles.

Saner-Yiu, L., & Saner-Yiu, R. (1985). Value dimensions in American counseling. *International Journal for the Advancement of Counseling, 8*, 137–146.

Sue, D. W., & Sue, D. (1990). *Counseling the culturally different* (2nd ed.). New York: Wiley.

Sue, S., & Zane, N. (1985). Academic achievement and socioemotional adjustment among Chinese university students. *Journal of Counseling Psychology, 32*, 570–579.

Tsui, P., & Schultz, G. L. (1988). Ethnic factors in group process: Cultural dynamics in multi-ethnic therapy groups. *American Journal of Orthopsychiatry, 58*, 136–142.

U.S. Government Accounting Office, Human Resources Division. (1990). *Asian Americans*. Washington, DC: Author.

White, G. M. (1982). The role of cultural explanations in "somatization" and "psychologization." *Social Science Medicine, 16*, 1519–1530.

6

UNIVERSITY-BASED GROUP THERAPY FOR FACULTY, STUDENTS, AND STAFF

GREGG A. EICHENFIELD

There has been much written in the past 15 years regarding men, therapy, and groups. Most of this information has been produced since the mid-1980s. Early work by Skovholt (1978), Scher (1981), and their collaborators has advanced the notion of successful group therapy work with men from a variety of perspectives. General work for men in groups has been discussed by such researchers as Washington (1982) and has been furthered by contributors to edited volumes, such as those by Scher, Stevens, Good, and Eichenfield (1987) and by Moore and Leafgren (1990). Recent writings have also included such special populations as African American teens (Lee, 1988), men who are violent (Long, 1987), veterans experiencing posttraumatic stress disorder (Carlson, 1987), and college men (Eichenfield, 1988; Good & May, 1987; Heppner & Gonzales, 1987). Another significant area where men's groups have shown positive outcomes and increasing usefulness has been in fathering groups (Levant & Kelly, 1990; Tedder & Scherman, 1987).

Although much has been written about therapy groups per se, there is a paucity of literature describing work with men in the context of counseling, support, and consciousness raising. Little has been published, and, primarily, conventions have been the arenas for promoting and disseminating such information (e.g., Andronico, 1993). It is my goal with this chapter to add to the published literature by describing and discussing a

81

particular group conducted for "men in transition." I describe the group in terms of its organization, leadership, membership, themes that have emerged over its 5 years of existence, and examples of successful and unsuccessful interventions. I hope that this chapter will promote thought and encouragement about how to use group work to intervene in a proactive, preventive manner for those men often described as the "walking wounded" or the "worried well" (Scher et al., 1987).

THE MEN IN TRANSITION GROUP

Description

This group was run continuously for 5 years at the mental health agency of a large midwestern university. It was described in its advertising and promotion as a Men in Transition (MIT) group, and included men ages 23 to 55 years as well as seven different therapists over the life of the group. What made this group unique was both its setting (a college mental health agency) and its composition. The agency served not only students but also staff, faculty, and their dependents; thus, it served as a mental health center for the entire university community.

The group included both undergraduate and graduate students, working-class staff from the university (e.g., painters, truckdrivers, and front-loader operators), professional staff (e.g., engineers and others with at least a bachelor's degree), and a number of university professors. Some group members were seen concurrently in individual or couples therapy; many group members were seen intermittently in individual therapy; and, occasionally, members belonged to other groups (e.g., psychoeducational groups concerned with assertiveness training and self-esteem enhancement). Several members had received group treatment prior to entering the men's group (e.g., in mixed-gender treatment groups or children of alcoholics groups).

The MIT group was formed around *transitions*, and its members were men experiencing life transitions, with the most common themes being relationships (e.g., divorce, separation, and other relationship endings). In addition, clients came in response to relocation concerns, starting or ending school, and stepparenting or parenting issues. Several men also dealt with a partner's psychological crisis during their participation in the group, and one man was preparing to retire and wanted help with this process.

The format of the group was a weekly meeting for 2 hours and—with the exception of scheduled university holidays and occasional breaks during the summer months—it continued for a 5-year period. Cotherapists generally rotated yearly, with a senior leader (either a seasoned psychologist or social worker with interest and experience in working with men) overlapping for 3 years; coleaders included doctoral interns, staff psychologists, and social workers whose ages ranged from 30 years to 42 years.

Meetings were conducted in an open-group format, which meant that group members could enter and leave at any time during the life of the group. An advantage to this model of group treatment was that it closely approximated the natural process of people coming and going in each other's lives (especially in a university community); this format also allowed for the addition of group members at any time that an opening occurred or a man entered the agency seeking assistance that could be provided by this group. However, the group leaders were cognizant of the need to provide continuity for group members and agreed not to add more than one new member per group meeting, with one or two new members per month being added during the busiest times of the year. As with the natural population flow at many college and university mental health agencies, group membership was highest during the fall (beginning of the school year) and winter (beginning of the second semester or quarter) and lowest during the summer months. Some men were self-referred to the group through word of mouth or responding to advertising in school or community newspapers; most were referred to the group on intake at the agency or received brief individual treatment before entering the group.

Components of Success

Intergenerational Issues

One of the unique components in the success of this group was its intergenerational nature. In the 5 years of continuous meetings, there were times when the group included three generations of men, and at least two generations were always represented. In describing the success of men's groups, a number of researchers (e.g., Rabinowitz & Cochran, 1987; Washington, 1982) have noted the importance of working with father–son themes. This clearly was the case in the MIT group, because much discussion of fathers, fathering, and the trials and tribulations of being a son occurred throughout the life of the group. The sharing of multiple roles, the pain of absent fathers, and wisdom between group members who were fathers and sons all brought a richness to the group that might have been missed with a more homogeneous (by age) group of men. In addition, the deference to age, life experience, and education all brought powerful issues of transference among group members to the forefront, so that conflicts could be raised, discussed, and resolved.

Intergenerational issues also created problems for the group at times. Some men in their 30s and 40s had difficulty allowing the younger members to go through the developmental struggles of young college men at their own pace. Impatience with these issues for younger members or with their inability to "move on" with emotional struggles often created conflicts in group and contributed to the lack of understanding between generations. Older men did not hide their impatience well for younger men who found themselves struggling with the complexities of postadolescent relationships, and many of the younger men had difficulties understanding issues of fathering and the decision to separate or divorce. And yet, these discussions were powerful, educational, and even brought some amusing insights (e.g., when a group member who was a humanities professor was able to say how he finally understood what was going on in his classes between men and women who dated and how what he observed was so different from his own experiences 30 years before).

Class and Classism

Being in the midst of a university community and having group members from all walks of life, it was inevitable that issues of class, elitism, and classism occurred in the life of the group. Having working-class men (e.g., truckdrivers and brick masons) as group members would regularly bring comments of "you just don't understand" from all members of the group. With these comments, the discussion of assumptions (and stereotypes) about both working-class men and the "elite" university professors and graduate students would help focus the energy of disagreements and personality conflicts in the group. What was helpful to the group members was that several of the group leaders had come from working-class backgrounds and could share their experiences and the difficulties of changing classes. In addition, one of the founding group leaders had been a fireman for a number of years (and had actually paid for graduate school by working as a fireman) and so gained credibility because of the nature of his work and the risks involved in such a profession.

OBSTACLES TO STARTING MEN'S GROUPS

The history of unsuccessful attempts at beginning this group went back to 5 years before its inception, when a male intern solicited clients from both the university community and the clinical staff. This group lacked sufficient membership to keep going. This early failure was followed the next year by the efforts of two male clinical staff members, who advertised the group both on campus and to the general town community (the reality of liability problems soon ended recruitment of this population). This early men's group ran for one and one half semesters. Because of low attendance and the need for resources to be allocated to clients with more severe problems, however, the group ended.

There was a 3-year hiatus for men's groups at the agency and, during this period of time, two significant components of a successful group program were added. First, a successful Women in Transition group was begun, and it was so popular that a second women's group was started. Second, a concerted effort was made on the part of the staff to begin to think about the group setting as the primary mode of treatment for many clients, rather than as adjunct therapy to individual treatment. This effort, which really was a change in attitude and beliefs about the successful outcomes of group treatment, took almost 6 years to accomplish. This process resulted in the agency serving 10%–15% of clients in group at Year 1 and 60%–80% of clients in group in Year 6. In addition, reduction in resources (staff cuts) also drove the agency to become more efficient, and group treatment was viewed as a way to increase efficiency without sacrificing quality.

Recruitment of Members

Most clients were initially recruited through their work in individual therapy with agency staff; interestingly, both male and female staff referred clients to the MIT group often. (This was partly, as was discussed frequently in staff meetings, because women's groups were successful and in demand and because there was a growing belief that men would also benefit from such a treatment format.) As the group gained recognition on campus (from regular advertising in the campus newspaper and from group members) referrals came directly, and male clients would present themselves at intake requesting membership in the group.

Disadvantages of an Open-Group Format

Although I have discussed the advantages of the open-group format, there are also noteworthy disadvantages of this model of group treatment. Such concerns may be significant for group leaders as they struggle to find a format that will work best with their clientele, their setting, and the greater community in which such groups would be offered.

What many successful group leaders acknowledge as the most successful component of effective groups—having a stable core of group members who set norms, develop and maintain group culture, and are regular in their attendance—may be initially missing or may rotate in an open-group format. The stability of membership is often cited as the reason for closed membership in groups, and this is certainly a critical component for groups operated through counseling centers and community agencies (because some therapists who run these men's groups view the changing of members as an advantage, in that newer members "step up" to assume leadership roles). However, this format also prevents groups from starting unless a "critical mass" (i.e., sufficient number to use staff time effectively and be profitable) is reached. In agencies that have busy and slow time cycles (as many agencies do), waiting for the critical mass may mean not having a group for a period of time.

Another disadvantage is the loss of the level of intensity that some group leaders describe having when a group is time limited and all members and leaders know how many weeks or sessions a group will exist. Finally, with ongoing, open-ended groups, the ability to provide a sequence to treatment may be lost. With time-limited groups, the opportunity to provide sequential treatment, or some combination of group and individual treatment, is easily accomplished. Some male clients would benefit from a men's group as well as psychoeducational group geared toward enhancing self-esteem, controlling violence, or addressing some other individualized need. Still others may benefit from a men's group for enhancing awareness of personal concerns and issues, and then might clearly be assisted by entering a mixed-gender group focusing on relationships (or a gay–bisexual men's group examining same-sex relationships). By having men in an ongoing group, opportunities to use other treatment models might be missed or postponed.

ESTABLISHING A THERAPEUTIC ENVIRONMENT

Establishing a successful group for men in transition requires focusing on the way in which an environment is created for the group as well as on how the logistics of the environment and the group leaders are managed. I next describe the MIT group environment and the significant issue of the rotation of therapists throughout the group's 5-year history.

Setting

The setting for the MIT group was a comfortable room used for group counseling and therapy in the agency. It contained a number of not-so-comfortable chairs (just as many group rooms in agencies are furnished). During the 3rd year of the group, new furniture was purchased, and the group spontaneously celebrated their new level of comfort with a ceremony and many jokes about the previous furniture.

Recording

Tape recording of the group, by both audio- and videotape, was a regular occurrence. Tapes were made available to group members on request, and some clients did take advantage of this opportunity. Video cameras were mounted in the corners of the room on the ceiling, and audiotaping was accomplished through a portable "boom box," with clients often taking responsibility for turning the tape over after the first side had ended.

Confidentiality

Confidentiality was guaranteed by the group leaders, and each client signed a statement promising to maintain group confidentiality prior to entering the group. Given that the group was composed of students, staff, and faculty, confidentiality was sometimes awkward to maintain. For example, the greatest fear was that an undergraduate student might enter as a new member and encounter a faculty member from his academic department. Neither could have been told about the other beforehand, but preference would always be given to the current group member. In the 5 years of the group, there were no incidents of confidentiality violations nor was any potential member ever prevented from attending the group.

New Members

A ritual was established that, when a new man entered the group, each member would say something about himself, including why he had joined. As mentioned above, the general rule was that no more than one member would be added during a group session, and, at most, new members entered approximately once or twice per month. Although the introduction ritual was time-consuming, it was also quite revealing and therapeutic. Watching men change the descriptions of themselves and their reasons for entering the group in successive rounds was helpful to the group and the leaders—revealing increases in levels of disclosure; an unfolding of group members and their lives; and, sometimes, a "shutting down" of a member. Several times during the life of the group, the introduction ritual resulted in interactions and therapeutic work that began when an existing member of the group would say something to the effect of "I didn't know that about you" or would make a link between group members. Thus, what was viewed as tedious by some members and leaders became another useful therapeutic tool to others.

Therapist Rotations

Given that the agency relied heavily on its training programs to provide service and given the small number of full-time clinical staff, it was common to rotate therapists in and out of groups after a semester or year. In addition, it was also important that senior staff could rotate in and out of groups on the basis of need, expertise, wanting a change, or because of leaving the agency. During its 5 years, the MIT group used seven different therapists. Many believed that the group would suffer from a lack of consistency. But one must remember that group members themselves came and went during those 5 years as well. Again, the issue of approximating "real life" was important to the conceptual goals of the group.

What allowed this group to maintain its continuity were the coleader postgroup debriefing sessions and opportunities to discuss the group and listen to or watch tapes with the entire staff during weekly group consultation meetings. In this way, when a group therapist would rotate out of the group, an incoming therapist was already familiar with the themes, leaders, members, and group issues that had developed over the past months or years. In addition, each semester, therapists presented a conceptualization model (Fuhriman, 1974) of the group to the entire consultation group (all groups in the agency were subjected to this model each semester). This format helped group leaders to think divergently about the group and receive input from other staff in a nonthreatening and supportive manner.

The rotation of therapists was conducted in a careful, thoughtful, and planned manner. Pregroup intakes with prospective members included a statement about the rotation of therapists, and rotations were announced well in advance. Overlap between entering and leaving therapists occurred for at least one session, with the outgoing therapist introducing the incoming therapist. The use of rituals again became important to the group during these transitions. Some groups gave parting gifts to the therapist (doughnuts, a card, or a poster); in others, each member would take time to describe how he had been affected by the therapist. One such "group leaving" turned into a comedy roast about the outgoing therapist, including imitations of the individual and funny stories. These responses were viewed as therapeutically important, and a great deal of freedom was given to group members as to how they might say goodbye. Experiencing the loss was significant for members, and it was not uncommon for members to coordinate leaving the group themselves with the leaving of a therapist, thus marking a significant point in the group's life and change.

The impact of therapist rotation on group members varied. Some members experienced such leavings as difficult and highly significant (from a transference perspective, often like the parting of the father–brother figure in their lives). For most members who stayed in the group for 12–18 months, this process was normalized, because it was discussed by both members and therapists as a natural occurrence. In reflecting on this process, I believe that the change process and the ending of therapeutic ties with individual therapists was quite helpful in assisting men to look at their lives in the context of change and transition.

Member Terminations

Members generally remained in the group for 1 year to 18 months, with some members leaving after a semester (4 months) and others remaining in the group for several years. At the pregroup intake, members were informed of the ground rules that they were to come to the group to say goodbye and to announce their departure to the group in advance. All but a few members held to this agreement, which is quite unusual in my experiences with groups (many group members simply disappear after a few sessions). Again, rituals were very important in the saying of goodbyes, and men sometimes gave gifts (cards, posters, or a baseball hat) to each other. Sharing the leaving member's impact on individuals and the group was also a common occurrence and provided for discussions that often carried over into the next few sessions. Because many of the men in the group had had poor experiences of saying goodbye to fathers and other important men in their lives, this process, which was ongoing, was profound and highly therapeutic.

CHANGING THEMES IN GROUP LIFE

Over the life of the MIT group, a number of themes ebbed and flowed. Consistent themes that were brought to the forefront by core members of the group (even as that core shifted over time) included relationships, substance use and abuse, anger at women, and power issues in relationships with other men (usually regarding bosses and fathers). However there were also themes that emerged from a particular group of men at a particular time that have been significant issues for most men's groups. The group leaders often discussed how powerful and pervasive some themes became in the group. There were at times tongue-in-cheek thoughts of renaming the group by its current pervasive theme, such as "Men and Codependency," "Men and Their Fathers," "Men and Their Mothers," and "Men Who Hate the Women Who Love/Hate Them" (à la *Oprah*). Although these changing themes elicited humor at the agency, they did warrant differing intervention strategies and different ways of working with the group (a few of which are discussed below). The discussion of some of these themes, and their concomitant interventions, should help others conduct more effective groups with men.

Relationships

Most discussions of relationships focused on women (relationships with men are also discussed below). This theme was the most consistent throughout the life of the group. Men struggled with divorces, separations, being dumped by partners, and behaving in ways that were destructive to male–female relationships. Discussions often would move from the sharing of painful emotions, to anger about how a client felt treated by his partner, and then would rapidly spiral into "women bashing." Much of the anger and pain was expressed through such tirades, and group leaders often learned to look for such catharsis from newly entering group members who wanted a forum in which to tell their story. Although this time was important for members to both share and be supportive, sometimes the anger would dwell. Successful interventions during these group sessions included much role-playing, role reversals, and discussion among members. What men most wanted at these times was support, and it was important for group leaders to facilitate links between men who shared similar concerns (e.g., between two men who were both struggling with limited visitation with their children, men who had divorced or separated, or men who were considering leaving a relationship).

Codependency

Some of the men described issues that had been defined as codependency (Beattie, 1987; Larsen, 1984) but, more recently, have been described as problems with boundaries and limits in relationships. Men with these concerns seemed unable to let go of relationships that had ended (even some who had ended the relationships themselves); they exhibited such behaviors as following former partners around town, monitoring their behavior, and constantly calling and hanging up before they would be recognized. Given new laws in many states, such behaviors might today be considered stalking or harassment, but the level of psychopathology of these men would preclude threats of harm. Along with relationship issues described above, men's dependency on their partners, their fear of these feelings and behaviors, the rage at seeing themselves as weak and their inability to let go of relationships brought the theme of anger about women and relationships to the group in every cycle. In some stages of the group, this theme remained for several months at a time. This was a theme that needed discussion and some resolution with each core of members throughout the life of the group.

Interventions that were successful with this theme were many and varied. Again, linking men with similar stories helped them to share the pain, anger, and fear. Talking directly about codependency and the inability to maintain or respect barriers also helped men come to terms with behavior that was ineffective and prevented them from establishing more satisfying relationships. Giving members a brief description or an audiotape about codependency and asking them to come and discuss it at the next session was also helpful. Much of this information can be found in the recovery movement (12-step programs) and includes the work of Melodie Beattie (1987) and Ernie Larsen (1984). Being able to work with men and to find humor in their pain and struggle was especially helpful in the group. I believe that accessing men's pain through humor is important because it allows men to feel their emotions more deeply and to share more of their fears.

Fathering

Being able to talk about relationships between fathers and sons is one of the critical issues in a men's group. It is a key to understanding the history and perceptions of men, and thus, is crucial to the success of any such group. Discussions of fathers either come spontaneously or can be programmed into group work. In the MIT group, this theme was brought forth at least yearly in the changing core of the group, and it often recurred throughout the experience of some members. Fathers who were emotionally or physically absent, abandoning fathers, abusive fathers and their stern ways (verbal, physical, and emotional abuse all played a part in such discussions), and loving fathers who had died became significant themes and important resolutions for the men.

The stories men brought to group regarding their fathers, and the nature of group composition at specific times, highlighted the struggles of men trying to be better fathers to their children. Especially poignant was the interchange between two men, neither of whom had custody of their children, and how they coped with the loss of daily contact. Joining the discussion were men whose fathers had divorced their mothers, who related what it was like from the child's perspective during these struggles.

Being a son was a perspective that all men could identify with, and this brought many hours of discussion. As the composition of the group changed over the years, this theme also took on several variations: being an adult son of an aging father (or aging parents); growing up without a father or other male role models (one young member grew up in a family with sisters, a mother, aunts, and a grandmother—all in one household— and never knew his father); and dealing with the loss of a father. One of the most powerful series of groups occurred when a group leader's father died during the middle of a semester. Not only was the leader able to share his struggles and grief but, in his absence to attend the funeral, the group began a journey of discovery about fathers that continued for many weeks.

Interventions included discussions as described above, sharing stories about fathers, and bringing pictures of fathers and other significant men to the group to share and aid in storytelling. A videotape of the 1990 public television special, *A Gathering of Men*, which featured the work of Robert Bly and was hosted by Bill Moyers, became a regular feature in the MIT group. Almost 90 minutes in length, this videotape provides the stories and poetry of Bly as well as discussions with participants in Bly's weekend retreats and with other therapists who had worked with men. The tape produced much discussion and enhanced awareness to the work of the group. Given that the MIT group met for 2 hours per session, leaders tried to use this tape in a variety of ways: (a) showing the whole tape and discussing it briefly; (b) showing the tape in two segments over 2 consecutive weeks, allowing more time for discussion; and (c) showing it over 3 consecutive weeks, so that group and individual concerns could also be addressed. The second format appears to have been most helpful. This work by Moyers and Bly continues to be a useful tool in bringing forth issues of men and their fathers and sons, and I continue to recommend it. Although some therapists who treat men have great difficulty with the premises of the mythopoetic men's movement, a willingness to use materials that facilitate men's growth should take precedent.

Men and Their Mothers

For some men, unresolved issues related to mothers had tremendous impact on their development and their relationships with significant women in their lives. For some men who grew up with emotionally or physically absent fathers, relationships with their mothers became even more significant. Talking about mothers was usually quite difficult for group members. This finding has been consistent for most men I have worked with, both in groups and as individuals. Family loyalty, protection of a mother viewed as helpless against the wishes of a brutal father, and concerns about sisters all figure significantly in the work that can be accomplished with men to improve the quality of their relationships and their lives (May & Eichenfield, 1987). The inclusion of sisters is noteworthy, because many men who were younger children in their families may have been raised by an older sister who served as a surrogate mother or became the parentified child for the family.

Allowing men to talk about the anger, pain, and sorrow of their relationships with women often led to conversations about the important women in their lives. Venting about the current women in their lives helped members share how important, significant, or difficult their relationships with mother, sisters, or grandmothers were. During the life of the group, a number of structured times were set aside to talk about mother–son relationships. Sharing photos or stories and making connections among members were all important sources of successful intervention. In addition, guided fantasies about past events with mothers (e.g., exercises such as recalling "the earliest memory of your mother" or "What was the moment in your growing up when your mother was most proud of you?") could elicit powerful emotions and fueled discussions that lasted for several group sessions.

In general (perhaps because of gender role socialization), men are less able to be angry at their mothers than at their fathers. This experience was not unique for the men in the MIT group and follows a pattern that many therapists (including myself) have found, even when the behavior of mothers was horribly abusive and left men emotionally scarred. What the MIT group leaders found, over the years, was that pushing men far about issues with fathers could be tolerated by many clients and the group, but pushing men to disclose or share their terrible experiences with women important in their lives when they were growing up was not tolerated. Therapists running men's groups should be aware of how these experiences with parents are different and that each is significant to the success of the group.

Making connections between the women in members' pasts and the women current in their lives is a critical issue in the success of any men's group (even in groups with gay and bisexual men). How this might be accomplished most effectively depends on, for example, the theoretical orientation of the leaders and awareness of these issues for the members. In the MIT group, because relationships with women were such a core issue and because of the rotating membership, men often asked each other (especially as new members entered the group) about their relationships with mothers and were willing to share their own experiences. Again, the belief that the most powerful interventions occur in group between members shows the wisdom of this form of intervention strategy.

FUTURE DIRECTIONS

Setting

It is my belief that the MIT model of a men's group for those who function adequately in the interpersonal arena can work effectively in a variety of settings. Most men's groups that have members of a variety of ages and classes generally are in the domestic violence venue, where men are often referred or mandated for treatment. Although therapy for men has traditionally been viewed as "therapy for rich White men," many agencies and practitioners are seeing increases in men from a variety of races, classes, ethnic groups, and circumstances; this anecdotal finding suggests that more men are getting the message about the need and benefit of counseling or therapy and are finding their way to our offices. Men generally do not stay in therapy for long (Scher, 1987); a group for men that emphasizes examining *transition* suggests that such treatment is time limited, and so men may be more likely to join.

Limitations

Clearly, most of the men in the MIT group were verbal, intelligent, and capable of expressing themselves fairly well. Not all groups of men in other settings will be as facile. Transition-oriented groups may not work in all settings, but agencies and private practice settings could benefit from this model. The model can also be adjusted to help group members benefit from treatment that may not require as much verbal facility. More structure and the use of psychoeducational exercises (Gertner & Harris, 1993) might assist men who have more serious psychological concerns than those I have described above.

The lack of minority men in the group and the use of only one African American group leader in its 5-year lifetime raises some questions about how well this group would work with minority men in a mixed group or with all-minority groups. In addition, the lack of gay or bisexual members or therapists in the group raises concerns about the model's generalizability. Several group therapists (Lee, 1988; Rabinowitz & Cochran, 1987; Washington, 1982) have recommended role-playing issues of race, ethnicity, class, and sexual orientation in such a group. It is unknown whether such simulations would be successful in the group I have described. In addition, there is some question about the availability of such therapies for diverse groups of men. Although such an issue is well beyond the scope of this chapter, it should be raised by agencies and group practices in the planning of services for men.

Future Research

Measuring the outcomes of groups for men in transition is, at best, quite difficult. Other chapters in this book relate insights into important issues in group-therapy-outcome research, and so, I do not cover this here. What can be investigated further are possible pre- and postgroup measures of members' self-concept and self-esteem; changes in behavior as reported by significant others in the lives of men; and opportunities to look at qualitative methods for reviewing self-reported outcomes of group members.

REFERENCES

Andronico, M. P. (Chair). (1993, August). *Men of minorities in group treatment.* Symposium presented at the 101st Annual Convention of the American Psychological Association, Toronto, Ontario, Canada.

Beattie, M. (1987). *Codependent no more: How to stop controlling others and start caring for yourself.* San Francisco: Harper & Row.

Carlson, T. A. (1987). Counseling with veterans. In M. Scher, M. Stevens, G. Good, & G. A. Eichenfield (Eds.), *Handbook of counseling and psychotherapy with men* (pp. 344–359). Newbury Park, CA: Sage.

Eichenfield, G. A. (1988). Needs of special populations of men. In R. J. May & M. Scher (Eds.), *Changing roles for men on campus* (*New Directions in Student Services, 42,* 35–51). San Francisco: Jossey-Bass.

Fuhriman, A. (1974). *Group conceptualization.* Unpublished manuscript, University of Utah.

Gertner, D. M., & Harris, J. E. (1993). *Experiencing masculinity: Exercises, activities, and resources for teaching and learning about men.* Unpublished manuscript.

Good, G., & May, R. (1987). Developmental issues, environmental influences and the nature of therapy with college men. In M. Scher, M. Stevens, G. Good, & G. A. Eichenfield (Eds.), *Handbook of counseling and psychotherapy with men* (pp. 150–164). Newbury Park, CA: Sage.

Heppner, P. P., & Gonzales, D. S. (1987). Men counseling men. In M. Scher, M. Stevens, G. Good, & G. A. Eichenfield (Eds.), *Handbook of counseling and psychotherapy with men* (pp. 30–38). Newbury Park, CA: Sage.

Larsen, E. (1984). *Stage two recovery: Life beyond addiction.* San Francisco: Harper & Row.

Lee, C. C. (1988). Black manhood training: Group counseling for male Blacks in grades 7–12. *Journal for Specialists in Group Work, 12,* 18–25.

Levant, R., & Kelly, J. (1990). *Between father and child: How to become the kind of father you want to be.* New York: Viking Press.

Long, D. C. (1987). Working with men who batter. In M. Scher, M. Stevens, G. Good, & G. A. Eichenfield (Eds.), *Handbook of counseling and psychotherapy with men* (pp. 305–320). Newbury Park, CA: Sage.

May, R., & Eichenfield, G. A. (1987, March). *Men and their mothers.* Workshop presented at the meeting of the American College Personnel Association, Chicago.

Moore, D., & Leafgren, F. (Eds.). (1990). *Problem-solving strategies and interventions for men in conflict.* Alexandria, VA: American Association for Counseling and Development.

Moyers, B. (Host). (1990). A gathering of men [videotape]. (Available from Public Broadcasting Service, New York.)

Rabinowitz, F., & Cochran, S. (1987). Counseling men in groups. In M. Scher, M. Stevens, G. Good, & G. Eichenfield (Eds.), *Handbook of counseling and psychotherapy with men* (pp. 51–67). Newbury Park, CA: Sage.

Scher, M. (1981). Men in hiding: A challenge for the counselor. *Personnel and Guidance Journal, 60,* 199–202.

Scher, M. (1987). Implications and future directions. In M. Scher, M. Stevens, G. Good, & G. A. Eichenfield (Eds.), *Handbook of counseling and psychotherapy with men* (pp. 388–390). Newbury Park, CA: Sage.

Scher, M., Stevens, M., Good, G., & Eichenfield, G. A. (Eds.). (1987). *Handbook of counseling and psychotherapy with men*. Newbury Park, CA: Sage.

Skovholt, T. (1978). Feminism and men's lives. *Counseling Psychologist, 7*, 3–10.

Tedder, S., & Scherman, A. (1987). Counseling single fathers. In M. Scher, M. Stevens, G. Good, & G. A. Eichenfield (Eds.), *Handbook of counseling and psychotherapy with men* (pp. 265–277). Newbury Park, CA: Sage.

Washington, C. S. (1982). Challenging men in groups. *Journal for Specialists in Group Work, 7*, 132–136.

7

MEN MENTORING MEN IN GROUPS

ARTHUR M. HORNE, DAVID L. JOLLIFF, and ERIC W. ROTH

Mentoring happens when a more experienced person provides guidance for a less experienced person. One often thinks of mentoring happening in the development of a young person's career, when an older, more experienced worker shares the "secrets of the trade" with the younger, more naive person. Such mentoring supports the career development of the novice and serves to provide continuity for the labors of the mentor, sometimes far beyond the mentor's working life. Although this process has long been thought important to the development and continuity of contributions in the workplace, there seems to be a shortage of mentoring in domains other than employed work. For young men, such other domains as being a father and husband or even such spiritual and emotional domains as developing a mature sense of their own masculinity are potential areas for mentoring. We begin this chapter by reviewing the current information on the concept and process of mentoring. Then, because mentoring is a stage in a wider context of developmental issues, we discuss and illustrate other critical

We acknowledge George Gazda's significant contributions to the field of group work, to mentoring, and to the personal and professional development of each of us. Through his leadership and creativity Gazda has helped shape group work to be the force it is today; in doing so, he served as a model for all of us and as a mentor for many, and he is now in the stage of sharing wisdom with us. We thank you for all you have been to us, for all you have done with us, and for the caring and sensitivity you shared as you directed us in our journeys.

stages. Finally, we specifically address the use of all-male groups to help meet the mentoring needs of selected male participants.

MENTORING RESEARCH

Mentoring is generally understood as the providing of good guidance from a more experienced to a less experienced person; however, depending on the context in which the term is used, it can mean different things to different people. This variability in defining the term makes it difficult to discuss mentoring in a concise and discriminating fashion, and the research to date has reflected this confusion and lack of consensus. Nonetheless, numerous studies have documented the importance of mentoring in adult life experience (see Carden, 1990, for a recent review), and much of the research is applicable to working with men in groups.

Although the term *mentor* goes back to ancient times, it was Daniel Levinson and his colleagues who recently focused attention on mentoring in their study of adult male development (Levinson, Darrow, Klein, Levinson, & McKee, 1978). They described a mentor as a transitional figure who welcomes the young man into the adult world and serves as a guide, teacher, and sponsor. The objective of the mentor–protégé relationship is to help a novice acquire a fuller sense of authority, autonomy, and responsibility—the essential elements of maturity. As Levinson et al. pointed out, "this relationship enables the recipient to identify with a person who exemplifies many of the qualities he seeks. It enables him to form an internal figure who offers love, admiration, and encouragement in his struggles" (1978, p. 334). The mentor supports the protégé in his self-definition, affirms the value of the protégé's "dream," and helps the protégé create a satisfactory life structure that serves as the vehicle for his aspirations, plans, and accomplishments.

Additional evidence of the importance of mentoring for men has come from a longitudinal study of men by Vaillant (1993). He discovered that men who had mentors were 2 to 3 times more likely to achieve a vocational identity—a prerequisite to career success—than men who did not have mentors. Other researchers have examined the effects of mentoring relationships on career development for both men and women. Results of recent studies have confirmed that the presence of mentoring is positively related to career attainment (Dreher & Ash, 1990), job satisfaction (Chao & Gardner, 1992), and career mobility (Scandura, 1992). Mentoring has also been linked to creative achievement in adult life (Torrance, 1983).

As the importance of mentoring has been recognized, there have been attempts to ensure that young people beginning their careers have opportunities to gain the benefits of a mentoring relationship. There has been a move to incorporate formal channels of mentoring into organizational structures (Alleman & Gray, 1986; Bernstein & Kaye, 1986; Lawrie, 1987; Zey, 1988), including providing for institutionalized incentives and evaluation of progress. There has been some disagreement about the effectiveness of this approach, and some feel that a successful mentoring relationship depends on mutual attractiveness and freely chosen involvement between mentor and protégé. As Kram (1987) explained, "research to date indicates that mentoring relationships cannot be engineered but must emerge from the spontaneous and mutual involvement of two individuals who see potential value in relating to each other" (p. 185). However, even if direct matchings are not effective as a way to promote mentoring, there are steps that men can take to increase the probability of getting and giving good mentoring. We discuss these steps later in the chapter.

A developmental cycle for mentoring has been suggested by several authors (e.g., Hobbs, 1982; Kram, 1987). Newby and Heide (1992) defined the following five phases of the mentoring process:

1. Goal Setting. In this first stage, the protégé explores the worth of having a mentoring relationship.
2. Initiation. Initially, the protégé needs support and guidance, and the mentor is in a position to provide that direction. Both members examine their respective roles and learn the boundaries of the roles, and each confronts concerns about commitment.
3. Cultivation. The partnership between protégé and mentor is expanded and grows. The mentor provides counsel, direction, and guidance, moving from direct teaching and leadership to becoming more of an adviser and consultant.
4. Separation. As the protégé develops confidence and ability, he or she moves toward increased autonomy and independence. The protégé demonstrates an ability to solve problems and address issues independently, turning to the mentor more for support and affirmation than for guidance.
5. Redefinition. The process of mentoring culminates in a relationship of peers, in which the mentor accepts the former protégé more as a colleague and partner than as a student.

Although there are clear advantages to being mentored, there has been some controversy about whether mentoring is always a pleasant and satisfying relationship. The process can and should be fulfilling for the parties involved, but reportedly, difficulties may develop (Kram, 1987; Ragins & Cotten, 1991). For example, Levinson et al. (1978) revealed that an overwhelming majority of mentor–protégé relationships have ended with "strong conflicts and bad feelings on both sides" (p. 100).

Mentoring relationships may entail some of the same conflicts and difficulties that are found in other important relationships. They can trigger struggles that are reminiscent of parental interactions and can lead to the same kinds of disappointments, recriminations, and violated expectations that occur whenever two people are intimately involved with one another. However, it also seems evident that mentoring relationships can grow into mutually rewarding peer relationships and friendships (Kram, 1987). In the discussion that follows about mentoring in groups, we point out how group work can facilitate the developmental cycle of a mentoring relationship.

MENTORING AND OTHER MALE-TO-MALE RELATIONSHIPS

Male mentoring is part of a lifelong pattern of influence of men on other men in service of the development of a mature masculinity. Until the early nineteenth century, fathers in America were responsible for training children for their life's work and directing their moral and spiritual growth (Rotundo, 1985). During the nineteenth and early twentieth centuries, fathers continued to be their sons' chief counselors in such areas as politics and economics and in the practical skills for survival in the world. Fathers had primary responsibility for providing career direction, for benchmarking the transitions into manhood, and for building character through discipline.

As men were forced by the economic realities of industrialization to pursue occupations that removed them from daily life at home, they tried to find more meaning in their work and invested more of themselves in their roles as providers (Yankelovich & Immerwahr, 1983). Their interaction with their children required more planning and deliberate attention and became less of a priority. Work eventually overshadowed the father's role in child rearing and reduced his opportunities to teach and participate directly in the development of his sons and daughters. Essentially, "the separation of the workplace from the home undermined the traditional authority of the father" (Rotundo, 1985, p. 13).

At the same time, the decline in extended family relations removed a significant source of male guidance from the lives of boys. Family relocation meant that uncles, grandfathers, and male relations were seen less often or not at all. Primary education became the province of a predominately female teaching staff (Beymer, 1995). Education at the elementary-school level has become highly populated with female teachers and administrators offering little male guidance and providing a learning environment that is not optimally conducive to the male learning style. As Moir and Jessell (1991) have pointed out, boys' orientation to the world is through action, exploration, and tangible things. In school, however, he is expected to sit quietly, to listen, to not fidget, and to pay attention to ideas. This is a contradiction between body–mind and school rules. Such limited contacts between young boys and mature men have resulted in impoverished social opportunities in terms of male developmental experiences with other, more senior men.

Researchers on development have examined the importance of strong character as being fundamental to psychological well-being and the ability to attain a mature and well-adjusted adulthood (Heath, 1991). The influences of other men are essential in the development of desired character traits and a healthy and robust masculine identity by boys. In fact, men both contribute to and benefit from relationships with other men that assist and enhance their growth and development. Men may provide nurturance, serve as models, initiate developmental transitions, guide the acquisition of mature competencies, and impart the wisdom of age and experience to other men throughout their lives. The presence or absence of their influence, and the quality of the relationships that form, have implications for the satisfaction and prosperity of men's lives.

Gilmore (1990) has found that the male maturation process, when fully and successfully completed, results in a consistent but flexible and open self-identity, as well as a cultural identity that connects the person strongly and reliably to his community roles and responsibilities. The positive influence of other men is to foster the acquisition of the psychological virtues or dimensions that constitute exemplary manhood—that is, to provide inspiration and validation along the way.

If maturity is attained through appropriate and effective guidance during development, then immaturity results when guidance is lacking, inappropriate, or inadequate. Lacking healthy figures to identify with, boys develop distorted images of masculinity and adopt stereotypical attitudes and behaviors. The behavior of immature males (which is sometimes mistakenly generalized to be the behavior of all males) can result in either dependent individuals who fear and reject masculine attributes or enraged individuals who engage in self-abuse and violence toward others (Beymer, 1995; Steinberg, 1993). We turn now to a discussion of the significant relationships between men that influence the course of their development.

FIVE DEVELOPMENTAL INFLUENCES ON MEN

Nurturing

The earliest influences of male development are found with fathers. Paternal relationships are the primary stimulant for male-to-male bonding and attachment. As boys begin to separate and individuate from their mothers, fathers become alternative nurturers—not replacing mothers, but extending the child's experience to fathering and, eventually, to other relationships as well. Fathers are a key part of the reciprocal nurturing attachments that are critical in early development (Pruett, 1988) and that have particularly beneficial effects for children in the areas of increased cognitive competence, empathy, and internal locus of control (Lamb, 1986).

Fathers provide a reliable source of empathic attachment for their children and are a primary source of identification for their sons. The father becomes part of the "holding environment" (Winnicott, 1965), stimulates individuation, and initiates the child into group relations (Osherson, 1995; Rotundo, 1985).

As gender identity develops, a boy begins to form a self-concept on the basis of similarity to his father and dissimilarity to his mother. This becomes the foundation for his personal sense of masculinity (Beymer, 1995). Paternal nurturance increases the willingness to take risks by providing the internal resources that lead to self-efficacy and confidence and by instilling a sense of strength, power, and solidity.

Inadequate bonding or attachment with the father can result in fear of intimacy and a preoccupation with autonomy. Successful bonding allows the boy to move into the next developmental task: selecting the role models that will provide a more diverse image of masculinity for the developing ego.

Role Modeling

Men other than the father become important in a boy's life at the time that he is becoming aware of a world that has importance beyond just his parents. They provide examples for the young boy that stimulate and foster his aspirations and ideals. Therefore, they serve as the stimuli for the internalization of desirable attributes and as reinforcements for the instrumental learning of competencies.

By seeing what is expected of other males, boys come to know what is expected of them. Older males demonstrate how to solve problems, handle adversity and failure, and recover from setbacks. This leads to resilience and the willingness to persevere. Role models impart permission to take risks, try new behaviors, and acquire new skills. Through their admiration of role models, boys begin to define and internalize the standards that will guide their own behavior.

Role models do not have to be personal acquaintances; they can be found in books, movies, comics, and other sources of powerful and appealing male prototypes. Good modeling results in boys with flexible and adaptive identities and confidence in their abilities. If such models are lacking, then boys tend to select stereotypical models of masculinity that are self-consciously imitated. Frequently, these are other boys, only slightly older, who have not progressed far enough themselves to act as adequate guides. Selecting such models can lead to the development of a rigid and exaggerated masculine social identity.

Initiation

As adolescent boys enter the periods in their lives that will lead to adulthood, they seek relationships with men who will initiate them into manhood (Raphael, 1988). The function of initiation is to provide the external validation for the change from child to man, to "overlay and counteract a hesitant and resisting nature" (Gilmore, 1990, p. 98) with the motivation to assume the responsibilities of adulthood. Historically, older men have constructed challenging and risky ceremonies and rituals designed to build a young man's confidence in his ability to perform. These rites of passage have stressed teamwork, loyalty, and group commitment as counterweights to individual achievement and excessive egocentricity.

Initiation moves a young man from a natural self-centeredness to a more mature, healthy inclusion of others. It facilitates the development of personal performance standards and self-validation skills through the internalization of competition as a natural part of self-motivation. These become critical factors in helping to ensure success at work (Weiss, 1990). Initiation focuses on goal setting and planning and helps the young man learn to identify priorities, to plan and execute strategies for achievement, and to defer gratification enough to begin accumulating a reservoir of resources.

In Gilmore's (1990) review of masculine initiation in non-Western societies and cultures, he found that public acknowledgment and validation of the initiate's rite of passage was consistently stressed. Developmental psychologists have also mentioned the importance of symbolic celebrations to mark the passing of childhood and transition into adulthood (e.g., Kegan, 1982). The social reality is that such occasions are rarely available for boys in contemporary American society. This results in poorly executed attempts by male peers to improvise rituals or to substitute ersatz initiation rituals (e.g., gang initiations, locker-room hazing, or fraternity beer fests; Raphael, 1988). These rituals generally fail to provide the full acknowledgment thought to be essential for a successful transition, because only mature men can initiate boys into manhood.

Failure to be successfully initiated can result in a kind of perpetual adolescence, with no sense of commitment to either self or community. It can leave the man with a perennial sense of not having arrived or "made it." If successful, initiation will lead to embarking on an adult life course and connection with a mentor who will guide the youth into his career.

Mentoring

The purpose of mentoring is to continue the process by which a young man grows and matures. In seeking a mentor, a young man is looking for a special relationship to help him become established as a productive and contributing member of his occupational and social community. Mentors continue to foster the skill development and knowledge acquisition that young men seek in order to thrive in the adult world. Levinson et al. (1978) have stated that "the true mentor serves as an analog in adulthood of the 'good enough' parent for the child" (p. 99), providing advice, sponsorship, and guidance.

A young man must first develop the capacity for intimacy before entering into a relationship with an older adult as a protégé. This means that he must have the interpersonal skills necesary to accept guidance, listen to advice, work collaboratively, and manage anger maturely (Vaillant, 1993). Other factors, such as higher autonomy and a sense of purpose, are also related to a readiness to be mentored (Rice & Brown, 1990).

Earlier in this chapter, we have discussed mentoring processes and the functions that mentoring plays during the early adulthood period. Levinson et al. (1978) found that mentoring was one of the most important relationships that young men could have. Failure to secure mentoring results in a man who does not thrive; it can create a sense of bitterness and failure, perhaps even a sense of abandonment. Unfortunately, there is a notable lack of mentoring in many areas of life, such as in community and family domains, which appear to be suffering from neglect and poor leadership.

As a man enters the second half of his life, there is a shift in overall focus from a preoccupation with his own achievements to concerns with the broader cultural context of his community and with establishing and guiding the next generation. He shifts from being mentored to becoming a mentor himself. His relationships with his peers become more egalitarian and less competitive, and his relationships with younger men become more reciprocal and nurturing. There is an increase in his reflective self-awareness, other-centeredness, the sense of reciprocity in his relationships, and his ability to discriminate the authentic from the superficial (Heath, 1991).

Becoming a mentor to younger men offers the opportunity to pass on personal values and wisdom to those who are following—what Erikson (1963) has called *generativity*, or "concern in establishing and guiding the next generation" (p. 267). Through mentoring, a man can attain a sense of accomplishment and move on to consider the larger context of his life in its spiritual and communal aspects. This permits him to begin the process we call *eldering*.

Eldering

As a man crosses the threshold of midlife, he becomes an elder of the community in which he lives. He develops an awareness that it is not just his achievement that is important but the returning of the fruits of this labor to the community. Advancing to more senior status invites a man to display his manhood through his generosity, by giving away that which he has acquired for himself. The process involves a shift from the outside to the inside, from the physical to the spiritual, and from egocentricity to community centeredness.

Borg (1994) has referred to these elders, these teachers of wisdom, as "sages." Sages speak of two types of wisdom: conventional and alternative. *Conventional wisdom* is the mainstream wisdom of a culture, a culture's understanding about what is real and how to live, or the dominant consciousness. Conventional wisdom is based on the dynamic of rewards and punishments. Socially, it creates a world of hierarchies and boundaries; psychologically, it becomes the basis for identity and self-esteem. One is to judge oneself in relation to others. Conventional wisdom is pervasive in all cultures; it is necessary for the survival of the culture and the self-understanding of individuals.

Alternative wisdom questions conventional wisdom, and speaks of another way, a road less traveled. It facilitates a cognitive shift to a new wisdom, an altered perception of truth, or an alternative lifestyle. Very often the shift in perception and focus is from outside the person to inside, that is, from the physical to the spiritual or from the individual to the community. The path of transformation requires a rebirth into a new awareness. Alternative wisdom directs people toward self-knowledge, intimacy, and fulfillment. The elder is the purveyor of both alternative and conventional wisdom in the culture.

Eldering is a vital role and identity for men in their later years that appears to have all but vanished from American life. The main preoccupation identified with older citizens has become degenerative disease and financial burden. The same social realities that work against finding rites of initiation or a mentor also prevent men from assuming the elder role. The decline in the sagacious influence of elders may be responsible for some of the malaise and cynicism that seems so prevalent nowadays.

MENTORING IN GROUPS

The most effective way of assisting men in their journey toward mature masculine development is through group work. (See Jolliff & Horne, chap. 4 of this book, for a discussion of specific group interventions relevant for men.) Group work provides the opportunity of learning from other men in a structured or semistructured environment designed to provide experiences of men working with men. On the basis of our experiences of working with men in groups, we have found that mentoring in groups takes three forms:

1. Groups designed to provide mentoring roles within the group setting;
2. Groups designed to provide direction to help men identify ways of becoming mentored;
3. Groups designed to provide support for men who are willing to take on one or more of the five facilitator roles.

Providing Roles Within the Group

Group work for men that will be focusing on providing mentoring and other facilitation roles needs to begin with a heterogeneous membership. Having men in a group at different levels of personal development, with varied life experiences and divergent worldviews, presents the best opportunity for the facilitation to occur. A group comprising homogeneous males does not allow the members to work with one another to build on life experiences that will lead to mature masculinity.

It is not necessary to have members at all levels of development in a group for men to address their masculine development. It is necessary, however, that the men in the group be open to guiding one another and to facilitating the growth process of others no matter what their level of development is. A given group may lack representatives from the chronological or developmental age of each stage, but the opportunity for group members to be introduced to stage-specific experiences can occur nonetheless. For example, in one of our groups, a young man who had attained considerable maturity in his relationships with women was able to provide guidance to an older member who lacked experience in this area. Also, men who were not adequately nurtured as children may, surprisingly, learn through group experiences that men can nurture other men. Even late-stage experiences such as mentoring or eldering can be had in a group on a limited basis from those who are not yet mentors or elders. Although these experiences may be of limited value, they provide a window into stages yet to come. Such experiences help prepare men to be receptive to their developmental needs and to opportunities they may have been inclined to overlook.

The group provides a safe place to ask for nurturing, role modeling, initiating, mentoring, and eldering. In general society, men are not in a position to seek out facilitators, particularly beyond work settings. The group—through the safety of confidentiality, mutual support, and facilitating growth of the self and others—allows the risk taking needed to identify areas of need and to ask for help. Also, supportive group members are able to help identify levels at which an individual appears to lack development, that is, where a person may need to seek help to meet a shortcoming that he has had in his life.

Finding a Mentor

A second function that groups may have is in helping find mentors. The group provides a safe and convenient setting in which men may express their concerns about not having satisfactorily worked through the developmental stages of mature masculinity because of a lack of a male facilitator in one or more stages of their development. This may include their current level of development, for which they may be interested in identifying a mentor to provide them support, leadership, training, and guidance in their work and personal life situations.

Men who have had traumatic or inadequate experiences during the nurturing stage or bad experiences with attempts at being mentored may be reluctant to ask for mentoring, or worse, they may fear reexperiencing the earlier wounding and are thus unwilling to receive mentoring even if it is offered. What is needed for them is new experiences with men: healing experiences that can provide evidence of the nurturing and mentoring qualities of genuine manhood.

The group setting can provide an opportunity to explore the advantages of having a mentor and to begin to examine ways of entering the process. As the group examines the advantages and disadvantages of mentoring, this can help clarify the process and provide direction in how to bring about the experience. It is also a place where members can begin role-playing and enacting methods of talking with potential mentors or other male facilitators that they may be interested in seeking out.

Related to fear of asking for mentoring is the reciprocal concern of rejections should the potential mentee not be accepted. By using the group to practice skills for identifying and seeking a mentor, a man can significantly reduce the likelihood of rejection and shame. The group provides an opportunity for information sharing as well, so that men can pool their knowledge of potential mentors and identify strengths and potential similarities between protégé and mentor.

Learning to Mentor

A third function of group work is to provide an opportunity for men to learn to become facilitators in other men's lives. There are no classes on how to become a mentor, there is no instruction on facilitating mature masculinity, and often men are unsure of whether they have enough to offer to take on the role or fear they would fail if they made themselves available. Also, men may see little benefit for themselves of becoming a mentor. The group is a good place to learn these benefits and to practice one's skills.

Rewards for Mentoring

Newby and Heide (1992) have suggested six potential intrinsic rewards of mentoring. The first is curiosity. The authors suggested that humans are motivated not only by novelty but also by the curiosity of a new and different role in the group. Second, humans are motivated by choice, and making decisions and directing the decisions of another gives one a sense of control over one's own life. Third, humans are motivated by complexity, and individuals focus on and invest effort in tasks of moderate complexity. Mentoring a fellow group member may provide this experience of complexity. Fourth, humans are motivated by cooperation. Working together for the growth of another individual can be highly rewarding. Fifth, humans are motivated by challenge. Mentors are challenged to discover the most effective ways to influence and facilitate the growth of another. Finally, humans are motivated by competence and confidence, and one's motivation is increased while performing tasks that demonstrate one's own knowledge and abilities.

By participating in group activities with other men, men can examine issues under a more reflective and safer "umbrella." In the group setting, men are able to share their interests in mentoring, to discuss their strengths and areas of concern, to provide feedback to one another, and to practice the skills necessary to begin facilitating other men's development.

GENERAL GROUP ISSUES

Issues related to all aspects of group work apply to working with men who seek mentoring in group work. The five stages of group development presented by Tuckman (1965) are important to consider when conducting men's mentoring groups: forming, storming, norming, performing, and adjourning.

Forming

In the forming stage of group work, attending to issues of safety and bonding around common themes is necessary. The leader must address boundaries, set limits, and establish positive goals for the group. These are sensitive issues for men, and in general, there can be considerable tension related to the beginning of the group. Forming a group that will focus on mentoring issues requires that participants come prepared to ask for help with the task of being facilitated, and this process is highly threatening to men—they worry about being taken advantage of, being rejected, and being shamed. The leader must have a high level of group formation skills to assist men in initiating the group process.

Storming

During the storming period of group work, participants begin to test the safety of the group—to explore issues and identify group members who can be helpful and those who are still not trusted. This is a period during which tension and concern about emotional safety and protection from shame are paramount. The leader must be able to encourage the exploration of fears, to draw members out, to cut off nontherapeutic participation, and to redirect communication lines to meet the focus of the group.

Norming

The norming stage continues from the storming stage. Members become familiar with one another, develop trust and confidence in one another, and begin to understand the rules of the group. During this period, the leader must help establish group norms, including identifying facilitator roles, individual needs for facilitators, and guidelines regarding group functions (such as safety, no shame, and willingness to help and support one another).

Performing

During the performing stage, group members begin identifying ways of serving as facilitators for one another. They help each member to clarify stages of development for which he has lacked an appropriate male facilitator and to understand what the process would have been like had a facilitator been present. From this discussion, the group develops ideas about how a member may be in need, what is needed, and who within the group may provide the functions to meet the need. During the working stage, men reach out to one another to provide the mature masculine roles they so frequently lacked in their early development. These may be developed through role-plays, enactments, dyadic work, or direct discussion among the members. The leader's job is to alert members to the work that is necessary and that is in process and to select methods of working together that will foster the nurturance, modeling, initiating, mentoring, or eldering that is called for in the moment of the group. The leader is also responsible for shifting the focus from one member or one facilitative role to another as is appropriate, for cutting off members who may be distracting from the facilitating, and to encourage the silence and reflection necessary for members to process their experiences.

Adjourning

During the adjourning stage, members identify changes they have made, express appreciation for other members who have reached out and facilitated their personal development in the area of mature masculinity, and begin the process of saying goodbye. The leader is responsible for alerting members to the closure, for encouraging men to process their feelings of loss, and for providing exercises that allow for effective group ending. Unlike therapy groups, many men's groups designed to address men's development through facilitative interactive group work do not simply stop. Our experience is that they frequently carry on in other forms and other models, for many of the men go on to have deep and lasting friendships, establish mentoring relationships beyond the group setting, and carry out the group involvement in other, non-therapy-oriented ways, such as camping, rafting, cookouts, backpacking, and related activities.

SUMMARY

Mentoring is an important part of male psychology, and it provides essential developmental experiences for men of all ages. We have expanded the concept to include a range of relationships between men that foster such things as nurturance, initiation, and the emergence of a mature masculinity. These developmental relationships, which appear to have been reasonably available in past times, are not easily found in today's society. Through group work, however, we believe many of these deficits can be effectively addressed and remediated. The group can provide a place for men to impart and receive mentoring as well as to receive support for seeking these relationships in their communities.

REFERENCES

Alleman, E., & Gray, W. (1986). *Designing productive mentoring programs.* Alexandria, VA: American Society for Training and Development.

Bernstein, B., & Kaye, B. (1986). Teacher, tutor, colleague, coach. *Personnel Journal, 65,* 44–51.

Beymer, L. (1995). *Meeting the guidance and counseling needs of boys.* Alexandria, VA: American Counseling Association.

Borg, M. J. (1994). *Meeting Jesus again for the first time.* New York: Harper Collins.

Carden, A. (1990). Mentoring and adult career development: The evolution of a theory. *Counseling Psychologist, 18,* 275–299.

Chao, G. T., & Gardner, P. D. (1992). Formal and informal mentorships: A comparison on mentoring functions and contrast with nonmentored counterparts. *Personnel Psychology, 45*, 619–636.

Dreher, G. F., & Ash, R. A. (1990). A comparative study of mentoring among men and women in managerial, professional, and technical positions. *Journal of Applied Psychology, 75*, 539–546.

Erikson, E. (1963). *Childhood and society.* New York: Norton.

Gilmore, D. D. (1990). *Manhood in the making.* New Haven, CT: Yale University Press.

Heath, D. H. (1991). *Fulfilling lives: Paths to maturity and success.* San Francisco: Jossey-Bass.

Hobbs, S. J. (1982). Male mentor relationships: A study of psychosocial development in early adulthood. (Unpublished dissertation, California School of Professional Psychology, Berkeley.) *Dissertation Abstracts International, 43,* 2016B.

Kegan, R. (1982). *The evolving self.* Cambridge, MA: Harvard University Press.

Kram, K. (1987). Mentoring in the workplace. In D. Hall & Associates (Eds.), *Career development in organizations* (pp. 160–201). San Francisco: Jossey-Bass.

Lamb, M. E. (1986). *The father's role: Applied perspectives.* New York: Wiley.

Lawrie, J. (1987). How to establish a mentoring program. *Training and Development Journal, 41,* 25–27.

Levinson, D., Darrow, C., Klein, E., Levinson, M., & McKee, B. (1978). *The seasons of a man's life.* New York: Knopf.

Moir, A., & Jessell, D. (1991). *Brain sex: The real difference between men and women.* New York: Dell.

Newby, T. J., & Heide, A. (1992). The value of mentoring. *Performance Improvement Quarterly, 5,* pp. 2–15.

Osherson, S. (1995). *The passions of fatherhood.* New York: Fawcett Columbine.

Pruett, K. D. (1988). *The nurturing father.* New York: Warner Books.

Ragins, B. R., & Cotten, J. L. (1991). Gender and willingness to mentor in organizations. *Journal of Management, 19,* 97–111.

Raphael, R. (1988). *The men from the boys: Rites of passage in male America.* Lincoln: University of Nebraska Press.

Rice, M. B., & Brown, R. D. (1990). Developmental factors associated with self-perceptions of mentoring competence and mentoring needs. *Journal of College Student Development, 31,* 293–299.

Rotundo, E. A. (1985). American fatherhood. *American Behavioral Scientist, 29,* 7–25.

Scandura, T. A. (1992). Mentorship and career mobility: An empirical investigation. *Journal of Organizational Behavior, 13,* 169–174.

Steinberg, W. S. (1993). *Masculinity: Identity conflict and transformation.* Boston: Shambhala.

Torrance, E. P. (1983). Role of mentors in creative achievement. *Creative Child and Adult Quarterly*, 8, 8–18.

Tuckman, B. (1965). Developmental sequence in small groups. *Psychological Bulletin*, 63, 384.

Vaillant, G. (1993). *The wisdom of the ego*. Cambridge, MA: Harvard University Press.

Weiss, R. S. (1990). *Staying the course*. New York: Free Press.

Winnicott, D. W. (1965). *The maturational processes and the facilitating environment*. New York: International Universities Press.

Yankelovich, D., & Immerwahr, J. (1983). *Putting the work ethic to work*. New York: Public Agenda Foundation.

Zey, M. (1988). A mentor for all reasons. *Personnel Journal*, 67, 46–51.

8

THE SOMERSET INSTITUTE'S MODERN MEN'S WEEKEND

GLENN W. WISSOCKI and MICHAEL P. ANDRONICO

The current men's movement that has developed over the past decades emphasizes that the modern world is not necessarily the "man's world" it was viewed as in the past. In many ways, this view is still present, but for the men who recently have been drawn to men's conferences and workshops, the world of their fathers no longer fits. The myth of maleness and its consequent roles have gone through serious reevaluation, leaving a majority of men searching for a new understanding of maleness that can help them meet the demands of their lives and replace a sense of general dissatisfaction with new patterns of meaning.

Politically motivated aspects of the movement, such as father's rights groups or groups like Men Against Rape, seek to change public policy or awareness regarding the male gender. They are important aspects of the masculine environment in modern times. They seem to focus on the behavior of men and on society's response to it.

Another broad division of the men's movement involves the internally focused men's groups, workshops, and literature. Within this subdivision is the "mythopoetic movement," which refers to a deep substrate of the unconscious structured by mythical motifs and expressed in poetic im-

We express our gratitude to Bill Bishop for his leadership participation in the Modern Men's Weekend and for his valuable ideas and contributions to this chapter. We also acknowledge Barbara Dazzo for her contributions to the development of the workshop and this chapter.

113

ages. Robert Bly, James Hillman, and Michael Meade are the central figures of mythopoeticism. Through their writings (e.g., Bly, 1990) and conferences they have used mythological, psychological, and spiritual information to help men find internal congruency and the strength to access empowering images of masculine energy.

Today's man finds himself confronted with significant challenges in both the external and internal spheres. Men's roles in society, particularly in the family, are shifting from a sole preoccupation with being protector–provider to include a nurturer–communicator role. This shift necessitates the development of additional skills and priorities. Traditional socialization of men to ignore emotions to accomplish their goals is no longer valued by all as courageous but, rather, is seen by many as insensitive. At the same time, however, the world of work for most men still rewards the "insensitive" qualities of a single-minded, unemotional approach to the task at hand.

In effect, modern men are faced with the conflicting demands of what is expected of them at home and work in this era. These challenges have created the context in which the men's movement exists. The large numbers of men attracted to the men's movement workshops, weekends, and conferences have had at least one strong commonality: They felt that something was missing in their lives as men. That missing piece might be called a sense of male identity, or a spiritual purpose, or just ordinary contentment. Unlike the political component of the men's movement, these groups sought internal change. It is one such internally focused group experience, the Modern Men's Weekend of the Somerset Institute (SMMW), that we focus on in this chapter.

One important aspect of the men's movement is the significance given to the beliefs and rituals of ancestral men. Modern men may find themselves confronted with a lack of commonly accepted information about being male. With the attitudes and behaviors of their fathers cast in doubtful light, men seek information in ancient ritual and belief. The men's movement provides opportunities for thousands of men to spend weekends in the woods, following rituals such as drumming and chanting in their search for an essential masculinity. Although the return to the images and rituals of the past has an obvious attraction to a great number of men, the modern, technological, and future-oriented culture of the present has difficulty supporting this approach. Thus, the media has tended to view this trend as simply "boys being boys."

The task for both the men's movement and individual men is to integrate the past with the present and to prepare for the future by reimagining masculinity in ways that meet the present challenges. A task for the mental health professional is to integrate traditional psychological practice with spirituality and mythology. Why?—because thousands of men do not flock to therapist's offices for traditional "talk therapy." This can easily be conceptualized as "resistance" and blamed historically, at best, on the socialization of men. In this chapter, we ask if it is possible that this so-called resistance represents not only, for instance, men's inability to ask for help, to reveal weaknesses, or to explore their feminine sides or fear of intimacy, but also a disagreement with the methods and perspectives of traditional therapy. That is, does the ritual of therapy fit all of today's men?

Moving therapy outside of the office was a significant contribution of the men's movement to the therapeutic process for men. The creation of a "sacred space" in which "soul" work could take place was an aspect of ritual contained in most of the male workshops. In an environment supportive of ritual and myth, a needed disruption is created in the routine cultural patterning that shapes men's lives. When done outdoors (most of the workshops spend at least some time outdoors), it reestablishes a conscious connection with nature. Although for some of the men a close connection with nature was and still remains a part of their lives, this vital and revitalizing relationship gets lost or blurred as one takes on the culturally determined tasks that define being male. Thus, the conceptualization for the SMMW includes the premise that a nature-oriented, nontraditional space is a fertile one for male exploration and discovery.

THE SMMW

Background and Ideology

The SMMW was conceived in 1986 by five members of the Somerset Institute for Psychotherapy, Education, and Research. The concept arose from a weekly group meeting designed to investigate and create nontraditional methods of helping individuals achieve life goals and overcome emotional or psychological difficulties. The Somerset Institute is a consortium of mental health practitioners from various orientations who work together to develop effective and innovative methods and strategies of psychotherapeutic intervention. The original concept of the SMMW was developed and refined by Michael Andronico, William Bishop, and Glenn Wissocki. The weekend was borne of ongoing discussions regarding men's issues and specific treatment approaches to working with men.

The SMMW was created around the universal paradigm of male initiation. According to Mircea Eliade (1958), "the history of religion distinguishes three categories or types of initiation" (p. 1). He went on to describe the similarities and differences between these three types, which include (a) puberty rites, (b) initiation into a secret society or cofraternity, and (c) "the type that occurs in connection with a mystical vocation; that is, on the level of primitive religion, the vocation of the medicine man or shaman" (Eliade, 1958, p. 3). The vision quest of the Native American (because of its focus on the discovery by each seeker of a deep personal myth that gives meaning to the individual life within the larger collective) became the structuring metaphor of this weekend. Included were aspects of both puberty rites and acceptance into a fraternity of fellow seekers.

The vision quest is a journey of spirit, courage, and discovery. It is a process of finding one's purpose or calling and requires an intimate and complete relationship with nature. This is a highly spiritual endeavor, because the purpose of the questor's life is communicated by forces outside of himself. In an actual vision quest, the man must be willing to die to achieve his vision of purpose (Foster & Little, 1989).

In many cultures, past and present, there exists a formal ritual that marks a male's transition into manhood. The lack of such formal rituals in Western culture has been well documented (Mahdi, Foster, & Little, 1988; Raphael, 1988). Informal rituals—such as boot camp in the armed services, fraternity initiations, or even college itself—approximate initiation, but these are not comprehensive enough to effect a complete transition. Emotionally, these rituals often demand courage and perseverance. Initiation is important in terms of the modern man because it is a process of dealing with and gaining mastery over childhood emotions and influences. In a very real sense, initiation rituals of the first type (puberty) prepare the male individual for all future development by forcefully and finally severing emotional attachment to childhood and painstakingly preparing him for adulthood, through indoctrination into the spiritual and cultural knowledge of his people. The modern Western world has become so complicated that there is no universal body of knowledge or experience that can be transmitted from one generation to the next that would adequately prepare initiates for the tasks ahead. Because of this, the burden of meaning has fallen on the individual and the small group of family and friends who can support him. Because of the lack of comprehensive rituals to effect this transition into adulthood, childhood adaptive patterns tend to remain and influence the search for deeper meaning. With this in mind, the SMMW proceeds developmentally by first uncovering these childhood adaptive patterns and then creating the opportunity to discover and articulate a new vision of the self.

The final important conceptual component of the SMMW is that of nature as an ally. On a very basic level, man has come to regard nature as an adversary—to be conquered, to be sheltered from, and to be apart from. At best, most men are able to connect with nature in a recreational manner. Beauty, space, fresh air, hunting, and fishing are typical experiences of male connectedness to nature. The experience of an interactional relationship with nature is outside of the day-to-day experience of most men. Yet, from an ancestral perspective, such an interactional relationship was once central to masculinity. The SMMW leads participants toward an interactional relationship with nature, with an eye on the most central tenet of the weekend: the integration of the psychological, mythical, and spiritual.

The Weekend

The SMMW begins on a Friday afternoon and ends on Sunday. In the following description, we address the content of the weekend as well as its rationale on several levels. Prior to the weekend, participants are given a list of supplies that they need to bring and are asked to arrive at a specified time. The SMMW is held at a local environmental center, in a wooded, secluded site. From the lodge, paths lead to woods and fields.

Friday Evening

The SMMW begins in a somewhat untraditional manner. After settling in on Friday evening, the men gather, and the three leaders each tell the story of their lives as men. They speak, in different ways, of their differentiation as men and as adults. Although the talks focus on how the sense of masculinity developed in each leader, they also reveal what meaning each leader holds for his presence and participation in the weekend. This has the effect of encouraging participants to contemplate their own stories of maturation as men and their reasons for being there, while raising anxiety in terms of the level of self-disclosure expected during the weekend. The anxiety of self-disclosure has roots in the deeper anxiety of the unknown and how each man will relate to it.

The tension created by the opening of the weekend is channeled into drawing rather than talking. After a brief meditation to access information about their own development, the participants are given crayons and markers and asked to draw symbols representative of their development. The relief of not being expected to verbalize their feelings increases the intensity of the visual representation. The act of drawing symbols, not words, puts each participant in relationship to the symbol-making parts of his psyche. This creates, from the beginning, a receptivity to nonverbal, symbolic information and prepares the men for later work that will call on this ability even more.

After being basically silent for quite some time, the participants are given an opportunity to talk about their drawings. With the parameters of self-disclosure expanded by the leaders opening talks, the participants' responses range from superficial to intense. Little feedback or comment is given during the description and explanation of each drawing. On one level this serves to reduce the defensiveness of the participants (particularly their sense of rationality, through which they reduce information into what is already known) and shapes the function of getting to know one another in such a way that participants are guided to reveal parts of themselves that they may not yet understand. This sets the stage for the style of group participation for the weekend. The weekend is one of individual discovery in a supportive group setting. As such, a group style develops that encourages interaction around the members' evolving experiences, creating an atmosphere in which exploration is supported.

Following this discussion of symbols, the participants are asked to walk around the room, allowing the symbols they have drawn and the emotions and sensations they've produced to guide their movement. This is a method of helping the men access and constellate information regarding their development as males that may be stored in their bodies. The goal of this exercise is for each man to develop a symbolic posture that communicates the essence of his masculine development. Each man then discusses the experience itself.

Having shared a common and somewhat uncomfortable experience, the men now feel more connected to each other. The next exercise is to have each man remember a name that he was called from childhood. Participants are given a light trance induction prior to this remembering, and the names are often funny or poignant. The man says the name or names out loud, and the group responds by chanting the name. This is a regressive device, and hearing the name often triggers strong emotion and memory.

The final intervention of Friday night is to plant a suggestion for each man to have an important dream about themselves. This gives the idea that work goes on even in sleep and that the process of achieving their goals for this weekend is arduous. Before the men retire for the night, they are asked to write an internal dialogue. Even though the hour is often late, most men stay up and write substantially. The initial evening is meant to stir up old feelings of being a boy and to help participants make connections between that boyhood self and the adult men that they have become.

From a psychological perspective, the activities of the first evening are geared toward accessing an awareness of the feelings and adaptive patterns that were created in childhood. From the perspective of initiation, the men have been given the opportunity, on different levels, to experience the lack of clear demarcation between childhood and adulthood. The blurred lines between childhood and adulthood become clearer in these exercises, and a sense of needing to put the past "in its place" arises. The awareness of the weight that boyhood still places on the adult male is the beginning of the work toward freeing the participant from the tangles and influences of boyhood emotion and memory.

The men are challenged in a variety of ways in this first evening. To be open to a visionary experience, they must use channels of information input other than those they are familiar with. They are encouraged to write down the inner dialogue in a journal style, so that there is a grounding in the more familiar means of communication.

Saturday

The first full day of the weekend begins with an early call to assemble and participation in what is called the "dream circle." This is a process in which the men are asked to recall the dreams they had the night before and, if they had dreams that they cannot recall, to tell of their experiences (thoughts, feelings, images, or memories) of the night after going to bed. Again, in this process, interaction is centered around discussing aspects of the self that are being discovered. As each man relates his experience or dream, the goal is that the participants get to know each other on levels that are not usually shared and, in this way, build an imaginary space in which the work of the weekend can take place. It is as though the stories that the men tell weave together to form a tapestry depicting what the particular SMMW will be like. This method of "interaction" conveys the message that the weekend is not the traditional "let's put our heads together" and solve a problem but, rather, a series of individual journeys of discovery supported by the group. This process helps disarm one's tendency to understand the experience in familiar ways. It creates a space in which parts of the self normally excluded in day-to-day life are encouraged to manifest. It also helps dilute the competitive aspect of the weekend, because interpretations and comments are absent. Competition among men in a setting such as this can be an avoidance of looking inward and doing the self-discovery and transformation that is the goal of the weekend.

After the dream circle and before breakfast, the men are sent out into the woods. The only instructions given them are that they are to wander through the woods, staying in earshot of the drum, and to allow themselves to be drawn to some particular object in the woods. The leaders explain that the object will select them, rather then vice versa. Many of the participants are confused by these instructions. It is a blatant statement of the potential interactional and allied relationship that each one of them can have with nature—both their own inner, unconscious nature and nature itself. They are encouraged to reject rational reasons for selecting an object and to use a more intuitional approach. This rather disorienting exercise often has dramatic results. Although many men leave on this quest with the attitude that "this is ridiculous," they all return with strong and significant tales of their search.

In this exercise, the participants are forced to be open to communication from the natural world. Almost without fail, the men return with what they describe as the perfect object for them. It often symbolizes their lives, or emotions, or conflicts. It is a concrete piece of evidence from the natural world that there is indeed an interactional and sympathetic relationship between man and nature.

Psychologically speaking, this exercise is one of projection. Each man finds an object that somehow represents an aspect of his internal and unconscious world. Because usual and rational methods of selection are thwarted, the unconscious has greater opportunity to exert influence.

After the men return from their hunt, they place their objects in their chairs on the circle and have a hearty breakfast prepared by the leaders. After breakfast, the men tell the stories of how the objects found them. Again, these are often poignant, relevant stories symbolizing the men's lives and conflicts.

Following this discussion, again involving little interpretation or feedback, the men are instructed to represent the story of their lives as men on their own "totems" through various decorative means. The totem is defined, for the sake of this weekend, as a symbol of one's life as a male to this point. Speaking of any kind is discouraged during this activity. The men carve, color, and decorate their totems. The common experience is one of men taking great pride in their work. An environment of reverence for this activity is created, both through the instructions given and the music played while this activity is underway. Music serves as a potent backdrop for many of the activities of the weekend. Music has always accompanied ritual activity, both to create a sacred space and to aid in the alteration of participants' consciousness.

The men are instructed and encouraged not only to symbolically represent their lives (development) as men, but also to represent the emotion of their lives as men in the totems. The leaders emphasize that they should "love" and value the object they are creating, encouraging the men to make it a complete reflection of their lives as men up to this point. Psychologically and emotionally, each man forms a strong attachment to his totem. Following this experience of transforming the object that nature has given them into a representation of their lives as men so far, they speak about the totem and the experiences of transforming it with each other in the now typical, noninterpretive style. This is often an emotionally charged session. The men have by now been immersed in the feelings, thoughts, and memories of boyhood and adult manhood, on both conscious and unconscious levels. At this point in the weekend, the men have come in contact with the influences and experiences that have shaped their identities as males on many levels. The vast majority of these influences have been external. To this point, there has been no focus on an intrinsic, essentially male self-definition.

The next experience attempts to create a space and situation in which the seeds of such self-definition can be sown. The men are instructed to again go out into the woods, wandering, being led and guided by their totems to a particular place of meaning and power. Again, no specific instruction about how to find such a place is given, other than that the totems will be their guides. The leaders state that, once the place is found, the totems will speak to them. The men are encouraged to attend to every thought, feeling, sensation, and experience that they have. The leaders caution that the totems will give each of them important information about their lives as men and that this information can arrive in a myriad of forms, so they must be open to everything.

This process again puts the men in a situation where nature is an active ally. The stage has been further set for them to be receptive to unconscious information. The men are now open and anticipating a communication from a source other than themselves, that is, other than their normal conscious sense of self. In this way, when they experience unfamiliar thoughts or feelings, they do not dismiss them as they might in day-to-day life but, rather, give them importance and attention. The workshop, thus far, has helped participants to evoke, articulate, and represent the history and development of their present self-concept. The totem "holds" this information, creating the possibility for "nature" to reveal information not presently a part of their identity.

Once this process is completed, the men convene to discuss the experiences they have had. By now the supportive and noninteractive norm has created a group culture and an atmosphere of individual discovery in the context of group support. This group norm typically elicits reflections of past events and influences as well as indications of future directions. These men clearly miss something in their lives, and in this type of process they begin to experience and articulate these missing pieces.

The men are now given their first and only free time of the weekend. It serves as a respite in what has been an intense and somewhat disorienting experience, in that usual and rational methods of problem solving have been stymied and alternative, nonlinear processes have been encouraged and supported.

Saturday Evening

After a dinner prepared by the men themselves, the group convenes. No information is given about what will transpire that evening, but several trance inductions are used, to still the rational part of the men and further open the intuitive, creative, nonlinear aspect of their process. As this induction is taking place, one of the group leaders is preparing a fire ring, on a distant hill. He not only prepares and starts a fire but also prepares himself for the evening's ritual, by using the fire as a trance-induction mechanism. He wears a mask made and decorated on his first SMMW, and he sits in meditative pose, waiting for the group to arrive.

The men are led to the fire ring while humming a zicker (a chantlike humming) to help maintain the level of trance they established in the lodge. The walk is dark and somewhat frightening. They must be aware of the man in front of them and use him as a guide through the darkness. The chanting helps increase the feeling of connectedness and diminishes the men's fear of walking through the woods at night with little light. The glow of the fire reaches out as a beacon, and soon the group arrives at the fire ring.

The group leader tending the fire tells the men a story. It is a story of man's connectedness to nature. The narrative weaves a cooperative and interactional relationship between man and animals as a metaphor for the potential and largely untapped benefits of such a relationship with the natural world. The story espouses the need for decay in the growth cycle of the natural world. It acknowledges, symbolically, that growth and change have inherent in their processes a letting go of past perceptions and patterns. The initiation process often includes a mourning, in some sense, of who the individual was before their transformation. The story is designed to sensitize the participants, on a variety of levels, to the full emotional breath of the change process. It is part of the ongoing goal of creating a sacred space in which transformational work can occur. In the narrative, the natural element of fire is used as the transformational catalyst. Following this story is an invocation which, again, bespeaks of transformation: A formal and dramatic prayer to the natural elements to assist the group in its transformation. A ceremony then ensues that helps to release the past, the influences, and the emotions—good and bad—that have defined the men's masculinity to this point in their lives.[1]

This is an intensely emotional and powerful moment. The purpose of the weekend is to systematically help the men achieve a state of mind where they are open to and focused on creative and nontraditional channels of information about themselves and their lives. This night's ritual is meant to create a psychological, symbolic, and actual space in which such a state of mind can exist.

The group aspect of the fireside ritual concludes with a "liberation" ceremony in which the freeing of the men's spiritual and creative selves is formally activated. This ceremony celebrates and acknowledges all aspects of human potential and formally removes the obstacles to their expression.

The men are next led into the woods once again and placed, individually, in locations apart from each other. They are encouraged to be open to whatever experience or vision might occur to them. This is their time to envision and for information regarding each participant's identity as a man to emerge. They are in the dark, with little to orient themselves. Unconscious material is brought into awareness by the unfamiliar environment. Rational, logical processes have little room in which to operate.

The men have experienced a symbolic loss of childhood and, through this exercise, must face the fear and uncertainty of the unknown with courage and perseverance. The characteristics central to the initiation pro-

---

[1]We have purposely omitted details of the ceremony here in our acknowledgment that an aspect of the creation of a sacred environment and the initiation paradigm is a sense of secrecy and privileged information. To detail the ceremony would thus risk diminishing the impact of the event on past and future participants.

cess are now central to the men's experience. Their allied relationship with nature is now tested by the darkness. Nature now shows, literally, its dark side, and the men must generate courage and self-assuredness to keep the interactional and sympathetic relationship with nature they have established to this point. A space fertile for change is not solely a comfortable one, and many men are not comfortable at this point. They have, however, been helped to achieve a state of mind in which they can positively harness this disequilibrium. They have been given tools to synthesize this experience into transformational energies. Rational understanding of the process, symbolic imagery, and trance induction have given each man multileveled means of using and incorporating the experience. The men have been prepared to use new channels of information, and a sacred space has been created in which this can occur. The men's experiences are varied and diverse. The common thread however, is the intensity, clarity, and significance of the experience.

The men are eventually led back to the lodge. There is little talk, and although ready for sleep, they are required to endure one more act of courage and perseverance. They are required to make a plaster life mask. This requires being still, often in the face of powerful feelings and reaction to the night's events. The experience itself builds in a period of calm and reflection as the men wait for the plaster to dry. Once the masks are done, they are set aside, and the men retire.

Sunday

In the morning, the men meet and discuss the experiences of the night before. The group connectedness is at a high point, as is the level of individual discovery and accomplishment. Following this discussion, the men are instructed to decorate and symbolize their masks. The mask now becomes the face of the vision; that is, the new man who emerged the night before is now represented for all to see. Like the first night, imagery and symbolism are used, but the tone and atmosphere have changed. Instead of the regressive experience of creating the totem, decorating the masks is an experience of empowerment. It is an act of external representation of the internal vision or essence of who they are as men. When the mask making is done, the men convene, and each takes a turn looking at the entire community while wearing his mask. It is a powerful experience. Something essential in each man, represented in his mask, has now taken the place of each participant's face—of his surface identity. The activity inevitably produces strong reactions in each participant.

When this is completed, the men are taken with their masks to an open field, where they are instructed to spontaneously engage in movement that embodies their new energy. The movement is joyous and powerful. These movements replace earlier ones, as the mask has the face. The awarenesses generated during the weekend are now grounded in physical movement.

The men are brought back to the lodge, where they are told a story of an Indian brave on a vision quest and the negative spirit that tries to take his vision away. It is a symbolic story that represents the fact that the current culture might not support and encourage their changes. The idea of an "entity" that stands at the threshold between the world of the weekend and the usual day-to-day world is developed. The men are given a workbook to use during the next 2 weeks, after which they will gather for a follow-up meeting. Focus now shifts to how each man can maintain the vision or energy he has gained during the weekend in his everyday life. The processes the men have experienced regarding alternative, creative methods of gaining information about themselves as men are defined and supported. The blending of ritual and day-to-day life is addressed, and this is pursued further in the follow-up meeting. The follow-up meeting, and the homework prepared for it, helps transfer the experience that the men have had into their everyday lives and practices. The men are made aware of the new tools for self-discovery they have learned throughout the weekend and are encouraged to continue to use them as an alternative, creative method of meeting life's challenges. At this point they also become aware of the hidden continuity of the workshop. The structure of the workshop can now be seen as a method for working toward changes in their identity.

SUMMARY

The SMMW has been shown, through both anecdotal observation and empirical study (Sussman, 1992), to be an effective vehicle for helping men gain clarity and insight into their lives. Men throughout America are discovering that traditional, linear methods of problem solving are limited in their ability to transform identity or evoke meaning. As men evolve into the twenty-first century, their need to be creative in solving conflicts of the internal and external worlds will grow in importance. The "twenty-first century man" (Andronico, 1993) will need to form a cooperative relationship with nature, women, and fellow men. The ability to be integrative will be paramount.

The SMMW was created within the space of the tension formed between understanding a process and trusting that process. This dichotomy is central to the distinction between psychology and spirituality and, to our minds, is fertile space for exploration into the process of helping men.

In a world where rational answers and expectations do not coincide with men's daily experiences, an emptiness can develop that leads to a lack of purpose and direction. The major perspectives of psychology and spirituality, instead of competing for ownership of this emptiness and longing, can be combined to create an integrative approach to the male psyche and to support transformational work. The terms *treatment* and *transformation* have distinct connotations that underscore the difference in these perspectives. The SMMW uses psychological rationale and understanding to contribute to the development of an environment and state of mind conducive to change and growth. A major contribution of the SMMW to work with men in groups is its understanding of the process enough to create environments, both external and internal, that heighten the potential for the process itself to unfold and reveal new and creative information. In addition to this central theme, the weekend experience also contributes other possibilities and modalities to working with men in groups.

Men are a physically oriented gender, and the enjoyment of "doing" appears to be an important component of successful work with men. Working together on a task, even a simple one such as preparing a meal, can bond men in a real and concrete way. Task accomplishment appears to come easily to most men, even when the tasks are of a decidedly nonrational type. Setting up emotional, psychological, and spiritual tasks for men can be an important tool in helping them to reach deeper levels of awareness—in themselves, others, and nature in general—and to become more comfortable and confident at these levels.

Talking among men can be of a formal, structured style and still hold powerful community-building potential. The presentation of one's ideas, feelings, and experiences without analysis and comment can be freeing and can lead to the establishment of a group culture of trust and mutual respect, as well as round out men's more overly rational and competitive experiences.

Movement also is an important dynamic to consider in men's groups. There is often a perceived injunction against movement in today's man. Movement is often related to action, which is in turn equated with fears of violence. In the supportive environment of a group that encourages movement and gives it logical credence, movement can become an integral part of the discovery and change process.

Much work is done symbolically in the SMMW. It is our experience that men seem to have a natural openness and ability to use the symbolic in the service of the concrete. This symbolizing aspect of men is used very little in traditional talk therapy, other than through the symbolic use of language. Yet, men have been using symbols to represent internal and external experiences for ages. Being symbol makers is one of the elements that separates man from the other species. The SMMW uses this affinity for symbols to help participants access aspects of their masculine selves that are not available through conscious, rational discussion.

As the lives of modern men become more fragmented and compartmentalized—requiring certain skills for the work place and others for effective interaction within the family and society—there is a growing need for an integrative process that can help men attain a deep and centered congruency between the varied aspects of their lives and roles as men. Work such as that done on the SMMW points to the need for further exploration of the construction of interventionist strategies that are both holistic and scientific. A place of integration between the polarities of rational understanding and divine intervention may well be the understanding and development of environments that promote growth and change in new and creative ways. Helping men to find completeness and purpose in this manner may lead to a fuller understanding of human growth, development, and potential, for men as well as for women.

REFERENCES

Andronico, M. P. (1993). Whither goes man? A vision for the 21st-century male. *New Jersey Psychologist, 23,* 11–14.

Bly, R. (1990). *Iron John: A book about men.* Reading, MA: Addison-Wesley.

Eliade, M. (1958). *Rites and symbols of initiation: The mysteries of birth and rebirth.* New York: Harper & Row.

Foster, S., & Little, M. (1989). *The roaring of the scared river: The wilderness quest for vision and healing.* Englewood Cliffs, NJ: Prentice Hall.

Mahdi, L. C., Foster, S., & Little, M. (Eds.). (1988). *Betwixt and between: Patterns of masculine and feminine initiation.* LaSalle, IL: Open Court.

Raphael, R. (1988). *The men from the boys: Rites of passage in male America.* Lincoln: University of Nebraska Press.

Sussman, B. (1992). *A program evaluation plan for male vision quest: A time-limited, structured group program for men.* Unpublished doctoral dissertation, Rutgers University, New Brunswick, New Jersey.

II

HETEROGENEOUS ALL-MALE AND MIXED-GENDER GROUPS

INTRODUCTION

HETEROGENEOUS ALL-MALE AND MIXED-GENDER GROUPS

In today's transitional times, with more people beginning to view psychological treatment as a possibility, no one approach or viewpoint works with all men. The second part of this book concentrates on issues of diversity. Heterogeneous groups offering assistance to men may consist of members who differ in cultural background, sexual orientation, or gender. Certainly, homogeneous groups and mixed groups deal with many common issues, but diversity adds a level of complexity to these groups. With the increasing emphasis on understanding cultural diversity in American society, this knowledge is becoming more crucial and will continue to grow in importance. Of course, some of the same men discussed in Part I can be found mentioned in these chapters.

The first three chapters of Part II provide insights into and techniques for working with men who are not from the White majority culture or who are homosexual. These chapters concentrate on identifying techniques that are the most effective in working with particular groups of men and those that should be avoided. The descriptions of the men in these groups are helpful from the viewpoints of leading groups composed entirely of a specific membership and of leading groups that may contain a mixture of members. Even though many threads of similarity run through these groups, it is the subtle nuances, pointed out by these authors, that are of particular value. Readers will be better able to understand, appreciate, and respond to the specific needs of individuals from these diverse groups.

African American men and Hispanic men have many commonalities of behavior in groups; however, the ways in which they tend to differ are important to the group therapist or to others who work with them. In his chapter on African American men in groups, Sutton emphasizes the cultural diversity within the African American community itself. He then explores the various ways in which African American men's unique cultural experience may influence how they react to group therapy, whether they are in groups with only African American members or in multiracial groups.

Next, Arcaya shows how Hispanic men are also often lumped together, despite originating from all over South America and Central America, and reveals similarities and differences within this group as well as with American and Puerto Rican men. He goes on to outline how men with Hispanic backgrounds may respond to the group experience.

A cultural population of males that is not bound by nationality or race is that of the American gay male. Frost deals with how gay men behave in group therapy situations, explaining the dynamics involved in relating to them and in helping them relate to others.

Although other chapters in this book mention involving women in group interventions, the next two chapters focus directly on this issue. There are advantages for men to having women included in groups, but one must realize that other complexities may arise from such mixed-gender situations.

For the female group psychotherapist, issues in relating to male clients in a psychotherapy group are different from those that male colleagues must confront. In her chapter, Bonds-White points out the real and counter-transferential issues that a female group psychotherapist might confront with men in her groups.

The last chapter in Part II is a detailed description of a university course designed to help students in a coeducational group setting gain better understanding of their own gender attitudes. O'Neil describes the Gender Role Journey Workshop, which sets the stage for changing and updating some of the participants' less conscious and more stereotypical attitudes. Given this book's focus, O'Neil deals primarily with the reaction of male participants in this group setting. His methods of facilitating this intensive group experience, by using multimedia presentations along with an expert knowledge of group process, help expand the awareness and knowledge of how to apply group process and group methods to a setting that, although not a psychotherapy group, has therapeutic goals and qualities. Such expanded knowledge will probably be more essential for future group psychotherapists as the role of the group therapist or group worker expands.

9

AFRICAN AMERICAN MEN IN GROUP THERAPY

ALEXANDER SUTTON

Research conducted on African Americans in psychotherapy has been limited by the fact that very little is known about how cultural factors affect their engagement and continuation in psychotherapy. Some research has focused on environmental and socioeconomic factors. Although hundreds of studies have looked at race as a variable in treatment, few have examined the dynamics of working with African American clients and the unique issues they bring to individual psychotherapy (A. Jenkins, 1990; Jones, 1990). In fact, research on how culture apart from socioeconomics affects therapeutic outcomes for African American clients has only been undertaken since 1983 (J. Jenkins & Hunter, 1983; Thompson, 1989). Only two clinical studies have contrasted how African Americans differ from Whites in group therapy. Boyd-Franklin (1991) conducted a study of treatment themes for African American women in group therapy, concluding that trust (particularly of African American men) and kinship ties are keys for successful treatment. However, with the exception of one study of African American Vietnam veterans in group therapy, no others have documented issues for African American men in group counseling.

Questions abound about how African American men present for group therapy. Why and under what conditions do African American men enter group psychotherapy? What are the rules for engaging these men as they enter the group? For what problems do African American men seek group therapy? What issues tend to surface? What impact do their own and others' reactions to race have in group situations for African American men? What are the origins of trust issues for these men? What unique life experiences do these men share and what meanings do these experiences have for them? What are some important cultural taboos and how might they be seen in group therapy? Do African American men's interactions change when groups are mixed (by gender, race, or both) as opposed to homogeneously African American? What is the basis of trust for these men? What unique life experiences do these men share, and what meanings do they hold? What rituals and styles are important to African American men in group therapy?

In this chapter, I address some of these and other questions about the impact of African American culture on African American men in group psychotherapy. In the absence of any substantial clinical research, my observations are drawn from my own 20-plus years of experience as a therapist with African American male groups in low-income communities and from existing theoretical literature. Central to this chapter is the thesis that the culture of being African American is defined in a much broader sense than just race. At the core of this must lie an understanding of the diversity within African American culture itself. *Culture* means those historical experiences, expectations, perceptions, values, belief systems, communication styles, taboos, and so on that are transmitted by families and institutions to children. Falicov (1988) defined culture as "those sets of shared world views and adaptive behaviors derived from simultaneous membership in a variety of contexts" (p. 336). Culture not only colors one's daily experiences but also determines the meaning and context of these experiences. In group therapy, the bonding that is necessary for change may not occur if cultural factors are ignored or left unexplored. Psychological literature examining reasons for the premature termination of therapy by African Americans has pointed to socioeconomic and racial factors as determinants. Until recently, prevailing notions of African Americans' reactions to therapy were governed by shortsighted theories like that by Kardiner and Oversey (1962), who believed that African American personality issues were solely derived from the people's common experience of oppression. They posited that no therapeutic issues exist outside of the African American experience with Whites and the dominant WASP, middle-class culture. I challenge this view here and assert that cultural referents are important in all aspects of participation in group psychotherapy for African American men, particularly in the engagement process.

CULTURAL CONSIDERATIONS IN THE TREATMENT OF AFRICAN AMERICANS

Intra- and cross-cultural studies have identified ways that culture may affect the interactions of African Americans in psychotherapeutic treatment. It is important to include manifestations of culture, like affirmation and engagement protocol, in therapy for African American men. Affirmation, as an example, refers to those ways that one seeks and gives validation. Among African Americans affirmations are expressed as verbal and visual acknowledgments, or "amens," if you will. Affirmation is acknowledging, empathizing, and validating another's experiences; it communicates understanding of one's logic and signifies that one's experiences and feelings are shared. Nanry (1970), a sociologist and business consultant on workplace diversity, conducted his doctoral study on how African Americans and Whites differ in their reactions to jazz. When White audiences listened to jazz, they listened quietly and politely applauded at the performance's end. When African American audiences listened to jazz, they shouted affirming messages throughout the performance. The quality of the performance was judged significantly better by African American audiences because vocal acknowledgments motivated performers. Similarly, affirmations are an important part of African American daily life and interactions. In group psychotherapy, African American men may affirm each other through such verbalizations as "yea" or "you got that right" or such physical gestures as hand slaps and nods. If these natural behaviors are viewed by therapists as strange and unacceptable and are discouraged in groups, then these men will disengage from the group, feeling that they cannot be themselves. This is only one aspect of how culture can affect interactions in group therapy. Other examples are explored later in this chapter.

Cultural patterns exist because they are needed to maintain connections among individuals with a common historical identity. Culture gives one a basis for comparing the known with the novel. It establishes the context for contrasting one's family and communal experiences with those of the outside world. Cultural messages are transmitted by families, friendship networks, and community institutions that prescribe how members should think, feel, and interact with fellow members and with outsiders. Although considerable variance exists among members of a given cultural group, the common threads that bind them are often stronger than subcultural group differences. Among African Americans, culture strongly influences personal and group identity. And, as McGoldrick (1982) pointed out, when they feel secure in their own (ethnic) identities, people act with greater freedom, flexibility, and openness toward those from different cultural backgrounds. In the following sections, I explore how culture-bound messages and behaviors affect stages of group participation.

ENGAGEMENT OF AFRICAN AMERICAN MEN IN GROUP PSYCHOTHERAPY

As is true in studies of White men's acceptance of therapy, African American men tend not to embrace psychotherapy. Many reasons exist for this. Psychotherapy is a process whereby clients allow themselves to be vulnerable, trusting, self-disclosing, and open to changing ways of operating in the world. Historically, men have difficulty giving up this kind of control, because maintaining control over one's feelings, affective expressions, and problem-solving abilities is perceived as being at the core of maleness. For men to seek psychotherapy they must admit to losing control of their lives, to failure in managing the family, and, ultimately, to losing their identity as men. J. Jenkins and Hunter (1983) have pointed to racism and socioeconomics as important factors in engagement and disengagement from psychotherapy among male African Americans. In reviewing the literature, they pointed to findings that dropout rates for African Americans are related to social class factors and not exclusively to race. Low-income clients are affected by such factors as crisis orientation, devaluing treatment against other life obligations, and weighing costs against the benefits of treatment. Although they alluded to cultural factors affecting both engagement in therapy and treatment outcomes, they did not identify specific factors. Washington (1987) has asserted that, for African American men, issues of engaging in group therapy are the same as for White men, except that additional racism and gender role constraints exist in African American culture.

Initial Resistance

African American men join and leave group therapy for various reasons. I have worked with African American men in community mental health settings in low-income communities for 20 years, and my experience has been that most African American men enter group psychotherapy unaware of its benefits, unaware of why they were referred, and with reservations about the value of any form of psychotherapy. In low-income settings, participation is often required by courts, social service agencies, and hospitals or because clients risk loss of freedom or sustenance. They may be cajoled and threatened by wives, parents, employers, and others to join group therapy as a last-ditch effort to make a change. Thus, group therapy is a treatment of choice, not for many African American clients, but for referring and receiving agencies that deal with them. Group therapy is often presented to these men as the only viable option in many situations. Exceptions are those African American men who voluntarily join self-help groups such as Narcotics Anonymous or Alcoholics Anonymous, who have made informed and carefully considered decisions.

One reason that African American men do not seek group therapy is that the notion itself may be foreign to them. When African American men need emotional support from peers on a day-to-day basis, there is no setting for it in the African American community. Pastoral counseling has always been available to support individual counseling needs, and short-term individual counseling with one's physician has also been a viable option within the African American community. Yet there is no institution within the community where men can meet, bond, and talk on an ongoing basis about life and personal growth issues in the way that they do in group psychotherapy. In addition, the concept of therapeutic groups may be seen not just as foreign but as a "White man's thing"—as one of my African American male clients put it—giving it a strange and ominous connotation. A second reason that African American men do not readily seek group therapy is that psychotherapy still carries the stigma of serious mental illness; the African American community has not widely adopted the value of seeking out group or individual psychotherapy for one's personal growth. Engaging in group therapy thus not only means that one has lost control as a man but that one is identified as being "crazy."

A third reason that African American men do not readily engage in group therapy is that many may not understand or acknowledge it as a viable form of treatment. Low-income African Americans may be steeped in the tradition of the medical treatment model and deal with health care professionals—be they MDs, PhDs, or MSWs—with a degree of reverence. They come to expect that these professionals will diagnose the problem, provide immediate relief in the form of medication or a prescribed set of activities, and give sound advice or orders that are to be followed to the letter (McGoldrick, 1982). Given this tradition, expectations of group therapy are that they will listen as the professional lectures to them and that somehow his or her words will heal. Such African Americans are not used to a healing activity in which the "prescription" is a free-flowing exchange with others and not exclusively with the expert. This is illustrated in another client's remark: "How can a group of dudes with the same problem as me be of any help?" Therapists may also neglect to explain what group therapy is, how it works, or what the expectations are for clients. Likewise, they may not explain the specific model of group therapy that is being used. Leaderless and unstructured situations are difficult for most people at least initially and are exceedingly difficult for men who are not familiar with the culture of group therapy. African American men may thus begin dropping out after the second or third session because they are uncomfortable, confused, and frustrated. (Again, however, this would not apply to the percentage of African American men with previous successful group therapy experiences, those who have been in addiction recovery programs, or those who have had a brief group growth experience in school or at work (e.g., sensitivity groups, assertiveness training, or synergy-styled groups at work).

At less conscious levels, African American men may resist group therapy for other reasons. Some fear revealing intimate, painful life events; others fear unleashing raw emotions in the presence of others, particularly among Whites. African Americans may, in particular, fear revealing angry and aggressive feelings that they have toward Whites. In the not-too-distant past, expressions of anger, sexual attraction, and aggression toward Whites warranted severe punishment, much of which was supported by law. Today's reality for many African American males can be that the most benign of confrontations with Whites can be life threatening; they may therefore learn to withhold and measure what is said around Whites for fear of terrible consequences. To emote or express oneself in "wrong ways"—that is, in openly assertive, demanding, or defensive ways—can get one in serious trouble with the White establishment (Hacker, 1992). A clear example of this is confrontation between African American males and White police. As illustrated in the Rodney King case, African American men who challenge White police may face brutal and sometimes deadly consequences.

Early Disengagement

Remnants of fears associated with aggression toward Whites, particularly toward White men, are present in racially mixed therapy groups. Working through these angry and aggressive feelings are important tasks in group therapy. In mixed groups African American men may become conspicuously passive, deny angry feelings, or become submissive in the presence of verbal attacks by White members, so group therapists need to be cognizant of underlying fears of White retaliation. Working through issues around anger and rage is critical to successful treatment for African Americans. Therapists should not assume that African American men are just resistant or emotionally removed from the group but should explore these fears and inhibitions and examine why anger is denied or projected onto a non-White member. Unless African American group members are supported in the same ways as White members in dealing with their aggressive impulses, their growth will be stunted. Group therapists need to validate African American male anger both when it surfaces at social injustices and systemic racism and when it is directed at individual group members. They should encourage African American men to explore what it means for them when they cannot say what they feel toward White members and what it feels like to challenge a White member who is making biased statements. Therapists too quickly rescue African American members when racism occurs in a group; yet such incidents are useful for the group and for the growth of the African American member. Finally therapists should be aware that African American men may react strongly to these anxieties and may simply leave the group instead of trying to deal with them.

Another problem affecting disengagement from therapy is the style of expression of African American men. Such styles vary with culture, and African American men are likely to express anger and hostility in a variety of ways, including direct verbal attacks, verbal jousting, competitive strivings, posturing, and satirical humor. They may, for example, loud talk, trash talk, "front off," stare down, "call out," make veiled threats, or engage in verbal one-upmanship. Therapists who are uncomfortable with these styles of relating may feel personally threatened and overreact by banning these styles of expression from group and admonishing African American men who continue to use them. My experience has been that African American men boisterously express feelings when they feel free to do so. In the excitement of the group, it is not uncommon for these men to loudly assert strongly held beliefs. Therapists inexperienced in working with such men may fear that high volume and high excitability will add up to potentially violent confrontations; they are not aware that their own unconscious racial fears are guiding their actions and that animated discussions are just another way of communicating. Thus, therapists may have to deal with their own fears of African American male aggression to be effective group therapists with this population. In mature therapy groups, members confront each other by pointing out and interpreting aggressive stances and are able to support a member's dealing with underlying issues that evoke aggressive gestures. Experienced, culturally competent group therapists know how to stay out of the way, know what to ignore, and know what to confront and when.

One sensitive issue that can affect premature termination of African American men in group work is discussion and disclosure of sexual issues (Gunnings & Lipscomb, 1986). A few years ago, many watched Clarence Thomas's confirmation hearing in shock as Anita Hill and a host of others revealed intimate details of her and Thomas's lives. Regardless of the validity of the sexual harassment charges, many in the African American community expressed shame and embarrassment because the televised spectacle resurrected old racial myths of African American sexual perversion and promiscuity. Early discussion in therapy groups of sexual issues may evoke fears in African American men that they will be stereotyped as having uncontrolled libidinal drives. African American men who believe these myths fear that their sexual energies will overwhelm them and potentially ruin budding relationships. They collude in silence with other African American men in group who do not consciously accept these myths but are aware that others do, fearing that sexual discussions will lead to promoting the myths. Consequently, all may be embarrassed when an African American member exposes sexual needs and inadequacies. In my groups, men have counterphobically boasted of sexual prowess, often cloaking intimacy and performance problems. Once sex issues are broached, therapists will find that many African American men who initially denied them believe in sexual myths, such as that African American men are not supposed to become impotent or have sexual arousal problems. Therefore, if sexual dysfunction issues are touched on before group members have had time to bond, some may drop out.

Thus far, I have focused on identifying cultural factors that affect attending and dropping out of group therapy for African American men. Some of the aforementioned behaviors are cross-cultural and so affect all men. It should be made clear that African American men are not unidimensional; participation in group is motivated by any number of factors. Thus, group leaders must attend to cultural issues if they hope to maintain African American men's commitment to group treatment. These men need to be welcomed and supported for who they are and how they present themselves in the group.

AFRICAN AMERICAN MEN IN DIFFERENT PHASES OF GROUP THERAPY

Once committed to the group and over the initial discomfort, African American men may complain of social isolation, problems in sustaining satisfying relationships, social anxiety, intimacy issues, anger management, and all the issues that other men bring up. How issues are communicated and the ways that men bond are largely determined by culture. Next, I explore how these men act as the group matures.

Initial Phase

African American men during the initial phases of group are apprehensive, vigilant, and racially sensitive, which are adaptive responses. White therapists may tend to pathologize the ways that these men interact in the White world rather than to try to understand and work within the context of their experiences. When entering mixed groups, these men remain distant from White members and leery of the group process until a certain level of comfort is reached. Next, they begin bonding with other African American members and may view group members' issues in racial terms. When asked to reveal their reasons for joining or to share something about themselves, they may be reticent, fearing that they will be prejudged by nonminority members. I have found African American men to be defensive when questioned and prodded by others to share presenting complaints with the group.

The initial phase of therapy is a time when all men are reticent. Men often engage in unproductive banter about sports, politics, and other topics unrelated to treatment. The beginning is a time when men jockey for favored status with the therapist, when they compete for power positions within the group. They are asserting their masculine identities. African American men's early engagement is also governed by cultural rules and protocol. Some of these rules follow.

- Elders and members with certain status are given deference.
- Interactions are formal until a level of familiarity is reached.
- Authority figures in the group, like the group leader, are addressed by title.
- One does not speak up until granted permission by the leader.
- One does not talk in ways that would be considered disrespectful.
- One does not disclose intimate details or secrets to strangers.
- One does not publicly chastise or challenge the group leader.

Therapists experienced in working with African American men in groups know how hard it is for some of these men to refer to the therapist by first name, preferring to use the title of "Doctor." This is not meant as a hostile or passive–aggressive act but, rather, as an act of respect and expression of the desire to establish boundaries in what they see as a doctor–patient relationship. Engagement rituals can serve to increase individual comfort and reinforce bonds between members. They may include a range of behaviors, from special handshakes to searching for common familial or friendship roots. Several years ago, I led therapy groups for Vietnam veterans where, at the beginning of each group, African American members greeted each other with elaborate handshakes. These were the same as those once given in combat. They signified not only survival of a terrible war experience but also a time of solidarity, loyalty, interdependence for daily survival, and intense feelings of intimacy among comrades. As an early bonding ritual, members could identify through a handshake the branch of service, unit, and period of time members had served in Vietnam as well as the locality served in. African American men today may often acknowledge each other with special handshakes and hugging rituals. Some therapists may deem such rules and rituals unimportant or an interference, but they should not feel threatened by these rituals and culturally based rules. If therapists disallow engagement rituals or misinterpret their meaning, then African American members may remain distant and guarded.

The initial stage of group is a time when members are at different periods of readiness for revealing issues. As they tell their stories and disclose conflicts, they seek support—first, exclusively from the leader and later from select members that they have bonded with. This is the phase of group when alliances are forged and subgroups are formed. Like most men, African American men readily complain about work-related and other external stressors, but they have difficulty disclosing inadequacies and exposing their intrapsychic lives. If comments are made at all, they are about feeling unappreciated and demeaned by women, families, and the White world (Franklin, 1986). Unless they become less guarded and more willing to share feelings, African American men will not offer support to others within the group. Those who do share form subgroups with other African American men and women as well as with other minority group participants.

Comfort level in the early phases of group therapy is also connected to how one's verbal communications are perceived. As Hoopes (1979) has pointed out, the ways that African Americans communicate may, to some Whites, seem to be odd, circumstantial, and not always following a clear line of logic. Many may speak street or Black English. Whites may conclude from the ways that African Americans communicate that they are concrete thinkers, function at a lower intellectual level, are not introspective, and have poor problem-solving capabilities. Whites may perceive African American men's style of thinking as rambling and disorganized, whereas African American men may experience White men as technical, intellectualizing, and overly analytic. Social scientists have pointed to other such differences in racial perception in linguistics, therapeutic orientation and treatment task (Lash, 1992), and affective reactions. Unknowledgeable group therapists may thus misinterpret African American men's style of thinking and speaking as evasive or as indicating an unwillingness to directly confront key issues. This can lead African American male group members to feel rejected and misunderstood.

African American men may talk about their experiences from a perspective that White members may not share, making it hard for the latter to empathize. As life stories are told, White members may not understand important metaphors, nuances, and underlying meanings in their counterparts' stories. African American men can become frustrated when they have to continue reexplaining and interpreting their stories for the benefit of White members, particularly when Whites are not asked to do the same for them. Therapists too may not recognize important nuances and, consequently, may overlook critical issues. In one group I led, an African American man told a childhood story of watching his sister being sexually assaulted. He related the story in an understated, matter-of-fact way. He said that the reason he revealed the story was to show how dangerous it is for women living in inner cities. I was amazed that group discussion continued and that none of the members asked how the experience affected him; no one acknowledged it as a traumatic life event. The underlying assumption seemed to be that life in the low-income community is fraught with traumas and that African American residents are immune or are not as affected as Whites would be. Of course, this is a racist assumption.

As men begin to discuss their experiences, sometimes issues of White male privilege and African American male disenfranchisement surface. If these are not acknowledged and made part of the group discussion early on, African American male members may feel alienated. For example, African American men in low-wage jobs will have a hard time empathizing with White men who talk about feeling unchallenged and unfulfilled in their high-paying jobs. A White member may talk about how long the taxi ride was to therapy, whereas the African American member talks about how hard it was to even hail a taxi, seeing Whites around him being picked up instead of him. A White member may talk about browsing at an expensive store for a gift whereas an African American member describes being followed in the same store by security as if he were a thief. These sorts of daily racial indignities are a fact of life for African American men, and such inequities need to be brought out in group so that victims can be empathized with. White members may even deny their privilege and accuse African American men of hypersensitivity or paranoia. Therapists have to be careful not to fall into this trap. It is relatively easy to side with the belief that African American members are setting themselves up for rejection by the group, that they are projecting anger for their own failures or inadequacies onto Whites, or that they see racial problems where none exist. Therapists need to validate the impact of racism and disenfranchisement while encouraging dialogue about different realities.

Middle Phase

The middle phase of group therapy is when members disclose their intrapsychic lives in more depth, articulate their needs, and begin to work on core issues. Alliances are cemented, and members seek subgroup support. It is also a time when gender and racial issues are more openly discussed and when members challenge each other and the leader. Often members disagree with the direction the group is heading and complain about the lack of growth by some participants. In this phase, the leader is no longer the focus of group attention, as members begin relying on each other for support. As African American men become more trusting and comfortable, they relax their rules. They are less formal and more involved in intergroup conflicts. In spirited exchanges these men may challenge each other in ways that seem like open verbal warfare: Voices are raised, fingers are pointed, and tones are angry; they may talk over each other as if to drown one another out (a departure from the reserved way they were at the start of therapy). These animated exchanges usually end in heightened excitement and humor and are not a prelude to violence or ongoing hostility.

This is also a phase during which these men express frustration, disappointment, and sorrow through anger, because it is the most available emotion. In one group of African American male schizophrenic clients that I led, members angrily blamed psychiatrists and the mental health system for their continuing need for medication. Later, some members asserted that they were really angry at themselves for being so sick. They were sad and frustrated that their lives revolved around medication and staying psychiatrically stable. Anger cloaked frustration, shame, and sadness over lost opportunities because of the illness. Discussion led to group acknowledgment of how difficult it is to manage one's chronic illness.

Trust issues surface at different stages of group evolution. Men at this stage need to trust that they can reveal painful experiences without being labeled "weak" or "cowardly." They must be able to trust that the private details of their lives will not be shared with others outside the group and that feelings and information shared will not be distorted in subsequent sessions. Men need to trust that when they are vulnerable, tearful, ashamed, or despondent the group will be supportive and not criticize them for being emotional. African American men are subject to these needs as well, particularly because African American participants in groups I have run live in proximity to each other or socialize in the same circles as other group members.

Demonstrations of trust vary. African American men demonstrate trust through verbalized affirming messages like "it's all right. . . go ahead and let it out" and through nonverbal gestures and rituals. Examples of support rituals are where group members pat each other on the back after a breakthrough or where members stand or sit close by a distraught member. The men sometimes offer to perform favors outside the group as an act of trust. In some support groups I have run, men have initiated rituals to enhance solidarity. An example is one group in which members asked me if they could hold hands and create a closing ritual at the conclusion of each meeting. Sometimes support groups end with a joint prayer.

It may be difficult for African Americans to accept that, after a history of superficial contact with Whites and dealing with all the fears and anxieties associated with intimacy with them, Whites want to befriend and entrust secrets to African Americans. It may be just as hard for African Americans to set aside their fears to befriend and trust Whites. African American men wait until overtures are made to them before revealing vulnerabilities and secrets. Even at this middle stage of the group, old racial fears remain. At this time, members may confront racial taboos about intimate contact. As members openly disclose intimate, painful experiences, open themselves for analysis by group members, and reveal aspects of themselves that they feel inadequate with, subtle issues of intimate contact between African Americans and Whites surface. Subconsciously, African American men may fear that play (particularly sexual play), affectionate embraces, and other intimate contact with White women will result in White male retaliation. Similarly, they fear that verbally attacking Whites will warrant punishment. In the past, intimate contact with Whites was fraught with danger for African Americans, particularly African American men. Numerous articles and books have been written about how African American men are viewed with trepidation by White authority. Intimate disclosures to White women in group therapy by African American men can evoke feelings of betrayal of African American women. African American men may fear women's disapproval and anger as they seek the attention of White women in the group. When there are no African American women in the group, such men may look for approval from other African American men, fearing that moving away from African American subgroups toward White ones will be viewed by others as disloyal. They run the risk of being ostracized by their own group and labeled an "Uncle Tom," a wanna-be, or a turncoat.

In group, self-esteem, masculine identity and dependency are closely tied. Men may fear that if insecurities and dependency needs are expressed, the resulting anxiety and guilt will be intolerable. They may want to avoid being labeled as weak, out of control, and effeminate. To affirm threatened masculinity, defend against inner conflicts over nurturing qualities, and defend against desires for attachment with other men, men may engage in homophobic behavior, aggressive displays, and counterdependent acts. Like other males, African American men initially present a veneer of unaffected and detached coolness. During the middle stage of the group, this facade begins to break down to reveal warmer, emotionally sensitive and needy men. During this phase, men may reveal past encounters with absentee and emotionally distant fathers. Those who grew up with no paternal figure in the home talk of early identity struggles and conflict with parental figures at different periods of their youth. Deeper insights for many men reveal the conflict between the need to remain close to overindulgent, overprotective mothers and the desire for attachment with absent or unavailable fathers. The more fragile a man's self-esteem and sexual identity, the more aggressive is his defense. For some African American men, being called "punk" evokes a violent confrontation, not only because this is considered a derogatory term for gay men, but also because it connotes immaturity, fragility, and weakness. It conjures up images of maternal attachment and dependence (i.e., like the term *mama's boy*).

The men at this stage of group therapy explore angry and ambivalent feelings toward the women in their lives, which, from a psychoanalytic perspective, are often displaced and repressed feelings toward their mothers. Their tasks are to work through conflicts over role expectations; to address origins of angry and ambivalent feelings arising from demands made by women in their lives; to come to terms with the gentle, nurturing side of themselves; to work through dependency issues; and to grow interpersonally. They need to come to grips with their own brand of stoic defensiveness and emotional unavailability. Some African American men need to learn how to swat a fly without using a baseball bat; that is, they need to learn how to cope without resorting to extreme measures in defense of honor. Consistent with this view is the growth of support groups for young men and boys desiring to learn nonviolent alternative behaviors.

Mature Phase

The mature phase of group therapy is a time when men are open to feedback from both the leader and other members. They respond in nondefensive ways to suggestions, insights, and interpretations from the group. Strong bonds develop among most members because subgroups no longer serve as important a support function. Men regularly support each other as deeper levels of need are acknowledged, and they share their vulnerabilities. Care is taken so that feedback is not punitive or castrating. Men are dependent without guilt. At this time, African American men comfortably expose aspects of their daily lives that they would have not shared earlier. They are relaxed, as if at home among friends. Although conscious of racial, ethnic, and gender differences, members are more cognizant of personality differences, common issues and repeating themes, and the availability of members for support. Having achieved a high level of trust, men (African American, White, and other) openly display affection for each other. Rituals such as the laying on of hands, may be adopted. In this ritual, when members want to demonstrate empathy for a fellow member, they reach out and touch him one at a time, symbolizing shared pain. Other rituals may also be developed. In one group of African American men, several members asked if they could all hold hands and pray for a hospitalized member. The prayer was for his speedy recovery and that "he return home to group to complete the work he started."

During this last phase, African American men sometimes use humorous stories as metaphors to illustrate an issue or use humor to reduce tension in sessions. They also use it in tactful ways, for pointing out misperceptions and maladaptive behavioral patterns. At times, these men will also tease or make satirical comments to draw in members who have chosen to remain on the outside. Humor is thus used to illustrate irony, inconsistency, and hypocrisy in nonthreatening ways. I have seen it effectively used to make White members conscious of subtle racist attitudes and behavior within the group.

Resolving life-domain issues and self-actualization motivates African American men's participation in group at this stage. The following may be key issues for young and middle-aged African American men: intergenerational problems, family religious tradition versus spiritualism, racial identity, assertiveness, confronting racism at work, reassessing gender role relationships with spouses and other significant women, sexism, confronting cultural taboos, conflicts over nurturing, parental relationships with children, inferiority complex, coping with loss, managing anger, culture shock in moving north (or south), guilt over moving away from a predominately African American community to a mostly White one, or dealing with the daily indignities of racism.

Conflict resolution and interpersonal skills are important developmental skills for young African American males. Other challenges for them in group therapy are identity issues, conflicts with mothers and significant females in their lives, dealing with racism, relationships with fathers, resentment toward authority figures, disinterest in school, value conflicts, dealing with aggressive impulses, anger management, and dealing with peer pressures. These are the same issues for many young males in this society, except that African American male growth is often complicated by poverty, high unemployment, gangs, pressure to engage in illegal drug sales, substance abuse, increasing levels of lethal violence among peers, and harassment by police. It is of great importance that young African American males at risk learn nonviolent means of coping and gain a stronger sense of self-worth at this phase of group therapy.

GUIDELINES FOR GROUP THERAPISTS

Racial and cultural factors should not be barriers to developing a strong therapeutic alliance between African American group members and their therapists. Openness, sensitivity, and the ability to empathize, along with therapeutic training and experience, should be more important than a difference in background. At the same time, the impact of cultural differences should not be understated. Too often, therapists blame premature termination of African American men from therapy on what they interpret as clients' inability to accept treatment. It is easier to identify client deficits and to blame them when they "talk with their feet" (i.e., drop out) than to examine how intimidating and unwelcoming the treatment environment sometimes is. Therapists have to want to work with clients who find group therapy foreign and pose interesting treatment challenges. With American treatment populations becoming increasingly more diverse, therapists can no longer afford to assume that one approach works for all clients. White therapists have to stop buying into the notion that, because they have not lived the African American male experience, they cannot work effectively with this population. Having biases and discomfort in treating these men does not disqualify a therapist. If therapists are clear about their own growth needs; are conscious throughout the group's evolution of how racism, White male privilege, and old racial fears are manifested; and are willing to become more culturally competent, then the risk of premature termination for African American men in their groups is minimal. Yes, therapists may have to work differently given these men's fears and unfamiliarity with the process. And therapists will need to make African American men feel that they can be themselves and do not have to "act White" or put on a performance to gain acceptance. I next discuss useful guidelines for facilitating therapy groups with African American male members.

First, therapists should study aspects of African American culture and history. Ignorance is a poor excuse for therapists making inaccurate statements. When they do this, they lose credibility with their African American clients, who may know more about American, European, and African American history and values than Whites know about theirs. Therapists would do well to learn about institutional racism and its impact on African American men. They also need to learn about regional and subcultural differences among African Americans. If, for example, tensions exist between African American men and African American men of West Indian descent over some issue in the group, an uninformed therapist would not understand how the source might be cultural.

Second, therapists should support cultural explorations by this population, particularly by young African American males. Afrocentricity and related cultural identification have been shown in preliminary studies to enhance self-expression and other forms of self-examination (Lash, 1992). Rites-of-passage programs and cultural education initiatives are widely used with African American boys and young men to enhance self-esteem and to reduce antisocial behavior. Therapists should not be put off or interpret cultural identification as a maneuver by individuals to distance themselves from others in the group.

Third, therapists must distinguish between a man's realistic complaints about racism and his attempts to blame racism for all of his problems in life. They must distinguish between the sensitivities to racial bias and discrimination that African Americans have and the defense that some men put up to intimidate and manipulate therapists. At the same time, therapists have to be careful not to pathologize the kinds of defensive reactions they are likely to encounter in these men, such as vigilance.

Fourth, therapists should allow African American male clients to teach them about their culture. This empowers clients to be special—to be teachers as well as clients. This will enhance men's sense of competence while allowing the therapist to demonstrate genuine interest.

Therapists should also be open to incorporating rituals into group practice. Greeting, support, and rite-of-passage rituals are important to consider. Including these or other aspects of African American culture enhances comfort and ownership for what occurs in the group.

Sixth, therapists should acknowledge their own prejudices. Many may deny having any racial prejudices until incidents in group therapy bring unconscious ones to the surface. The practitioner should trust that African American male clients will make him or her aware when a group member has said something offensive or when he or she has done something they see as racially biased. There must be room for these men to express their sensitivities in group and with the therapist.

Therapists must be aware that cultural nuances are important. No one psychology or anthropology text yet covers the myriad of values, mores, and taboos of all African Americans. Therapists may need to read literary works about African American life to gain more of this information. For instance, I read psychological literature on posttraumatic stress disorder as well as Goff, Sanders, and Smith's (1982) *Brothers*—a nonfictional story of African American men's combat experiences in Vietnam—to prepare me to understand qualitative differences in experiences of African American and White combat soldiers when I facilitated a mostly African American therapy group of Vietnam combat veterans. Also, for me, no other book captures the fears associated with intimacy between African Americans and Whites like Richard Wright's *Native Son* (1969).

Finally, it is important that therapists not idealize or infantilize the African American male experience. Therapists who overidentify try to convince these men and themselves that they are not part of the racist system or will overprotect them while refusing to confront them on critical issues in what has been referred to as "oversolicitous caring." If White therapists are comfortable using street slang in group with men who use it, this can enhance bonding between the therapist and African American members. Inappropriate use makes these men feel patronized, however.

CONCLUSIONS

In this chapter, I have explored some aspects of culture as they affect the dynamics of conducting group psychotherapy with African American men. Many important nuances were left unexplored here and yet are important in ensuring that these men feel accepted. The most culturally sensitive therapist is not always aware of how his or her socialization (both personal and professional) can jaundice his or her approach and interactions. To talk about single-parent families as if they are inherently dysfunctional is an example of a clinical misnomer, just as presuming that African American men are prone to violence when angered is an example of racial bias. With racial fears fostered by daily, negative media denoting

African American men as murderers, rapists, and violent gang members, it is easy to understand why therapists may be unconsciously fearful of confronting some African American men in group therapy when they need to. It is my hope that this chapter has portrayed these men as similar to others in many respects but contextually different. Certainly, one advantage for low-income African American men participating in racially mixed groups is that they may inevitably learn how to function more effectively in, for example, White middle-class environments. They can come to grips with their fears and biases toward Whites, and for many, it may be the first time in their lives that they will have forged honest, open friendships with Whites. For White men there are also advantages to participating in such mixed groups. They are brought to realize the impact of White male power and privilege on men of other racial and ethnic backgrounds. In addition, they confront their own biases and come to appreciate stylized differences between themselves and African American men. For many, it may be the first time that they are able to establish open, honest relationships with African American men. As J. Jenkins and Hunter (1983) pointed out, group therapists need to understand that minorities understand the values and behavior of the majority culture much more than Whites understand the minority culture.

A repeated theme in this chapter has been that cultural differences are important. It is my hope that group therapists do not make the mistake of assuming that all African American men have the same cultural referents. As writers on West Indian culture have pointed out, there are many differences among people of African descent. African American men from Trinidad are culturally different from African American men from North America, just as African American men from New York have important cultural differences from African American men from Texas. The key is to explore what those differences are. Although there has been little scientific literature to turn to, there are many literary works available on African American life to jump-start study of these cultural experiences. Some recent works have been published from the African American male's perspective. Cross-cultural issues are important to take note of, in that the numbers of U.S. immigrants of African descent from such places as Cuba, South and Central America, England, and the Middle East are on the rise.

I also hope that this chapter has shed some light on the need for further scientific study in this area. More therapists treating African American men need to document critical, clinical treatment issues. Empirical studies need to be conducted to discern which client cultural factors are key to African American men continuing in group treatment. Equally important is identifying those therapist and situational cultural factors that are impediments. Other African American male therapists are encouraged to write about the experiences and techniques that they have successfully applied in ensuring maximum therapeutic benefit for these clients.

REFERENCES

Boyd-Franklin, N. (1991). Recurrent themes in the treatment of African American women in group therapy. *Women and Therapy, 11*(2), 25–40.

Falicov, C. J. (1988). Learning to think culturally. In H. A. Liddle, D. C. Breunlin, & R. C. Schwartz (Eds.), *Handbook of family therapy training and supervision* (pp. 335–357). New York: Guilford Press.

Franklin, C. (1986). Conceptual and logical issues in theory and research related to Black masculinity. *Western Journal of Black Studies, 10*, 161–166.

Goff, S., Sanders, R., & Smith, C. (1982). *Brothers.* Novato, CA: Presidio Press.

Gunnings, T., & Lipscomb, W. (1986). Psychotherapy for Black men: A systemic approach [Special issue]. *Journal of Multicultural Counseling and Development, 14*, 17–24.

Hacker, A. (1992). *Two nations: Black and White, separate, hostile and unequal.* New York: Random House.

Hoopes, D. S. (1979). Intercultural communications concepts: Psychology of intercultural experience. In M. D. Psych (Ed.), *Multicultural education: A cross-cultural training approach.* La Grange, IL: Intercultural Network.

Jenkins, A. (1990). Dynamics of the relationship in clinical work with African American clients. *Group, 14*, 36–42.

Jenkins, J., & Hunter, K. (1983). Minorities. In M. Hersen, A. Kazdin, & A. Bellack, *The clinical psychology handbook.* New York: Pergamon Press.

Jones, N. L. (1990). Black/White issues in psychotherapy: A framework for clinical practice. *Journal of Social Behavior and Personality, 5*, 305–322.

Kardiner, A., & Oversey, L. (1962). *The mark of oppression.* New York: World.

Lash, S. (1992). *Effects of racial identity and cultural communications style on the evaluation of clinical involvement in psychotherapy of Black students.* Unpublished doctoral dissertation, University of Pennsylvania.

McGoldrick, M. (1982). Normal families: An ethnic perspective. In F. Walsh (Ed.), *Normal family processes.* New York: Guilford Press.

Nanry, C. A. (1970). *The occupational subculture of the jazz musician.* Unpublished doctoral dissertation, Rutgers University.

Thompson, C. (1989). Psychoanalytic psychotherapy with inner-city patients. *Journal of Contemporary Psychotherapy, 19*, 137–148.

Washington, C. (1987). Counseling Black men. In M. Scher, M. Stevens, & G. Good (Eds.), *Handbook of counseling and psychotherapy with men.* Newbury Park, CA: Sage.

Wright, R. (1969). *Native son.* New York: Harper & Row.

10

THE HISPANIC MALE IN GROUP PSYCHOTHERAPY

JOSE M. ARCAYA

Despite the prevalence of Spanish-speaking individuals in the U.S. population, no report, article, or investigation exists in the current literature describing the unique characteristics of the Hispanic membership participating in group psychotherapy. By extension, no mention has been made regarding the characteristics of Hispanic males involved in group psychotherapy. Therefore, this chapter represents the first attempt to describe the way that Hispanic males view group therapy and how their response differs from that of other group members from mainstream European cultures or backgrounds.

In the following pages of this chapter, I attempt (a) to describe the main social characteristics of the Hispanic population as a whole, (b) to depict how these are manifested in the group therapy situation of Hispanic men, and (c) to suggest some forms of intervention that, in deference to the cultural aspects of this group, might improve the participation of Hispanic men in group treatment. These remarks are intended only as preliminary observations about their involvement in a kind of psychotherapy that has only recently gained some acceptance within the ranks of this ethnic group. Furthermore, they are based on my personal experience as a practicing group psychotherapist who has dealt with numerous Hispanics over the years as well as on my history as an assimilated, South American man who has lived many years in the United States. Nevertheless, despite the somewhat anecdotal nature of my remarks, I hope that they will prompt more formal forms of research in the near future that would empirically confirm or disconfirm such observations. Finally, it should be noted that I use the term *Hispanic* throughout this chapter to refer to individuals of Spanish-speaking extraction, rather than the more ambiguous term *Latino*.

HISPANIC CULTURE

Unlike other immigrant groups, Hispanics have always been part of the American scene, even preceding the English arrival to these shores (Acosta-Belen & Sjostrom, 1988). It is thus a mistake to differentiate the separateness or uniqueness of Spanish culture from American life or values, because this very ethnic group (as evidenced by the presence of fifth- and sixth-generation Spanish Americans in the American Southwest) has had an active hand in shaping this country's consciousness from its beginnings (Shorris, 1992). Such observations are also made to stress the point that the Hispanic culture is not a uniform or monolithic structure but a composite of many influences, ranging from the well-established Mexican presence in the Southwest to the South American impact on the cities of the Eastern Seaboard. Nevertheless, some broad generalizations can be made about this social group, the knowledge of which might assist in advancing psychological services for Hispanics.

United only by a common language and religion, as well as a broad set of cultural expectations, the many nationalities and subcultures that make up the Hispanic heritage can be best depicted as being tribes within a loose confederacy rather than states of a unified country. As such, Hispanic people may be seen as being more united because of their dissimilarities from some of the Anglo-Saxon ideals or aspirations than because of a unifying mind set. In other words, in the course of ordinary transactions between members of different Hispanic subgroups (e.g., Cubans and Mexicans) almost as many differences can be noted between these Spanish speakers as exist between mainstream, European-derived Americans. Therefore, when they are considered as prospective members for group therapy, Hispanics must be evaluated not only in light of their broadly defined ethnicity, but also in terms of their economic status, education, historical legacy, and the length of their residency in the United States (Wyer, 1988).

As an example, the psychological mindedness that can be expected of an Argentinean (in a country devoid of indigenous natives, European in orientation, and sophisticated in its appreciation of psychoanalysis) is quite different from that which can be anticipated from someone from the Dominican Republic (with its mixed strain of races, where psychology is barely practiced, and where a strong Afrocentric heritage prevails). Thus, although in the following paragraphs I present a list of five characteristics that distinguish the Hispanic psychological personality from its American counterpart, these must be viewed only as broad set of generalities, not as an enumeration of specific attributes. Given the numerous qualifications that must be borne in mind whenever one deals with an individual Hispanic, abstractions must never be allowed to overshadow the idiosyncrasies of the actual person.

HISPANIC PSYCHOLOGY

First, Hispanics can be said to be more formal in their dealings with the world at large than assimilated Americans. Because of the grammatical structure of the Spanish language (based on a formal, second-person form of *you*) and the authoritarian legacy willed from Spain (as the former colonial ruler), role distinctions between intimates (i.e., friends or family) and nonintimates (e.g., authority figures, strangers, or acquaintances) are more clearly defined for Hispanics than they are for mainstream Americans. This sense of propriety not only leads Hispanics to behave in a more conservative and reserved fashion than assimilated Americans during initial meetings but also conditions them to be highly respectful of authority, particularly of doctors and other professionals. In this regard, Hispanics often view treatment only as a means for acquiring expert help rather than as a collaborative effort of joint problem solving. The Hispanic is thus more often than not inclined to take a somewhat docile and obedient attitude in such instances rather than one of equality or independent questioning of what he or she is told. This feature in the Hispanic mentality would, of course, significantly affect an individual's participation in the group therapy situation, with the Hispanic being more likely to approach treatment in a less critical or questioning fashion than an American counterpart.

Second, the notion of personal reputation, or "face," is highly important to the Hispanic mentality, especially among males. This characteristic compels the Hispanic man to act in a strong, definite, and physically intimidating manner to resolve disputes if diplomatic tact fails to achieve his goals or objectives. In this respect, bald confrontation and bluntness is rarely tolerated in polite Hispanic society. Instead, reprimands tend to be issued through understatement, asides, and low-key, face-saving comments. Public declarations of personal dissatisfaction toward others are seen to be in bad taste. Indeed, the kind of confrontational bluntness or frankness sometimes exhibited in mainstream U.S. society is frequently viewed as insulting or personally degrading by the prideful Hispanic.

Third, the Hispanic ethos promotes an outlook supportive of family and group solidarity in the face of external attacks or threats. In this regard, no one has the right to critically question any failings of an individual's family (particularly of parents) except other family members themselves. Hispanics are therefore prone to project a public view of harmony or cooperativeness of their domestic situation, for fear that they might become an object of gossip and derision by others. Moreover, this idealization of the family is both a cultural and an internalized-object phenomenon, which often prevents any objective discussion of parents' good or bad attributes (e.g., leading to such statements as "My mother was a saint and my father was very hardworking"). Furthermore, within the group therapy situation, Hispanic participants are apt to remain sanguine not only about their family of origin but also about any other primary organizations with which they are closely allied (e.g., clubs, schools, or neighborhoods). In this regard, Hispanic males may voice quite chauvinistic or parochial beliefs about their origins, culture, or roots (e.g., "The people in my country [town, street] are much more lively [friendly, respectful] than they are here").

Fourth, although laughter is often just a simple expression of good feelings and the recognition of the absurdities of everyday life, Hispanics can also use cool mockery or irony to exact conformity to group norms through ridicule. In its more benign manifestation, humor is used as a way of broaching uncomfortable topics and of making a bridge between individuals regarding matters of possible controversy (i.e., with the idea that people that laugh together cannot be dangerous adversaries). In its more cruel manifestation, it shows up as derision. Regardless, Hispanic humor is often experienced as puzzling or frustrating to non-Hispanics because, in group settings, Hispanics may seem to be "laughing all the time." The impression is thus given that no serious transactions are taking place because an air of levity and frivolousness predominates the scene or situation. As a result, outsiders at Hispanic gatherings often walk away, scratching their heads and wondering "what's so funny?"

Finally, Hispanic culture, following from its group-centered viewpoint, tends to emphasize cohesion and conformity rather than the individualism so strikingly observed in a mainstream American type of family perspective. Dissension, controversy, and individual protests are thus not characteristics that are as valued in Hispanic culture as they are in mainstream American life. Whereas people are expected to parade their strengths, accomplishments, and virtues in American business life, Hispanics—reared with a more humble outlook—might judge such displays as self-assertive, egotistical behavior. Instead, their tradition emphasizes the subjugation of the self for the sake of larger family obligations or social propriety. It opposes the questioning of presuppositions and assumptions of daily existence if such a critique would reposition the lines of traditional family authority. It is for this reason that young Hispanics are taught to obey their elders without the type of democratic debate often encouraged in mainstream American households.

THE HISPANIC MALE CHARACTER AND
PSYCHOTHERAPEUTIC SITUATION

These cultural characteristics of respect for authority, dignified communication, time-worn formality, and reverence for established patterns of living account for the Hispanic male's unique way of interacting in the group psychotherapy situation. Whereas the standard group therapy approach would have it that the group process should help members recognize the nature of their self-defeating character traits (i.e., those blocking participants from adapting successfully to their social situation), the Hispanic influence operates to diminish the impact of any method that would uncover these maladaptive individual traits. As such, it promotes conformity rather than emancipation from restrictive norms (e.g., "Don't talk disrespectfully about your father"). Moreover, to the extent that the entire psychotherapeutic enterprise is aimed at helping individuals differentiate from enmeshed family systems or to otherwise learn ways of distinguishing self-defeating family involvements from those which are more positive or promoting of personal adjustment, Hispanic culture emphasizes displacement of blame on external causes rather than purposeful decision making. It can be said, then, that a sort of fatalism characterizes much Hispanic thinking, leading members of this culture to believe that their destinies are dictated by impersonal forces (e.g., religion, custom, or family expectations) rather than by voluntary, immediate choices within their control.

This propensity means that Hispanic males are more likely than average American participants to assume a defensive stance when they are required to examine their identities or customs critically in group therapy. Indeed, an often-heard refrain of Hispanic male group members is that, in their country of origin, life is much more tranquil and respectful than in the United States; that is, there is too much freedom in America. They seem threatened by the notion that a decision could arise from independent choice and self-determination rather than according to prescribed habit or custom. In summary, a profoundly hierarchical and tradition-bound outlook courses through the mentality of many Hispanics, particularly those who have immigrated relatively recently.

According to Hispanic culture, the course taken in one's individual life, particularly if psychopathology or personal problems are hallmarks of one's existence, is often conceived to be the consequence of trauma rather than to result from learned behavior. Fate, deemed to be the controlling factor of life, is thought to be best placated through external behavior (e.g., prayer, ritual, or medicinal potions) instead of intrapsychic change. Commensurate with this passive outlook is the frequent view of Hispanic males that they are the guardians of secrets rather than agents of responsible choices that account for their emotional distress. They may therefore see their problems as something that has happened to them (e.g., divorce, financial ruin, rebellious children, or childhood abuse), instead of badly made decisions that led them to their present, unhappy circumstances. Often rather wary of professionals and other strangers who presume to inquire into their personal lives, Hispanic males in particular may tend to superficially accommodate the demands of outside authority or otherwise affirm what they anticipate to be the clinician's wishes, keeping hidden their authentic skepticisms, doubts, and ambivalences. This "me–them" outlook, although couched in the conservative formalism of traditional Hispanic culture, presents an appreciable mode of resistance to any therapeutic method premised on self-revelation and uncovering techniques. It is at this juncture—between the values exalted by authoritarian Hispanic culture and the democratic spirit of the American tradition—that the greatest difference between the male Hispanic and his American counterpart can be seen. I explore the concrete implications of this disparity further in the concluding section of this chapter.

The foregoing comments suggest that there is something deeply private about the personality of the male Hispanic that prevents his easy assimilation into a group subculture. Although it is likely that this individual would partake socially in group projects, his participation would probably tend to be superficial and calculated rather than spontaneous and uninhibited. In this respect, the character makeup of the Hispanic male defies the rather open and democratic spirit of an American mentality. Deeply distrustful of organized groups beyond the confines of his family and community, the Hispanic male integrates only slowly into artificial or foreign groups not of his own making. In this respect, the Hispanic male holds a somewhat cynical and skeptical attitude toward all political systems, extending to the intentions of the group psychotherapy situation.

Therefore, a prime consideration in any attempt to effect change in the functioning of the Hispanic male character would be helping these individuals recognize the degree to which they control the course, impact, and effectiveness of their psychotherapeutic experiences. Before the psychotherapeutic experience can be truly transformative, they must learn to adopt a nonalienated or otherwise emotionally invested role in their treatment, rather than one merely following social expectations or the dictates of polite behavior. From a treatment perspective, then, the Hispanic male often needs to learn how to move from an outward to an inward locus of control to gain from therapy. Within the group therapy situation, he must come to realize that—as an equal member of a spontaneous social alliance (i.e., the psychotherapeutic group)—it is he who determines the destiny of the therapeutic agenda, not the other way around.

A main contributing factor to such isolation from social organization, apart from the Hispanic male's immediate family or environmental circumstances, is the well-known personality attribute of *machismo*. This exaggerated evaluation of one's maleness and sexual virility is based in the idea that self-worth emerges from the individual's seductive powers as well as from his capacity to "go it alone."

Such psychic separateness would at first seem to contradict the earlier observation that Hispanics are sociable, community-minded individuals. However, an important paradox to consider when understanding the Hispanic mentality is that pride and honor are sacrosanct ideals—that is, one does not want to be a *pendejo* (a weak-willed individual). Thus, basic to the Hispanic male's way of thinking is the importance of protecting his social reputation at all costs and fighting any insinuation that he cannot meet his personal or social responsibilities. Therefore, if the typical, wage-earning Hispanic male were confronted about his failure to fulfill family requirements, financial obligations, or personal promises (however justified), he would likely respond with vigorous denial or defensiveness rather than with open self-reflection. Forced by his cultural ideal to guard a view of himself as someone capable of carrying off the demands of caretaker, provider, and responsible parent without external help, favors, or special treatment from others (yet often the member of an enmeshed and deeply intertwined family), the Hispanic male often presents himself to the therapy situation with marked ambivalent feelings about his dependency strivings. On the one hand he is strongly tied to the lives of others (e.g., mother, father, brothers, sisters, and cousins). On the other, he feels diminished when he must admit that he harbors the same level of neediness as he sees displayed by others around him (evidenced by this comment from one group participant: "I wish I could just run away from the whole lot of them and never come back").

His idealization of self-sufficiency often has the effect of keeping the Hispanic male from learning about his faults, difficulties, or limitations from others. As such, he invests in conveying to others the image of invincibility. Unaccustomed to self-introspection or objective appraisal of his failings in the public arena, the Hispanic male may have particular problems revealing his doubts and uncertainties within the context of the group situation (because he cannot be seen as "weak or soft").

Although it can cause therapeutic opposition, this manly pridefulness can also be a source of therapeutic transformation, because once he has given his word, the Hispanic male is quite likely to abide by his promises. However, such cooperativeness must be carefully distinguished from superficial placations or gestures made to temporarily accommodate the therapist's desires. Awareness of this difference is difficult unless the clinician first realizes the subtleties at work in the Hispanic male's communication system; namely, when words are used for the convenience of the moment and when they reflect the genuine commitment to change or involvement. A therapist can only draw this distinction over a period of time by observing the degree of congruence between the client's statements and deeds.

THERAPEUTIC IMPLICATIONS FOR GROUP PSYCHOTHERAPY

On the basis of the observations made above about the character structure of the Hispanic male, several suggestions for treatment in the group therapy context are relevant to an analysis of Hispanic male psychology. First, therapists should not view the formality and politeness manifested by these clients as mere modes of resistance but, instead, should accept these as natural means by which men establish intimacy or interpersonal trust. As such, for Hispanic males, authentic personal relationships should be seen as growing in a stepwise fashion rather than through sudden leaps or "breakthroughs." For example, it may very well be that in the course of group therapy the leader is never addressed by his or her first name by the Hispanic participant, but only by formal title. However, such propriety does not necessarily mean that the male participant is detached or alienated from the emotional roots of the therapeutic process, only that he is relying on a formal structure to feel secure within the often-ambiguous dynamics of the treatment process. This type of etiquette should thus not be cause for analysis or discussion; it should be accepted as part and parcel of the common ways in which Hispanic males establish their bearings within social settings organized or directed by authority figures.

Second, interventions should be aimed at expanding the choices that these clients have at their disposal but may have overlooked because of unquestioned obligations or being enmeshed in their families of origin. Indeed, this conundrum of conflicting obligations to self and others is a perennial problem confronting Hispanic males.

In one group that I led, a Hispanic member insisted that he was "trapped" in a lower economic circle, making it highly improbable that he would ever be able to meet a "higher" type of woman or more ambitious group of friends than those with whom he was associating. The client saw himself as fated to exist in a crime-ridden neighborhood and to be surrounded by individuals whose only aspiration in life was drinking or carousing (saying, "the only type of people I know want to party and have a good time"). After some commentary by the other members, who themselves came from a variety of ethnic backgrounds, I remarked on this client's easy resignation and generally fatalistic outlook. In particular, I questioned him about what prevented him from changing his life (i.e., making his circle of friends or acquaintances more congruent with his personal values). His answer was that this possibility was nonexistent because "no one wants anything to do with a poor Latin man." He expressed the lament of being a victim of the wider society's anti-Hispanic prejudice.

This intervention was one of many of the same type that were brought repeatedly to this client's attention, focusing on his self-disparaging and passive style of dealing with his social status. It eventually led to more pointed inquiries into this man's unconscious fears of abandonment by his unrecognized parental introjects. Links were made between the client's tendency to see himself without choice and his propensity to remain tied uncritically to his family of origin, helping him to appreciate the taken-for-granted quality of his passive attitude. My approach consisted of tactfully working through or otherwise illuminating the ways in which this man limited himself to a certain array of possibilities because of his enmeshed family situation—that is, preferring to conceive of a life without choice rather than one characterized by ambiguity and anxiety. Eventually this had the liberating effect of helping the client connect with individuals who were markedly different than those compelled by his transferential influences.

Third, humor must be used as the "coin of the realm" in Hispanic groups as a means of coding or making statements that might otherwise be threatening if delivered in a blunt or serious fashion. This method requires a therapist to have a certain amount of flexibility in using group defenses to gain advantage against participants' tendencies toward emotional detachment. The group therapist has to be able to stay at the level of humor, using irony, paradox, or reverse mockery (aimed at the client's defenses, never at his character or self-respect) to outwit those aforementioned resistances. The following example illustrates an appropriate use of humor.

In one of my group sessions, laughter was taking place between two Hispanic group members engaged in private conversation while a third was speaking about matters of intimacy to the entire group. I intervened and stated to the members who were talking, "you should really get what you're saying published because, judging from the laughter, it would certainly be a bestseller for those wanting comedy." This somewhat sarcastic remark had the effect of drawing attention to the laughter without actually having to confront those who were engaged in the disruptive behavior. Hearing that their conduct had had that type of noxious influence on the other participants, the two men began to explain why they were engaged in their unsettling conduct, bringing into group focus the extraneous communication without my needing to be forceful or shaming.

Fourth, the therapist should emphasize the burdens and responsibilities that Hispanic men see in carrying out their sometimes unrealistic visions of manliness rather than berate them for being excessively authoritarian, sexist, or rigid. In this respect, an empathic approach rather than a condemnatory attitude is more likely to help foster a working therapeutic alliance between the therapist and Hispanic male group member.

All too often group therapists—particularly those running short-term, focused, or theme-centered rehabilitative groups—report that they resort to criticism to bring about change in their participants. In particular, they may remind the Hispanic male that he now lives in a new society where his old customs are no longer tolerated. For example, he might be chided for his harsh child disciplinary practices, intemperate drinking and driving, sexist outlook, or lackadaisical attitudes toward his children's education. Nevertheless, however true the Hispanic male's shortcomings may be, interventions highlighting only negative characteristics are, in the bulk of cases, likely only to result in a hardening of the client's defensive system. Their effect would likely make these individuals more proud and rigid than might otherwise be the case. Instead of encouraging openness about their role confusion or difficulties adapting to the norms of a new culture, this type of commentary would serve only to close them down further. The Hispanic male is more likely to reorganize his thinking around culturally relevant lines if he is coaxed into awareness about the social contradictions in which he finds himself, thereby giving him an opportunity to integrate old ideals with new realities of U.S. society.

In summary, the group leader must bring into consideration not only the frustrations and shortcomings of Hispanic group members in carrying out their responsibilities in American society, but also their abiding sense of disappointment and disillusionment at not being able to live up to their own unrealistic ideals as men who are strong, autonomous, or otherwise absolute in their authority. It is this identification with the unattainable ideal that can serve as a powerful rallying point or common topic in group discussions, especially with recent emigrants from Latin American countries.

In one group I led, consisting of court-referred Hispanic males charged with spousal abuse, several decried the "injustice" of the American system that took it upon itself to intervene in their private affairs. This complaint expanded into a general criticism of the "liberalism" rampant in the country, which robbed families (particularly male-headed households) of their right to manage their affairs according to their best judgment. After a prolonged period of fault finding about the unfairness of the American social system, the group leader drew attention to the difficulties that all of these men seemed to be having in adapting to the new expectations while attempting to preserve their old identities, formed by their traditional cultures (e.g., saying, "It's sort of hard to be two people at the same time when one culture demands one thing and another something else"). In general, this form of empathic intervention lessened the men's defensive stance, making it less necessary for them to justify their maladaptive behavior than would have been the case were they censured outright.

CONCLUSION

The Hispanic male certainly has the emotional structure and self-awareness to be a productive participant in traditional group therapy. However, clinicians ignorant of Hispanic culture can commit many needless errors resulting from unthinking value judgments and destructive comparisons with other ethnic groups drawn from narrow, mainstream beliefs. Many Hispanic males are united by common characteristics of conservatism, respect for authority, suspiciousness of crass individualism, and reluctance to admit vulnerabilities beyond the bounds of their most intimate family circles. These characteristics, while leading to significant resistances to participating in group processes, can be managed to a productive end if the group leader avoids direct confrontation of the Hispanic male's defenses, uses humor in a strategic fashion, and discerns clearly superficial flattery from genuine interpersonal communication.

Moreover, I have stressed that the common experiences of cultural displacement and role confusion are particularly important themes for psychotherapeutic analysis throughout the treatment process. Interventions that recognize these common dilemmas (e.g., marginalization and unclear sources of personal identity) are more likely to advance the process of group cohesion than those focusing on the deficiencies of the participants relative to the larger U.S. society.

Finally, all therapists dealing with this population must bear in mind that a multiculturalism already exists within the Hispanic community itself, because it comprises a diversity of national origins, economic backgrounds, and educational attainments. The preceding guidelines must be used cautiously, given that no specific individual ever manifests only the general attributes ascribed to a diffuse ethnic group. Thus, the Hispanic male is probably more similar than different to the other men discussed in this book. Because they require affirmation of their strength and determination, group therapy for these individuals should acknowledge and support their quest for respect as individuals rather than approach them as mindless objects of stereotypic prejudice.

REFERENCES

Acosta-Belen, I., & Sjostrom, B. R. (1988). *The Hispanic experience in the United States*. New York: Praeger.

Shorris, E. (1992). *Latinos: A biography of the people* New York: Norton.

Wyer, T. (1988). *Hispanic U.S.A.: Breaking the melting pot*. New York: Harper & Row.

11

WORKING WITH GAY MEN IN PSYCHOTHERAPY GROUPS

JOEL C. FROST

Much is written throughout the chapters of this book about the struggle for men to understand what it means to be a man, with attention given to class, culture, race, and ethnicity. There is also much written about men wanting to relate with other men, even in ways that are intimate and affectionate. At this point in the various discussions, however, there will likely be a line drawn. This is a line of discomfort that seems to occur when the depth of male–male yearning moves from affectional to sexual. There are areas of commonality among all men, but there also exists a clear demarcation, with gay men either on the outside or, at least, on the other side. This is because the ways in which gay men yearn for intimacy and connection with other men often seem different and frightening.

Heterosexual, or straight men, often feel uncomfortable with gay men. Slavson (1964) wrote this regarding the types of people that he thought were inappropriate for group psychotherapy: "The presence of a homosexual patient, whether active or latent, in a group of non-homosexuals, greatly intensifies anxiety in the latter. . . . the climate of the group reflects a sort of fear resembling the restlessness of a herd of animals who sense the proximity of a dangerous enemy" (p. 216). This is an old attitude; yet, it seems in some ways to be as true a feeling and perception today as 30 years ago. Gay men are often seen not only as different but as a threat.

Being gay is seen as separate from, rather than a variant of, normal human sexuality.

At the time of this writing, the state of Colorado is presenting a legal argument that homosexuality is simply a behavior (i.e., an action devoid of its implication for core identity); thus, homosexuals are not seen as an identifiable group that would merit protection. At the heart of this argument are the perceptions of (a) choice versus orientation, (b) homosexuality as a behavior versus an identity, (c) the exclusive focus on sexual behavior versus an expression of love and affection, and (d) the unacceptability of homosexuality as a normal variant of human sexuality.

I believe that to understand the issue of gay men in psychotherapy groups one must first understand what it is to be a gay man and what histories gay men bring of their experiences of groups. This may be the only chapter that many therapists read about gay men in groups; thus, I have included a fairly extensive amount of background material.

I am writing about what I have experienced both as a gay man and as a therapist working predominantly with White gay men in a large urban setting. I can speak neither for all gay men nor for all types of group experiences for gay men, because the community of gay men is as heterogeneous as any other.

As is true for all men, each gay man needs to struggle to understand what it means to be a man. Gay men are raised with the same social expectations and interpersonal training as other men. Yet, in addition, these men must struggle with what it means to be gay men, within a society that teaches exclusively negative stereotypes about them. The greater society reinforces the view that sexual behavior is the single most important element that defines a man as gay, as if there are no other significant defining characteristics of merit and worth. To know themselves, gay men need a climate in which they can shift through stereotypes, character issues, projections, and internalizations to find out who they are from the inside. In terms of psychotherapy, a climate of safety and clarity depends on the type and composition of the psychotherapy group, as well as on the beliefs of the group psychotherapist. I believe that it is the attitude and objectivity of the group therapist that makes a group safe. Thus, group therapists need to develop their knowledge about the contexts in which gay men live and develop.

BACKGROUND

Although much talked and written about, gay men are not a well-known group. Historically subjected to persecution or harassment, gay men have felt the need to hide their identity. This reality has played some part in the difficulty of mental health professionals to understand gay men. The clinical populations available to mental health professionals for earlier study were only those gay men who had been arrested or were in mental institutions. With such a pathologically skewed subject group, the larger group of gay men was often perceived as inappropriate for mixed psychotherapy groups (Bromberg & Franklin, 1952; Eliasberg, 1954; Fried, 1955; Hadden, 1958, 1966, 1968; Litman, 1961; Nobler, 1972; Pittman & DeYoung, 1971; Powdermaker & Frank, 1953; Resnick & Peters, 1967; Singer & Fischer, 1967; Slavson, 1964).

Pre-dating the gay movement, homosexual men were seen in homogeneous therapy groups, for two reasons: Homosexual men made heterosexual men and group therapists too anxious in mixed groups, and shame could be more effectively fostered in an all-homosexual-male group. The group therapist would intentionally foster shame regarding men's sexual acts, as well as their identification as homosexual, while fostering the belief that homosexual men were incapable of forming lasting and loving primary relationships as long as they remained homosexual. No positive self-references as homosexual men were allowed to be spoken in the group sessions (Hadden, 1958, 1966, 1968). Conversion to heterosexuality was the group therapist's primary goal for each member, regardless of the client's stated goals.

The 25th anniversary of the Stonewall Riot, which marked the beginning of the gay movement in the United States, was in 1994. This year also marked the twenty-first anniversary of the deletion of homosexuality as a distinct pathology per se in the *Diagnostic and Statistical Manual of Mental Disorders* (American Psychiatric Association, 1968). These are significant events because they heralded a change within American culture: Gay men had begun to take a more active role in defining themselves.

As the larger culture has changed, as more gay men and lesbians have come out and been known in nonpathological ways, and as more gay and lesbian mental health professionals have furthered clinical understanding, the mental health culture has shifted with regard to gay men (Berzon, 1979; Dank, 1971; Fassinger, 1991; Garnets, Hancock, Cochran, Goodchilds, & Peplau, 1991; Gonsiorek, 1981–1982; Graham, Rawlings, Halpern, & Hermes, 1984; Herek, Kimmel, Amaro, & Melton, 1991; Herron, Kinter, Sollinger, & Trubowitz, 1980, 1981–1982; Lee, 1977; A. Martin, 1982; Neisen, 1990). These changes have been reflected in the development of gay-affirmative psychotherapy (Shannon & Woods, 1991). Premises of gay-affirmative psychotherapy are that being gay is a normal variant of human sexuality and that one can successfully complete psychotherapy or psychoanalysis while identifying as a lesbian or a gay man. It also encompasses the belief in the capacity of gay men and lesbians to form and maintain lasting and healthy same-sex primary relationships. Furthermore, gay-affirmative psychotherapy respects gay men's and lesbians' underlying yearning and capacity to parent children. In short, it affirms gay men to be the same as all men and simply different in object choice.

Thus, there has been a change in the cultural context in which gay men are developing their core identities. Social supports, role models, and many of the definitions are different. This is most true within large urban centers, however; it is still a very different world in smaller and more rural communities for a gay boy growing into a gay man.

GROWING UP GAY

Before there is a gay man, there is a gay boy. Some know at an early age that they are gay, but some just know that they are different. Shame is an ever-present companion for most gay men, and it is related to the fact of being gay or questions of how one got to be gay. Because the etiology of homosexuality remains unclear, confusion continues about whether being gay is a preference or an orientation. This distinction is of central importance when a boy understands a primary part of his identity to be internally derived, whereas the larger culture perceives his being gay as a choice.

Boys must integrate their gender before their sexuality, first in the context of play and "boy things" (with no girls allowed) and later in competition and sports. In the attempt to solidify their identities as masculine, boys often eschew things feminine, or "sissy," and bond through aggression and competition. This creates problems for many boys who are gay. Some gay boys are fine with these vehicles, but most are not. Experiences with other boys centered around sports are uniformly shame-filled memories for almost all gay men.

Gay men talk about feeling different as boys. For purposes of discussion, I separate gay boys along these two variables: inner awareness and outer awareness.

Inner awareness denotes only that known to oneself. This category may be further divided into (a) those who know that they are different, and define that as gay, and (b) those who do not inwardly define that difference as being gay. Boys of the former group begin to develop a gay identity early in life. These boys need to define what sets them apart and do so differently depending on their age of awareness—as effeminate, as strongly attached to other boys, or through sexual feelings for other boys. Boys in the latter group may grow up, marry, have children, and only later realize their inner identity.

Outer awareness denotes that which is detectable by others. Gay boys either can pass as any other boys or cannot pass because others see them as different. For the latter, their external characteristics or mannerisms give them away. They are thus defined as gay by the larger group, whether this was an acknowledged awareness or not.

The first distinction is between those who know inside that they are different, and the second is between those whose difference can be noted by other boys from outward appearance or actions. There are actually four separate groupings, with variations amidst all four. These realities create very different developmental paths for various gay boys, both in the manner in which they develop and in what it means to them to be gay. What is common is that all gay boys learn to develop both strong defenses against intimacy and the consequent anticipation of the shame of rejection. Gay boys struggle to hide their inner realities and to tone down or hide external manifestations. After a lifetime of hiding, gay men often have great difficulty relating intimately, even with other gay men and especially in groups.

Some gay boys' outward appearances do not betray them, and they can continue to be perceived as heterosexual boys by their peers. These boys grow up much like others: They have male reference groups, participate in sports, and, yet, maintain a hidden inner secret. This is called *passing*. Passing is the ability to be accepted as belonging to the dominant culture, and it is the basis for being "in the closet." (This phenomenon is also not unusual for a light-skinned African American or an Anglo-looking Latino man.) By passing, gay men learn to live a dual existence: one public and one private; one life a lie and one life real. This creates both a fear of being found out and a yearning for a community of one's own, a reference group.

Some boys' outward appearance betrays them. These boys may talk, look, or act in ways that set them apart as sensitive. As a consequence, they are often called "sissy," "chicken," "queer," or "faggot" and are rejected by their male peers. They more actively seek a reference group in which they can be themselves and not be judged. Such boys often seek solace in friendships with girls. The following five things may happen in the development of boys with such outer awareness.

First, these boys may lose the opportunity to integrate inner experiences of themselves with external bodily experiences of themselves in culturally prescribed ways. This lack of integration often makes these boys highly dependent on sexual affirmation later in life, needing constant reassurance through sexual admiration.

> I always have felt odd with my body. I was always skinny and slight, and no one ever wanted me to be on their team. They picked on me, and I could never fight back. I never felt good about my body until I started to have sex (with other boys).

Second, they may lose a sense of themselves as being like other boys; in other words, they may not sufficiently differentiate themselves from girls as do other boys. Boys are encouraged to differentiate from girls in American culture, yet many gay boys find a comfortable receptivity in either a less masculine or a more feminine experience. Working with gay men, one sees fine distinctions between maleness and femaleness, masculine and feminine, erotic and affectional, gender role stereotypes, and the ability to tolerate dependency.

> When I was younger, I used to draw women with many different outfits. I was quite good at it, and I enjoyed it a great deal. My parents forbade me to do this, and would always be on the watch to catch me. I had to sneak when they were out of the house and then destroy the drawings before they found them. I never knew why they thought it was so bad. I could have been a great dress designer if I had been allowed to continue; instead, I am in a job that I hate.

Third, gay boys seek nurturing and physical contact with other boys. However, the usual modes of physical contact available to young males are based on competition and aggression. Thus, interactions can involve significant risk of rejection, failure, or exploitation by heterosexual boys.

> I wanted so much to be liked by my brother and his friends. In order to be accepted by them, they made me have sex with all of them, and then they made fun of me and rejected me. I still hate them. I still get anxious around men.

Fourth, many gay boys miss out on opportunities to engage in peer activities where boys learn how to successfully and safely be in groups with other boys. In mixed groups, gay boys need to hide what might mark them as different or threatening. Hiding one's true self is a fundamental reality for gay boys and, later, for gay men. Hiding goes much beyond a coping skill; it is a learned survival technique. Rejection, humiliation, physical intimidation, physical assault, and the possibility of death are realistic expectations when faced with heterosexual boys and men. Hiding is a psychological means of managing shame, anxiety, and panic. Thus, there is a strong need to have safe places where a gay boy or gay man can explore his true self.

> I am always aware of who I am around. I never say anything more than I have to say. I have learned that it is best to tell people as little as possible. That is one reason why I don't trust groups; I can't control everything that people know.

Finally, what is often cited as a precursor to the later realization of being gay is a boy's sense of himself as being more like a girl. It is not clear if gay males occupy a position between male and female, have a different blend, or occupy a different position altogether. Nevertheless, gay men need to be able to integrate their femaleness in a way that is separate from effeminacy. Yet another group member had this to say:

I feel ashamed to talk about this, even here in a group of gay men. I like being a "bottom," and I think that you will all see me as no longer being "butch." I feel safer talking with my individual therapist about this, because she will not judge me. I feel like I have always had to hide what I really like to do sexually; maybe that is why I have so much anonymous sex.[1]

HOMOPHOBIA

Growing up gay means internalizing society's stereotypes. Homophobia has to do with a fear of homosexuality or of gays and lesbians, "the dread of being in close quarters with homosexuals" (Weinberg, 1972, p. 4). Homophobia also often involves the fear of things feminine (Blumenfeld, 1992). It exists in all people and is not just a set of attitudes that heterosexuals feel toward gays and lesbians. Homophobia is a system of projections and introjections. In that most people are raised in a society that is heterosexist, everyone has internalized negative beliefs and attitudes about homosexuality and femaleness (Blumenfeld, 1992). *Heterosexism* has to do with heterosexuality being considered the norm and *sexism* (conflict and inequality between the genders) being fundamental to the culture (Neisen, 1990). These attitudes about homosexuality and femaleness come together in people's reactions to gay men and in gay men's reactions to each other and to themselves. In the absence of positive gay role models, society's negative stereotypes have enormous power. Thus, there is a critically important need for gay men to have a positive and supportive reference group.

DEVELOPMENT OF A POSITIVE GAY IDENTITY

As one can see, growing up from a gay boy to a gay man requires additional developmental imperatives. Gay men must not only struggle with what it means to be a man, they must also resolve internalized homophobia, integrate aspects of femaleness, integrate dependency and passivity, and develop a positive gay identity. Heterosexual males do not have to question the etiology and meaning of their sexual orientation, and reference groups are readily available to them.

---

[1]In gay culture, "top" (active, masculine, or inserter) and "bottom" (passive, feminine, or insertee) refer to more than just sexual positions; they are references to status, role, character, and value. Many elements of gay culture parallel stereotypically heterosexual male attitudes toward women; in this case, there is an added element of shame for the gay man who is a "bottom."

COMING OUT

Coming out is a developmental process whereby the sense of identity as a gay man or lesbian is solidified internally and then revealed to and lived out externally in the world (Cass, 1979; Coleman, 1981–1982; Hencken & O'Dowd, 1977; Isay, 1986, 1989; Larson, 1981; Malyon, 1982; H. P. Martin, 1991; McDonald, 1982; Minton & McDonald, 1983–1984; Troiden, 1979, 1989). This is not a linear process, nor is it a one-time thing. Gay men go back and forth along the stages in this process and experience some anxiety every time they need to come out to a new person in a new situation.

If homophobia relates to the negative attitudes about gay men and lesbians, then shame relates to the underlying experience of being gay. Homosexuality and shame go hand in hand. Coming out is a process of living on the outside what is real and honest on the inside. Often, the cost is rejection, even by one's biological family. Most gay men feel sure that homosexuality is beyond a parent's capacity for unconditional love; therefore, coming out to one's parents is often the most difficult task that confronts a gay man. Gay men often expect rejection by their own families, and, consequently, they establish a chosen family. This may include friends, coworkers, accepting parents of gay friends, and others who form a sense of family, on the basis of acceptance, emotional bonding, a sense of watching out for each other, and having a family group with which to share holidays. It is within the context of the gay culture, through the gay reference group, that gay men have found support and encouragement in the development of a positive gay identity. Psychotherapy groups can take on some of the functions of a chosen family, with the result that the meaning of members to each other can be very intense.

PSYCHOTHERAPY GROUPS

Men do not generally join psychotherapy groups, and when they do, they are reluctant to talk about their own feelings and often insensitive to the feelings of others. Men more readily join sports-related groups and groups based on action as opposed to affect, valuing competition versus intimacy, and concentrating on bonding as a group goal only when applied to the group task. The sports group task is to win the competition. In psychotherapy groups, the group task is to bond in openly emotional intimacy. Being emotionally vulnerable is less comfortable for men, less familiar, and more ascribed to the ways that women are typically thought to interact. If men are to relate in these ways, then it is often easier if they relate with women. Gay men are not very different than heterosexual men in these regards. One must remember that gay men are still raised as men and thereby manifest many of the same resistance as any other man regarding being in a group. The specter of being openly emotional in a group of men is doubly horrifying for gay men.

TYPES OF PSYCHOTHERAPY GROUPS FOR GAY MEN

There are many variables to consider when deciding which group placement is appropriate for a gay male: psychological and developmental characteristics as well as the expressed goals of the client. The stage of development of the man's gay identity should be considered, as well as the presence or absence of a reference group (Frost, 1990). Often a good predictor is whether a man has had some previous positive experience in a group format.

There have been many effects on the gay and lesbian community from HIV and AIDS. The community has had to pull together for its very survival, and out of this a stronger positive experience of belonging to a group has evolved. There has also been a dramatic upsurge in the use of group interventions, in the form of psychoeducational and support groups (Frost, 1993). Although this chapter is about gay men in psychotherapy groups, it must be stated that the increased willingness of gay-affirmative therapists to provide psychotherapy groups for gay men and gay men's increased willingness to join these groups must be in some measure related to the increased positive presence of gay and lesbian support groups in the community. Gay men have so long felt excluded, or potentially excluded, from male groups; this change shows that positive experiences of acceptance can go a long way in promoting their nascent yearning to join with other men in intimate relationships. Another side effect of AIDS has been an increased desire for primary relationships among gay men; this means having to learn how to be intimate with other men, which is best done in a group setting.

ALL-GAY-MALE GROUPS

Short-term groups composed entirely of gay men have historically worked well for such tasks as coming out, getting sober, or managing sexual behavior, or when there is no available reference group (such as in small communities). The current focus for a long-term all-gay-male psychotherapy group is on those gay men who have had a significant amount of psychotherapy, have reference groups, and want to deeply probe why they do not yet have lasting relationships.

The world of gay men is firmly centered around the constancy of reject or be rejected. Modes of relating often are highly sexualized, and the route to self-definition as well as to intimacy with others is primarily through sexual expression. All-gay-male psychotherapy groups are helpful in that, deprived of the usual method of bonding sexually, members can begin to see how frightened they are of other gay men emotionally and find new ways to relate intimately.

There are two main choices for single gay men: (a) to take the risk of trying to establish a loving relationship, which requires tolerating sadness, despair, vulnerability, and the fear of rejection; and (b) to live alone and settle for short affairs that are exciting and involve less intimacy, along with much less risk of loss or rejection.

A long-term group setting provides men the opportunity to work on establishing loving relationships. All-gay-male psychotherapy groups can provide a safe setting in which there is more rapid and significant self-disclosure than in mixed groups (Schwartz & Hartstein, 1986). There is a greater degree of identification between members; thus, superficial bonding occurs more quickly, on the basis of shared similarities. When the group process deepens and expands to include ways in which members are different from each other, the level of anxiety rises, and members begin to feel the urge to flee. Feeling safe enough to more openly discuss sexual orientation does not mean that all gay men will readily talk about their own sense of femininity, vulnerability, despair, or wellsprings of internalized homophobia and shame. As stated above, gay men have practiced hiding their feelings for most of their lives, so they do not easily open up and disclose, even to other gay men. Knowledge that the therapist is also gay can encourage more rapid disclosure. This knowledge sets the stage for positive role modeling as well as for a complex set of transference and countertransference reactions.

STAGES OF DEVELOPMENT IN ALL-GAY-MALE PSYCHOTHERAPY GROUPS

In general, gay men approach joining a psychotherapy group with great trepidation. They most often prefer the safety and privacy of individual psychotherapy, because their experiences with groups have been uniformly terrible, marked by exclusion rather than inclusion. Gay men have been conditioned to feel that being alone is safer, that revealing any deep truths risks betrayal and exposure, and that being emotional only makes you seem more effeminate. As a result of their life experiences, gay men are often more self-absorbed and more self-conscious. They do not expect acceptance, nor do they expect trust in others to be fulfilled. Gay men are also conditioned to feel that they are flawed in an unredeemable way, which is manifested in a deeply held shame that interferes with establishing and maintaining loving and mutually trusting relationships.

Deepening the intimacy of the gay male group depends on one's ability to manage levels of anxiety as members begin group psychotherapy. The following is an account of one such new group, its various levels of anxiety, and the importance of a contract and an alliance with the therapist. The contract that I use covers an agreement to be at all sessions, to participate, to stay until the work is done, and to announce any decisions to leave in a way that allows the group to look at and work on the decision before it is acted on.

THE GROUP

I now describe a group I facilitated in my private practice in Boston, which met weekly at the office. This was my first all-gay-male group; my other therapy groups have been mixed by gender, sexual orientation, and race.

Four gay men met for the first session of the new psychotherapy group. They were all between the ages of 35 and 50 years and were single, White, middle-class, professional men within a large urban area. All but one man was either presently in, or had previously been in, individual psychotherapy with me. In the first session, there was much talk about the powerful influence of first impressions. Each man talked about feeling isolated and alone in his life and wishing to become more connected and develop greater intimacy. In the second session, members talked about how surprised they were that everyone had returned. They were aware of the constant phenomenon of either rejecting or of being rejected following first impressions. The men initially thought that they had all made it back because they were all so alike. They began to tell stories about their growing up and of the unhappy results of being with others in groups. These stories were also quite similar.

Following sessions included themes of wanting to be liked and fearing that they would not be and how they kept their barriers up so as not to be hurt, as well as indirect references to myself and what type of gay men I might like. The fifth session began with the announcement that there would be a new member. This announcement initiated a discussion about obligation versus commitment and prompted some thoughts about leaving the group (on the part of the member who had not been in individual psychotherapy with me). This man began to talk about how much he felt rejected by his father and how all of the men he had pursued sexually had in some way looked like his father.

In the next few sessions, the men looked more deeply into what factors were most powerful in first impressions. They focused on physical characteristics and fantasy, and they were struck with why they all felt so unattractive and desperate. It was agreed that first impressions constituted a "10-second test" and that if one failed this test it was all over. Indeed, when asked to reflect on the process of this group, the men agreed that, had it not been for their commitment to the contract, they would not have stayed together. This was a powerful moment, in that they all had experienced a deepening sense of affection for and connection with each other specifically because they had stayed beyond their initial impulse that it was not right to do so. As they talked further about intimacy, they determined that it had three requirements: sufficient time together (to force oneself past the 10-second test), honesty, and the capacity to work through conflict. Indeed, the next critical stage of development appeared as the members began to experience greater differences, which created strain, anxiety, and experiences of feeling misunderstood.

Open conflict is an important stage in the development of trust within the group, because gay men often have difficulty managing conflict. As mentioned earlier, gay men have often missed out on opportunities to become familiar with and work through situations of conflict and aggression. This is also an important stage when individual differences can be tolerated. One such difference was raised in this group with the introduction of the sixth member at the 18th session:

> Jerry, a 39-year-old gay man, joined the group with some hesitation. He was concerned that there were no women in the group. He had always relied on a sense of comfort that he felt with women. He heavily identified with women, feeling his character to be one of much femaleness. When he began to talk about this characteristic in the group, the other men began to laugh and appear uncomfortable. Jerry introduced an entirely new area of discussion for the group. What followed were themes of gender roles, sexual behavior, dependency, and the continuing confusion around masculinity.

This group initially bonded quickly, with similarity being an important element in this process. Being a relatively new group, its members experienced increased anxiety as greater dissimilarity began to appear. Increased levels of anxiety were also tied to the content of dissimilarity, different styles, levels of comfort with femaleness, and discomfort with conflict.

MIXED GAY-MALE AND LESBIAN GROUPS

It is a myth that gay men and lesbians form a homogeneous group based solely on the reality that both are homosexual. What is shared is that people of both orientations are the subject of discrimination within the larger society. There are actually wide differences between gay men and lesbians, just as there are between heterosexual men and women. This leads to increased anxiety as researchers search for lines of similarity and attempt to resolve the differences. Because there are so many differences, this type of group composition has more often been successful in work groups, political groups, or family groups.

There are, however, many gay men and lesbians who prefer being in a mixed gay and lesbian psychotherapy group. The advantages of this type of group are enumerated below:

1. More rapid development of interrelatedness because of a line of similarity and shared safety that is based on discrimination from the larger societal group;
2. A shared wish to develop and foster a more broadly based gay and lesbian chosen family;
3. An ability to work on opposite-gender relationships without the fear of a pull to "convert" to heterosexuality;
4. The opportunity to look at shared wishes and conflicts regarding parenting;
5. A place to continually work on the development of relationship models for gay male and lesbian relationships that are not based on the heterosexual model;
6. The opportunity to share the grief in both gay and lesbian lives from the loss of so many to AIDS, violence, and suicide.

HETEROGENEOUS GROUPS

Most groups led by therapists who are not gay tend to be heterogeneous, as do most groups outside of a larger urban center. The kinds of groups that can be offered are highly affected by the nature and extent of one's referral base. In addition, heterogeneous groups are also the group of choice for many gay men; they may feel too uncomfortable with other gay men, may be too "closeted," may not even have come out to themselves, or may prefer a group that better reflects the larger society.

When a group is predominantly heterosexual, there are pitfalls that a therapist must consider. This is particularly true if a gay member is not out to a significant degree in other areas of his life; the more closeted he is outside, the more closeted he will remain in the group. It is best if he has at least one other gay man as an ally, or that role will fall too often to the therapist. Another pitfall is the tendency of groups to scapegoat gay men (e.g., point out attributes such as narcissism in a member, but not see it in themselves) and gay men's willingness to accept the role because it is so familiar. When scapegoating occurs, it provides an opportunity to help the group see what they are wishing to get rid of within themselves.

Gay men sometimes prefer heterogeneous groups because of the opportunity they provide to engage in more intimate relationships with heterosexual women. They have often experienced a greater history of trust with women or, at least, less betrayal and rejection. The fact that this intimacy is nonsexual makes boundaries more clear. The subsequent development of trust and intimacy with a woman and with the group therapist often creates a safer environment in which to begin work on greater intimacy with the men in the group. A gay male member of one of my groups had this to say: "I like working with straight women. We always have something in common. At the very least we can sit and talk about how difficult men are."

COUNTERTRANSFERENCE

Gay-affirmative psychotherapy means the appreciation of homosexuality as a normal variant of human sexuality and an assertion of the basic potential healthiness of a person's identification as gay. Yet, even a gay-affirmative and gay male psychotherapist can be brought up short when he hears about the intricacies of various group members' sexual and emotional relationships. Sexual expression can be immensely varied and fluid. What is clear is that the group generally will not reveal more than what they sense the therapist is ready to hear. As the gay culture continues to develop in a more "out" style, sexual experimentation and expression broaden; thus, group therapists can experience much protective anxiety as members risk exposure to HIV.

It is difficult but critically important for the group therapist to remain nonjudgmental regarding individual differences in sexual and affectional expression. This is also true as gay men attempt to construct primary relationships in the style and manner that works for them. The group therapist may be male or female, straight or gay, and may thus have differing countertransferential reactions. What is common is that everyone is more comfortable with what is familiar to them.

SUMMARY: WHAT KINDS OF GROUPS DO GAY MEN NEED?

First, gay men need safe groups. Gay-affirmative psychotherapy does not mean that the therapist has to be gay, only that she or he should feel comfortable, knowledgeable, and objective when working with gay men. Second, gay men do need a gay-affirmative therapist, who believes that gay men are capable of establishing lasting, mutual, nurturing, and loving primary relationships. Third, it is best to have more than one gay man in the group and, if this does not happen, that the group therapist actively keep a chair open for another gay man. Finally, gay men need therapists who are able to feel fine about letting each member decide on the type of relationship that he wants, even if that means no relationship at all.

REFERENCES

American Psychiatric Association. (1968). *Diagnostic and statistical manual of mental disorders* (2nd ed.). Washington, DC: Author.

Berzon, B. (1979). *Positively gay: New approaches in gay and lesbian life.* Los Angeles: Mediamix.

Blumenfeld, W. J. (1992). *Homophobia: How we all pay the price.* Boston: Beacon Press.

Bromberg, W., & Franklin, G. H. (1952). The treatment of sexual deviates with group psychodrama. *Group Psychotherapy, 4,* 274–289.

Cass, V. C. (1979). Homosexual identity formation: A theoretical model. *Journal of Homosexuality, 4,* 219–235.

Coleman, E. (1981–1982). Developmental stages of the coming out process. *Journal of Homosexuality, 7,* 31–43.

Dank, B. M. (1971). Coming out in the gay world. *Psychiatry, 34,* 180–197.

Eliasberg, W. C. (1954). Group treatment of homosexuals on probation. *Group Psychotherapy, 7,* 218–226.

Fassinger, R. E. (1991). The hidden minority: Issues and challenges in working with lesbian women and gay men. *Counseling Psychologist, 19,* 157–176.

Fried, E. (1955). Combined group and individual therapy with passive–narcissistic patients. *International Journal of Group Psychotherapy, 5,* 194–203.

Frost, J. C. (1990). A developmentally keyed scheme for the placement of gay men into psychotherapy groups. *International Journal of Group Psychotherapy, 42,* 155–167.

Frost, J. C. (1993). Group psychotherapy with HIV-positive and AIDS patients. In A. Alonso & H. I. Swiller (Eds.), *Group therapy in clinical practice* (pp. 255–270). Washington, DC: American Psychiatric Press.

Garnets, L., Hancock, K. A., Cochran, S. D., Goodchilds, J., & Peplau, L. A. (1991). Issues in psychotherapy with lesbians and gay men: A survey of psychologists. *American Psychologist, 46,* 964–972.

Gonsiorek, J. (1981–1982). The use of diagnostic concepts in working with gay and lesbian populations. *Journal of Homosexuality, 7,* 9–20.

Graham, D. L., Rawlings, E. I., Halpern, H. S., & Hermes, J. (1984). Therapists' needs for training in counseling lesbians and gay men. *Professional Psychology: Research and Practice, 15,* 482–496.

Hadden, S. B. (1958). Treatment of homosexuality by individual and group psychotherapy. *American Journal of Psychiatry, 114,* 810–815.

Hadden, S. B. (1966). Treatment of male homosexuals in groups. *International Journal of Group Psychotherapy, 6,* 177–186.

Hadden, S. B. (1968). Group psychotherapy for sexual maladjustments. *American Journal of Psychiatry, 125,* 83–88.

Hencken, J. D., & O'Dowd, W. T. (1977). Coming out as an aspect of identity formation. *Gai Saber, 1,* 18–22.

Herek, G. M., Kimmel, D. C., Amaro, H., & Melton, G. B. (1991). Avoiding heterosexist bias in psychological research. *American Psychologist, 46,* 957–963.

Herron, W. G., Kinter, T., Sollinger, I., & Trubowitz, J. (1980). New psychoanalytic perspectives on the treatment of the homosexual male. *Journal of Homosexuality, 5,* 393–403.

Herron, W. G., Kinter, T., Sollinger, I., & Trubowitz, J. (1981–1982). Psychoanalytic psychotherapy for homosexual clients: New concepts. *Journal of Homosexuality, 7,* 177–192.

Isay, R. A. (1986). The development of sexual identity in homosexual men. In *The psychoanalytic study of the child* (pp. 467–489). New Haven, CT: Yale University Press.

Isay, R. A. (1989). *Being homosexual: Gay men and their development.* New York: Farrar, Straus, & Giroux.

Larson, P. C. (1981). Sexual identity and self-concept. *Journal of Homosexuality, 7,* 15–32.

Lee, J. A. (1977). Going public: A study in the sociology of homosexual liberation. *Journal of Homosexuality, 3,* 49–78.

Litman, R. E. (1961). Psychotherapy of a homosexual man in a heterosexual group. *International Journal of Group Psychotherapy, 11,* 440–448.

Malyon, A. K. (1982). Biphasic aspects of homosexual identity formation. *Psychotherapy: Theory, Research and Practice, 19,* 335–340.

Martin, A. (1982). Some issues in the treatment of gay and lesbian patients. *Psychotherapy: Theory, Research and Practice, 19,* 341–348.

Martin, H. P. (1991). The coming-out process for homosexuals. *Hospital and Community Psychiatry, 42,* 158–162.

McDonald, G. J. (1982). Individual differences in the coming out process for gay men: Implications for theoretical models. *Journal of Homosexuality, 8,* 47–60.

Minton, H. L., & McDonald, G. J. (1983–1984). Homosexual identity formation as a developmental process. *Journal of Homosexuality, 9,* 91–104.

Neisen, J. H. (1990). Heterosexism: Redefining homophobia for the 1990s. *Journal of Gay and Lesbian Psychotherapy, 1,* 21–35.

Nobler, H. (1972). Group therapy with homosexuals. *Comparative Group Studies, 3,* 161–178.

Pittman, F. S., & DeYoung, C. D. (1971). The treatment of homosexuals in heterogeneous groups. *International Journal of Group Psychotherapy, 21,* 62–73.

Powdermaker, F. B., & Frank, J. D. (1953). *Group psychotherapy: Studies in methodology of research and therapy.* Cambridge, MA: Harvard University Press.

Resnick, H. L. P., & Peters, J. J. (1967). Outpatient group therapy with convicted pedophiles. *International Journal of Group Psychotherapy, 17,* 151–158.

Schwartz, R. D., & Hartstein, N. B. (1986). Group psychotherapy with gay men: Theoretical and clinical considerations. In T. S. Stein & C. J. Cohen (Eds.), *Contemporary perspectives on psychotherapy with lesbians and gay men* (pp. 157–177). New York: Plenum.

Shannon, J. W., & Woods, W. J. (1991). Affirmative psychotherapy with gay men. *Counseling Psychologist, 19,* 197–215.

Singer, M., & Fischer, R. (1967). Group psychotherapy of male homosexuals by a male and female co-therapy team. *International Journal of Group Psychotherapy, 17,* 44–52.

Slavson, S. R. (1964). *A textbook in analytic group psychotherapy.* New York: International Universities Press.

Troiden, R. R. (1979). Becoming homosexual: A model for gay identity acquisition. *Psychiatry, 42,* 362–373.

Troiden, R. R. (1989). The formation of homosexual identities. *Journal of Homosexuality, 17,* 43–73.

Weinberg, G. (1972). *Society and the healthy homosexual.* New York: St. Martin's Press.

12

WORKING WITH MEN IN GROUPS: A FEMALE THERAPIST'S PERSPECTIVE

FRANCES BONDS-WHITE

My purpose in writing this chapter is to describe what is involved when a female psychotherapist works with men in group psychotherapy. My personal theoretical frame of reference is based in transactional analysis, psychoanalysis, and the Tavistock model of group work. It is my conviction that group psychotherapy is a primary therapy that can be supplemented with individual therapy as needed and that individual therapy is usually enhanced and made more efficient with the addition of group psychotherapy. I think that group psychotherapy provides the most efficient and economical way to do both short- and long-term psychotherapy. The group becomes the container, within the boundaries of which members can play out and realize the purpose of their defensive structures, experiment with rewriting their life scripts, and implement deep structural change in an interactive microcosm of their larger world. Because most of my therapeutic work has been done in an outpatient private-practice setting, I do not discuss the treatment of all-male groups by a single female therapist here.

For me, three issues emerged as relevant to this chapter: (a) considerations of the physical safety of the female therapist and its impact on patient selection (especially male patients), (b) male-to-male identification and bonding and confrontation of male–female stereotypes in group psychotherapy with a female leader, and (c) the group environment as a setting for the resolution of female therapist–male patient transference and countertransference issues.

The topic of female leadership of psychotherapy groups and its implications for the members of the group, especially the male members of the group, has seldom been discussed. In a survey of the literature, I found only two articles—by Conlon (1991) and by Wallach (1994)—that spoke to the effects of gender on the female group therapist. Conlon pointed out that the social and cultural expectations of women have a dynamic impact on female leaders in the beginning stages of a group, when selection of members, composition of the group, the responsibility for the setting, and maintenance of boundaries are of key importance. She suggested that the male group will see the female leader as the primordial mother parent, with a dual nature, and that men will be likely to lead the fights to test the boundaries and the authority of the leader. Transference and countertransference issues between female therapists and male patients in individual therapy, particularly the impact of gender on the female therapist's view of herself, have been discussed by Fuerstein (1992), Guttman (1984), and Lukton (1992). Karme (1979) has focused on the negative oedipal transference between female therapist and male patient, whereas Russ (1993) and Woodley (1988) have discussed the difficulties that female therapists may have both in dealing with and in getting adequate supervision for working with erotic transferences with male clients. Wallach (1994) has pointed out that female group leaders may have difficulty dealing with issues of competition and underlying envy, greed, and jealousy because of their fear of loss of relationship. Finally, discussion of the female leadership of heterogeneous psychotherapy groups is minimal in the literature.

SAFETY AND THE FEMALE THERAPIST: WHAT MEN DO WE SEE?

I work with groups comprising eight patients of both genders that meet once a week. These groups are held in a private office, and I am in a group practice with two other women and one man. Four out of five weekly groups are heterogeneous, with a balance of heterosexual and homosexual men and women who range in age from their early 20s to mid-50s in most groups. This mix reflects both the location in a large city and my aim to have groups that are as diverse as possible. Some clients are in individual therapy with me, one of my colleagues, or other individual therapists outside the practice. Others supplement group attendance with only an occasional individual session or a cluster of sessions as needed.

Obviously, some clients that are initially seen in private practice are not good candidates for treatment, either because of a lack of facilities for dealing with them adequately or because the client's safety and well-being are best managed in institutions that can provide shelter, emergency housing, detoxification facilities, medical care, or other such services that make for ethical and responsible case management. Not so obviously, one of the criteria that a female therapist in private practice must think about in her work with male clients is her own physical safety.

As a private practitioner, my office telephone numbers and address are listed in the telephone book. I give public lectures and teach seminars to help build my practice, and I distribute my card to people for referral purposes and send out flyers on workshops. I and other female therapists in private practice are therefore public figures in the community and need to be visible to develop professionally and economically. This public exposure that enables us to earn a living also puts us at some measure of risk, however. In the community mental health setting, a therapist is, to an extent, anonymous. Moreover, one is seldom alone in an agency; even during evening hours, other therapists or security personnel are present. However, in an individual or small group practice, this is not necessarily so. Thus, I have developed some ways of screening new clients that have, I think, contributed to my having a safe clinical practice. Getting a clear statement of the presenting problem, learning about client expectations, and discussing fees and schedules overtly in the initial telephone contact emphasizes that this will be a serious working relationship and gives me this opportunity to screen potential clients.

Recently, a man called for an appointment. He was referred to me by someone in California—he could not really remember the therapist's name, he had only seen him once in the Los Angeles area. When I asked for his address, he told me that he had just moved east and was staying with his girlfriend. I asked what made him seek therapy right now, and he informed me that he was having a problem with cocaine, but that really he wanted to come to therapy because he was angry with his wife, who he thought was cheating on him and would not tell him whether or not she had a boyfriend. I quickly suggested that he seek a drug rehabilitation program and gave him the name of several in the area. The interaction on the telephone raised several red flags about seeing this client in private practice. His inability to remember the referring therapist, the discounting of his drug use as a problem, and the anger with his wife all indicated a client who was acting out and at risk of escalating the acting out to a higher level. A referral to a drug rehabilitation agency seemed both the responsible and the self-protective thing to do.

WORKING WITH MEN IN GROUPS

One of the advantages of group psychotherapy for men working with a female therapist is that the group environment gives men a chance to explore many facets of their relationships to other men and to examine how their stereotypes about both masculine and feminine gender roles get played out in group situations. Sometimes this can be done in group therapy more effectively than in individual therapy. Men's violence against women (Watts & Courtois, 1981); a lack of intimacy in men's lives (Lewis, 1978); the inability to express the "softer sides" of themselves (O'Neil, 1981b); and restrictions in emotional expressiveness, homophobia, restricted sexual and affectional behavior, obsession with achievement and success, and power and control problems (O'Neil, 1981a, 1981b; Rabinowitz, 1991)—all have been related to gender role socialization. Every one of these issues can be worked with in group psychotherapy.

Fuerstein (1992), writing about individual therapy, pointed out that one of the difficulties of male patients working with female therapists is the problem of the client expressing paternal transference wishes toward the therapist that arise from a feared loss of masculinity that may accompany identification with the female therapist. In group psychotherapy, therapists can use the ways that men relate to each other to resolve this problem. Upon entry into a group, a man is more likely to look to the women in the group, including the female therapist, for nurturing and support. A female therapist who is attuned to the ways in which men avoid intimate contact with other men in the group and notes this can help men use their here-and-now interactions in the group to change the ways they relate to other significant men in their lives. The following group example illustrates this point.

> In a group of three men and four women, a new man entered the group. He immediately began to build alliances with the women and barely acknowledged any overtures made to him by the men. When one of the men in the group began to express anger at me (the female leader) because I had canceled his individual session and "forced him to rearrange at an inconvenient time," the new man immediately began defending me. I wondered aloud what his behavior meant for the group. The group members began to explore their anger at me for leaving them and their sense of my unreliability (I had canceled a group because of illness 2 weeks before this incident). The new man began to defend my right to be sick, to criticize the other members (especially the men, for being so dependent), and to protest the unrealistic expectations of the group members on me. Later work revealed that this man had as an only child spent a great deal of time in childhood and adolescence defending his mother against criticisms from his father and that he saw his father's criticalness as covering dependency and neediness. The male split between being aggressive (expressing anger) toward the therapist and needing to subdue aggressive impulses toward a woman (protecting and idealizing) was worked out in the group as each person explored what it meant to work with me, as an

active female leader who both pointed out the contradictions and drew the anger of the group toward me and my desertion of the group.

The men identified with each other about their fears of expressing aggressiveness toward a woman. Next, they explored their wishes to strike out at women who disappointed them. This strengthened their identification with each other. As the women in the group took sides, they too could begin to express some of their aggressive impulses toward me and to explore the female role demands that they nurture the "sick" therapist at their own expense. The final result of the work was that both men and women could explore their fantasies of needing to take care of the authority figure (mother) to get their needs met and to survive. This confronted the pre-oedipal transference projections of both genders in the group and enabled the entire group to reach across gender roles to their basic needs as human beings.

As the female leader of heterogeneous psychotherapy groups, I must always confront my own sociocultural stereotypes about gender to facilitate my work. Schachtel (1986) has pointed out that women have been socially trained to respond to others in a way that often conflicts with the analytic (group leadership) stance. It is also known that therapists respond to a client's gender when making treatment plans (Bowman, 1982). Bearing this in mind, the group psychotherapist needs to monitor herself regularly to be sure that she is not helping men avoid group treatment and that she looks for and challenges stereotypical gender behaviors in her groups. The following example illustrates how essential this is.

> For several weeks, the female members of a mixed-gender group kept returning to work-related problems—in particular, the difficulty of asking for raises and applying for promotions. The men would sit out this part of the group, acting on the surface (at least) as if they had no concerns in this area. Although I kept pointing out that these conversations had something to do with what was presently happening in the group, the members consistently discounted these interpretations. The women were developing patterns of empathy and emotional expression with each other, whereas the men gave advice to the women about these work-related concerns. The women were acting out the expressive–communion half of the problem while the men acted out the instrumental–agency half, as described by Levant (1993). As I continued to point out the almost caricatured nature of the split in the group and to insist that the discussions had to do with life in the group, not with extratherapy work, both the men and the women became angry at my need to "center everything on myself." With time and persistence, the issues of competition with the leader began to emerge. The ways in which women expressed fears of competition and the men denied their wish to compete with the female leader in the group were expressed, and we began some serious work on power and authority issues.

This paradigm of focusing on the here and now of the group interaction, of moving extragroup events into the context of the group, of confronting gender divisions and gender role behaviors, of containing the group's anger, and of persisting in the face of the group's attempts to discount and demean me and my willingness to be seen as a strong authority helped the members to move out of stereotypical gender behaviors. The men acknowledged the difficulty of living locked in a role that demanded denial of competition with and envy of women. They were also able to explore the limitations of a gender role that demanded that they be competitive. Gender role demands for male competition that interfere with male–male intimacy and trust were explored. Similar gains were made by the women in the group, and both men and women were able to move beyond gender expectations and identify on issues of competition, greed, and envy. Both men and women worked with the feelings aroused when I (a female leader) behaved in an atypical way for a female and confronted their attempts to make me into an all-nurturing "fantasy mother" who would give them whatever they wished for.

TRANSFERENCE AND COUNTERTRANSFERENCE ISSUES

It has been suggested by Fuerstein (1992), in writing about individual therapy, that men fear the potential destructiveness of a female therapist, particularly a passive female therapist. Conlon (1991) asserted that men tend to deal with the threatening aspect of the female group leader's power by devaluing her interpretations and attacking the boundaries of the group to express hostility to the leader as an authority figure. Such interpretations view male attacks on the competency and creativity of the female group leader as a way of dealing with the dual nature of the primordial transference onto the female leader in the opening phases of a group. The obverse has been suggested by Lukton (1992), who asserted that men experience a core psychic terror, as well as persecution and dread, as a residue of their very early self and object experience with their mothers. Thus, if a male patient identifies with a female therapist, then he must sacrifice the sense of difference he has had to achieve to have a core identity as a man. This may lead to either male devaluation and contempt for women or an idealized and exalted view of women—both of which keep women at a distance and circumvent the fear of engulfment and loss of self.

The opening stage of a group has been referred to as a chaotic (Usandivaras, 1993) or unintegrated (Bonds-White, 1987) stage. It has been said that on entrance to a new group, all members regress to the toddler stage of development (Coleman, 1975), where developmentally they first experienced moving from the triad into group life in the family. The emergence of the men as the "attackers" or the "idealizers" in the opening phases of a group can provoke pre-oedipal countertransference issues in the female leader. Either the unrealistic positive, superior, giving, and loving mother or the negative, castrating, and withholding mother impulses can be provoked. The female therapist may avoid confronting boundary violations, may be unclear about fees, may run overtime on ending the group, or may fall into a pattern of availability and vagueness, which will feed the group's fears. Alternately, to avoid showing signs of weakness, the female therapist may become overly rigid or sarcastic with the whole group or may turn the hostility onto the men and invite the women in the group to project the gender stereotype of "mean, aggressive men" while denying their own frustration and anger at the female leader.

The personal task of the female group leader is to come to terms with her own power and competition. This clearly involves the mastery of and acceptance of one's own aggressive drives, acknowledgment of the pleasure of being able to influence others in one's role as therapist, and comfort with one's acquisition of competence and knowledge. The group task of the female leader is twofold. First, she must ensure that her discomfort with any of these issues does not get projected into and acted out by the women in the group. Second, she must not exploit the gender acculturation of the male and female members of her group by ignoring issues of aggression. This means being alert to and facilitating expression and exploration of any material that hints of power, competence, anger, and aggression.

The issue of the erotic transference and countertransference between female therapists and male patients in individual therapy has been discussed by Fuerstein (1992), Guttman (1984), and Russ (1993). However, these same issues have not been examined with regard to group therapy treatment. In group situations, men may avoid the subject because of their fears of the pre-oedipal seductive mother figure or their wishes that the female therapist would be seductive. Fears of destructive wishes toward the mother figure or social prohibitions on expressing sexual feelings toward a "lady" and the incongruence of having sexual feelings toward a dominant woman may also cause men to avoid expressing erotic feelings toward the female therapist. Avoiding erotic transference feelings toward the therapist may also be a defense against underlying feelings of envy and greed, with the concomitant wishes to destroy, devour, and merge with the therapist.

There is a danger that the female group therapist may avoid focusing on or calling attention to material that arises in the group because of her own fears of being seen as seductive by the group's male members. These reactions may cause the female therapist to mute sexuality and ignore material in the group that would lead to exploration of sexual issues. She may lessen eye contact with men in an effort to avoid being seen as seductive, may dress or carry herself in an asexual manner, and may miss clues expressed by the women in the group about sexual issues. Stereotypical projections onto men as violent, sexually demanding, and abusive or as needy and demanding children may also lead to avoidance of erotic material in the group.

Uncertainty about one's own sense of power as a female group leader may lead to rigid responses to male seductiveness in group therapy with male clients. In my first few years in private practice, a colleague moved out of the area and handed his groups over to me. I became aware that whenever one of the men in the group started talking I stiffened physically. As he described some of the difficulties in the relationship with his wife, my internal responses were very different from the responses of the group members, yet I felt hesitant to speak, and when I did speak I became very formal. Upon reflection, I realized that I found him physically very attractive and that he had a style of verbal interaction that I found seductive. My fear of losing power and authority in the new group and my inexperience were responsible for my rigidity.

Another set of transference and countertransference variables interact with the gender acculturation of men and women in Western society. Take, for example, the cultural idea that men are expected to control more power and wealth than women. With this worldview, a female therapist may support the dependency of male group members while displaying contempt for that behavior as a way of denying her envy. That is, if she were to cast the men in her group as inadequate little boys, she would be denying her feelings of triumph about being in the position of treating socially powerful men (Gornick, 1988). If she were to focus only on the pre-oedipal issues of the men and women in the group, then she would continue to deny her feelings of power over the men and avoid dealing with the issues of competition. By subverting work that brings envy and greed to the surface in the group, the female therapist would avoid the challenge herself and support the group's male–female split. Certainly, one of my more difficult moments in group was listening to a male client, who was unable to describe his feelings at all, tell that he had just earned $500,000 by settling one legal suit. The internal reactions of despair (I will never make that much, even in years of work), envy (I want to make that much money), greed and anger (I am going to increase his fees), and the urge to put down his achievement (it cannot mean anything when you do not even "know yourself") were intense and had to be digested in order to support the strength of his achievement and help group members move into acknowledgments of all of those feelings within themselves. By being aware of my own countertransference reactions, I was able to listen for the attempts that group members made to deny envy and disparage him and to help the man get in touch with his pleasure at the achievement and his sense of power in his work. In large part, he was able to experience his pleasure because others could own the envy and greed they felt at his good news.

Levant (1993) proposed that men need to learn certain skills in therapy to move beyond the restrictions of male gender role socialization. Some of these skills—emotional sensitivity and self-awareness, the ability to be comfortable with mature dependency, the ability to nurture, the acceptance of the feminine side of themselves, and the ability to move beyond competition to identification with other men—are ready-made for group therapy. Or perhaps it is more accurate to say that group psychotherapy is the ready-made environment for developing these skills. Levant and others have suggested that men need all-male groups to learn these things. It is also possible that mixed-gender groups offer an equally strong opportunity to learn such skills. Certainly, this is an area where more in-depth research is needed.

The female therapist who works with men in heterogeneous groups must think through how she will make herself both physically and emotionally secure to bring a full person into the group leadership role. She certainly needs to closely examine her own gender bias to understand the ways that she may be projecting cultural stereotypes onto the men in her groups. In supervision, I sometimes ask group therapists to write such headings as "men should," "men always," or "men never" and "women should," "women always," or "women never" on a piece of paper and to write out 25 sentence-completion responses to each of these. The underlying pattern that emerges will more often than not be very revealing of personal gender stereotypes. The interaction of the cultural gender roles of men and women and the developmental vicissitudes of both genders contribute to the transference and countertransference issues that arise in the work of female group therapists with male patients. Gornick (1988) and Woodley (1988) have initiated research about the transference and countertransference issues that arise between male patients and female therapists in individual therapy. No research has been done on this interaction in group therapy.

ADVICE TO BEGINNING FEMALE THERAPISTS

This chapter was based on my clinical experiences as a female therapist working with men in groups for 20 years. The impact of the therapist's experience, training, and age in such situations cannot be denied. Certainly my issues and awarenesses are not the same as those of a younger or less experienced female therapist. For beginning female therapists leading groups with men, my advice is simple and direct: know thyself, know thyself, know thyself, and supervision, supervision, supervision.

Under the category of knowing oneself, the experience of being a member of either a heterogeneous treatment group or experiential training group is essential. The opportunity to explore one's own gender stereotypes and biases in the environment of the treatment or experiential training group can produce a sense of awareness and security unsurpassed by any other experience. Second, the female therapist has to examine who she is physically (Is she indeed pretty and attractive?) and what message will be perceived by her physical appearance, manner of dress, or style of speech. An examination of these attributes appears to emphasize cultural gender stereotypes of women. This is important because cultural stereotypes are pervasive—they cannot be ignored or denied—and so the female therapist needs to think about how she as a person will be "seen by the other" to prepare herself for these reactions.

A thorough grounding in at least one theoretical model and intensive supervision by both male and female advanced therapists who use that model is also essential for the beginning therapist. The advantage of being grounded in one model rather than eclectic in one's approach to groups is that when exceptions occur, the boundary violations are clear. Intensive supervision, especially when beginning to work with groups, is a must. Knowing that help is at hand between each group or every couple of groups gives a sense of confidence that enables a beginning therapist to face the chaos of working with new groups.

SUMMARY

Group therapists need to examine some of the gender role and transferential activities in group therapy as they relate to the variables of age and the experience of female therapists, and we need to study how these phenomena are dealt with in supervision and training programs for group psychotherapists. The task of the therapist is to keep the group focused on its goals and to bring into awareness the ways in which members conspire to avoid that goal. For the female group therapist, an additional part of the task is to be willing to recognize how her femaleness and the group members' freedom to be aware of and use both the negative and positive aspects of that femaleness contribute to or hinder the group from reaching its goals.

REFERENCES

Bonds-White, F. (1987). *Through roles to the self in group psychotherapy*. Unpublished manuscript.

Bowman, P. (1982). Clinical bias against "activity" in women and implications for female self-concept. *International Journal for the Advancement of Counseling, 5*, 63–71.

Coleman, A. (1975). Group consciousness as a developmental phase. In A. Coleman & W. Bexton (Eds.), *Group relations reader* (Vol. 1, pp. 35–42). Sausalito, CA: GREX.

Conlon, I. (1991). The effect of gender on the role of the female group conductor. *Group Analysis, 24,* 187–200.

Fuerstein, L. (1992). The male patient's erotic transference: Female countertransference issues. *Psychoanalytic Review, 79,* 55–71.

Gornick, L. (1988). Turning the tables: Transference and countertransference themes in the dyad of female therapist and male patient. *Dissertation Abstracts International, 50*(2), 5315B.

Guttman, H. (1984). Sexual issues in the transference and countertransference between female therapists and male patients. *Journal of the American Academy of Psychoanalysis, 12,* 187–191.

Karme, L. (1979). The analysis of a male patient by a female analyst: The problem of the negative oedipal transference. *International Journal of Psychoanalysis, 60,* 253–261.

Levant, R. (1993). A marital couples communication program based on gender socialization. *Psychotherapy Bulletin, 28,* 27–30.

Lewis, R. (1978). Emotional intimacy among men. *Journal of Social Issues, 34,* 108–121.

Lukton, R. (1992). Gender as an element in the intersubjective field: The female therapist and the male patient. *Clinical Social Work Journal, 20,* 153–167.

O'Neil, J. (1981a). Male sex-role conflicts, sexism and masculinity: Psychological implications for men, women and the counseling psychologist. *Counseling Psychologist, 9,* 61–80.

O'Neil, J. (1981b). Patterns of gender role conflict and strain: The fear of femininity in men's lives. *Personnel and Guidance Journal, 60,* 203–210.

Rabinowitz, F. (1991). The male to male embrace: Breaking the taboo in a men's therapy group. *Journal of Counseling and Development, 69,* 574–576.

Russ, H. (1993). Erotic transference through countertransference: The female therapist and the male patient. *Psychoanalytic Psychology, 10,* 393–406.

Schachtel, Z. (1986). The "impossible profession" considered from a gender perspective. In J. Alpert (Ed.), *Psychoanalysis and women* (pp. 237–256). Hillsdale, NJ: Analytic Press.

Usandivaras, R. (1993). A new perspective in group analysis. *Group Analysis, 26,* 269–276.

Wallach, T. (1991). Competition and gender in group psychotherapy. *Group, 18,* 29–36.

Watts, D., & Courtois, C. (1981). Trends in the treatment of men who commit violence against women. *Personnel and Guidance Journal, 60,* 245–248.

Woodley, T. (1988). Transference, countertransference: Erotic issues and the female therapist. *Dissertation Abstracts International, 50*(1), 357B.

13

THE GENDER ROLE JOURNEY WORKSHOP: EXPLORING SEXISM AND GENDER ROLE CONFLICT IN A COEDUCATIONAL SETTING

JAMES M. O'NEIL

Over the past decade, increasing polarization has existed between men and women on vital issues of mutual concern. Dialogues between men and women on sexism, male violence, feminism, and the respective men's and women's movements have been too infrequent. When dialogues have occurred, they have usually been brief, fragmented, conflictual, and emotionally charged. Many men and women politely avoid these topics rather than directly discuss them. Psychologists have been surprisingly slow in

Parts of this chapter were presented at the 95th Annual Convention of the American Psychological Association, September 1987, in New York in the paper "Evaluation of the Gender Role Journey Workshop: Three Years of Follow-Up Data."

I thank Marianne Roberts Carroll and Ellen Rosoff for their contributions in developing the workshop from 1985 to 1990, Fran Archambault and Steve Owen of the University of Connecticut for their support in developing and evaluating the workshop, and the 350 students at the University of Connecticut who have provided critiques and feedback over the past 10 years. Jean Egan of Asnuntuck Community College was instrumental in helping to better define the phases of the gender role journey outlined in Exhibit 1 and in stimulating the development of the Gender Role Journey Measure (O'Neil et al., 1993). Louise Silverstein (Yeshiva University) provided very useful comments on drafts of the chapter, and both her and Roy Scrivner's (Dallas Veterans Administration) ongoing influence with multicultural and diversity issues is evident throughout. Rod Nadeau's (University of Connecticut) critical comments and editing are also appreciated. Special thanks also go to the Office of Residential Life at the University of Connecticut (especially Kim Beckwith and Rich Bova) for providing the resident hall lounges in which the majority of the workshops were conducted. More information about the gender role journey workshop can be obtained by writing me at the School of Family Studies, U-Box 58, University of Connecticut, Storrs, CT 06269-2058.

developing programs for both men and women to discuss gender role issues in coeducational settings. Therefore, educational and therapeutic environments are needed to facilitate men's and women's dialogues about changing gender roles.

In the fall of 1984, I developed a course proposal for men and women to analyze their gender role conflict and sexism in an intensive workshop setting. When the course proposal was reviewed by the faculty there was an organized attempt to defeat it. Criticisms were based on negative biases about the inclusion of the new psychology of men in the workshop. Questions were also raised about whether the psychology of women would be fully integrated into the workshop. I worked with the criticism, resistances, and controversy. Eventually, the proposal passed, and the course was offered in 1985 on an experimental basis. Over the next 10 years, the course evolved and was institutionalized as the gender role journey workshop, which is the topic of this chapter.

The gender role journey workshop combines traditional lecturing with psychoeducational group interventions (Ivey & Alschuler, 1973), experiential learning (Kolb, 1984), and hypermedia learning (Jensen, 1993). The workshop was developed to explore whether men and women could talk about sexism and gender role conflict in an informal, academic setting without victimizing each other in the process. A full description of the workshop and the effects of the workshop over extended periods of time can be found elsewhere (O'Neil, 1994; O'Neil & Egan, 1992b; O'Neil & Roberts Carroll, 1987, 1988a, 1988b).

In this chapter, I first describe the workshop content, methodology, process, assumptions, curriculum, and outcomes. In the second part of the chapter, I provide insights and recommendations for educators offering similar workshops in coeducational settings. I also discuss the complexity of the group dynamics for men, women, and diverse participants[1] engaged in this kind of intense group experience.

METAPHOR AND PHASES OF THE GENDER ROLE JOURNEY

The gender role journey metaphor is the primary conceptualization of the workshop (O'Neil & Egan, 1992b; O'Neil, Egan, Owen, & Murry, 1993; O'Neil & Roberts Carroll, 1987, 1988a, 1988b). The journey metaphor helps people examine how early gender role socialization experiences and sexism have affected their lives. The gender role journey provides a framework for evaluating thoughts, feelings, and behaviors about gender

---

[1] In this chapter, participants from different races, classes, ethnic or national backgrounds, or sexual orientations are described as *diverse participants*, because no single term covers this wide array of diversity adequately.

roles, sexism, and gender role conflict (O'Neil & Egan, 1992b). The journey includes a retrospective analysis of early family experiences with gender roles, assessment of one's present situation with sexism, and decisions about how to act in the future. Overall, the process includes evaluating how gender roles and sexism have affected one's life personally, professionally, and politically.

The five phases of the gender role journey form the major workshop paradigm that helps participants assess and discuss sexism and gender role conflict. Exhibit 1 shows the five phases of the gender role journey that represent periods of transition for gender roles and sexism. A careful reading of the different phases in Exhibit 1 provides the psychological and personal dimensions of the gender role journey. Full theoretical and empirical descriptions of these phases can be found in previous publications (O'Neil & Egan, 1992b; O'Neil et al., 1993; O'Neil & Roberts Carroll, 1987, 1988b). As shown in Exhibit 1, the phases include (a) acceptance of traditional gender roles, (b) ambivalence about gender roles, (c) anger, (d) activism, and (e) celebration and integration of gender roles. Empirical support for three of the phases has been found with the Gender Role Journey Measure (see O'Neil et al., 1993). These phases help workshop members personally assess their experiences with gender role conflict and sexism by using the assumptions and processes described below.

THE GENDER ROLE JOURNEY WORKSHOP

Premises, Assumptions, and Foundations

The workshop design assumes that men and women need to talk with each other about their sexist gender role socialization as part of the healing process. Sexism is assumed to be a form of psychopathology that is dangerous and delusional (Albee, 1981). Healing alliances between men and women (Birk, 1981) can be created if safe group environments are developed for both intellectual and emotional dialogues. In the workshop, psychologically violent interpersonal interactions, "gender bashing," and authoritarian and politically correct attitudes that are potentially coercive are prohibited. The leader addresses this issue in the following way:

> Diversity and differences in the workshop can make the dialogue rich. Tensions that emerge should be recognized [and] worked through when possible, without harm to anyone. There will be no victims from our dialogue here today. (O'Neil, 1988, p. 4)

Journeying with gender roles is considered potentially dynamic, difficult, and painful. Consequently, special workshop norms are established to provide a safe and communal atmosphere. These norms are considered critical

EXHIBIT 1
Phases of the Gender Role Journey

Phase 1: Acceptance of Traditional Gender Roles

Accepts traditional notions of masculinity and femininity
Endorses restrictive view of gender roles
Endorses strength, control, power, and restrictive emotionality for men
Endorses warmth, expressiveness, nurturance, and passivity for women
Experiences limited awareness of how restrictive gender roles limit human
    potential
Lacks awareness of how sexism restricts and violates people
Receives rewards for acting in stereotypical ways
Fears questioning authority
Lacks information about how gender roles are learned
Feels powerless and dependent
Feels anger when others violate gender role stereotypes

Phase 2: Ambivalence About Gender Roles

Experiences dissatisfaction with stereotypical notions of gender roles
Questions restrictiveness of gender roles through exposure to new ideas
    about sexism
Experiences increased awareness of how gender roles and sexism violate
    people
Experiences some fear of what it would mean to change one's gender role
    ideas or behaviors
Vacillates between the safety of stereotypical gender roles and the
    excitement and anxiety of possible gender role change
Feels confusion about masculine–feminine identities
Begins to recognize the lost potential from restrictive gender roles in
    Phase 1
Experiences sporadic irritation about sexism
Begins to contemplate making gender role changes
Needs support from others to make changes or may regress to Phase 1

Phase 3: Anger

Experiences negative emotions about sexism and expresses them to
    individuals and groups
Experiences limited outlets for negative emotions, isolation, and personal
    pain about sexism
Expresses negative emotions in ways that produce conflict, anxiety, and
    depression
Restricts circle of friends to those who accept and understand the anger
Recognizes that sexism is a form of interpersonal violence
Recognizes that sexism produces male or female victims
Experiences more interpersonal conflict with others regarding gender role
    issues
Remains "stuck in the anger" and immobilized
Experiences difficulties pinpointing the multiple sources of the anger
Begins to use anger to make personal changes

Phase 4: Activism

Pursues an active exploration of how gender roles and sexism have affected his or her life

Deals directly with the pain of sexism and gender role conflict

Increases self-communication and feedback about gender role issues in his or her life

Makes gender role changes in his or her life that are less restrictive and conflictual

Takes personal responsibility for reducing sexism in personal or professional life

Uses the anger about sexism in positive ways

Commits to social, political, or educational courses of action

Makes personal, professional, and political plans of action related to gender roles and sexism

Feels confirmed or disconfirmed by activism regarding gender role and sexism

Needs role models and support from others to continue the activism

Phase 5: Celebration and Integration of Gender Roles

Experiences new awareness and satisfaction of viewing self and the world as unrestricted by gender roles

Integrates anger about sexism regularly with efficiency and effectiveness

Works against sexism regularly with efficiency and effectiveness, not out of anger but out of commitment to positive change

Understands other people's gender role journeys and their views of sexism and gender roles

Experiences increased "gender role freedom" in personal and professional relationships

Continues active efforts to educate the public about gender roles and the violence of sexism

Experiences greater compassion for other people's gender role journeys and transitions

Experiences increased personal power, autonomy, and strength

Commits to gender role egalitarianism in personal, professional, and political areas of life

---

Note. From *Gender Issues Across the Life Cycle* (pp. 114–115), by B. Wainrib (Ed.), 1992, New York: Springer. Copyright 1992 by Springer. Adapted with permission.

for having any constructive dialogue that avoids destructive conflict between group members. Given the confusion with gender roles, an established set of conceptual definitions and workshop assumptions are offered as a starting point for the 6 days of dialogue (O'Neil, 1994). First, personal self-disclosure and "being real" in the group are considered prerequisites for the development of trust and cohesive group dynamics. Second, group members are invited to participate in the workshop process at their own "optimal comfort level." Third, it must be recognized that working with the pain of sexism and other forms of oppression requires commitment, honesty, and mutual community support from the group. These assumptions are communicated to all participants before and during the workshop.

Description, Participants, and Curriculum

The workshop's course title is Gender Role Conflict Issues for Helping Professionals. This graduate-level course has been offered every summer since 1985 as part of the Counseling Psychology Program in the Department of Educational Psychology at the University of Connecticut. The workshop is implemented on 6 consecutive days, for 3 hours in the morning and 3 hours in each afternoon. Between 20 and 25 students enroll in the workshop; a majority of them have been graduate students in their 20s and 30s. Women have usually outnumbered men by a ratio of 3:1. There are usually two or three ethnically or racially diverse participants in the workshop (African Americans, Asian Americans, or international students).

The specific curriculum of the workshop is summarized in Table 1. On the left, five workshop dimensions represent the range of themes and activities in the workshop. Across the top, the 6 days of the workshop are listed. As shown, lectures, music, movie clips, structured exercises, and group activities are used throughout the workshop.

Preparation, Readings, and Media

The workshop syllabus, objectives, transparencies, and small group activities have been collated into separate sources for others' access (O'Neil, 1994; O'Neil & Roberts Carroll, 1987). Before the workshop, participants are sent an 18-item questionnaire that assesses their needs and preferences regarding the workshop process. These data help shape the workshop around student needs and are reported to the group on the first day. Students are asked to read nine chapters in Basow's (1992) *Gender Stereotypes: Traditions and Alternatives,* as well as seven other articles (Albee, 1981; Kahn, 1984; O'Neil, 1981a, 1981b; O'Neil & Egan, 1992a, 1992b, 1993), before attending the workshop.

Lectures, movie clips, music videos, self-assessments, small and large groups, and discussions are used continuously throughout the workshop. Four of the video presentations, prepared specifically for the workshop, examine the gender role journeys of famous men and women, including John Lennon, Marilyn Monroe, Jane Fonda, and Marvin Gaye. The journeys of these individuals are conceptually connected to the course concepts and allow the ideas to be personalized by the participants. I share my own gender role journey through a 30-minute videotape that uses family photos and detailed analyses of how gender role conflict and sexism have negatively affected my life. Throughout this presentation, I model personal dis-

TABLE 1
Dimensions and Curriculum of Gender Role Journey Workshop

Workshop dimension	Day 1	Day 2	Day 3	Day 4	Day 5	Day 6
Themes	Workshop norms & expectancies Gender role journey phases How to access the workshop Stages of a group Understanding the group process Power & oppression Men & women as victims of sexism Metaphors for healing Power & control issues in the workshop	Research on sex differences, gender role socialization, & stereotyping Patriarchy, sexism, oppression, & violence Working with emotional pain Working with defense mechanisms	Patterns of men's & women's gender role conflict	Adult life cycle & gender role Transitions & themes	Family socialization & mothers, fathers, sons, & daughters Sexual orientation, race, class, ethnic background, & gender role socialization	How to keep the gender role journey going Action plans & goals Summary of workshop Community lunch closure & goodbyes
Lecture topics	Rationale & norms for workshop Summary of need assessment data Gender role vocabulary Four kinds of violence Sexism, racism, classism, homophobism, & ethnocentrism as violence The gender role journey Leader's disclosure on gender role journey	Research on sex differences & gender role socialization Gender role restrictions, devaluations, & violations Pleck's (1981) sex role strain analysis Gilligan's (1982) *In a Different Voice* Jeanne Block's research Matthew Fox's via negativa	Men's perceived losses of power Men's patterns of gender role conflict (O'Neil, 1981a, 1981b) Men's fears of femininity & masculine mystique Women's patterns of gender role conflict Research on men's gender role conflict Leader's disclosure on patterns of gender role conflict	Adult life cycle stages Gender role transition & themes John Lennon's gender role journey Methods of transformation & gender role transitions	Data on victimization & violence in the United States Marvin Gaye's gender role journey Leader disclosures: father–daughter relationships Jane Fonda's or Marilyn Monroe's gender role journey Healing the wounds Definitions of racism & classism	Working with pain over time Developing action plans How to use the workshop content Reentry issues & problems Purpose & function of action plans

(table continues)

TABLE 1 (*contd.*)
Dimensions and Curriculum of Gender Role Journey Workshop

Workshop dimension	Day 1	Day 2	Day 3	Day 4	Day 5	Day 6
Music & media used	Music Concerto no. 1 in A Minor (Bach) "Unity" (Holly Near) Four Seasons (Vivaldi) "Homecoming Queen's Got a Gun"; "I Like 'em Big and Stupid" (Julie Brown) "The Way We Were" (Barbara Streisand) Music videos "That's What Friends Are For" (D. Warwick, E. John, S. Wonder, & G. Knight) Movie clips *Nine to Five*	Music "Between Two Worlds and Forever the Optimist" (Patrick O'Hearn) "Candle in the Wind" (Elton John) Music videos "Cry" (Godley and Creme) "Oh Father" (Madonna) Movie clips *Thelma and Louise*	Music "Free to Grow"; "Feeling Better" (Holly Near) Music videos "I Want to Know What Love Is" (Foreigner) Movie clips *Tootsie* *Superman III*	Music "American Tune"; "A Bridge Over Troubled Water" (Simon & Garfunkel) "Double Fantasy" (John Lennon & Yoko Ono) "From the Goddess" (On the Wings of Song and Robert Gass) Music videos "Woman is the Nigger of the World"; "Mother"; "Woman"; "Imagine" (John Lennon) Movie clips *Kramer vs. Kramer*	Music "Child" (Holly Near) Music videos "Motown Anniversary Video"; "What's Going On"; "Sexual Healing" (Marvin Gaye) "Missing You" (Diana Ross) "The River" (Bruce Springsteen) Movie clips *On Golden Pond* *Ordinary People* *The Honeymooners* (Jackie Gleason) *Mississippi Burning*	Music Bach Concerto in D Minor for Two Violins (Isaac Stern) "Comfort Zone" (Steven Halpern) "Wrap the Sun Around You"; "Voices" (Holly Near)
Structured exercises	Guided imagery summary sheet Psychological violence checklist	Sex differences checklist Identifying gender role stereotypes exercises	Men's & women's gender role conflict inventories	How to improve male–female relationships Gender role themes checklist	Gender role restrictions, devaluations, & violations questionnaire	Letting pain be pain and letting pain go exercise Generating action plans & goals exercise Overall workshop evaluations
Large- or small-group discussions	Small-group processing of psychological violence checklist Large- & Small-group disclosures & discussion about guided imagery experience	Small-group exercise: identifying gender role stereotypes Large-group discussion of identified stereotypes	Large-group discussion of patterns of gender role conflict	Small-group discussions: improving male–female relationships Large-group discussion: improving male–female relationships	Small-group discussion on family socialization	Large group discussion on future plans & goals Closing statements by workshop participants

Note. Lecture materials, transparencies, and structured activities can be found in O'Neil & Roberts Carroll (1987) and O'Neil (1994).

JAMES M. O'NEIL

closure, vulnerability, and possibilities for personal renewal and transformation.

Atmosphere, Leader's Roles, and Group Norms

The workshop is held in a carpeted room that is comfortable and private. Participants sit in a "learning circle" in comfortable armchairs or on the floor. I sometimes refer to this as a "sacred space" or an area of possible transformation. Face-to-face learning makes the workshop environment more conducive to dialogue, cohesiveness, and personal care. The leader provides coffee, ice water, fruit, freshly cut flowers, and calming music to enhance the learning environment. The atmosphere is informal, but the pace of activities is continuous and preplanned.

For the first 5 years, I conducted the workshop with a female coleader, but over the past 5 years I have implemented the workshop by myself. Ideally, these coeducational interventions should be implemented with a male–female team that models positive cooperation and alliances between the sexes. Leaders who have ample experience and who understand the complexity of the group process may be able to effectively implement these workshops by themselves.

The leader is primarily a teacher and facilitator who presents the workshop content and process simultaneously. Moving from cognitive content to personal process instantaneously requires constant assessment and interpretation of overall group dynamics. Decisions on what content to emphasize and when require insights into the group's personality, as well as some calculated risk taking. Personal self-disclosures by the leader model aspects of the gender role journey for participants. The leader constantly identifies and works with personal power, control, and competition issues that emerge from group dynamics. He or she also prepares refreshments, maintains media equipment, and serves as the daily cleanup crew for the learning environment.

Group norms provide the expected or optimal code of conduct during the group. These norms also legitimatize a wide variety of means of self-expression and personal involvement. Thirteen norms (listed below) are established early in the gender role journey workshop.

1. Participants are encouraged to find personal comfort and safety in the workshop environment.
2. Freedom of movement and self-expression are given high priority.
3. Interpersonal respect is recommended as a positive norm for personal interactions.
4. Permission is given for both emotional and intellectual expressions.

5. Psychological violence (O'Neil & Egan, 1993) and destructive interactions are prohibited.
6. Participants are encouraged to develop alliances in the group (Birk, 1981) and within themselves to support their own gender role journeys.
7. Self-assessment and self-disclosure are encouraged and modeled by the leader.
8. Appropriate (meaning nonviolent) expression of anger, as described in Phase 3 (see Exhibit 1), is established as legitimate.
9. Participants are told that the workshop can be experienced personally, professionally, and politically.
10. Participants are encouraged to give each other support and to listen carefully to each person's disclosures.
11. Tuckman's (1965) stages of group development (forming, storming, norming, performing, and adjourning) are presented so that individuals can track the group process.
12. Each participant is asked to monitor his or her own "talk time" in the group.
13. Group members are encouraged to work constructively with someone they dislike or who annoys them during the workshop.

My availability and constant evaluation give the participants the security that I am aware of what is happening and available to them if needed.

Content and Process

What exactly occurs in the these gender role journey workshops? How are the workshop curricula in Table 1 implemented over the 6 days? Discerning the actual workshop process from a quick perusal of Table 1 is difficult, but the following discussion should provide more explanation.

Overall, the workshop alternates between academic content and group process in a cyclical fashion. I direct the cyclical nature of the content and process in the first 2 days. Gradually, I turn some of the responsibility for the group's direction over to the group, through democratic votes and collective decision making.

The content of the workshop includes the assigned readings, lectures on gender role theory and research, music, media, and participants' own ideas. The process of the workshop includes the ongoing verbalizations, self-disclosures, confrontations, and evaluations that are read every morning. As the workshop develops, the group process becomes part of the workshop content. In this regard, the leader continuously points out how the naturally occurring events in the group process relate to the overall workshop concepts (i.e., sexism, phases of the gender role journey, gender role conflicts, and stages of groups). Students actually observe the workshop concepts "coming to life" in the ongoing dialogues, self-disclosures, and group conflicts.

The workshop processes are activated by five different, but related, process dimensions: (a) stimulus diversity, (b) personalization of the workshop process, (c) paper-and-pencil exercises, (d) large- and small-group processing sessions, and (e) using daily evaluations and feedback to understand group process.

Stimulus diversity is defined as using multiple teaching modalities and alternating the sequencing of these interventions. For example, a brief conceptual lecture may be immediately followed by a video that deepens the concept in a significant way. Next, a self-assessment checklist is administered, followed by a period of reflection in which classical music is played. Finally, a focused, large- or small-group discussion allows participants to verbalize their thoughts and feelings across these numerous stimuli. The ultimate goal of stimulus diversity is to activate as many senses as possible, to enhance group cohesion, and to increase the group's empowerment of itself.

Personalization of the workshop concepts is encouraged each day. I model this on the first day when I play the 30-minute videotape of my own gender role journey. Additionally, the personalization is increased with structured exercises and checklists that help participants internalize the workshop content and process. Furthermore, alternating between the use of small- and large-group discussions to process the workshop also shapes the workshop process. Finally, reading daily evaluations each morning allows group members to communicate and assess where they have been and where they want to go next with the process.

The leader's role is to decide the order and the sequence of the interventions, using the process dimensions described above. There is some variability in the actual sequence of events depending on the group's personality, but Table 1 represents the most consistent use of workshop content across the 6 days.

To provide readers with more concrete ideas about what happens in the workshop, I describe numerous interventions below.

On the first day, presenting my own gender role journey significantly increases the intensity of the workshop. Group members observe my own struggle and my growth and pain through the gender role journey phases. This intervention prepares group members for memories of their own childhood and adult experiences with gender roles. After systematically relaxing the group, I provide a 20-minute guided-imagery experience. Participants are asked to call up images of gender roles in early childhood as well as adulthood conflicts with gender roles. This guided-imagery experience usually prompts memories of experiences in the first three phases of the gender role journey and evokes strong emotions.

On the second day, the structured exercise "Identifying Gender Role Stereotypes" is completed and discussed in gender-specific groups. This exercise increases the intensity and polarization in the group. Both sexes are confronted with the potential viciousness of each other's stereotyping. Deep and negative emotions are usually felt (e.g., anger, loss, and shame), and gender role ambivalence may be experienced in the group (see phases 2 and 3 in Exhibit 1).

I disperse media presentations throughout the workshop to introduce new topics, to regulate the intensity of sessions, or to orient the group. For example, I have used video clips from the movie *Mississippi Burning* or from the music video of *The River*, by Bruce Springsteen, to help introduce the difficult topics of racism and classism into the workshop process. These tapes focus attention on how sexism interacts with other forms of oppression. As mentioned above, the gender role journeys of John Lennon, Marilyn Monroe, and Marvin Gaye are presented during the week through lectures and videotapes (which I have created on the basis of reviews of biographies, movies, and music of the artists). These interventions allow participants to understand how others have "journeyed with their gender roles" as they simultaneously evaluate their own journeys. The lecture and an exercise on working with pain help group members deal with heightened emotions that may been have developed in the workshop. This intervention is designed to help participants move past their pain and anger to personal and professional activism (see Phase 4 in Exhibit 1).

The workshop leader orchestrates the sequences of these interventions to raise or lower the group intensity as the process unfolds. Concurrent with these interventions, the large group dynamics—particularly the group's growth, conflicts, and resistances—are discussed and integrated into the group process. During the last 2 days, the use of such structured activities as the Gender Role Restriction Questionnaire, Workshop Action Plans and Goals Exercise, and the community lunch provides further personalization and closure to the workshop.

Evaluations and Follow-Up Data

Daily evaluation questionnaires are completed by the participants to assess individual reactions to the workshop. These evaluations are read each morning and allow group members to communicate through their written comments. The daily feedback provides both positive and negative perspectives on the collective group process and on how individuals are personally experiencing the group.

Comprehensive workshop evaluations are completed on the last day, and two long-term follow-ups are completed months and years later (the exact time period for follow-ups has varied over the years). Results of these evaluations have indicated that the workshop has had an impact on most participants. Over 87% of the participants have indicated that the workshop continued to influence their lives either 1 or 2 years later. Extensive evaluations and follow-up data can be found in my other publications (O'Neil & Roberts Carroll, 1987, 1988a, 1988b).

IMPLEMENTING GENDER ROLE JOURNEY WORKSHOPS: INSIGHTS, LESSONS LEARNED, AND RECOMMENDATIONS

The 10 gender role workshops I have led have been the most exciting teaching and group experiences of my career. I have learned much about myself and about the complexity of intergender dialogue. I have been surprised by how much intensity can be developed in the group process. The evaluations and follow-up data have indicated that the workshop can touch some deep emotions and have long-term effects (O'Neil & Roberts Carroll, 1988a, 1988b). Painful stories about family violence, rape, incest, alcoholism, divorce, tragic deaths of family members, and other losses are common. Observing some group members' struggle, receive support from others, and finally break through their defenses to new dimensions of themselves has been very moving. It is difficult to capture in words how these healing transformations have occurred. I can only attest that acts of personal courage and strength have been witnessed in these gender role journey workshops.

Next, I enumerate recommendations for implementing these workshops, including necessary preparation; required knowledge and skills; how to facilitate group dynamics; and the special problems faced by men, women, and diverse participants. These recommendations may be useful for colleagues developing gender role journey interventions or similar gender role groups.

Recommendations: Preparation, Knowledge, and Important Skills

Preworkshop preparation is critical to the overall success of the 6-day workshop. Lectures, media, and experiential activities need to be easily accessible and precisely cued. Furthermore, each year, I have needed to prepare myself psychologically for leading the group. I call this "getting up for the workshop on a psychological level." Thus, I take time to review my own emotional processes with sexism, racism, classism, and homophobism. Examining my own personal and professional vulnerabilities gives me confidence in objectively interpreting the workshop process free from most of my own issues. Implementing coeducational workshops requires leaders to have their own gender role journey and emotional issues in clear focus.

To lead a gender role journey workshop, one must be a skilled facilitator with knowledge about how to work with complex group dynamics. Specifically, the leader needs special sensitivity to the complexity of intergender dialogue as well as skills in processing conflict, resistance, anger, and people's pain. Having compassion for the struggles of both men and women with sexism and gender role conflict is essential. Leaders need to be knowledgeable of both the psychology of women and the new psychology of men (Levant & Pollack, 1995; O'Neil, Good, & Holmes, 1995). This includes knowledge of theory and research as well as the way that gender role conflict is experienced in people's everyday lives. Knowledge and skill in conflict resolution, family systems, feminist pedagogy, and race relations are also essential. An understanding of how sexism interacts with other forms of oppression (i.e., racism, classism, ethnocentrism, anti-Semitism, and homophobism) is important because participants often discuss their personal experiences with multiple forms of discrimination. Leaders should be well read in the multiple areas of oppression and have some special supervisory relationship (or training) wherein they have worked out their own issues related to sexism, racism, homophobism, classism, and ethnocentrism.

Facilitating the Group and Assessing Its Complex Dynamics

Facilitating these groups is very challenging, stimulating, and, at times, quite exhausting. Many times I have been unsure what exactly is happening in the group. My tolerance for ambiguity has thus been severely tested. Patience and restraint are needed as the process unfolds. Ambiguous but important issues may simmer beneath the surface for hours or days before finally surfacing in significant ways. So much thought and emotion can be stirred up by the group process that keen attention needs to be paid to all verbal and nonverbal interactions.

I encourage each group to reflect on itself by closely observing individual group members as well as overall group dynamics and processes. I model nurturing support, personal disclosure, vulnerability, and constructive confrontations to the group during the first few days. The overall goal is to have the group facilitate itself without going through the leader. Allowing for processing time every morning and afternoon helps the group observe itself and consider its direction. When there are conflicting needs about group process or workshop activities, democratic votes are conducted to decide how to proceed.

Challenging interpersonal dynamics occur in the workshop that require careful diagnostic assessment and decision making. Every group is different and has a life of its own. Consequently, there are only a few specific prescriptions on how to facilitate this kind of group. First, the overall intensity of the group needs to be carefully monitored. Enough tension should exist for the intergender or personal issues to be activated. Yet, too much early conflict or intensity can scare inexperienced group members and derail (or delay) the group process. Prepackaged media or activities can be used to regulate the intensity. A careful reading of the daily evaluations and "checking in with the group" frequently can provide the necessary information for guiding the optimal group process.

Power, control, and competition issues usually emerge in the group as individuals express their thoughts and feelings. I acknowledge and legitimize these issues in the group. On the first day, I indicate that one of the more interesting aspects of the workshop is how power and control might operate in the dynamics of the group. I encourage participants to observe the power and control dynamics in the group from a gender role perspective. Allowing covert power and control issues to become overt encourages group members to communicate more effectively with each other and with the leader. I emphasize that understanding power and control issues within the group can help us understand conflict and misunderstandings in our personal and professional lives.

I acknowledge my own power needs, which are to "get the group going" and to empower the group members to work toward helping each other. In this regard, I challenge the group to empower itself by accepting responsibility for its evolution into a therapeutic and caring community. I express the impossibility of developing group cohesiveness merely through the actions of the leader. In this way, shared responsibility for the workshop's cohesion and therapeutic potential is directly placed on the group members by Day 3.

The leader may still need to intervene in critical ways when the group is facilitating itself. Conflicts and tensions are inevitable as group members and the leader self-disclose about sexism and other forms of oppression. Some group members inexperienced with group conflict or expressed anger may be frightened or anxious by these intense exchanges. In pursuit of more intensity, other group members may challenge members to take more risks by confronting each other more directly. When this happens, my primary concern is to ensure that there are no victims or casualties in the group process. I remind the group that the goal of the workshop is to expose and examine gender role conflicts without victimization. When the group is unable to facilitate itself, the leader needs to intervene. Usually this means stopping the group process and letting the group members reflect on themselves until there is some understanding of what has transpired. Other times, direct interpretation of the group's dynamics is required. Checking the comfort levels and needs of "stressed" or vulnerable individuals communicates care for those who are struggling with their own issues or with other group members.

The leader also helps the group to label resistances, projections, and other defense mechanisms that occur. The major defense mechanisms are defined at the beginning of the workshops for those unfamiliar with psychological resistance and other unconscious processes. Labeling and observing defensive posturing during the workshop can help explain some of the more complicated group behavior. I usually discuss my own resistance and defensive structure to model the deeper and more psychological aspects of the gender role journey.

Participants' positive and negative projections on the group leader or other group members are frequently observed. Negative projections usually focus on the leader or other group members being sexist, unfair, or the "bad parent." Usually, some negative emotion (i.e., anger, fear, or shame) is projected on the leader or individuals in the group. When negative projections or feelings occur between group members, expert processing skills are required. When these projections occur between the leader and group members, it is sometimes useful to describe the complexity of possible transference and countertransference in the group's dynamics.

Specific Issues of Men, Women, and Diverse Participants

Men, women, and diverse participants experience the workshop differently depending on their own personal gender role journeys and their consciousness about sexism and other forms of oppression.

Men's Gender Role Journeys

Men face some personal issues during the workshop that deserve special attention. Men usually assess their personal sexism in the context of the workshop definitions and group process. For some men, this is the first time that they "own" their sexism. The question is not whether men are sexist, because most men have learned sexist attitudes and behaviors. The more critical questions are When did men learn their sexism? From whom? And what contemporary costs and consequences have resulted? Some men fear that their sexism will be observed during the group process. Anxiety about being sexist can produce worry, withdrawal, and passivity in the group. These men can be helped with the explanation that men's sexism is usually a result of men's sexist socialization into a patriarchal society. These explanations are not given to condone men's sexism. To the contrary, men should be asked to take responsibility for their sexism and to hold other men accountable for their sexism and abuses of power and privilege.

Furthermore, men usually hear women disclose about men who have victimized them personally, professionally, and sexually. These disclosures usually stimulate defensiveness, guilt, fear, and shame by some men in the workshop. These disclosures can also be an opportunity for men to fully experience and empathize with "women as victims" in much deeper ways than reading the newspaper or hearing about violence against women on television. Men may also worry about male bashing or losing their temper when confrontations occur. Leaders can acknowledge all of these feelings as a natural part of men and women "journeying with their gender roles" together. Furthermore, the workshop norms of "no victims or violence in the workshop" can be repeated as the workshop intensity increases.

Men sometimes feel out of control, powerless, and outnumbered during the workshop process. They may have to face being a minority in the group, because women usually outnumber men by a ratio of 3:1. Many men experience ambivalence with their gender roles during the workshop, as defined by Phase 2 of the gender role journey (see Exhibit 1). I encourage insecure and vulnerable men to engage the process more personally and explore new ways to communicate without their usual positions of privilege, power, and control. Some men may feel competitiveness with the group leader, who may be perceived as having all the power. There may also be ambivalence about asserting power or showing their masculine qualities for fear of being labeled as sexist. Many times, power struggles become the focus of the group process either overtly or covertly. Redefining power not as "power over others," but as the ability to "empower others" in the process of personal transformation can open up new notions of power, control, and healing for the group.

Some men have intense emotions as they recognize how the sexist patriarchy has also contributed to their being victims of sexism (O'Neil, 1991). Many men do not have an emotional vocabulary for labeling, experiencing, and expressing these feelings during the workshop process. Furthermore, they fear being devalued by other group members if they express deep emotions. Still others feel a sense of relief as they recognize that there are some significant sociopolitical reasons why they are (or have been) sexist.

Women's Gender Role Journeys

Like men, women's reactions to the workshop are dependent on their knowledge about sexism, feminism, and oppression against women. Helping women understand which phase of the gender role journey they most identify with can be very useful. Most women admit that the anger phase is the most difficult place to be. Those who have been "stuck in their anger" for a long time seek release and healing. For those women who have been directly victimized by men (i.e., through rape, incest, or battering), the workshop content and process usually brings up very painful memories. Leaders therefore need to be experts in understanding posttraumatic stress disorder and the complexities of being victimized. Approaches to helping victims recover and heal can be incorporated into the workshop design (e.g., see McCann & Pearlman, 1990; Root, 1992). Some women fear being revictimized by men (or other women) during the workshop process. It is therefore critical that the leader ensures careful processing of all interpersonal exchanges and remains personally available to group members.

Some women take issue with the notion of men as victims of sexism. Usually, these women are unable to move out of the anger phase of the gender role journey. Anger at men and other emotions (i.e., fear) may limit compassion for men who have been victimized by sexism. Expressed and unexpressed anger is usually near the surface with most women who have been directly hurt by men. Some critical event usually occurs in the workshop that allows this anger to be expressed at men, at other women, or at the leader. Positively facilitating this anger toward mutual understanding and healing is the leader's and group's responsibility. Some women have difficulty developing any compassion for men and seem to want to remain angry. In some cases, the presentation of John Lennon's and Marvin Gaye's gender role journeys have promoted consideration of possible compassion for men as victims. Some women openly discuss their sexism toward men and how they reinforce destructive stereotypes in men. These disclosures can bring cohesion to the group, because sexism is conceptualized as a destructive force that harms both sexes.

Gender Role Journeys of Diverse Participants

A majority of the workshop members over the years have been White, middle-class, heterosexual Americans in their 20s, 30s, and 40s. Diverse participants frequently experience the workshop differently, having had gender role experiences that are distinct from those of White, American, heterosexual members. Furthermore, these participants usually bring less trust of others to the workshop because of their past experiences with oppression (racism, classism, ethnocentrism, and homophobism).

The majority of group members may have limited awareness and appreciation for how these cultural, racial, and sexual differences affect someone's gender role journey. Majority group members may have limited compassion for diverse participants' pain resulting from multiple oppressions during their gender role journeys. These participants usually have some difficulty separating the effects of sexism from how they have been victimized by racism, classism, homophobism, and ethnocentrism. The "double duty" to which they have been subjected can intensify the workshop experience for these members. Many times, the pain of other oppressions is stronger than their pain from sexism.

Diverse participants are usually faced with assessing multiple layers of oppression as they examine their gender role socialization. To effectively deal with the racial and multicultural issues of these members, workshops need to incorporate content on how other forms of oppression interact with sexism. I have typically presented information about how racism, classism, homophobism, and ethnocentrism are critical to the gender role dialogue during the first 2 days of the workshop.

Many times, diverse participants are unwilling to bring up other forms of oppression for fear of being misunderstood, revictimized, or minimized. For example, in terms of race and ethnicity, White American workshop members may want to consciously or unconsciously deny the true effects of racism and ethnocentrism in American society. Defensiveness, shame, and White guilt may prohibit race and ethnicity from being discussed as important issues in the gender role dialogue. These group dynamics can activate deep negative emotions and immediate distrust, if not paranoia, in all group members. Under these conditions, the workshop intensity increases, cohesiveness decreases, and the commitment to community building and healing can evaporate. Some group members may fear that the workshop is out of control and on a "slippery slope" when race, class, ethnicity, and sexual orientation enter the group dynamics. Leaders need to anticipate these dynamics and label the group's struggle to discuss other forms of personal oppression that interact with sexism. Most important is that these issues not be avoided but be faced directly.

Vital and unexplored topics of critical importance emerge in the group process when sexism is discussed in the context of race, class, ethnicity, and sexual orientation, reinforcing that the gender role journey is not just about sexism and relationships between men and women. Of course, these issues need to be discussed simultaneously with special care and compassion.

CONCLUSION

Over the past 10 years, the gender role journey workshop has evolved into an intervention that can alter the "gender role consciousness" of both men and women. From my experience, it is clear that under the right group conditions men and women can journey together with their gender roles. However, there is a continued need for segregated men's and women's groups that facilitate the gender role journey. Simultaneously, coeducational workshops need to be created that help men and women understand their mutual perils and pains from patriarchal sexism and other forms of oppression. The gender role journey metaphor holds promise for a more humane, nonviolent relationship between men and women. I hope that this chapter encourages therapists to develop other interventions that facilitate the gender role journeys of all people.

REFERENCES

Albee, G. W. (1981). The prevention of sexism. *Professional Psychology, 12,* 20–28.

Basow, S. A. (1992). *Gender stereotypes: Traditions and alternatives.* Monterey, CA: Brooks/Cole.

Birk, J. (1981). Relevance and alliances: Cornerstone in training counselors of men. *Personnel and Guidance Journal, 60,* 254–262.

Gilligan, C. (1982). *In a different voice: Psychological theory and women's development.* Cambridge, MA: Harvard University Press.

Ivey, A., & Alschuler, A. (Eds.). (1973). Psychological education [Special issue]. *Personnel and Guidance Journal, 51*(Whole No. 9).

Jensen, R. E. (1993). The technology of the future is already here. *Academe, 79*(4), 8–13.

Kahn, A. (1984). The power war: Male response to power loss under equality. *Psychology of Women Quarterly, 8,* 234–247.

Kolb, D. (1984). *Experiential learning.* Englewood Cliffs, NJ: Prentice Hall.

Levant, R., & Pollack, W. (1995). *A new psychology of men.* New York: Basic Books.

McCann, I. L., & Pearlman, L. A. (1990). *Psychological trauma and the adult survivor: Theory, therapy, and transformation.* New York: Brunner/Mazel.

O'Neil, J. M. (1981a). Male sex-role conflict, sexism, and masculinity: Implications for men, women, and the counseling psychologist. *Counseling Psychologist, 9,* 61–80.

O'Neil, J. M. (1981b). Patterns of gender role conflict and strain and fears of femininity in men's lives. *Personnel and Guidance Journal, 60,* 203–210.

O'Neil, J. M. (1988). *The gender role journey: A context for the workshop.* Unpublished manuscript, Counseling Psychology Program, University of Connecticut, Storrs.

O'Neil, J. M. (1991, August). Men and women as victims of sexism: Metaphors for healing. In G. Brooks (Chair), *Practitioners' perspectives on male–female relations in the 90's.* Symposium conducted at the 99th Annual Convention of the American Psychological Association, San Francisco, CA.

O'Neil, J. M. (1994). *Resource manual for workshop: Gender role issues for helping professionals.* (Available from Educational Psychology 325, School of Family Studies, University of Connecticut, Storrs, CT 06269.)

O'Neil, J. M., & Egan, J. (1992a). Men's gender role transitions over the life span: Transformation and fears of femininity. *Journal of Mental Health Counseling, 14,* 305–324.

O'Neil, J. M., & Egan, J. (1992b). Men's and women's gender role journeys: Metaphors for healing, transition, and transformation. In B. Wainrib (Ed.), *Gender issues across the life cycle* (pp. 107–123). New York: Springer.

O'Neil, J. M., & Egan, J. (1993). Abuses of power against women: Sexism, gender role conflict, and psychological violence. In E. Cook (Ed.), *Women, relation-*

ships, and power: Implications for counseling (pp. 49–78). Alexandria, VA: American Counseling Association Press.

O'Neil, J. M., Egan, J., Owen, S. V., & Murry, V. M. (1993). The Gender Role Journey Measure: Scale development and psychometric evaluation. *Sex Roles, 28,* 167–185.

O'Neil, J. M., Good, G. E., & Holmes, S. (1995). Fifteen years of theory and research on men's gender role conflict: New paradigms for empirical research. In R. Levant & W. Pollack (Eds.), *A new psychology of men* (pp. 164–206). New York: Basic Books.

O'Neil, J. M., & Roberts Carroll, M. (1987). A six-day workshop on gender role conflict and strain: Helping men and women take the gender role journey. Storrs, CT: University of Connecticut, Department of Educational Psychology, Counseling Psychology Program. (ERIC Document Reproduction Service No. ED 287121)

O'Neil, J. M., & Roberts Carroll, M. (1988a). *Evaluation of gender role workshop: Three years of follow-up data.* Paper presented at the 95th Annual Convention of the American Psychological Association, New York. (ERIC Document Reproduction Service No. ED 287121)

O'Neil, J. M., & Roberts Carroll, M. (1988b). A gender role workshop focused on sexism, gender role conflict, and the gender role journey. *Journal of Counseling and Development, 67,* 193–197.

Pleck, J. H. (1981). *The myth of masculinity.* Cambridge, MA: MIT Press.

Root, M. M. P. (1992). Reconstructing the impact of trauma on personality. In L. S. Brown & M. S. Ballou (Eds.), *Personality and psychopathology: Feminist reappraisals* (pp. 229–265). New York: Guilford Press.

Tuckman, B. (1965). Developmental changes in small groups. *Psychological Bulletin, 63,* 384–399.

III

FATHERING AND BEING FATHERED

INTRODUCTION

FATHERING AND BEING FATHERED

Whether fathers were absent, abusive, present, pathetic, or wonderful, men's feelings and attitudes about them may be the single most important issue that men struggle with in their lives. It is high on women's lists as well. Men's fears about their own abilities to be adequate fathers often reflect their struggles to come to grips with their feelings about their own fathers.

Part III contains chapters examining men's relationships with their fathers and the wide range of feelings involved in this crucial relationship. This part starts with a chapter on a workshop specifically geared to exploring men's feelings toward their fathers and ends with another workshop designed to teach teenage fathers valuable parenting skills. The work of this group of chapter authors has the common theme of seeking to help males develop and improve on their fathering skills, both directly (e.g., through skills training) and indirectly (e.g., through therapeutic explorations). This body of work contributes toward meeting a great void in American society—helping fathers from a variety of viewpoints to develop and improve their fathering skills, in the present as well as the future.

In the first chapter, Sternbach relates his experiences of leading men's groups in dealing with their deeply felt emotions toward their fathers and, often, toward themselves as fathers. The poignant stories and important methods of his workshop reveal valuable insight into the nature of working through fatherhood issues.

Next, Levant provides a wonderful concrete example of a male parenting workshop. He shows how presenting group activities in a psychoeducational format can be of valuable assistance to conscientious fathers who wish to become better fathers but are reluctant to get involved at a deeper level of exploration of their feelings. Levant usefully describes how to gradually introduce such men into the world of feelings in nonthreatening ways.

Hall and Kelly enlighten readers next on the subject of helping divorced noncustodial fathers maintain ties to their children. With the increased alienation of society—particularly, the lack of cohesiveness of many nuclear families—it is even more important to encourage noncustodial fathers to retain close ties to their children. The authors not only cover specifics of informing these men about their all-important roles as fathers and advocacy resources, but also illustrate how the group setting can be used to help them better deal with their feelings.

Barret's chapter on gay fathers in groups informs on the need for work with this important but neglected population. Citing sparse research literature and the reasons for this void, he points out the need for more programs to help gay men to follow their desires to become fathers or to be better fathers. He also provides clinical research that can be used to evaluate and improve future programs that target this population.

Focusing on his pioneering work with fathers and their adolescent sons, Ginsberg describes a program aimed at helping both parties to relate more closely. He details the Parent–Adolescent Relationship Program and discusses other useful group methods designed to tighten the father–son bond at this crucial time.

The next chapter—the last in this part of the book—continues the theme of adolescence and fathering. Kiselica presents an exciting and innovative program for teaching adolescent fathers the skills of parenting. In his well-designed program, he emphasizes ways of relating specifically to adolescent fathers and channeling their motivations to be good fathers. Moreover, this chapter provides documentation that teenage fathers should not be stereotyped as irresponsible and unmotivated.

14

THE FATHER THEME IN GROUP THERAPY WITH MEN

JACK STERNBACH

Received models of fatherhood are not writ in the stars or in our genes. Our ancestors knew a very different pattern from our own, and our descendants may well have another that is no less different. Fatherhood, history reminds us, is a cultural invention. (Demos, 1986, p. 64).

A truly reconstructive experience in a men's group inevitably requires a new and more positive experience of fathering and being fathered by one's peers. The need to do this is built, in large measure, on the ashes of *failed fathering*. In using this phrase I refer to the actual experience of men in their families of origin. This also refers to the dehumanizing impact of the larger sociopolitical system on the young males in its care. The fathers who so badly injured these sons were themselves victims of those same forces.

In this chapter, I confine my discussion to the immediate and intimate process within the all-male therapy group. I also maintain an awareness of the pathogenic effect of structural forces on men, especially how such forces affect their capacity to parent. This awareness is brought into the group, often by the men themselves, as a context for understanding (Sternbach, 1977). More comprehensive discussions of economic forces, men's sense of powerlessness, and distortions in family life are available from others (e.g., see Connell, 1987; De La Cancela, 1986; Kupers, 1993; Pleck, 1984).

In the group process with peers there is the potential for a male-to-male nurturing that encompasses the fathering that all men wish for: fathering that rests on mutuality, rational authority, openness to feedback, and vulnerability. (For information on fathers and fathering, in addition to the well-known work of Osherson [1986], see Biller [1974], Cath, Gurwitt, & Ross [1982], Chodorow [1978], Gary [1981], Lamb [1986], Levant & Kelly [1989], Levinson [1978], Lewis & Salt [1986], Pasick [1992], Pruitt [1987], and, most recently, Real [in press], who presents a new and challenging model of fathering.)

Attracting men to such an experience with other males—given the pain, neglect, mistrust, and competitiveness that flows from the masculinization process—is itself a demanding professional task (Brooks, 1991; Kupers, 1993; Pasick, 1992; Silverberg, 1986; Sternbach, 1992). Building each men's group is a matter of months of preparation with men on my caseload and careful orientation of referrals. Attracting men to an intensive weekend workshop also involves considerable outreach energy.

I have found that providing a clear, formatted structure, at least in the initial stages of group therapy, helps men with their preaffiliation anxiety and sets limits on the recapitulation of destructive male patterns in the group. I explicitly convey the message that our main task is to create a safe structure for one another. I have written to this effect elsewhere (Sternbach, 1990).

A vivid illustration of the link between prior experience with one's father and initial pregroup anxiety is revealed in these words from one man's journal, describing his preparation for a weekend workshop:

> Excited—anxious—Where will I fit in—What will others think of me? I know there are so many barriers for "men" in dealing with themselves. I find an emptiness when it comes to connecting with another man—has a lot to do with Dad.

The naming of the emptiness that this man felt is at the core of normative male socialization. It provides a necessary and powerful focus throughout the duration of the men's group.

In this chapter, I bring a multidimensional framework to the father theme in men's groups that is anchored in four interdependent processes: (a) direct discussion and sharing about fathers, (b) generating and experiencing new norms of male-to-male fathering as expressed in mutual nurturance, (c) recognizing and declaring ownership of toxic fathering, and (d) reconstructing fatherhood in life space outside the group.

The material I present here consists of a flowing narrative that weaves a texture from these themes as they emerge in clinical vignettes from group sessions. These vignettes were drawn from work with six of my most recent men's groups. There were 5–7 men in each group, for a total of 32. The men were all White, and most were either Protestant or Catholic. There were equal numbers of blue-collar and white-collar workers. Each group ran from 1 to 5 years.[1] In doing this, I wish to mirror the actual group process. It is in the interaction between the men—which may, at times, include the therapist—that the healing occurs. The interventions of the therapist may facilitate this interaction, but they will never substitute for it.

FIRST STAGE: INTRODUCTION OF THE FATHER THEME

In all of my men's groups, I deliberately introduce the father theme after the first few sessions. The results are predictable. I quote from the notes of the man cited above:

> Damn! It really hurts not to have Dad in the way I so badly want. It's frightening how many of us struggle with these same hurts. It feels so good to share so openly feelings of shame and weakness.

In an ongoing group, seven men are gathered together. This is their fourth session. I suggest that they go around the circle and complete this sentence: "When I think of my father, I feel _____," filling in the blank. It is important that they say the whole sentence each time. It builds a cadence, a rhythm, rather like a chant in the men's lodge or by the campfire. With many pauses, usually in somber voices, they begin, with comments such as these:

> When I think of my father I feel the tip of the iceberg—anger, abandoned, lonely, curious, emptiness, sad, confusion, my own death, unimportant, inadequate, cheated, pity, cold, uneasy.

After going around from 5 to 10 times, the men begin to amplify their statements. Two of the men never knew their fathers, because of death and desertion; their grief is almost beyond bearing. Another man says he now begins to feel love for his father, but that there is still anger. Another speaks of his father as a shadow, saying that he would like to feel anger but it would go right through his father. When asked how he is feeling, he says: "disconnected—like a brick wall away from my feelings." (Bergman [1991] has explored this theme of lost connection in male development.)

This format becomes one of several "a-ha" experiences that I try to build into initial sessions to help men find common ground. They can then begin to reach for connection across the emptiness and mistrust that otherwise separates them.

---

[1]Readers interested in demographic data on these men and more detailed information on the groups are invited to contact me. However, the intertwining of fatherhood and alcoholism demands special note. Those in the addictions field have been saying for years that children of alcoholic families are overrepresented in their caseloads. They are surely correct in this instance. Nineteen of 32 fathers of these group members, or almost 60%, had been alcoholics. Seventeen of the 32 group members, or 53%, were either in recovery or had suffered serious disabilities in earlier years due to substance abuse.

SECOND STAGE: NEW NORMS OF FATHERING

A different group has been together for about 20 sessions. They are discussing whether they wish to make member-to-member feedback part of their process:

> Jerry: "I am concerned about when a group of men get into negatives—we could lose the support part."
> Therapist: "Can we think of any men in our lives who have been able to give us feedback that may have been difficult—but in a way we could accept and gain from?"
> Donny: "Isn't that what a father does?"
> Frank: "Not too many fathers like that around . . . and I wish I could say I had been that kind of father . . . but I haven't been."
> Richard: "This is very difficult and scary for me. Criticism in my life has been humiliating and hurtful."
> Donny: "I want more feedback. I get a feeling of strength—that I'm not by myself . . . but I want it to be from the heart. And if I can't hear it from those of you in this group I don't know who I could hear it from!"

With those words, Donny helps the group quiet the ghosts of their fathers—fathers from whom the men learned mistrust and despair at their capacity to be loving with other men.

In this second stage of group development, one sees the group beginning to clearly identify what feels nurturing and what does not. This is also an important stage for the leader. I consciously choose to ask for feedback about my role and use of authority—about my fathering in the group. The following vignette provides an example of such group processing.

> In a long-term group, one member told me, with great affect, that he felt picked on by me and that his feelings were hurt. I was touched by his sincerity and openness. I also knew how much he had suffered at the hands of a terribly abusive and alcoholic father. I looked at him and said:
> "I'm sorry, Matthew, if I have hurt your feelings."
> Blane interjected to Matthew: "Does Jack remind you of *your* father?"
> Before he could respond, Jason jumped in, tears welling in his eyes, and said "My father never in his life apologized to anyone, especially me!"
> Matthew sat in stunned but appreciative silence. I know that my response to him was one of many critical incidents in his recovery from abusive fathering. For Jason, as well as Matthew, this seemed to be a corrective emotional experience. Jason's spontaneous response was a reminder of the impact that the group process can have, even for the group member not directly engaged in the particular interaction.

Inviting feedback is hard work, but it is fundamental to change. The corrective emotional experience will only occur to the extent that the therapist, or another member who is a transference object at a specific point in time, can engage the group member. It is only then that the old template can start to give way to a new, freer possibility. It is my belief that one does this best if in touch with and acknowledging one's own wounds as a son and a father, as well as one's capacity to wound others. I also think that this kind of authentic interchange is a sine qua non regardless of one's theoretical orientation or general approach when leading a men's group.

THIRD STAGE: RECOGNIZING AND REWORKING TOXIC FATHERING

In its third stage, the group develops into a powerful vehicle for working through fathering material. Sometimes our work begins by identifying the ways in which men in the group may be furthering their father's toxic legacy. One man told us of staying up late at night and drinking bourbon, feeling lonely and depressed. This was how he found communion with his alcoholic father, who had deserted him when he was a child.

Another man's wife had confronted him, pointing out that his driven behavior would surely lead him to the same sad fate as his father. Although appalled by his broken, alcoholic father he also admitted how powerful he felt when he "walked in [his] father's shoes."

Even in the first father go-around, another member, Roy, had said "pass," and he continued this through 6–7 turns. I eventually asked him about his silence. Roy replied, "I have no memories and feelings about my father. He is dead these many years; I helped him die in a decent manner and I have forgiven him. Nothing is left and that's just as well." I was stunned; tears came to my eyes. As I sat, wondering if I dared risk a comment, Mart and Pete (both a generation older than Roy) turned to him and, with infinite gentleness, invited him to tell them a little about his father. In the ensuing weeks, a painful account of disinterest combined with something worse emerged: "I was at war with my mom and misbehaving in school and he came up to my room. I was 16. He started to talk to me and all of a sudden punched me in the mouth and left."

Roy also revealed how he experienced periodic suicidal urges. All were concerned by this. At that point, I suggested an intervention that, when used appropriately and with good timing, has a powerful impact. Roy moved his chair to the middle of the room and sat quietly with his eyes closed. All of us moved our chairs close and made gentle, physical contact with Roy. I suggested we say to him the things we wished we had heard as very young boys from our fathers. For a full 10 minutes, the men slowly, and then with greater ease, said to Roy, "you are beautiful, you are perfect, you are my dear little boy, I cherish you, I protect you, I love you," and so on. Roy was not a demonstrative man, and he took this in quietly, breathing slowly throughout the process. At the end, he wiped a few tears and thanked the group with a sweet and very young smile. After that, there were no recurrent suicide urges or thoughts from Roy over the next 4 years.

The group develops into a powerful vehicle for a variety of imaginative re-creations of the father–son linkage. Men in my groups have invoked their fathers in situ, speaking aloud to their long-dead fathers. They speak the words, both loving and angry, that they never had the opportunity to say when their fathers were alive. I have also used the "empty chair" technique associated with the gestalt therapy of Fritz Perls (1969), as well as some modified psychodrama techniques tailored to the uniqueness of the father–son situation. Beyond technique, however, it is remarkable to me how readily men can allow themselves to be fully in touch with their own father–son experiences. It is almost as if they were in a trance state at such times.

Writing a letter to one's father is one of the techniques most likely to evoke affective responses. Excerpts from some of these letters appear below. The first is from a young man in his 20s, whose father committed suicide when he was in college.

> Dear Dad, . . . I wish you were here so I could talk to you about art
> . . . so I could ask your advice about what I should do next in my life
> . . . I wish you were [sic] so you could meet Charlotte and eventually
> our children.

At that point, the letter ended (this was written during group, and the man dissolved into tears). How could such a young man bear to confront the question that he choked out?: "Why didn't he think about me when he did it?" All the men leaned forward. Everyone was very quiet. Finally, he wiped his eyes, saying, "Thanks, that's all I can do right now." He knew he could come back to this again.

The reading aloud of these letters is punctuated with tears, with sobs. It often takes quite a while to get through the readings. Sometimes the letter writing moves the writer through to a new and unexpected place:

> I'm supposed to write a letter to you and read it out at therapy. That's
> a place to get help dealing with life's problems, a place you never went
> to. Our relationship was full of anger, beating, threats, and fear. All of
> which you gave me. Not hugs, praise, [or] ever saying "I love you."

The writer continued in that vein for a page or two and then surprised himself by what he wrote at the end:

> I miss you and wish we were getting old together and caring for each other. . . . No matter how much you hurt me, I love you, and wish only that we had more time. I'll talk to you again sometimes. Be well.

At the end of that group session, this middle-aged man, whose father had been dead for many years, said how glad he was to find that he could feel love for his father. He had not known it was there.

Neither age nor death are barriers to a reworking of the father–son relationship. One of the most touching examples was a 50-year-old man whose father had died quite suddenly when he was 9. He told us, at a weekend workshop, of an experience he had when meditating. He found himself in the familiar space where he usually found his spirit guide—a deer or an owl. This time, he discerned a figure seated in a chair. When he approached there, the figure revealed itself as his father, who said to him, "I have been waiting for you all these years."

FOURTH STAGE: RECONSTRUCTING FATHERHOOD OUTSIDE THE GROUP

The following letter was addressed to a father still living, who visited his son yearly. Each time, he created an ugly scene as his temper and irritation were fueled by alcohol.

> I love you, Dad. I like your company; but you still have this power over me when you drink. Most every year when you visit we have a fight, and it takes me right back to when I was a kid. I get the same sick feelings and I carry them around for a long, long time. . . . So, please, for the sake of our relationship, it is important to you—us—don't drink when you come to visit us.

With much encouragement from the group, this man was able to actually send this letter to his father. To his surprise, he received a phone call from his father, thanking him for the letter. Even better, his father was pleasant and agreeable on the next fishing trip. In telling us this, he acknowledged how sad and lonely he still felt, knowing that his father's alcoholism kept them from any real intimacy. However, he no longer felt intimidated and like a little boy. That was a real gift for him.

In every group there is at least one member, sometimes several, who have adolescent or adult children. They are faced with the extra sadness of grieving their failures as fathers as well as their hurts as sons. The group can be very powerful in helping men to stay with the pain and to reach for something more giving and open with their children.

Thomas had told us of his son, whom he had left behind as a little boy with his exwife. They seldom saw each other once his son became a young man. He felt that his son did not want to have much to do with him. At one group session, he mentioned that his son's birthday just passed and he had not sent him a card or called him.

Karl, who was the same age as Thomas, turned toward him, placed his hand on Thomas's shoulder, and said, "Thomas, I'm disappointed in you. It just doesn't sound like you to do something like that."

Thomas looked up with gratitude in his eyes and acknowledged his shame and impotence. From that point on, the group could work with him on options and possibilities. At the next session, Thomas mentioned that he took one man's advice, found a "late" birthday card, sent it off, and would be calling his son soon.

As is so often the case, an experience of empowerment with peers can generalize beyond the group. Karl emerged in one group as a man with considerable capacity to father other men, as he did with Thomas above. When his 16-year-old son started dating, Karl talked with him about it, saying, "I told him to be who he was and treat her like a person." His son said, "Of course, I know that." When we asked Karl what he had been told at that age, he told us of his three uncles, who would nudge him, smirk, and ask "Have you gotten a piece yet?"

In the same group, six of the seven men had sons, and their concerns as parents were paramount. Pete's sons (and daughters) were adults in their 30s. He focused with much intensity on how he was that father whom other men in the group spoke about: the father who wounded and hurt his children. He reflected, somberly, on the years of loneliness that resulted as he sequestered himself from family life.

This man had been in three successive groups over a number of years. In each one he was an elder and quickly assumed a role as social–emotional support person to the other, younger men. He found appropriate opportunities to share how cut off, controlling, and distant he was when his children were young. The message always got through to the younger fathers in the group.

Over these same years, Pete's wife reported on how much his partnering and parenting had changed and how delighted she was. It was as if the practice parenting he had done in the group became part of a reintegrative reconstruction of his role as husband and father.

CONCLUSION

I have illustrated the process by which men in small groups struggle to make sense and find connection to their fathers, alive or dead. I have found, time and again, that the collective power of the group to induce a member to take risks is often well beyond the impact possible in individual or couples therapy. The group can make the difference in moving a man forward and helping him find his way through this very painful, necessary journey. As I have indicated, some of these men have worked very hard to father their own children in a more connected, sustained, and caring manner.

I have also described some of the different channels through which the father theme works and reworks itself. Sometimes it is sufficient to simply open the subject, and some members may not revisit this issue for quite a while. But, inevitably, they will. I suggest that failing to work purposively with this father theme may well lead to impasse. Whether or not the therapist introduces the topic, the father is always present—his is one of the major narratives in a men's group. Whether spoken or left silent, avowed or denied, within or outside awareness, he is often at the center of the group process. If not consciously evoked, he will remain as a shadow, undercutting the therapeutic process.

The very act of giving voice to the father and exploring his presence provides a centering focus around which the men's group can realize its potential for reconstructing a more humane masculinity. In this regard, the group is not only the means but also the medium through which this hard work proceeds. The group nourishes, supports, demands, and contains. As an assemblage of men, its very presence stimulates powerful feelings. As the men work with these feelings—so familiar, so evocative of father–son issues—a resocialization process can take place within the group. Through both action and reflection, a new kind of fathering experience evolves in the group that can be carried to life beyond therapy.

REFERENCES

Bergman, S. (1991). Men's psychological development: A relational perspective. In *Work in Progress*, 48 (pp. 1–13). Wellesley, MA: Stone Center Working Paper Series.

Biller, H. (1974). *Fatherhood: A sociological perspective*. Lexington, MA: Heath.

Brooks, G. (1991). Traditional men in marital and family therapy. In M. Bograd (Ed.), *Feminist approaches for men in family therapy* (pp. 51–73). New York: Harrington Park Press.

Cath, S., Gurwitt, A., & Ross, J. (1982). *Father and child: Developmental and clinical perspectives*. New York: Basil Blackwell.

Chodorow, N. (1978). *The reproduction of mothering*. Berkeley: University of California Press.

Connell, R. W. (1987). *Gender and power*. Stanford, CA: Stanford University Press.

De La Cancela, V. (1986). A critical analysis of Puerto Rican machismo: Implications for clinical practice. *Psychotherapy*, 23, 291–296.

Demos, J. (1986). *Past, present and personal: The family and the life course in American history*. New York: Oxford University Press.

Gary, L. (1981). *Black men*. Beverly Hills, CA: Sage.

Kupers, T. (1993). *Revisioning men's lives*. New York: Guilford Press.

Lamb, M. (Ed.). (1986). *The father's role: Applied perspectives*. New York: Wiley.

Levant, R., & Kelly, J. (1989). *Between father and child*. New York: Penguin.

Levinson, D. (1978). *The seasons of a man's life*. New York: Knopf.

Lewis, R., & Salt, R. (Eds.). (1986). *Men in families*. Newbury Park, CA: Sage.

Osherson, S. (1986). *Finding our fathers*. New York: Fawcett Columbine.

Pasick, R. (1992). *Awakening from the deep sleep: A guide for courageous men*. San Francisco: Harper.

Perls, F. (1969). *Gestalt therapy verbatim*. Lafayette, CA: Real People's Press.

Pleck, J. E. (1984). Men's power with women, other men, and society: A men's movement analysis. In P. P. Rieker & E. H. Carmen (Eds.), *The gender gap in psychotherapy* (pp. 79–89). New York: Plenum Press.

Pruitt, K. (1987). *The nurturing father: Journey toward the complete man*. New York: Warner Books.

Real, T. (in press). Fathering our sons, fathering ourselves: Some thoughts on transforming masculine legacies. *Journal of Feminist Family Therapy*.

Silverberg, R. A. (1986). *Psychotherapy with men: Transcending the masculine mystique*. Springfield, IL: Charles C Thomas.

Sternbach, J. (1977). Men's awareness. *State and Mind, 1*, 28–29.

Sternbach, J. (1990). The men's seminar: An educational and support group for men. *Social Work With Groups, 2*, 23–29.

Sternbach, J. (1992). A men's studies approach to group treatment with all-male groups. *Men's Studies Review, 9*, 21–28.

15

THE MALE CODE AND PARENTING: A PSYCHOEDUCATIONAL APPROACH

RONALD F. LEVANT

Traditional masculinity ideology (also known as the "male code") requires that men be independent, strong, self-reliant, competitive, achievement-oriented, powerful, adventurous, and emotionally restrained. These characteristics both take a toll on men's physical and mental health and make it difficult for men to seek and use psychological services. In this article, I first examine the male code and its consequences. Using as a point of departure Brannon's (1985) delineation of traditional masculinity, I consider, in turn, the effect of the male code on men's health and the difficulties that the code creates for men in seeking and using psychological services. I then present a psychoeducationally structured group program for men as an example of how psychological services might be designed to be more accessible and useful to men.

An earlier version of this chapter was published in *Psychotherapy, 27*, pp. 309–315. Copyright 1990 by the Division of Psychotherapy (Division 29) of the American Psychological Association. Adapted with permission.

THE MALE CODE AND ITS CONSEQUENCES

Brannon's Model of Traditional Masculinity

Brannon (1985) has identified four components of the traditional ideology of masculinity: (a) that men should not be feminine (labeled by Brannon as "no sissy stuff"); (b) that men should strive to be respected for successful achievement ("the big wheel"); (c) that men should never show weakness ("the sturdy oak"); and (d) that men should seek adventure and risk, even accepting violence if necessary ("give 'em hell").

These traditional role prescriptions may be changing somewhat. In a study of college men in New England, Thompson, Grisanti, and Pleck (1985) found that their subjects tended to endorse the norms of adventure seeking and not showing weakness, but did not endorse norms of avoidance of femininity and respect through achievement. Levant et al. (1992) have obtained similar results using the Male Role Norms Inventory. These findings suggest that, at least in these samples, recent cultural changes seem to have weakened the avoidance-of-femininity and achievement norms but that role prescriptions to conceal weakness and take risks seem to have been affected much less. As I shall show, these two dimensions have important implications for the mental health of men. In addition, Thompson et al. (1985) found that college men who endorsed traditional male role norms also tended to show higher than average levels of homophobia and Type A behavior, lower self-disclosure, and greater dominance over partners in intimate relationships.

Moreover, new evidence has been emerging that the ideology of masculinity and the norms for the male role vary among different ethnic groups. Lazur and Majors (1995), on the basis of a literature review, described the differences in male role norms and male role strain among African American, Latino, American Indian, and Asian American men. And Pleck (1995), in an empirical study, found variations in masculinity ideology among White, African American, and Latino males.

Effects on Men's Physical and Mental Health

The traditional male role is a self-denying and stoic–heroic combination of characteristics that takes its toll on men's physical and mental health. There are three facets to this. First, there is the well-known finding that men have higher mortality rates than women. Harrison (1978) examined the differences in life expectancy for American men versus women (which is about 8 years on the average; U.S. Bureau of the Census, 1990) and attempted to partial out the effects of biogenetic and psychosocial factors. He concluded that gender role norms, and socialization along those norms, account for most of men's shorter life expectancies in comparison with women.

Second, there is the equally well known finding that women are reported to have more physical and emotional illnesses than men. At first, one might think that this higher illness rate would be associated with a higher death rate. One must remember, however, that illness rates are often measured in terms of visits to physicians and clinics. Hence, what appears to be at work is that the traditional male role inhibits men both from seeking help in the early stages of illness and from being sufficiently attuned to their own internal processes to be able to detect the early warning signals of illness (Waldron & Johnson, 1976). Thus, it seems that "the male role may be hazardous to your health" (Harrison, 1978, p. 65).

Third, with regard to mental health, although women have more reported psychological distress, men are closing the gap. Kessler and McRae (1981) analyzed five national surveys on mental health conducted between 1957 and 1976. They found that men's rates of symptoms of psychological distress increased 3 times as much as women's and that, as a result, the "gender gap" in symptoms was 38% smaller at the end of the 2-decade period. In a later study, Kessler and McRae (1983) found a similar process occurring with regard to attempted suicides. Generalizing across a group of studies, they reported that the ratio of females to males attempting suicide dropped from 2.3:1 in 1960 to 1.3:1 in 1980. It should also be noted that men continue to have substantially higher rates of completed suicides than women. Finally, a recent large-scale study by the National Institute of Mental Health revealed that, although women have higher rates of affective, anxiety, and somatization disorders, men have higher rates of substance abuse and antisocial personality disorders (Landers, 1989).

Obstacles to Psychological Services

There can be no question that men need a variety of preventive and therapeutic psychological health services. However, men do not use psychological services readily. There are four major factors that stand in their way, and all have to do with the norms and prescriptions of the traditional male role. The first is difficulty in admitting the existence of a problem. This stems from the "sturdy oak" trait, in which the man feels he must conceal weakness, even from himself. It is interesting that this is one of the two traditional-male-role prescriptions that Thompson et al. (1985) found to still be endorsed by their college student sample.

The second factor, closely related to the first, is difficulty in asking for help. Scher (1979) has noted the costs to the self-esteem of a man who is forced to admit that he cannot solve a life problem.

The third factor is difficulty identifying and processing emotional states. This is a direct result of the male socialization process, in which boys are taught to tune out painful feelings, both physical and emotional. No doubt many men can remember being told in sports to learn to "play with pain" or that "big boys don't cry." Heppner and Gonzales (1987) described a man who recalled "the tragedy he felt in seeing the bloody and lifeless body of the first gopher he killed as a boy. His male friend, seeing the boy's emotional reactions, told him to 'just think about all the grain they eat' " (p. 32).

As a result of such socialization experiences, men may often be genuinely unaware of their emotions. In my experience, this is more often a result of trained incompetence and skill deficits than of repression and denial, although those dynamics are certainly part of it. In the absence of emotional awareness, men tend to rely on their cognition and try to "logically deduce how they should feel" (Heppner & Gonzales, 1987, p. 32). In a recent article, I discussed these widespread problems as a mild form of alexithymia (Levant, 1992), which literally means "without words for emotions."

However, it is not accurate to say that men's lack of emotional awareness is complete; rather, it is selective. Men are allowed to feel and become aware of emotions in the anger and rage part of the spectrum, as prescribed in Brannon's (1985) "give 'em hell" injunction. Also, the fact that these emotions are sanctioned by the male code may account for men's higher rates of completed suicides and antisocial personality disorders. Men's higher rates of substance abuse may also be attributable to their difficulty in experiencing and releasing painful emotions through talking or crying, combined with the risk-taking norm, which is the second of the two traditional role prescriptions endorsed by students studied by Thompson et al. (1985).

The final factor that interferes with men seeking and using psychological help is their fear of intimacy. This, again, is a result of the male socialization process. An anecdote from a magazine story is illustrative. Titled "Daddy's Home," the story described how a father drove into the driveway of his home after work, and his three small children bounded out to greet him. He first hugged and kissed one daughter and then the other daughter, while 4-year-old Jimmy stood waiting to be hugged. Daddy then said, "No, Jimmy. Men don't hug." Slowly, Jimmy got reorganized and extended a stiff, manly little hand for a handshake.

As a result of experiences of this type, boys may grow up to be adults who are not comfortable with intimacy; such men will experience difficulty in the intimate therapeutic encounter. Men often equate intimacy with sexuality, and this may cause difficulties in the therapeutic relationship. With a female therapist, the transference may be eroticized, whereas transference with a male therapist can lead to fears of homosexuality.

Good, Dell, and Mintz (1989) attempted to test the hypothesis that aspects of the male role stand as impediments to men seeking psychological help, using a scale that conceptualizes the male role differently than in Brannon's (1985) model. In a sample of undergraduate men, Good et al. found that traditional attitudes about the male role, difficulty expressing emotions, and concern about expressing affection toward other men were each significantly related to negative attitudes toward seeking psychological services. There is thus empirical support for the proposition that the male role makes it difficult for men to seek and use psychological services.

Despite these obstacles, in my work as director of the Fatherhood Project at Boston University I have found that men will seek out and use psychological services if these services are designed with sensitivity to the male role (Levant & Doyle, 1983; Levant & Kelly, 1991).

The task of designing psychological services for men can be conceptualized as a kind of cross-cultural process, in which it is recognized that the culture of traditional psychological services requires behaviors that conflict with aspects of the male role. Then the service can be modified to whatever extent possible to reduce or remove these conflicts. In this context, one should recognize that traditional therapy was designed primarily by men to treat women (Levant, 1990); thus, it has long reflected male assumptions about female personality development. In recent years, feminist psychotherapists have pointed out the flaws in these assumptions and offered correctives. The next step is to design therapy for men, on the basis of an accurate understanding of male personality development.

I offer the Fatherhood Course, centerpiece of the Fatherhood Project at Boston University, as an illustration of how one might go about designing gender-aware psychological services for men. The Fatherhood Course was designed to fit men's traditional learning styles and to help men develop certain psychological skills that many men do not ordinarily acquire, because of the male socialization process. Although this course was intended to primarily be educational, therapeutic processes have occurred from its use. It may therefore be possible to extrapolate from this experience and adapt some of the techniques used in this program in designing new therapeutic approaches for men.

THE FATHERHOOD COURSE

The typical Fatherhood Course meets one evening a week for 8 weeks and teaches fathers communication skills—particularly, learning to listen to their children's feelings and to express their own feelings in a constructive manner. In addition, it teaches fathers about child development (stages and norms) and child management. The course uses a skill-training format, in which fathers role-play the particular skills using examples from their own family situations; videotapes are used to provide instant feedback. In addition, each father receives a workbook containing exercises that can be done at home with his children.

The program is designed to fit men's traditional learning styles. It is not held out as counseling, and men are not initially required to talk about their feelings (although most eventually do). Instead, it is offered as an educational program with an opportunity to develop skills. When men first walk into the room, hardware is immediately in evidence in the form of video equipment, which may provide a feeling of familiarity given men's traditional relationship to machinery. Furthermore, they are told that they will be taught to be better fathers in a manner comfortable to them, in much the same way that they might have learned to play a sport, such as football or tennis.

The Fathers

The fathers who participate in the course come from all walks of life, from laborer to plumber to lawyer to stockbroker. As a rule, they are not men with careers in the human services and who therefore might have overcome some of the communicational limitations that result from the male-role-socialization process. Ages of participants have ranged from the late 20s to the mid-50s, with their children's ages ranging from early infancy to young adulthood. Usually, about half of the men are married and half are divorced, with a few remarried and functioning as stepfathers in a "reconstituted" family. Those who are divorced often have custody arrangements ranging from visitation to joint custody to sole custody.

The fathers enter the program voluntarily, learning about it from public service announcements in the media. Many of them come to the project because their wives bought their tuitions as birthday or Christmas gifts.

Although these men tend to be successful in the workplace and fulfill the "good provider" role, they experience discomfort and dissatisfaction in the nurturing role. Some speak with sadness of the distance in their relationships with their own fathers, saying that they never really knew them. Others remember the conflict they experienced with their fathers and articulate a fierce desire to avoid the mistakes their fathers made with them. Still others feel inadequate with their children and marvel at how well their wives perform when it comes to such seemingly simple tasks as getting 10-year-old Timmy to bed: Mom can do it with four words, yet for Dad it is often a half-hour struggle that usually ends with Dad losing his temper and yelling at Timmy, and Timmy bursting into tears.

Most of the men are uncomfortable with feelings, both their own and their children's. And many get caught in the "anger trap," becoming ensnared in unproductive repetitive patterns of limit testing followed by punishment.

Some assume at the outset that they know how to communicate with their children. Two fathers in particular in one group, who thought their communication skills were adequate, were shocked to see videotaped replays of role-playing sessions. One saw himself towering over his child, and the other witnessed himself talking from behind a newspaper. Another father has noted: "the idea that being a father is a learned skill never occurred to me."

The Course

The Fatherhood Course is a psychoeducational structured group and is part of the emerging field of psychoeducational programs for families (Guerney, 1977; L'Abate & Weinstein, 1987; Levant, 1986). It also draws on the theory and practice of structured groups, a subfield of group therapy (Drum & Knott, 1977). Such programs are designed for treatment, for prevention, or for facilitating development over the life cycle. The last aim, informed by life-span developmental psychology, has been the focus of the Fatherhood Course. Although the aim of the course is to facilitate development, some very important therapeutic work occurs in the process.

The approach to fostering fathers' development in the course comes from (a) the person-centered literature on the characteristics of effective relationships in counseling (Rogers, 1951) and parenting (Gordon, 1970), which highlights the importance of empathy and genuineness; and (b) the cognitive social development literature, which describes how social perspective taking in parents develops through a sequence of stages (Newberger, 1977). Both literatures were used to design a program aimed at helping fathers learn to take their children's perspective with increasing degrees of empathic sensitivity, to become more aware and expressive of their own perspective (and, in particular, their feelings), and to balance their children's perspectives with their own on particular issues.

I usually coteach the course with a male advanced doctoral student in counseling psychology who has had training in family psychology and in leading groups. I am a father, and the coteacher may or may not be a father himself. It is essential that at least one of the leaders be a father, to establish credibility with the group.

The first half of the course focuses on listening and responding to children, beginning with a session on nonverbal parental behavior that can facilitate communication, such as staying at eye level with the child and maintaining an open body posture. In the next session, fathers learn about responding attentively to the content of a child's message. In this session, the men discover that they have been taking listening for granted. Most think of themselves as good listeners, but in the role-plays and homework exercises they discover that instead of listening they were thinking of their next response, telling themselves that they had heard this before, or listening to their own reaction to what their child was saying. In the third session, fathers learn to listen empathically to a child's feelings. This session builds on the previous one and reinforces the idea that children have minds of their own. For some men this is a revelation; like many parents, they think of their children as extensions of themselves. Once this idea sinks in, teaching fathers to tune in to their children's internal frames of reference becomes relatively straightforward. The approach taken is to teach the fathers the client-centered method of reflecting feelings. This session also covers topics of how children often express feelings through action and how to identify children's feelings in their nonverbal behavior. The fourth session is devoted to review, integration, and practice.

In the second half of the course, fathers work on speaking for themselves, beginning with a session on increasing their awareness of the thoughts and feelings that emerge while interacting with their children. This is one of the most difficult sessions, because, as I have noted, many men have been socialized to tune out most of their feelings. The leaders begin by developing a lexicon of the full spectrum of feelings. This is done by asking men what kinds of feelings they had in the previous week with their children. As a leader writes the reported feelings on the blackboard, a pattern emerges: The feelings are all in the irritation, anger, and rage part of the spectrum. This then becomes a consciousness-raising exercise, as the leaders ask if there is not a man among them who has felt fear, or sadness, or hurt, or vulnerability. Following some discussion, fathers are taught to tune in to their feelings through watching and discussing immediate playbacks of role-plays in which feelings were engendered. With leaders pointing out nonverbal cues and asking questions (e.g., "What were your feelings, Don, when you grimaced in that last segment?"), fathers learn how to access the ongoing flow of emotions within themselves.

Next comes a session on learning to express thoughts and feelings in a nondefensive manner and to catch certain feelings such as anger earlier in the sequence, when they are at the level of irritation and can be talked about. In the session on acceptance (the seventh), fathers examine their own personal sensitivities in order to become more accepting of their children's feelings and behavior. In this session, some men do significant work on deeply seated feelings about their own fathers and begin the process of coming to terms with their fathers' limitations. This sort of emotional work has the potential of interrupting the multigenerational transmission process, whereby parents pass on to their children the impairment that has resulted from limitations in their own upbringing. The final session is devoted to wrapping up loose ends and terminating; it includes a small graduation ceremony. It should be noted that most groups do not stop at this point. Some groups organize a larger get-together that includes the men's families, such as a Christmas party or a picnic. Others continue to meet, without the leaders, on a biweekly or monthly basis. Periodically, leaders would hear from one of these groups, through a phone call from one of its members, who would provide an update on the changes in the men's lives.

Group Dynamics

Structured groups provide benefits to participants by guiding them through a set of experiences that result in what Yalom (1985) has referred to as "interpersonal learning." For this to occur, these groups require a significant degree of group cohesiveness. Cohesiveness is facilitated in several ways. First, the homogeneity of the group (all male, all fathers) serves to create a feeling of "sameness." Second, the uniqueness of a group of men getting together to discuss fathering issues serves to set these men off as special, perhaps even as "pioneers." Third, a warm-up exercise conducted at the beginning of the first session (wherein participants pair off and interview each other to introduce one another to the group) provides each participant with the feeling that he has a "buddy" in the group. Fourth, the sharing of personal experiences that takes place in early sessions serves to bond the men together. This sharing often begins in the very first session. For example, I recall one man who, bottom lip quivering and struggling to maintain control, said: "You want to know why I'm here. I'll tell you why I'm here. I'm here so that my little son Jimmy doesn't grow up to feel as bad about me as I feel about my own dad." His revelation evoked a rich mixture of empathy and identification from the assembled fathers.

Interpersonal learning is achieved through the experiential aspects of the course: the homework exercises and the in-class role-plays. The in-class role-plays are drawn from the previous week's homework, in particular, from the interactional exercises between group members and their children. It is not uncommon that several fathers will have experienced difficulties in carrying out these exercises with their children, and it is also likely that these difficulties will reflect long-term problems in the father–child relationship. Selecting the role-plays in this manner serves several purposes. For one thing, difficulties are attended to so that hurdles are overcome and motivation remains high. It is possible in such short-term structured groups for unsatisfactory experiences with the homework to lead to discouragement, which can be expressed either in the form of dropping out of the group or participating at a shallow level. For another, by focusing on the longer term issues as they have emerged during the homework, the leaders foster interpersonal learning, but do so in a way that an optimal balance between safety and depth is achieved. Ostensibly we are working on the fathers' difficulties in learning the skills; but in the process, the fathers enact the difficulties in their relationships with their children, which then become available for modification. An additional benefit of focusing on such longer term issues is that it creates a climate of engagement and genuineness in the group.

Most meetings begin with a discussion of the previous week's homework, which sets the stage for the role-plays by providing fresh examples of difficult father–child interactions. The role-plays are videotaped and played back to the group, which provides a focus for discussion. Staging the meetings in this way serves to facilitate men's active participation.

Evaluation

Empirical evaluation of the Fatherhood Course has been favorable (Levant & Doyle, 1983). Experimental group fathers, their wives, and one of their children were compared to a control group before and after training on several paper-and-pencil measures. The evaluation found that training resulted in an improvement of fathers' communication skills. In addition, a complex pattern of findings on the Family Concept Test suggested that, as a result of training, fathers underwent a cognitive restructuring, changing their views of the ideal family. My interpretation of these findings is that the men took their families for granted before the course, but, as a result of the course, became more invested in their families and thus began to form views of how they would like their families to be.

When the Fatherhood Course was in the design stage, colleagues cautioned that if the program successfully helped fathers become more involved with their children, then it might threaten the mothers, who might then work to undercut the gains of the program. To assess such systemic effects, it was necessary to build in an evaluation of the mothers (Levant & Doyle, 1983). Happily, this revealed that experimental group mothers' sense of satisfaction with their families did not decline. Furthermore, posttest interviews with experimental group wives indicated that most felt closer to their husbands after the course. These wives mentioned such benefits as feeling more like a parental team, reductions in role overload, and improved communication.

Changes were also seen in children's perceptions of their fathers, with significantly more experimental than control group children perceiving positive changes in their relationships. A telling example was the change in one boy's pre- and postcourse Kinetic Family Drawings. Before the course began, he drew a picture of a roller coaster, with the tracks filling most of the page. At the top was a tiny little car. In the front seat was the boy, legs and arms akimbo; in the next seat was Mom; and then Dad; and in the last seat was his brother, who appeared to be falling out of the car. After the end of the course, the boy drew a picture of a spaceship running diagonally across the page, in which the cockpit filled about 40% of the page. Seated at the controls was Dad; next to him, with her own steering wheel, was Mom. At opposite sides, looking out the windows, were him and his brother. There is a systematic way to score these drawings, but I think anyone can see that this sequence of drawings represents a remarkable transformation of family structure and emotional climate.

SUMMARY

In this chapter, I first considered men's need for psychological services in the light of Brannon's (1985) definition of masculinity ideology, which includes four components: "no sissy stuff," "the big wheel," "the sturdy oak," and "give 'em hell." I have shown, using studies of men's physical and emotional health, that men are in great need of psychological services. However, because of the male-role-socialization process and traditional masculinity ideology, many men do not find it easy to seek out and use psychological services. This is due to such impediments as men's difficulty in admitting the existence of a problem, their difficulty in asking for help, their difficulty identifying and processing emotions, and their fear of intimacy.

Next, I considered the matter of whether it might be possible to design services that might be more accessible to men. To this end, I presented a psychoeducational structured group known as the Fatherhood Course, based on client-centered and cognitive social developmental principles, as an example of how psychological services might be developed that have as their aim improving their accessibility to men. The ensuing discussion revealed how the Fatherhood Course created group cohesion through its homogeneity, uniqueness, the fostering of a "buddy" system, and the sharing of personal experience. I also observed the manner in which such a group promotes interpersonal learning through the use of in-class role-plays of the previous week's assignment, with particular attention to those aspects of the course that the fathers found difficult. Ironically, although the Fatherhood Course was designed to be "experience near" to men, by focusing on the development of skills rather than the expression of feelings, its major effect has been to improve men's ability to be aware of and sensitive to feelings, both their own and those of their children.

REFERENCES

Brannon, R. (1985). A scale for measuring attitudes about masculinity. In A. Sargent (Ed.), *Beyond sex roles* (pp. 110–116). St. Paul, MN: West.

Drum, D. J., & Knott, J. E. (1977). *Structured groups for facilitating development: Acquiring life skills, resolving life themes, and making life transitions.* New York: Human Sciences Press.

Good, G. E., Dell, D. M., & Mintz, L. B. (1989). Male role and gender role conflict: Relations to help seeking in men. *Journal of Counseling Psychology*, 36, 295–300.

Gordon, T. (1970). *P.E.T.: Parent effectiveness training*. New York: Peter H. Wyden.

Guerney, B. G., Jr. (1977). *Relationship enhancement*. San Francisco: Jossey-Bass.

Harrison, J. (1978). Warning: The male role may be dangerous to your health. *Journal of Social Issues*, 34, 65–86.

Heppner, P. P., & Gonzales, D. S. (1987). Men counseling men. In M. Scher, M. Stevens, G. Good, & G. A. Eichenfield (Eds.), *Handbook of counseling and psychotherapy with men* (pp. 30–38). Newbury Park, CA: Sage.

Kessler, R., & McRae, J. (1981). Trends in the relationship between sex and psychological distress: 1957–1976. *American Sociological Review*, 46, 443–452.

Kessler, R., & McRae, J. (1983). Trends in the relationship between sex and attempted suicide. *Journal of Health and Social Behavior*, 24, 98–110.

L'Abate, L., & Weinstein, S. E. (1987). *Structured enrichment programs for couples and families*. New York: Brunner/Mazel.

Landers, S. (1989, December). In U.S., mental disorders affect 15 percent of adults. *APA Monitor*, p. 16.

Lazur, R. F., & Majors, R. (1995). Men of color: Ethnocultural variations of male gender role strain. In R. F. Levant & W. S. Pollack (Eds.), *A new psychology of men* (pp. 337–358). New York: Basic Books.

Levant, R. F. (Ed.). (1986). *Psychoeducational approaches to family therapy and counseling*. New York: Springer.

Levant, R. F. (1990). Psychological services designed for men: A psychoeducational approach. *Psychotherapy*, 27, 309–315.

Levant, R. F. (1992). Toward the reconstruction of masculinity. *Journal of Family Psychology*, 5, 379–402.

Levant, R. F., & Doyle, G. F. (1983). An evaluation of a parent education program for fathers of school-aged children. *Family Relations*, 32, 29–37.

Levant, R. F., Hirsch, L. S., Celentano, E., Cozza, T. M., Hill, S., MacEachern, M., Marty, N., & Schnedeker, J. (1992). The male role: An investigation of contemporary norms. *Journal of Mental Health Counseling*, 14, 325–337.

Levant, R. F., & Kelly, J. (1991). *Between father and child*. New York: Penguin.

Newberger, C. M. (1977). *Parental conceptions of children and child rearing: A structural–developmental analysis*. Unpublished doctoral dissertation, Harvard University, Cambridge, Massachusetts.

Pleck, J. H. (1995). The gender role strain paradigm: An update. In R. F. Levant & W. S. Pollack (Eds.), *A new psychology of men* (pp. 11–32). New York: Basic Books.

Rogers, C. R. (1951). *Client-centered therapy*. Boston: Houghton Mifflin.

Scher, M. (1979). On counseling men. *Personnel and Guidance Journal*, 58, 252–254.

Thompson, E. H., Jr., Grisanti, C., & Pleck, J. H. (1985). Attitudes toward the male role and their correlates. *Sex Roles, 13,* 413–427.

U.S. Bureau of the Census. (1990). *Statistical abstract of the United States: 1990.* Washington, DC: U.S. Government Printing Office.

Waldron, I., & Johnson, S. (1976). Why do women live longer than men? *Journal of Human Stress, 2,* 19–29.

Yalom, I. D. (1985). *Theory and practice of group psychotherapy* (3rd ed.) New York: Basic Books.

16

NONCUSTODIAL FATHERS IN GROUPS: MAINTAINING THE PARENTING BOND

ALEX S. HALL and KEVIN R. KELLY

There is both a science and an art to counseling noncustodial fathers in groups. A highly skilled psychotherapist is one who knows not only the current psychological literature about noncustodial fathers but also the skills involved in crafting cognitive, affective, and behavioral interventions that work for men in groups. The purpose of this chapter is threefold. First, we provide antecedent information about noncustodial fathers and group work, including a definition of the noncustodial father, the central issues for fathers and therapists involved in group work, and the importance of a therapist having a wide therapeutic base from which to draw to effectively help noncustodial fathers reconstruct their lives. Second, we review what the literature says about noncustodial fathers—who they are, what they want, and how therapists can help them adjust to their loss so that they can rebuild their lives. Third, we provide specific guidelines for group interventions, so that group therapists can increase both their range and their effectiveness in group work. In short, after reading this chapter, you will know the research, theory, and practice related to the art and the science of being a group therapist with noncustodial fathers; in addition, you will be able to teach the members of your group key skills involved in successful noncustodial fathering.

Through our own trial and error, we have become convinced that working with fathers in groups must be congruent, consistent, and cohesive not only for fathers to feel safe in a group context, but also for fathers to understand the value of counseling in their lives. Congruence is evident when therapists represent themselves as whole people working with whole men, in a way that accesses their own and their membership's expression of honest feelings, thoughts, and actions in the group context. Consistency is evident when therapists reliably respond in the same way to similar cognitive, affective, or behavioral stimuli from either a member of the group or the group itself, in a way that demonstrates equality, fairness, and justice. Cohesiveness is a reality when the group experiences safety in the strength of therapists who act with courage when responding to members' feelings, thoughts, and actions.

Congruence, consistency, and cohesiveness are best accomplished in the delivery of practice informed by theory. Taken together, theory-driven interventions establish immediately that the therapist is the expert, is in charge of structuring each session, and is powerful enough to handle the pain of the individual group member as well as the pain of the collective membership. In short, practice and theory along with art and science are partners in a therapeutic dance. It matters less whether practice or theory lead than that they remain partners.

COUNSELING NONCUSTODIAL FATHERS IN GROUPS

Because there is no knowledge without comparison, definitions of both *fathering* and *noncustodial fathering* are needed. There are two kinds of fathering: traditional and nontraditional. In addition, there are two ways to father: biologically and psychologically.

Traditional fathers include those fathers who are married, who are physically present and accessible to their children, and who are able to provide to their children immediate and direct fathering: nurturing, guiding, disciplining, and providing moral training. Nontraditional fathers are mirror images of traditional fathers; these are fathers who are not married, who live away from the family home for extended periods of time and are largely inaccessible to their children, and who are not able to directly nurture, guide, discipline, or morally instruct their children.

The difference between biological and psychological fathering is simple. In contrast to biological fathering—which is brief, easy, and generally involves a minimal emotional investment—psychological fathering is extended throughout the lifespan, is difficult to do well, and is characterized by peaks and valleys of immeasurable euphoria and anguish. So, a father can be biological only and traditional; biological only and nontraditional; biological, psychological, and traditional; or biological, psychological, and nontraditional.

This chapter is concerned with biological, psychological, and nontraditional fathers. In short, these are fathers without legal custodial rights to their children who choose to be psychologically invested in them over the lifespan, despite nearly insurmountable intrapersonal, interpersonal, familial, social, legal, and national policy obstacles.

Such noncustodial fathers face a central issue in their group therapy work, whereas their therapists face another. The central issue for noncustodial fathers is this: How can I continue to be a father to my children when I rarely see them and when my rights to parent them have not only been curtailed, but abrogated? Because noncustodial fathers have few institutional supports, the nonresidential parent–child subsystem can move rather quickly from a "vital" relationship involving recurring interaction and cohesiveness to an "empty shell" relationship involving erratic and infrequent interaction (Thompson & Gongla, 1983). Although the quality of the noncustodial parent–child relationship may improve initially (Earl & Lohmann, 1978; Earls & Siegel, 1980), this eventually decomposes when custody is not shared (Ahrons, 1980), when loss of everyday contact with family rituals and routines is either blocked by visitation restrictions or strained relations with the custodial parent (Weiss, 1979), or when the noncustodial parent was marginally involved with the family before the divorce (Keshet, 1980). Many noncustodial fathers gain strength from group therapy to continue visiting their children when they otherwise would give up in despair, because of the supportive presence of other noncustodial fathers who also experience difficulty adjusting to visitation schedules either because it means contact with a hostile exwife or because it is too painful to repeatedly say goodbye to their children. Simply learning that they are not alone in their struggle and pain is a curative factor derived from being in a group, known as *universality* (Yalom, 1975). Whatever the group can do to help members maintain contact with their children is directly therapeutic and responds to their most central concern: the physical and psychological loss of their children and the need to restore themselves to full fatherhood status, albeit on a part-time basis.

The central issue for group therapists working with noncustodial fathers is this: How can I best use the group to restore to disenfranchised fathers both the perception and the reality of fathering. Furthermore, how can I increase support for fathers so that I can meet their basic social parenting needs for power, competence, and affiliation? If fathers are to have authority over their children, then they need to have the power to parent so that they can influence their children. If fathers are to parent their children with authority, then they must achieve competence in basic parenting skills so that they can competently nurture and discipline their children. If fathers are to have the power to parent and the competence for parenting well, then they will need to have reasonable and reliable contact with their children so that they can have a close and enduring relationship. Essentially, when fathers have influence over their children (power), basic parenting skills (achievement), and meaningful contact with their children (affiliation), then they are able to meet their basic social needs as parents. The degree to which therapists can use the group context to meet these three basic social needs of fathers as parents is the measure of how successful group therapy can ultimately be.

Working in groups is highly complex, and working with noncustodial fathers in groups is highly emotional for members. It is therefore essential that group therapists have a thorough therapeutic base from which to draw in facilitating men's experience of healing and their reconstruction of a parenting identity associated with noncustodial fathering. A foundation for effective group work can be found in Yalom's (1975) 11 primary categories of curative factors:

1. instillation of hope
2. universality
3. imparting of information
4. altruism
5. corrective recapitulation of the primary family group
6. development of socializing techniques
7. imitative behavior
8. interpersonal learning
9. group cohesiveness
10. catharsis
11. existential factors.

These 11 categories of curative factors identify some of the most crucial aspects of the change process. They also serve as a rational basis for deriving tactics and strategies that help men help each other do two things: (a) stay psychologically involved as fathers and (b) restore their paternal power, competence, and affiliation with their children. The task of the group therapist is to make sure that these curative factors are evidenced within the group and that noncustodial fathers are actively involved in helping each other reconceptualize their feelings, thoughts, and actions so that they can become whole, effective, and involved fathers once again. In summary, when a therapist begins with a strong therapeutic base (by using, for example, Yalom's (1975) curative factors in group) and ensures the congruent, consistent, and cohesive orchestration of the group process so that members can help each other, then the task of demonstrating both the science and the art of effective group intervention is accomplished.

CHARACTERISTICS OF THE NONCUSTODIAL FATHER

In this section, we present a brief discussion of what the literature says about noncustodial fathers: who they are, what they want, and how therapists can help them adjust to their losses and rebuild their lives following divorce. It is imperative for the group therapist to know the characteristics, drives, and motives of noncustodial fathers, and how these change over time, so that group interventions will be relevant, timely, and effective.

Who Are They?

Research has clearly shown that, in general, noncustodial fathers are men who usually do not initiate divorce (Ahrons, 1994), love their children and want to spend time with them, and are at greater risk for illness and suicide than women.

Powerlessness

Men in general experience a greater sense of powerlessness and pain following divorce than do women and, therefore, have greater emotional difficulty adjusting to divorce than do women (McHenry & Price, 1990). Results of two studies have shown that husbands were more satisfied with marriage than their wives (J. B. Kelly, 1982) and initiated divorce less frequently than did their wives, at the rate of 35% versus 65%, respectively (Wallerstein & Blakeslee, 1990). Because men generally initiate separation less often than women do, they more often experience a loss of personal control over their lives (Petit & Bloom, 1984) and a sense of powerlessness because they are unable to prevent the leaving. Perhaps this is why some researchers have found that men experience more emotional difficulties than women, as evidenced by (a) greater emotional upheaval for men in the immediate postdivorce period (Albrecht, 1980); (b) higher admission rates for men into psychiatric facilities following divorce (Goetting, 1981); (c) greater severe depression rates among men, and (d) men's greater general distress.

Alienation

It is not just that men do not initiate divorce, but that they also may find their marriages over without ever knowing why. For example, in one study (Kitson & Sussman, 1982), 18% of divorced husbands, in comparison with 2% of divorced wives, said that they "were not sure what happened" when asked the reason for the divorce. In addition, because husbands benefit more from the socioemotional features of marriage, they may have more difficulty replacing what a wife and family provided; therefore, divorce creates expressive hardships unique to men (Reissman, 1990). Fathers must deal not only with the loss of their marriage and new financial strains but also with the loss of their children from their daily lives. As a result, noncustodial fathers have described themselves feeling "rootless" after divorce (Hetherington, Cox, & Cox, 1976). Again, the loss of their children is the most central issue for most newly divorced fathers.

Higher Rates of Suicide

Suicide rates are 5 times higher for divorced men than for married men and much higher for divorced men than for divorced women (Price & McHenry, 1988), and divorced men do not appear to be disproportionately economically disadvantaged following divorce. Therefore, it seems logical to conclude that there may be a relation between the emotional aspects of losing a marriage and children and higher suicide rates for men than for women following divorce. However, because women also lose their marriages, yet have lower suicide rates than men following divorce, it seems logical to conclude that, for some men, it is the loss of their children (more than the loss of their marriage) that may literally make a difference for men between life and death.

What Do They Want?

It seems, from the literature reviewed as well as from our clinical observations, that noncustodial fathers most want either shared custody of their children or liberal, unobstructed visitation access to their children when they are able to be with them. Along with this, fathers want to be informed and involved in all aspects of their children's lives, especially those that concern their children's education. Where shared custody is desired but not granted, fathers want help managing their feelings related to the loss of their children; these feelings include helplessness, alienation, anger, and despair. In addition, fathers may want a less conflicted relationship with their former spouse. Finally, fathers want improved knowledge and competencies related to parenting their children.

Shared Custody

Although a presumption of maternal preference in custody decisions remains potent and permeates custody proceedings (Schutz, Dixon, Lindenberger, & Ruther, 1989), fathers are gaining some rights regarding their continued meaningful involvement with their children, as evidenced by a 180% increase in single fathers from 1970 to 1983, in comparison with a 105% increase in single mothers. This indicates that the court system is changing and that fathers are beginning to be considered viable parents in custodial court rulings (Greif, 1985).

Help Managing Feelings of Loss

Two group therapy strategies can minimize the loss experienced by noncustodial fathers. The first is to assist fathers in identifying the full extent of legal options available to them to ensure shared parenting. When all chances of shared parenting options are exhausted, then fathers can be taught how to negotiate maximum legal contact with their children. This requires therapists to work proactively for noncustodial fathers. There are at least three important areas of impact that therapists with a proactive stance can explore with noncustodial fathers to help generate increased parenting opportunities and options. A proactive stance includes the use of specific interventions that examine fathers' gender role socialization history, perceptions of power and control in the legal process, and beliefs about factors related to children's adjustment following divorce (Tillitski, 1992). Specifically, noncustodial fathers who have not requested joint custody need to challenge the socialization messages that may have convinced them that children are better parented by their mothers as well as the myth that mother custody is the best arrangement. Next, noncustodial fathers need to know their legal rights, so that their rights to parent their children are maximally used and safeguarded. Finally, noncustodial fathers need to be taught to visualize the ideal custody arrangement for their individual situations. For example, if joint physical custody is a legal possibility, then what are the perceived obstacles in a man's life, and what must be done to overcome them? If joint physical custody is not a viable option, then informal ways for increasing fathers' involvement in parenting must be explored. Therapists can recommend to their group members the following options for enlarging their parenting role within the typical parameters of the noncustodial father: (a) volunteering as room parent in the child's school; (b) assisting the mother by taking the child to the doctor; (c) assisting the mother by offering to stay home with the sick child; (d) requesting additional visitation under the legal rule of "reasonable times and places"; (e) signing the child up for specialty lessons in such areas as music, drama, art, or dance during regularly scheduled visitation times; (f) hiring a tutor, again, during regularly scheduled visitation times; (g) attending parent conferences separately or along with the former spouse; (h) attending special programs at school in which the child has a part; and (i) requesting extra copies of information related to school activities, functions, or grade reports.

Improved Relationships With Former Spouses

Feminist theory has argued against sharing custody of children even though empirical studies have determined that "joint custody at its best is superior to sole custody at its best" (Luepnitz, 1986, p. 11), because of the argument that frequent child transfers give fathers excessive opportunities to harm their former wives. Contrary to this speculative, wild overstatement from one feminist faction regarding the motives of noncustodial fathers, we have found from clinical observation that fathers want a positive interaction with former spouses during transfer situations and are puzzled at the level of hostility directed toward them when such transfers are made. Spousal abuse is gender equivalent, not only during marriage but also during courtship (K. R. Kelly & Hall, 1992; Strauss & Gelles, 1986); men, more often than women, marry for love (Cancian, 1986); men fall in love more rapidly and fall out of love more slowly than women (Hill, Rubin, & Poplau, 1976); and, although women initiate breakups more often than men, when men do initiate a breakup they more often tend to remain friends (Hill et al., 1976). It therefore seems that men are more motivated toward positive relationships with former spouses than toward conflictual relationships. Poor communication during marriages predicts both divorce and conflictual parenting relations following divorce. Poor communication competence on the part of both parents results in an inability to defuse heated verbal interchanges when they occur, to solve unexpected problems, to negotiate changes in the visitation schedule, to establish backup plans and maintain a flexible approach when unexpected events occur, and to resolve interpersonal conflicts between parenting partners and between parents and children. For these reasons, there is a high value in teaching communication skills to noncustodial fathers. It is particularly valuable to divide into smaller groups for role-play practice of anticipated visitation transfer conversations between fathers and mothers and of anticipated conversations with children related to visitation.

Knowledge and Competencies in Parenting

There are three factors related to paternal involvement after divorce: satisfaction with parenting, fathers' perceptions of their influence on their children, and fathers' geographic proximity to their children (McHenry, Price, Fine, & Serovich, 1992). Noncustodial fathers experience varying degrees of access to their children following divorce; contact with their children may vary from every day, to several times a month, to very occasionally, to not at all. For example, a statewide survey in Wisconsin found that 33% of noncustodial fathers saw their children only once a week and that over 40% saw their children less than once a month, or never (Seltzer, Schaeffer, & Charng, 1989). Parenting competence diminishes following divorce for several months to a year or more, not only for noncustodial fathers but for custodial mothers as well (Wallerstein & Blakeslee, 1990).

It has become apparent from our clinical observations that fathers want their visiting time to be a positive experience. As a result, there can be a tendency for noncustodial fathers to discipline less at a time when there is a need to discipline more. So, to increase single noncustodial fathers' physical involvement with their children, satisfaction with parenting, and influence on their children, therapists must ensure that fathers develop and practice minimal competencies in parenting, such as those recommended by Stover and Hope (1993) and outlined below. These minimal parenting competencies will reduce the stress that children experience in the first 2 years following their parents' divorce. Each can be learned and role-played in the group context.

1. Fathers can learn to minimize disruption in the lives of their children, especially disruption in the relationship between the child and the father.

2. Fathers can establish specific, consistent, reliable times for seeing their children and then follow through without fail. The loss of reliable contact with either parent has both short-term and long-term negative effects on children.

3. Fathers can encourage close relationships with other adult relatives as a way of increasing the support base for children during a time when parents are caught up in conflict.

4. Fathers can provide as much economic security for their children as possible.

5. Fathers can work to develop and sustain a low-stress, low-conflict divorce and postdivorce relationship with the other parent.

6. Fathers can maintain a well-structured, organized life for their children. In addition, fathers can work with the former spouse to set and maintain common expectations for chores, bedtimes, quality of schoolwork, and methods of discipline that are similar to what children had before the divorce.

GUIDELINES FOR GROUP INTERVENTIONS

We next look at global guidelines for group interventions that we have used with noncustodial fathers that seem highly promising, in the areas of therapeutic structure, content, and outcomes.

Structure

It is important to provide the group with a rough outline of what should typically be accomplished in each session and to briefly discuss how the tasks for each session are expected to be accomplished. In our group work with noncustodial fathers, we limit the first, closed group to a life of thirteen 3-hour sessions. Session 1 is for testing and screening, and Session 2 is for introduction of the group membership, the cotherapists, group work in general, and group work with noncustodial fathers in particular. Sessions 3, 4, and 5 deal with power issues, whereas Sessions 6, 7, and 8 are reserved for achievement of personal and parenting talents. Sessions 9, 10, and 11 address affiliation needs and skills, and Session 12 is a review and practice session. Finally, Session 13 is reserved for termination rituals.

Each of the 13 sessions is divided into 3 therapeutic hours, which are used in different ways. The first hour is for cognitive interventions, the second hour is for affective interventions, and the third hour is for behavioral practice.

Every session is led by two therapists, one male and one female. Prior to every session, the therapists determine who will act as the primary versus secondary therapist. The primary therapist is responsible for structuring the sessions and the activities in a typical session; the secondary therapist is charged with the task of observing and commenting on process variables evidenced during that session. In other words, the primary therapist is responsible for task leadership, and the secondary therapist is responsible for relationship leadership. Cotherapist role responsibilities alternate after every session.

Content

As stated above, each 3-hour session is divided into three 1-hour sections, in which cognitive work, affective work, and, finally, behavioral work is accomplished. This is because we have found that affective work is more productive after men have been introduced to didactic information and shown a way to conceptualize their experience that is consistent with psychological theory. For example, once men learn the facts about non-custodial fathers (from handouts cogently and succinctly identifying the main themes they face) and know how to structure their thinking (e.g., from handouts on rational emotive thinking, describing how it is not the event but one's perceptions of the event that direct both feelings and behavior), they are able to articulate their feelings in ways that leave them in control of the therapeutic process, rather than feeling overpowered by it. In this way, more than catharsis is accomplished. Instead of simply venting during the affective component of group therapy, these men are informed about their emotions in a way that gives them some choice about how to respond to their feelings and their life situations.

When noncustodial fathers learn information that is relevant to them as a group, they are less likely to feel as alienated and as powerless and, therefore, are less likely to feel as depressed. As a result, they are more likely to behave in ways that can build a healthier, reorganized family unit.

The keys to deciding what information to give noncustodial fathers are revealed by answering the following questions:

1. Is the information relevant to these fathers?
2. Is the information able to guide and direct their behavior toward healthy outcomes for the entire family system?
3. Is the information useful for legal interventions for continued involvement with their children?
4. Is the information useful for increasing their parenting skills?
5. Is the information a guide for building closer relationships with their children?
6. Is the information helpful in building a dual-parent relationship with the former spouse?
7. Is the information suggestive of ways to increase their sense of power, achievement, and affiliation as parents?

Outcomes

Therapeutic outcomes must match the needs of the men attending the group session. As we discussed earlier, noncustodial fathers have their own specific concerns and desires. From empirical research, it is known that noncustodial fathers (a) experience powerlessness, (b) become alienated, (c) have higher rates of suicide than custodial parents, (d) want shared custody of children, (e) need help in managing feelings of loss, (f) desire improved relationships with former spouses, and (g) want knowledge and competencies in parenting skills. Knowing this, therapists must work with noncustodial fathers in ways that directly address these specific concerns and desires. Every group intervention must therefore be designed so that these issues are the central focus. Also, every group counseling effort must culminate in improved knowledge, awareness of feeling, and an increased behavioral repertoire for noncustodial fathers; otherwise, such efforts are likely to be perceived by men as a waste of time. In addition, every group counseling session must result in an enhanced sense of power, achievement, and affiliation if the social needs of these noncustodial fathers are to be met. Finally, every group session must end with each noncustodial father feeling more like a parent, as opposed to less than a parent.

These outcomes are difficult to achieve. However, when attention in therapy is directed to the whole person (i.e., to cognitive, affective, and behavioral components of personality and behavior), when the focus of therapy is to develop awareness of choices that are available to noncustodial fathers (by emphasizing their own control over their thoughts, feelings, and behaviors), and when the ultimate goal of therapy is to help fathers find ways to increase involvement with their children in spite of situational constraints, then these outcomes are very likely to be achieved. We are confident that if therapists circumscribe their tasks to legally, emotionally, and behaviorally empower noncustodial fathers within the full context of the law, fathers can adapt and can cope with their new status as parents.

CONCLUSION

There is no one way to do group work with noncustodial fathers. There is no one school of psychology that is superior in helping fathers regain influence over their children and maintain viable relationships with them when their visitation rights are severely curtailed. Regardless of whether the clinician is operating from a perspective that is predominantly psychodynamic, behavioral, humanistic, cognitive, or integrative, three aspects of the person must be developed: the affective, the cognitive, and the behavioral. Furthermore, three areas of the social needs of noncustodial fathers must be met: the need for power (influence over the lives of their children), the need for achievement (learning to be competent parents), and the need for affiliation (maintaining a viable parenting bond with their children). It is our hope that the information and suggestions contained within this chapter will enable therapists working in groups with noncustodial fathers to help their clients become fathers once again.

REFERENCES

Ahrons, C. R. (1980). Redefining the divorced family: A conceptual framework. *Social Work, 25,* 437–441.

Ahrons, C. R. (1994). *The good divorce.* New York: Harper Collins.

Albrecht, S. L. (1980). Reactions and adjustments to divorce: Differences in the experiences of males and females. *Family Relations, 29,* 59–68.

Cancian, F. M. (1986). The feminization of love. *Signs: Journal of Women in Culture and Society, 11,* 692–709.

Earl, L., & Lohmann, N. (1978). Absent fathers and Black male children. *Social Work, 28,* 413–415.

Earls, F., & Siegel, B. (1980). Precocious fathers. *American Journal of Orthopsychiatry, 50,* 469–480.

Goetting, A. (1981). Divorce outcome research. *Journal of Family Issues, 2,* 213–222.

Greif, G. (1985). Single fathers rearing children. *Journal of Marriage and the Family, 47,* 185–191.

Hetherington, E. M., Cox, M., & Cox, R. (1976). Divorced fathers. *The Family Coordinator, 25,* 417–428.

Hill, C. T., Rubin, Z., & Poplau, L. A. (1976). Breakups before marriage: The end of 103 affairs. *Journal of Social Issues, 32,* 147–168.

Kelly, J. B. (1982). Divorce: The adult perspective. In A. S. Skolnick & J. H. Skolnick (Eds.), *Family in transition* (5th ed., pp. 304–337). Boston: Little, Brown.

Kelly, K. R., & Hall, A. S. (1992). Toward a developmental model for counseling men. *Journal of Mental Health Counseling, 14,* 257–273.

Keshet, J. (1980). From separation to stepfamily. *Journal of Family Issues, 1,* 517–532.

Kitson, G., & Sussman, M. (1982). Marital complaints, demographic characteristics, and symptoms of mental distress in divorce. *Journal of Marriage and the Family, 44,* 87–101.

Luepnitz, D. A. (1986). A comparison of maternal, paternal, and joint custody: Understanding the varieties of post-divorce family life. *Journal of Divorce, 9*(3), 1–12.

McHenry, P. C., & Price, S. J. (1990). Divorce: Are men at risk? In D. Moore & F. Leafgren (Eds.), *Problem-solving strategies and interventions for men in conflict* (pp. 95–112). Alexandria, VA: American Association for Counseling and Development.

McHenry, P. C., Price, S. J., Fine, M. A., & Serovich, J. (1992). Predictors of single, noncustodial fathers' physical involvement with their children. *Journal of Genetic Psychology, 153,* 305–319.

Petit, E., & Bloom, B. (1984). Whose decision was it? The effects of initiator status on adjustment of marital disruption. *Journal of Marriage and the Family, 46,* 587–595.

Price, S. J., & McHenry, P. C. (1988). *Divorce.* Newbury Park, CA: Sage.

Reissman, C. K. (1990). *Divorce talk: Women and men make sense of personal relationships.* New Brunswick, NJ: Rutgers University Press.

Schutz, B. M., Dixon, E. B., Lindenberger, J. C., & Ruther, N. J. (1989). *Solomon's sword: A practical guide to conducting child custody evaluations.* San Francisco: Jossey-Bass.

Seltzer, J. A., Schaeffer, N. C., & Charng, H. (1989). Family ties after divorce: The relationship between visiting and paying child support. *Journal of Marriage and the Family, 51,* 1013–1032.

Stover, R. G., & Hope, C. A. (1993). *Marriage, family, and intimate relationships.* Fort Worth, TX: Harcourt, Brace & Jovanovich.

Strauss, M., & Gelles, R. (1986). Societal change and change in family violence from 1975 to 1985 as revealed by two national surveys. *Journal of Marriage and the Family, 48,* 465–479.

Thompson, E., Jr., & Gongla, P. (1983). Single-parent families: In the mainstream of American society. In E. Macklin & R. Rubin (Eds.), *Contemporary families and alternative life-styles.* Beverly Hills, CA: Sage.

Tillitski, C. J. (1992). Fathers and child custody: Issues, trends, and implications for counseling. *Journal of Mental Health Counseling, 14*, 351–361.

Wallerstein, J. S., & Blakeslee, S. (1990). *Second chances: Men, women, and children a decade after divorce.* New York: Ticknor and Fields.

Weiss, R. (1979). *Going it alone.* New York: Basic Books.

Yalom, I. D. (1975). *The theory and practice of group psychotherapy* (2nd ed.). New York: Basic Books.

17

GAY FATHERS IN GROUPS

ROBERT L. BARRET

In the past 2 decades, both the professional and popular literatures have noted an increased interest in the role of the father. Formerly restricted to being breadwinners, men are learning that they can find much satisfaction as fathers, and it is not uncommon to see fathers awarded primary custody when a divorce occurs (Robinson & Barret, 1986). The newest development in this trend is the many gay men who are now choosing to be more active and more visible as fathers. The old notion that being gay and a father was impossible has changed along with the increased visibility and diversity of gay communities. And today, there is a growing realization that gay men make good fathers too (Barret & Robinson, 1990).

In the past, most of the gay fathers who participated in research studies were men who had become fathers through marriage. They had their children primarily while living heterosexual lifestyles and either continued to parent through joint-custody arrangements or by remaining in the closet. Recently, more and more gay men who have never married are choosing to become fathers. As gay communities mature in major metropolitan areas, the notion that men who have exclusively self-identified as gay can be effective parents is becoming more widespread. Some gay men have served as adoptive parents or foster parents to babies with HIV. Also, as social service workers become more familiar with gay men's parenting skills and the stable home lives they provide, adoption of healthy children has be-

257

come more of a choice. Private adoption, financial support of a surrogate mother, and cooperative parenting with lesbians who want to be parents provide other ways for gay men to become parents.

Still, what is known about these fathers and their families comes primarily from anecdotal reports. Finding gay fathers who are willing to participate in research is a formidable task. Most of these men keep a low profile out of fear that too much exposure will result in loss of contact with their children, either because of court orders or because the extended family may be uninformed about the richness and depth in the gay community and thus discourage father participation in child rearing.

Because the court system may be uneasy about such arrangements, many formerly married gay fathers tend to keep a low profile and do not let their sexual orientation become known. Distrust of the courts is a frequently cited reason for not openly living as gay once active parenting is chosen.

In this chapter, I present an overview of the research findings about gay fathers in general and then review what is known about their participation in groups. Data from research studies are complemented with information I have gleaned from discussions with gay fathers in clinical settings in California and North Carolina.

PROFILE OF GAY FATHERS

Gay fathers are like any other fathers. They may be young or old, professional or blue-collar, healthy or terminally ill, emotionally stable or unstable, financially secure or on welfare, or in committed relationships or single. Gay fathers across the country clearly have strong commitments to their children and, like other parents, organize their lives to maximize their children's well-being. However, unlike heterosexual fathers, they have the additional challenge of protecting their children from the prevailing discrimination and prejudice directed toward homosexuals in America, to minimize its negative impact on their children.

Like the question of what percentage of the general population is homosexual, exact figures on the numbers of gay fathers do not exist, and projections are just guesses. Previous estimates of the percentage of the total population that is gay or lesbian appear to have been exaggerated, but gay men and lesbians are a visible community in most large cities. Harry (1983) has suggested that 20% of the homosexual population is composed of heterosexually married gay men. Earlier, Bell and Weinberg (1978) posited that approximately half of such marriages result in children. It has been estimated that over 1 million gay fathers live in the United States and Canada (Bozett, 1984).

Interest in fathering is growing in gay communities throughout the nation. With access to more of the activities of mainstream America, it is not surprising that many gay men choose fathering as one way to participate more fully in the whole range of family activities that typically accompany adulthood. Unfortunately, controversy is a frequent companion of the creative ways that gay men find to experience fatherhood. Heterosexual former spouses, social service agencies, and the legal system are not altogether comfortable with the idea of gay men as parents. More conservative Christian groups actually target gay parents as a major threat to family life and the "American way." The growing body of research indicating that gay men can serve adequately in the fathering role is not widely reported in the media (Barret & Robinson, 1990).

Often, formerly married gay men turn to the courts to gain access to their children. In some of these cases, custody is awarded to men reluctantly when it is clear that the natural mother is an inadequate parent. Although the court may be uneasy about awarding custody to a gay father, it is more common today for sole or joint custody to be awarded to these fathers, many of whom are openly gay. In addition, some legal systems are placing homosexual children who have been abandoned by their natural parents with gay foster parents. The hope in these instances is that the gay parents will provide a positive role model for gay youth (Harry, 1983).

More conservative groups that are threatened by the growing gay rights movement serve as watchdogs in the legal system and challenge these changes by depicting the gay rights movement as antifamily. In Oregon, Idaho, and Colorado, recent advances in antidiscrimination legislation are being challenged in the courts or before the electorate. The Virginia Supreme Court recently awarded custody of one lesbian's son to his grandmother. Many state legislatures are passing laws that forbid adoption by gay men. Often the prejudice inherent in these laws is buried through the use of language that bans adoption by single people who live with a "significant other." Conversely, other states and communities are enacting antidiscrimination legislation that can be used to block the courts from preventing visitation and custody solely on the basis of sexual orientation. Still, the acquisition of political power by more conservative groups threatens to create an even harsher environment for gay and lesbian parents.

Learning about gay fathers in groups necessitates learning about the research reported on their children. In reading the section below, one must keep in mind that although the studies I discuss generally involved few subjects, they represent the empirical research that exists.

CHILDREN OF GAY FATHERS

The children of gay fathers are like children from all families: Some are academically talented, some struggle to get through school, some are model students, and some are constantly in trouble. In thinking about the children of gay fathers, it is essential to recognize that many of them have experienced the divorce of their parents, others have grown up in single-parent homes, and still others have been caught in a major cross fire between parents, grandparents, and, perhaps, the community over the appropriateness of gay men serving in the father role. Much of the distress that one might see in the child living with a gay father may, in fact, be the result of divorce or other family tensions. Legitimate concerns about households headed by gay fathers include (a) the developmental impact on the child of the knowledge that his or her father is gay, (b) reasonable worries by fathers about the timing of disclosing their orientation to children, and (c) fathers' need to create sensitivity to the ways children will experience society's generally negative attitudes about homosexuality.

To understand the behavior of gay fathers in groups more fully, it is also important to know something about their experiences as fathers. Issues that typically come up when groups of gay fathers are formed include coming out to children, parenting and coparenting styles, and dealing with the outside world.

Coming out to children is usually an emotion-laden event for gay fathers. The disclosure of one's homosexuality creates anxiety about rejection, fear of hurting or damaging children's self-esteem, and grieving over the loss of innocence. Some gay fathers never accomplish this task and never disclose, citing legal and emotional reasons (Bozett, 1980, 1981; Humphreys, 1979; Spada, 1979). Recent publications have reported on the intricacies of this question (Corley, 1990). Those who never disclose often lead deeply conflicted lives and present parenting styles that are characterized by psychological distance (Miller, 1979). Those who do disclose to their children do so because of their desire to be more of a whole person as a father. As they try to merge their gayness with the father role, these men encounter a different kind of conflict. Deciding how open to be about their sexual relationships and how much to expose children to the gay community are frequently mentioned issues (Robinson & Barret, 1986).

Fathers in group therapy often report that the first concern they have about disclosing their homosexuality is for the well-being and healthy adjustment of their children. Many gay fathers seek the help of counselors or specialists in child development as they decide when to tell and how to tell about their homosexuality. Fathers and children have both reported feeling closer after disclosure about the father's sexual orientation (Bozett, 1980; Miller, 1979). Bigner and Bozett (1990) studied the reasons that gay fathers give for coming out to their children. Among the most cited items were wanting their children to know them as they are, being aware that children will usually discover for themselves if there is frequent contact, and the presence of a male partner in the home.

The parenting styles of gay fathers are not markedly different from those of other single fathers. Research has revealed, however, that gay fathers try to create a more stable home environment and more positive relationships with their children than traditional heterosexual parents (Bigner & Jacobsen, 1989a; Bozett, 1989). Studies also show that gay parents are both like and unlike their heterosexual counterparts (Barret & Robinson, 1990; Bigner & Jacobsen, 1989b; Scallen, 1981). The same is true for their children (Bozett, 1980; Lewis, 1980; Miller, 1979). Most researchers conclude that being homosexual is compatible with effective parenting and is not usually a major issue in parental relationships with children (Harris & Turner, 1986).

Issues of parenting when there is a gay coparent can likewise be complex. Decisions about where to live, how much time to spend away from children, displays of affection, and other situations common to all parents create stress for gay fathers as well.

Dealing with the outside world is a task that gay fathers and their children must master. Gay families live in social systems that are generally uncomfortable with homosexuality and certainly do not overtly support gay parenting. One reality for gay fathers is figuring out how to successfully interact with people in children's schools, after-school activities, parent–teacher associations, churches, and social networks. Many gay fathers see no choice other than to continue living relatively closeted lives (Bozett, 1988; Miller, 1979). Others, fearing the damage that exposure may bring to their children or possible custody battles arising from their homosexuality, live rigidly controlled lives and may never develop a gay identity. Those who are more open about their gayness struggle to help their children develop a positive attitude about homosexuality while cautioning them about the dangers of disclosure to teachers and friends. Teaching their children to manage these two tasks is a major challenge for gay fathers (Morin & Schultz, 1978; Riddle, 1978). Accomplishing this despite having virtually no visible role models frequently leaves these fathers and children feeling extremely isolated.

Some children limit or attempt to control the content of interactions with their gay fathers. One father we talked with reported that he had offered to introduce his teenage daughter to some of his gay friends in the hope that she would see how normal they are. Her reply was a curt, "Dad, that will never happen!" Another father told of trying to reconcile with his son and being rebuffed by the comment "I don't want to hear anything about your personal life. I can't handle it."

Children of gay fathers do sometimes worry that their own sexual orientation may become contaminated by their fathers' homosexuality. Either they or their friends may begin to question if they are gay as well. Those children who do disclose their father's sexual orientation report being called "queer" and "fag." Naturally, this concern is greatest during their teenage years (Riddle & Arguelles, 1981). Obviously, the children of gay fathers need to carefully consider the consequences of disclosing their father's homosexuality. Keeping this aspect of their lives secret can have the same negative impact on their development as isolation, alienation, and compartmentalization does for gay men.

Although public understanding of gay communities continues to expand and the general public is more comfortable interacting with gay people, there are still significant barriers for gay fathers to overcome before their fathering role will be widely accepted. Two major issues—both myths—are most frequently cited as reasons to bar gay men from becoming fathers. First, many believe that gay fathers will "recruit" their children into homosexuality. Second, it is thought that gay men, being unable to control their sexual energy, will inevitably sexually molest their sons (Barret & Robinson, 1990).

HOMOSEXUAL INCEST AND RECRUITMENT

Recent interest in incest has led to the speculation that it is not uncommon for children to be sexually abused by their parents. As often as this issue is discussed in the media, the point is rarely made that most of the reports involved identified heterosexual parents who molest their own and others' children. Incest research that focuses on gay fathers is virtually absent from the literature, and police records rarely indicate that an incest perpetrator is gay. This may be because few gay fathers have been studied at all, because few gay fathers have molested their children, or because the incest taboo is so strong among gay men that they do not speak of their experiences. However, it is generally believed that the vast number of child molesters identify as heterosexual, because virtually no cases of child sexual abuse have been reported involving gay parents and their lovers (DeFrancis, 1976; Gebhard, Gagnon, Pomeroy, & Christenson, 1965; Geiser, 1979; Richardson, 1981). Although the evidence is scant, at this time it appears that children living with heterosexual parents are more at risk for incest than children living with gay fathers.

The concerns that gay fathers will pass along their homosexuality or molest their children suggest the general negative attitude that exists toward homosexuality—namely, that gay men are less sexually reliable with their children than heterosexual parents and that homosexuality would be a "bad" thing to "catch." Gay fathers usually point to their own heterosexual parents to refute both of these concerns. One gay father in my group said, "I get so tired of responding to questions from people who recently find out I am a gay father. They almost always ask if I think my son is gay. They would never ask a nongay father if he thought his son was straight!"

Of course, although there are no data to suggest that children with gay parents are at risk for incest or for "catching" homosexuality, reports will ultimately surface where this does, in fact, happen. The challenge is for professionals and the public to understand that a few cases do not make a statement about the parenting ability of all gay fathers, just as cases of incest among heterosexual families do not indict all heterosexual fathers.

GAY FATHERS IN GROUPS

A gay father seeking help in a group setting has a formidable challenge. Outside large urban areas, gay men live much more in the shadows, and gay fathers are virtually invisible. However, mental health professionals with gay clients will become familiar with both the diversity and resources that exist within most gay communities. Finding creative ways to reach out to these men will be essential in order to create effective groups.

The situation is different in large cities. For example, the San Francisco *Bay Times*, a newspaper with a gay, lesbian, and bisexual readership, advertises opportunities for coparenting as well as the following support groups for gay fathers: Gay/Lesbian Parenting Group, Prospective Queer Parents, Southbay Gay Parents, and Adoption Support Groups. There is even an organization for children of gay parents that reports more than 1,500 members. As more and more services are made available to assist gay fathers, it is probable that these men will become more visible in schools, churches, and the other social service agencies with which parents routinely interact.

Few psychotherapists offer therapy groups exclusively for gay fathers, although in working with gay couples who have children in the home, discussions about the unique stresses of gay fathering are common. I worked with one gay couple who had moved to the suburbs to normalize the experiences of one partner's children, and the stepfather had this to say:

> I really am having a hard time living in the 'burbs. I miss the energy and challenge of the city and especially the connections with my gay friends. We've worked it out so that I spend one weekend night each week in the city. This helps, but I feel like I've given up lots of my identity because I love and support Jeff and his kids.

There is an international support organization that offers the opportunity for gay fathers to mingle with each other and with their lesbian counterparts. The Gay and Lesbian Parents Coalition International,[1] based in Washington, DC, offers many services to gay parents. This organization encourages the establishment of gay parent groups in cities throughout the

[1]The Gay and Lesbian Parents Coalition International can be contacted at P.O. Box 50360, Washington, DC 20091 (202-583-8029).

world. Through their newsletter, they offer tips on legal issues, updates on federal legislation, and information about the growing literature on gay parenting. They also hold annual meetings in such places as Disney World, where gay parents can bring their children and have fun while reducing some of the isolation that typifies this kind of parenting.

Although the behavior of gay fathers in support groups has not been researched, anecdotal reports indicate that they find emotional support as they discuss their parenting duties with others who face similar challenges. They also routinely plan social activities that include their children. The groups provide a place for the exchange of information on ways to interact with school officials, tap legal resources, and manage family reunions. These gay fathers are also seen with their children marching in gay pride celebrations around the country. When identifying themselves as gay fathers like this, it is not unusual for onlookers to cheer and encourage them.

The psychologist who wants to reach out to gay fathers has several opportunities. First, one must become aware of internalized negative attitudes about gay men and gay fathers. Homophobia and the negativity associated with it is present to some extent in everyone. Being aware of one's own biases and prejudices will help to minimize their negative impact. It is also important to learn to recognize and celebrate significant events that occur in gay clients' lives. Silence in the face of these events may be interpreted as disapproval (McHenry & Johnson, 1993). Second, learning about the local gay community is essential. Calling a gay and lesbian switchboard or placing ads in gay newspapers are other ways to gain access to this population. Offering training on the mental health needs of gay men to the staffs of mental hospitals and other mental health groups also helps one gain a presence. Basically, gay fathers are unlikely to show up for group experiences led by someone whose pro-gay stance is not obvious.

Groups organized around themes might attract more participants. Topics such as improving parenting skills, dealing with schools and churches, the impact of children on gay relationships, and discipline from a gay perspective are likely to be of interest. Of course, discussions of disclosing homosexuality to one's children are popular, as are discussions about integrating children into gay community activities. Many gay men live in isolation and rarely have an opportunity to discuss issues like these. Psychoeducational or structured groups can be the first step toward starting therapy groups for gay fathers. Announcing a gay fathering group with advertisements in the gay media and through flyers sent to other mental health professionals are ways to get the word out.

Leading a therapy or support group with gay men is not unlike leading any other group. It is important to conduct a screening interview and to obtain a verbal or written commitment from members to attend at least a limited number of sessions. Anticipating that there may be other therapeutic issues that complicate parenting is one thing to watch for in screening. Special attention might also be paid to the issue of sexual relationships between group members.

In the beginning stages of the group there is likely to be a sense of euphoria as these men find some companionship in the difficult and often isolated experience of being gay fathers. For many men, parenting complicates dating, and discussion of this topic is common. Others simply need to hear other gay men talk about their fathering experiences. One gay father told a group,

> Until I came to this group, I had refused to have any relationship with my daughter. I thought she was better off without me and that I should just leave her alone. Now I see her each week, and she is coming to spend the night at my place soon. I never knew that there was a way for me to be gay and a father at the same time.

What will happen in a group for gay fathers is that many men will find role models for the first time. They have wondered how to handle family events, such as graduations, weddings, and funerals. They have struggled to try to learn more effective ways to parent. One father talked about going to see a photographer for his daughter's wedding.

> We sat and talked about the kinds of pictures she wanted, and the man was very helpful. As we were getting ready to leave he looked up and asked if there was anything unusual about our family that he needed to know. My daughter just rolled her eyes, and I quickly told him that there was much more than we would go into at this time but that we will fill him in later. This gave my daughter and me the chance to talk about some of the things that we will have to do to make sure that the presence of my lover and my exwife don't take too much attention from my daughter. My other daughter is a lesbian, and she will be there with her girl friend. I have been wondering how we will handle all of this and have not been able to find a book for gay fathers planning a wedding. Later when I went to my group, I learned of a couple of people I could call who had already been through this. Their suggestions helped make Laura's wedding a success.

Group leaders need to understand the importance of networking and passing along information. Time in the group must be devoted to these activities.

It is also probable that group members will want to plan outside social activities that include their children. Having an opportunity to introduce their kids to others who have gay fathers helps to strengthen the entire family system. The therapist or support group leader may be invited to attend these events, as well as other family celebrations.

Certain exercises can be useful in groups composed of gay fathers, such as sentence stems, value clarifications, and other experiences that help develop insight into family dynamics. Other techniques, such as role-plays, setting aside time to identify major issues, learning different communication styles, and prepackaged parenting programs based on particular theoretical orientations and adjusted for gay fathers will help. Publishing one's experience as a leader of a group for gay fathers will also help other professionals who are interested in this work. Therapists should remind themselves that they are working on a frontier where little has been done; this will enable them to relate more fully to the experience of group members. The therapist's struggle to find resources mirrors the struggle of the group. The kind of creativity that one models will encourage them.

Just as HIV pervades the lives of most gay men, it also is a frequently ignored issue for gay fathers. Some gay fathers give up their sex lives entirely out of the fear that they will get sick and orphan or lose their children. It is therefore important for them to learn ways to deal with staying HIV negative. It is critical for HIV-positive gay fathers to figure out ways to integrate their health issues with fathering. One gay father told a group, "I am sending my son away without telling him I am sick. He will be better off creating a relationship with new parents now rather than trying to do that after I am dead." It was only with the encouragement of other HIV-positive gay fathers that this man was able to talk to his son about his illness so that they could plan the future together.

Basically, these support activities provide a sense of hope as gay fathers become aware that others are successfully blending their fathering duties with their sexual orientation. This is apparent from these statements made by one father:

> I had about given up on ever having my family together again. But, after hearing other fathers talk about their own family reunions, I began to work toward my own. One of my daughters told me that having the whole family together was just too hard. But when I told her it was hard for all of us and we needed her to be a part of the family once again, she agreed to come. We only had an afternoon together, but for my exwife and me, it was the beginning of learning how to coparent and cograndparent. My mother was there, my children and son-in-law, and my grandson. I never thought this would happen, and I now know that there is a way for us to be a family again. We may be different from other families, but that's no reason for us to give up. I would have never done this without having seen that others have done it too.

In anticipating the future, it is clear that gay fathers will be participating in more groups. Research studies on gay fathers are expanding as doctoral studies seek unexplored populations for their dissertations. Once the media publicizes models of gay parenting, more and more gay men will be investigating parenting as a viable option. Finally, as the numbers grow, the demand for services for this population of fathers will likewise expand.

Gay fathering groups will become more commonplace, and mental health professionals will see more of these men among their clientele.

Learning about the gay, lesbian, and bisexual community will certainly become a more essential task for psychologists. Supporting research studies of this population will likewise result in improved services. On the most basic level, simply starting a support or therapy group for gay fathers will help reduce their isolation and improve their parenting ability. Although little may be known about the experience of gay fathers in groups, it is clear that a need exists for psychologists to extend a hand to this hard-to-reach but richly deserving population.

REFERENCES

Barret, R., & Robinson, B. (1990). *Gay fathers*. New York: Free Press.

Bell, A., & Weinberg, M. (1978). *Homosexualities: A study of diversity among men and women*. New York: Simon & Schuster.

Bigner, J., & Bozett, F. (1990). Parenting by gay fathers. *Marriage and Family Review, 18*, 163–172.

Bigner, J., & Jacobsen, R. (1989a). Parenting behaviors of homosexual and heterosexual fathers. *Journal of Homosexuality, 18*, 173–186.

Bigner, J., & Jacobsen, R. (1989b). The value of children to gay and heterosexual fathers. *Journal of Homosexuality, 18*, 163–172.

Bozett, F. (1980). Gay fathers: How and why they disclose their homosexuality to their children. *Family Relations: Journal of Applied Family and Child Studies, 29*, 173–179.

Bozett, F. (1981). Gay fathers: Evolution of the gay father identity. *American Journal of Orthopsychiatry, 51*, 552–559.

Bozett, F. (1984). Parenting concerns of gay fathers. *Topics in Clinical Nursing, 6*, 60–71.

Bozett, F. (1988). Social control of identity of gay fathers. *Western Journal of Nursing Research, 10*, 550–565.

Bozett, F. (1989). Gay fathers: A review of the literature. *Journal of Homosexuality, 18*, 137–162.

Corley, R. (1990). *The final closet: The gay parent's guide to coming out to their children*. Miami, FL: Editech Press.

DeFrancis, V. (1976). *Protecting the child victim of sex crimes committed by adults*. Denver, CO: American Humane Society, Children's Division.

Gebhard, P., Gagnon, J., Pomeroy, W., & Christenson, C. (1965). *Sex offenders: An analysis of types*. New York: Harper & Row.

Geiser, R. (1979). *Hidden victims: The sexual abuse of children*. Boston: Beacon Press.

Harris, M., & Turner, P. (1986). Gay and lesbian parents. *Journal of Homosexuality, 18*, 101–113.

Harry, J. (1983). Gay male and lesbian relationships. In E. Macklin & R. Rubin (Eds.), *Contemporary families and alternative lifestyles* (pp. 216–234). Beverly Hills, CA: Sage.

Humphreys, L. (1979). *Tearoom trade.* Chicago: Aldine.

Lewis, K. (1980). Children of lesbians: Their point of view. *Social Work, 25,* 200.

McHenry, S. S., & Johnson, J. W. (1993). Homophobia in the therapist and gay or lesbian client: Conscious and unconscious collusions in self-hate. *Psychotherapy, 30,* 141–151.

Miller, B. (1979, October). Gay fathers and their children. *Family Coordinator, 28,* 544–551.

Morin, S., & Schultz, S. (1978). The gay movement and the rights of children. *Journal of Social Issues, 34,* 137–148.

Richardson, D. (1981). Lesbian mothers. In J. Hart & D. Richardson (Eds.), *The theory and practice of homosexuality* (pp. 139–158). London: Routledge & Kegan Paul.

Riddle, D. (1978). Relating to children: Gays as role models. *Journal of Social Issues, 34,* 38–58.

Riddle, D., & Arguelles, M. (1981). Children of gay parents: Homophobia's victims. In I. Stuart & L. Abt (Eds.), *Children of separation and divorce* (pp. 174–197). New York: Van Nostrand Reinhold.

Robinson, B., & Barret, R. (1986). *The developing father.* New York: Guilford Press.

Scallen, R. (1981). An investigation of paternal attitudes and behaviors in homosexual and heterosexual fathers. (Doctoral dissertation, California School of Professional Psychology, San Diego, 1981). *Dissertation Abstracts International, 42,* 3809B.

Spada, J. (1979). *The Spada report.* New York: Signet Books.

18

TOGETHER IN GROUP THERAPY: FATHERS AND THEIR ADOLESCENT SONS

BARRY G. GINSBERG

It is common to find in therapy with men that their experiences with their fathers are dotted with dissatisfactions and yearnings for what has been missed in this significant relationship. In the adolescent years, the father–son relationship becomes particularly acute. A struggle for separation and individuation becomes important developmentally, yet the adolescent wants to know that his father is there for him and accepts him for the emerging adult that he is becoming. At the same time, the father—struggling with his own midlife change, years of variable involvement with his son, and difficulties with expressing feelings and closeness—is also looking for acceptance from his adolescent son. He is confronting what it means to him to be a "good" father. What happens to adolescents in the father–son relationship remains significant throughout the balance of the son's (and father's) life. Any efforts to enhance this relationship during the dynamic period of adolescence are significant. In this chapter, I describe a group therapy program for adolescent sons and their fathers to help them relate to each other more intimately, with greater expression of feeling and increased acceptance of each other.

In the psychological literature, the male role as father has largely been ignored or given significantly less importance in the development of children. According to Parke (1981), fathers have not been forgotten by accident but have been purposely ignored because of psychologists' beliefs

269

that they were less important than mothers in influencing children's development. Psychologists have only recently acknowledged the importance of fathers in the lives of their children and made attempts to understand the value of this role. Even now, the emphasis seems to be more on the effects of a father's absence, psychological or physical, rather than on how a father's presence affects the family. L. B. Feldman (1990) has suggested that the most common dysfunctional pattern of father–child relationships is the disengagement or absence of the father. Osherson (1986) has stated, "we know that the boy is searching deeply throughout his childhood, beginning around age 3, for a masculine model on which to build his sense of self" (p. 3). Osherson has further suggested that perceptions of fathers arise from distortion and myths, so that males grow into men with a conflicted sense of masculinity that is based on the experience of their fathers as rejecting, incompetent, or absent. A complicating factor of this is that within the last 20 years or more, men's gender role relationships have changed dramatically, making it even harder for them to understand what it means to be a man and further confounding their relationships with their own fathers and sons.

Werrbach, Grotevant, and Cooper (1992) identified a decrease of connectedness expressed in the father–son relationship in adolescence, noting that this may result from adolescents' increasing efforts to differentiate and develop a separate identity. Other studies of adolescent identity development (Cooper & Grotevant, 1987; Grotevant & Cooper, 1985) have suggested that mutuality expressed from father to son is important. They hypothesized that decreased connectedness during adolescence may simply reflect adolescents' overall emotional distance.

Campbell and Snow (1992) found that men with more constricted emotions and more conflict between work and family relations were less satisfied in their marriages. Men with more constricted emotions had less family cohesiveness as well. It is likely that this decrease of connectedness and increased emotional distance exacerbates the difficulties that fathers and adolescent sons have with each other.

It is interesting how the role of father and the father's involvement with his children seem to have changed dramatically in recent years. A survey conducted by *Child* magazine in March 1993 (Levine, 1993) found that more than half of the fathers considered themselves to be "well-rounded" and willing to help with child care, whereas more than one third of both men and women described their own fathers as "backseat" dads.

Levant, Slattery, and Loiselle (1987) indicated that fathers they studied were spending more time involved in housework and child care, tended to spend more interactive time with their children, and were more aware of their parental role. McBride (1991) found that fathers increased their amount of involvement, accessibility, and responsibility in child care after completing an education program. The fathers who went through this program also reported feeling more competent in their roles. As Lamb (1993) has stated:

> psychological research shows that male and female individuals can be equivalently responsive and sensitive to their young (see Lamb, Pleck, Charnon, & Levine, 1987, for a review). Behavioral differences between mothers and fathers seem to represent responses to societal pressures and expectations, not the product of endogenous differences and responsiveness to infants. (Lamb, 1993, p. 230)

Grossman, Pollack, and Golding (1988) found that it was the quality rather than the quantity of fathering that was associated with children's psychological well-being. Therefore, a program designed to help improve the father–adolescent relationship seems particularly pertinent today.

COMMUNICATION IN THE FATHER–SON RELATIONSHIP

Communication within the context of the family appears to be important during the adolescent years, particularly because it affects adolescent identity formation and role-taking ability (Barnes & Olson, 1985; Cooper, Grotevant, Moore, & Condon, 1982; Grotevant & Cooper, 1983). According to Allen, Hauser, Bell, and O'Connor (1994), "there is growing evidence that a state of 'autonomous–relatedness,' a term coined by John Bowlby, is an optimal outcome for the adolescent–parent relationship" (p. 179). The concept of autonomous–relatedness holds that achieving autonomy and maintaining a positive relationship should occur concurrently within the parent–adolescent relationship.

It is interesting that, in the findings noted above, male adolescents' self-development was enhanced by fathers challenging aspects of their development and communicating that to their sons, but this only occurred when the father also modeled autonomous–relatedness for his son. Levi, Stierlin, and Savard (1972) wrote of a "loving fight," in which father and son engage openly about their differences with mutual respect. This leads to greater integrity for the father and increasing identity for the son.

In their book *The New Masculinity*, Fanning and McKay (1993) have suggested that it is the avoidance of certain factors that fosters distance in the father–son relationship. I remember a poignant moment in which a father was sharing with his son his own past experience with his father. He said,

> You know my father never told me he loved me, and one time we were in a bar having a beer together (and this was long after I had

grown up), and I asked him, "Why couldn't you ever tell me that you loved me?" And he said, "men don't talk like that to each other."

FATHERS AND ADOLESCENT SONS IN GROUP THERAPY

A review of the psychological literature reveals little information about studies on working with fathers and adolescent sons in group together. Bowman (1993) developed an intergenerational experience that involved men with their fathers and sons. He planned a three-generational men's retreat that focused on enrichment rather than therapy. Bowman found that the retreat had fostered improved communication and sharing among family members. Werdinger (1981), described the benefit of using a simulated father–son group composed of men in their 20s and 30s combined with an older group of men in their 40s and 50s, to facilitate differentiation. He found that the 1 1/2-hour sessions did assist the younger men in improving their individuation.

Raubolt and Rachman (1980) raised the idea that, just as the male adolescent comes into his own, his father is experiencing midlife transitions. Florsheim and Gutmann (1992) suggested that as the father loses his instrumental functioning within the family and his feeling of being responsible for or having some control over his children he loses the sense of his identity as father. Raubolt and Rachman (1980) engaged fathers through an educational group seminar. Among other methods, they used role-playing of father–son interactions and meditation techniques and videotape examples to help fathers learn how to communicate more effectively with their adolescent sons. The fathers were open and shared many of their perspectives with each other. There was a dramatic decrease in school absence, fewer reported incidents of disruptive classroom behavior, and improved academic performance in sons following the program. The fathers all indicated that their relationship with their sons had improved.

Levant (1990) has developed the Fatherhood Course, an educational program for men that he elaborates on in chapter 15 of this book. Levant and Doyle (1983) have empirically evaluated the Fatherhood Course and found that training resulted in improvement of fathers' communication skills and that fathers changed their views of the ideal family. Informally, they also found that fathers became more involved with their families. Empirical investigation also revealed positive changes in children's perceptions of their fathers.

Burnett (1992) developed a structured 15-session program to improve the parent–adolescent relationship. He led multifamily groups for parents and adolescents in inpatient and outpatient settings, as well as in juvenile court diversion programs. Families preferred the structured, hands-on skill training to generalized, unstructured discussion groups. Because this was a multifamily group approach, both fathers and their sons attended these sessions. Burnett emphasized that having the adolescents and parents participating together was a positive feature of his program. He quoted one adolescent participant: "We didn't have to 'role-play' what we would say to our parents if they were there. They were there! And we got to practice face to face with them!" (1992, p. vi). He also quoted a parent as follows: "Just having our son in the same room practicing the activities with us made the whole program seem more like a 'family' activity, not an 'us vs. him' situation" (1992, p. vi).

I developed a group therapy program specifically for adolescent boys and their fathers (see Ginsberg, 1971, 1977) that has been elaborated on over the years (see Grando, 1972; Grando & Ginsberg, 1976). Called the Parent–Adolescent Relationship Development Program (PARD), this program is directed toward helping all parents and adolescents come together to learn more effective ways of relating to each other, although it was originally designed for sons and their fathers. Its objective is to help foster a relationship of mutual trust, acceptance, and understanding. Under these conditions, optimum levels of differentiation and independence can be achieved in both father and son without sacrificing the intimacy of their relationship.

PARD

PARD originated in the late 1960s along with the evolving approach that later was called relationship enhancement therapy (Guerney, 1977, 1984). Relationship enhancement therapy integrates major principles and practices from psychodynamic, behavioral, experiential, interpersonal, and relationship systems schools of psychotherapy. What makes relationship enhancement therapy unique is its emphasis on skill learning as therapy. With its structured, systematic, and "time-designated" components, it has continued to be a viable approach to therapy.

The first relationship enhancement therapy program was filial therapy (Guerney & Stover, 1971). In this approach, parents are taught client-centered play therapy skills as well as how to conduct weekly play sessions at home. The outcomes of this approach have been significant; for example, there was a low dropout rate, parents learned to be more accepting of their children, and children reduced aggressive and problem behaviors (see Guerney & Stover, 1971; Oxman, 1971; Sensue, 1981; Sywulak, 1977). This was followed by the development of a program for couples, called *conjugal therapy*, and, eventually, by relationship enhancement therapy with couples (Ely, Guerney, & Stover, 1973; Guerney, 1977). The outcomes of this approach have been significant as well (see Collins, 1977; Guerney, 1977; Rappaport, 1976), have been equal to or better than comparable approaches (Brock & Joanning, 1983; Jessee & Guerney, 1981; Wieman, 1973), and have been significant even in comparison with therapists' preferred approaches (Ross, Baker, & Guerney, 1985).

From these origins, a framework emerged for a program for adolescent sons and their fathers that would reduce their negative responses to each other and enable them to become more open and accepting in their relationship. It was thought that if they could learn new constructive relationship skills to replace or change the habits undermining the way they related to each other, then they would have greater opportunities to strengthen their bond with each other while accepting their increasing differentiation.

Basic Format

There are some essential attitudes or beliefs that are important to the relationship enhancement approach. The first is an emphasis on the importance of primary and significant relationships in the development of self-mastery, coping, and personal satisfaction. Another principle concerns the relationship between judgment and defensiveness. A context of nonjudgment is essential for the establishment of the trust necessary for participants to feel safe and secure, to be open to one another, and to respect one another's separateness. A third attitude is that emotions or feelings must motivate all behavior and that any expression or acknowledgment that occurs in a relationship must include expression of the feeling, so that the meaning of the expression or acknowledgment can be understood.

Five essential skills form the basis of relationship enhancement therapies: speaking (expressive skill), listening (receptive and empathic skill), conversive (interactive and engagement skill), generalization, and maintenance. Expressive skill has two major purposes. The first is to be able to recognize and understand one's own motivations and meaning; this has to do with understanding one's self. The second is to be able to skillfully and efficiently convey one's understanding of oneself, one's motivations, and one's meanings to others, so that others will better understand and respond. To do this, a person must "own" the meaning of his or her statements. This means that the person acknowledges and accepts that what he or she is saying comes from a unique perspective and does not necessarily represent a shared meaning with another person. Acknowledging the feeling that pertains to the expression conveys the motivation for it to oneself and the other. This is true "owning."

The second of the three essential skills is listening, or receptive or empathic skills. A person learns to take in and be receptive to another person's meaning without confounding it with his or her own perspective and judgment. Acknowledging the feeling of the other person fosters self-concept and trust between listener and speaker. Learning how to do this helps create an environment of safety, security, and trust.

The third skill, conversive skill, often can be the most difficult. In mastering this skill, one must learn to negotiate a relationship and its conversation by determining when to be a listener and when to be a speaker. In addition, this skill includes the ability to acknowledge the meaning of the relationship in the process of the conversation. In essence, the new speaker must state how he or she feels in order to know the other person's feeling.

A Vignette

An example of dialogue drawn from a father–son group will help to clarify this process.

> Father (as speaker): A lot of things that you can do, son, are important. It'll make you a better individual as you grow up. So the activities at home could make you feel important. That's why I'm *concerned* that you're not doing the chores at home.
>
> Son (as listener): Okay, you think that things are really *important* growing up. You're not *happy* with me about my chores.
>
> Father (as speaker): Yes, and *I don't like* having to list the chores. I'd rather see you accept them without my having to spell them out day in and day out. That would make me feel *good*.
>
> Son (as listener): So you think that, uh, that I . . . it would be more helpful to you if I got into the habit of doing these things; *you'd like* that.
>
> Father (as speaker): Yes. Switch [meaning for them to switch speaker–listener roles].
>
> Son (now as speaker): Well, I just can't see that much importance in it. It *frustrates* me that you put so much importance on chores. I'd rather do outside things more.
>
> Father (as listener): So you're *frustrated* 'cause you like to do outside things more.
>
> Son (as speaker): Yeah!

Obviously, this is the beginning of a dialogue between father and son that deals with intimacy and differentiation. Talking this way can over time lead to improved conversation and a better relationship.

The fourth and fifth skills, generalization and maintenance, respectively, are related. They promote transferring relationship skills to everyday use. From the beginning of the program, father–son pairs are encouraged to begin the generalization. At first, this is done by having fathers and sons establish a special time every week with one another, then trying that time to see if it can be kept every week, and then beginning to practice at home. Toward the end of the program, strategies to keep the special time and practice of the relationship skills are encouraged. The therapist guides discussion to help clients use the skills in more informal and spontaneous ways. The longer they can continue applying the skills, the more long lasting the effects of this program will be.

Fathers and Adolescent Sons

In PARD, fathers and adolescent sons are brought together in a group made up of three or four pairs. The program is systematic and structured around skill learning and practice and then generalized to participants' everyday lives.

The program is time-limited; it runs for ten 2-hour sessions. The first session is introductory, didactic, and dynamic. After an initial introduction and sharing by the participants, the therapist provides a didactic presentation of the skills to be learned and their importance in the relationship between father and son and leads a discussion of them. Next, the therapist models each of the three basic modes. After some discussion, the therapist suggests a homework assignment. It is important to establish some kind of home practice or task to act as a bridge between one session and the next.

In the second session, fathers and sons begin to practice their skills, using issues that both have identified at the beginning of the session. It is helpful, if possible, to get an adolescent to volunteer to be the first speaker, and it is usually useful to ask another father to double (role-play) for that boy's natural father. This helps to take some of the anxiety and defensiveness away from the beginning of this interaction. With the therapist's guidance and support, participants try to practice one of the more positive issues in the son's relationship with the father. After a short practice of the three basic skills, each participant can begin to practice talking directly with his own father or son. An alternative way to begin practicing these communication relationship skills is for only the sons to role-play the fathers' roles with one another and only the fathers to role-play the sons' parts with one another. Both of these methods of practice help to build a greater empathy and understanding of the other person's feelings and experience. This helps to reduce some initial defensiveness, discomfort, and anxiety. Practice continues in the third, fourth, and fifth sessions, with the therapist making sure that every father–son dyad has a chance to practice with each other under supervision. While each father–son pair has a turn to practice, the other fathers and sons participate as facilitators or, sometimes, take the place of one of the participants if defensiveness is high. This is when a therapist's skill is most important. It is vital that the therapist be patient and sensitive to the quick defensiveness and discomfort that emerges when fathers and sons work together. Modeling receptivity and empathy during these times is essential. Accepting an adolescent's initial unwillingness to talk is very important. Role-playing as the adolescent (doubling) in a conversation with his father can be helpful, as is having other sons or fathers role-play.

Power is a very important variable present in work with adolescent sons and their fathers. S. S. Feldman and Gehring (1988) found that adolescents perceive parental power as gradually declining over time, particularly with their fathers. The father's own concern for his declining power (Raubolt & Rachman, 1980) fosters a climate in which either son or father could be threatened by the perceived loss of power. Nevertheless, they care about each other, need to be accepted by each other, and wish for a closer relationship with improved communication (Grando & Ginsberg, 1976). It is particularly important that the therapist use various skills, role-playing, and doubling to keep these underlying positive issues apparent and reduce the defensiveness brought about by perceived threats of loss of power. It is a satisfying experience to observe the engagement between father and son when the father learns to accept the son's perspective and the son spontaneously acknowledges the father's importance to him and respect for him.

Homework

Homework (although the use of this word might not be received positively by the adolescents) is important for several reasons: (a) It provides continuity from session to session, (b) it helps clients take responsibility for their own change, and (c) it promotes generalization of skills. Beginning from the 1st session, fathers and sons are asked to meet with each other at an appointed time at home and do something together. This might be to play a game, to go over something important with one another, or anything else that might help to establish a regular time together, which eventually could be used for skill practice at home. They are also asked to complete a home practice session report (Guerney, 1977, pp. 378–379), to be handed in at the next session. By the 6th session, they are asked to practice their skills at home. They receive a handout that helps remind them of the skills they have been practicing and includes other suggestions that help create a safe context for their structured conversations. Each father–son pair is then asked to tape-record the practice and bring the audiotapes back for feedback and supervision. In the 7th session, the emphasis is on listening to the home practices and role-playing practice to identify a particular issue or problem and help participants learn how to avoid such problems. In the 10th session, the emphasis is on how to continue to practice, generalize, and maintain the skills after the program is over. Each father–son pair identifies their own way of going about this. At the end of the program, the group is encouraged to meet for a session in 3 to 6 months as a review and reinforcement.

ISSUES TO CONSIDER IN FATHER–SON GROUP WORK

There is already a great deal of insecurity, anxiety, and discomfort in the relationship between adolescent sons and their fathers. One aspect that makes leading such groups so sensitive is the difficulty that the members have communicating with one another, particularly in openly expressing feelings. It is much more comfortable for fathers and adolescent sons to do something physical or active together, such as going to a ball game. These too, are important aspects of the relationship, but all too often these activities do not allow for the open communication of feelings. Because of fathers' and sons' stages of development, there is a great deal of vulnerability on both parts in the potential change that communication will foster in their relationship. Men often will express this vulnerability through defensiveness and anger. This certainly is a component in the father–adolescent son relationship. Furthermore, bringing fathers and adolescent sons together may initially exacerbate the sense of vulnerability in each. Intimacy conveyed through love and affection is also something that is hard to express. These are some aspects that acknowledge the sensitivity of bringing fathers and adolescent sons together. Skillful therapist leadership and involvement is thus essential to the success of any father–son program. Engaging fathers and sons in a structured and time-limited group can help ease some of this discomfort. Furthermore, because this is an educational group focused on skill learning, it may be more acceptable for fathers and sons to participate and may produce less anxiety than a less structured and more dynamic approach.

Therapist's Skills

In a structured, systematic, and time-limited group, such as that used in the PARD program, the therapist balances didactic and dynamic elements into an integrated whole (Andronico, Fidler, Guerney, & Guerney, 1967). In the early sessions, the therapist is very involved, providing a great deal of structuring, didactic, and dynamic efforts to create a secure context for fathers and sons to learn and practice their communication and relationship skills. The primary purpose of the therapist's skill is to help keep them motivated to continue practicing and applying the skills that they are learning. The therapist uses a number of methods to motivate participants: administering, structuring, prompting, modeling, reinforcing, and troubleshooting (see Guerney, 1984).

Research Outcomes

In evaluations of the PARD program (Ginsberg, 1971, 1977), the outcomes were quite positive. Both fathers and sons showed improvement in patterns of general communication. The quality of the relationship improved and sons and fathers evidenced significant improvement in self-concept. They also were shown to improve in empathy, acceptance, awareness, and acknowledgment of their own feelings as well as in making less judgmental expressions.

A program for mothers and their adolescent daughters that was fashioned after the PARD program was found to show similar outcomes (Guerney, Coufal, & Vogelsong, 1981). Guerney et al. compared a PARD format with traditional discussion-based group treatment and a no-treatment control group. The PARD-format groups showed improvement in empathic and expressive skills, in general communication skills, and in the quality of the general relationship between daughter and mother. These gains were maintained at a 6-month follow-up.

The PARD group format has also been followed for a whole family approach, in which all family members participate (Ginsberg, in press). This has been quite effective as well and particularly useful for clinical referrals and when there are not enough people to constitute a formal PARD group.

SUMMARY

Working with adolescent sons and their fathers together in small groups can be difficult and frustrating. Yet, offering a program that is structured, systematic, and time designated can begin to open up this sensitive relationship at a crucial time. Although the original program was developed and researched in the 1970s, sons and their fathers still seem to suffer from the same pressures in the 1990s that spurred this development. Autonomous–relatedness (Allen et al., 1994) continues to operate today in the father–adolescent son relationship. Pertinent to this is the ability of the father to challenge aspects of his son's development while acknowledging acceptance of the son's developing autonomy. This is best accomplished when the son continues to convey how important his father is to him. Bringing father and son together in a PARD group offers an excellent opportunity to accomplish this.

The stresses between fathers and sons do not vanish after participation in the PARD program and learning the skills. Accomplishments of the program are that father and son remain engaged, continue to express the positive feelings in their relationship, and are able to communicate a respectful acceptance of each other's perspective. As a result, they can feel good about each other and their relationship while continuing to be differentiated and autonomous. Bringing fathers and sons together in a group to learn communication and relationship skills provides a context that enhances their relationship and improves their self-concepts.

REFERENCES

Allen, J. P., Hauser, S. T., Bell, K. L., & O'Connor, T. G. (1994). Longitudinal assessment of autonomy and relatedness in adolescent–family interactions as predictions of adolescent ego development and self-esteem. *Child Development*, 65, 179–194.

Andronico, M. P., Fidler, J., Guerney, B. G., Jr., & Guerney, L. (1967). The combination of didactic and dynamic elements in filial therapy. *International Journal of Group Psychotherapy*, 17, 10–17.

Barnes, H. L., & Olson, D. H. (1985). Parent–adolescent communication and the circumplex model. *Child Development*, 56, 438–447.

Bowman, T. (1993). The father–son project. *Families in Society: The Journal of Contemporary Human Services*, 74, 22–27.

Brock, G. W., & Joanning, H. (1983). A comparison of the relationship enhancement program and the Minnesota couple communication program. *Journal of Marital and Family Therapy*, 9, 413–421.

Burnett, D. J. (1992). Improving parent–adolescent relationships: Learning activities for parents and adolescents participant workshop, Muncie, IN. [Available from Accelerated Development, Inc., 300 Kilgore Avenue, Muncie, Indiana 47304-4896.]

Campbell, J. L., & Snow, B. M. (1992). Gender role conflict and family environment as predictors of marital satisfaction. *Journal of Family Psychology*, 6, 84–87.

Collins, J. D. (1977). Experimental evaluation of a six-month conjugal therapy and relationship enhancement program. In B. G. Guerney, Jr. (Ed.), *Relationship enhancement: Skill-training programs for therapy, problem prevention, and enrichment* (pp. 192–226). San Francisco: Jossey-Bass.

Cooper, C. R., & Grotevant, H. D. (1987). Gender issues in the interface of family experience in adolescence, friendship and dating identity. *Journal of Youth and Adolescence*, 16, 247–264.

Cooper, C. R., Grotevant, H. D., Moore, M. S., & Condon, S. M. (1982, August). Family support and conflict: Both foster adolescent identity and role taking. Paper presented at the 90th Annual Convention of the American Psychological Association, Washington, DC.

Ely, A. L., Guerney, B. G., Jr., & Stover, L. (1973). Efficacy of the training phase of conjugal therapy. *Psychotherapy: Theory, Research, and Practice*, 10, 201–207.

Fanning, P., & McKay, M. (1993). Being a man: A guide to the new masculinity. Oakland, CA: New Harbinger Publications.

Feldman, L. B. (1990). Fathers and fathering. In R. L. Meth & R. S. Pasick (Eds.), *Men in therapy: The challenge of change* (pp. 220–256). New York: Guilford Press.

Feldman, S. S., & Gehring, T. M. (1988). Changing perceptions of family cohesion and power across adolescence. *Child Development*, 59, 1034–1045.

Florsheim, P., & Gutmann, D. (1992). Mourning the loss of "self as father." A longitudinal study of fatherhood among the Druze. *Psychiatry: Interpersonal and Biological Processes, 55,* 160–176.

Ginsberg, B. G. (1971). *Parent–adolescent relationship development: A therapeutic and preventative mental health program.* Unpublished doctoral dissertation, Pennsylvania State University.

Ginsberg, B. G. (1977). Parent–adolescent relationship development program. In B. G. Guerney, Jr. (Ed.), *Relationship enhancement: Skill training programs for therapy, problem prevention, and enrichment* (pp. 227–267). San Francisco: Jossey-Bass.

Ginsberg, B. G. (in press). *Relationship enhancement family therapy.* New York: Wiley.

Grando, R. (1972). *Parent–adolescent relationship development program: Relationships among pretraining variables, role performance and improvement.* Unpublished doctoral dissertation, Pennsylvania State University.

Grando, R., & Ginsberg, B. G. (1976). Communication in the father–son relationship: The parent–adolescent relationship development program. *The Family Coordinator,* 465–473.

Grossman, F. K., Pollack, W. S., & Golding, E. (1988). Fathers and children: Predicting the quantity and quality of fathering. *Developmental Psychology, 24,* 82–91.

Grotevant, H. D., & Cooper, C. R. (1983). The role of family communication patterns in adolescent identity and role taking. Paper presented at the meeting of the Society for Research in Child Development, Detroit, MI.

Grotevant, H. D., & Cooper, C. R. (1985). Patterns of interaction in family relationships and the development of identity exploration in adolescents. *Child Development, 56,* 415–428.

Guerney, B. G., Jr. (1977). *Relationship enhancement: Skill training programs for therapy, problem prevention, and enrichment.* San Francisco: Jossey-Bass.

Guerney, B. G., Jr. (1984). Relationship enhancement therapy and training. In D. Larson (Ed.), *Teaching psychological skills: Models for giving psychology away* (pp. 171–206). Monterey, CA: Brooks/Cole.

Guerney, B. G., Jr., Coufal, J., & Vogelsong, E. (1981). Relationship enhancement versus a traditional approach to a therapeutic/preventative/enrichment parent–adolescent program. *Journal of Consulting and Clinical Psychology, 49,* 927–939.

Guerney, B. G., Jr., & Stover, L. (1971). *Filial therapy: Final report on MH 1826401.* Unpublished manuscript, Pennsylvania State University, College of Human Development.

Jessee, R., & Guerney, B. G., Jr. (1981). A comparison of gestalt and relationship enhancement treatments with married couples. *American Journal of Family Therapy, 9,* 31–41.

Lamb, M. E. (1993). Biological determinism redux: Comment on Silverstein (1993). *Journal of Family Psychology, 7,* 301–304.

Lamb, M. E., Pleck, J., Charnon, E., & Levine, J. (1987). A biosocial perspective on paternal behavior and involvement. In J. Lancaster, J. Altman, A. Rossi, & L. R. Sherrod (Eds.), *Parenting across the lifespan: Biosocial dimensions* (pp. 111–142). New York: Aldine de Gruyter.

Levant, R. F. (1990). Psychological services designed for men: A psychoeducational approach. *Psychotherapy, 27,* 309–315.

Levant, R. F., & Doyle, G. F. (1983). An evaluation of a parent education program for fathers of school aged children. *Family Relations, 32,* 29–37.

Levant, R. F., Slattery, S. C., & Loiselle, J. E. (1987). Fathers' involvement in housework and childcare with school age daughters. *Family Relations, 36,* 152–157.

Levi, L. D., Stierlin, H., & Savard, R. J. (1972). Fathers and sons: The interlocking crisis of integrity and identity. *Psychiatry, 35,* 48–56.

Levine, J. A. (1993). Is your husband a good enough father? *Child, 8,* 96–99.

McBride, B. (1991). Parent education and support programs for fathers: Outcome effects of paternal involvement. *Early Child Development and Care, 67,* 73–85.

Osherson, S. (1986). *Finding our fathers: The unfinished business of manhood.* New York: Free Press.

Oxman, L. (1971). *The effectiveness of filial therapy: A controlled study.* Unpublished doctoral dissertation, Rutgers University.

Parke, R. D. (1981). *Fathers.* Cambridge, MA: Harvard University Press.

Rappaport, A. F. (1976). Conjugal relationship enhancement program. In D. H. Olson (Ed.), *Treating relationships* (pp. 41–66). Lake Mills, IA: Graphic Publishing.

Raubolt, R. R., & Rachman, A. W. (1980). A therapeutic group experience for fathers. *International Journal of Group Psychotherapy, 30,* 229–239.

Ross, E. R., Baker, S. B., & Guerney, B. G., Jr. (1985). Effectiveness of relationship enhancement therapy versus therapist's preferred therapy. *American Journal of Family Therapy, 13,* 11–21.

Sensue, M. E. (1981). *Filial therapy follow-up study: Effects on parental acceptance and child adjustment.* Unpublished doctoral dissertation, Pennsylvania State University.

Sywulak, A. E. (1977). *The effect of filial therapy on parental acceptance and child adjustment.* Unpublished doctoral dissertation, Pennsylvania State University.

Werdinger, I. F. (1981). The use of the simulated father–son group to facilitate separation–individualization. *Clinical Social Work Journal, 9,* 282–292.

Werrbach, G. B., Grotevant, H. D., & Cooper, C. R. (1992). Patterns of family interaction and adolescence as role concepts. *Journal of Youth and Adolescence, 21,* 609–623.

Wieman, R. J. (1973). *Conjugal relationship modification and reciprocal reinforcement: A comparison of treatments for marital discord.* Unpublished doctoral dissertation, Pennsylvania State University.

19

PARENTING SKILLS TRAINING WITH TEENAGE FATHERS

MARK S. KISELICA

Since the 1970s there has been a dramatic increase in the number of out-of-wedlock, adolescent pregnancies in the United States. In response to this trend, scholars began to systematically study adolescent childbearing and parenthood (Kiselica & Murphy, 1994). The results of 2 decades of research have indicated that out-of-wedlock child rearing poses numerous emotional and financial hardships for teenage mothers (see e.g., Fursten-berg, 1976; Furstenberg, Brooks-Gunn, & Morgan, 1987). These findings prompted the development of special service programs designed to prevent many of the problems associated with unwed, adolescent parenthood (Kis-elica & Sturmer, 1993a).

Initial adolescent parenting programs focused almost exclusively on the important challenge of helping teenage mothers (see Children's Defense Fund, 1986; Kiselica, 1992; Kiselica & Sturmer, 1993b; Smollar & Ooms, 1987; U.S. Congress, Select Committee on Children, Youth, and Families, 1986). Consequently, little effort was made to address the needs of teenage fathers, until several pioneering writers (e.g., Allen-Meares, 1984; Elster & Lamb, 1986; Hendricks, 1980, 1981, 1982, 1983, 1988; Robinson, 1988) raised an awareness among service providers regarding teenage parenthood from the father's perspective.

Although the emerging interest in teenage fathers has inspired numerous suggestions for how to conduct outreach and individual counseling with this population (see Allen-Meares, 1984; Barth, Claycomb, & Loomis, 1988; Hendricks, 1988; Kiselica, Stroud, Stroud, & Rotzien, 1992; Robinson, 1988; Sander & Rosen, 1987), it has failed to adequately address what might be the most important challenge for counseling professionals who work with these youths, that is, how to sensitively help teenage fathers become caring, committed, and effective parents (Kiselica, Rotzien, & Doms, 1994). In addition, the literature lacks information on how to effectively work with teenage fathers in groups.

The purpose of this chapter is to address these shortcomings of the literature by describing a group psychotherapeutic approach to preparing adolescent fathers for parenthood. Based on the original work of Kiselica, Doms, and Rotzien (1992) and several refinements suggested by Kiselica et al. (1994) and by Kiselica (1995), this approach uses a group-support process to help teenage fathers clarify their attitudes about fatherhood (especially their reactions to their own fathers), learn about child development and child care (particularly the importance of the father–child relationship), and develop sexually responsible behavior.

As a preliminary note, I recommend that all counseling professionals acquire important background information about teenage fathers before working with this population, including an understanding of societal stereotypes regarding teenage fathers, the adjustment difficulties of this population, and pertinent outreach considerations. An overview of these topics is presented here in a brief profile of the teenage father. For more detailed information, the reader is encouraged to consult other useful resources (e.g., Elster & Lamb, 1986; Hendricks, 1988; Kiselica, 1995; Kiselica, Stroud, et al., 1992; Robinson, 1988).

PROFILE OF THE TEENAGE FATHER

According to Robinson (1988) and Rotzien (1992), societal stereotypes have depicted an inaccurate, pathological picture of the adolescent father. Typically, the teenage father is viewed as a psychologically maladjusted male who first exploits an adolescent girl and then abandons her and his child. Findings from recent research in which teenage fathers were directly studied have challenged such stereotypical views of this population. For example, in his review of the literature, Robinson cited numerous studies suggesting that adolescent fathers generally are well-adjusted individuals prior to becoming involved in unplanned pregnancies. Although premature parenthood represents a developmental crisis that places teenage fathers at risk for later adjustment difficulties, most young fathers report feeling genuine concern for their children and for the mothers of their children. In addition, teenage fathers typically provide emotional and financial support to their children and the children's mothers (Hendricks, 1988; Robinson, 1988).

Other recent research on teenage fathers has identified their many adjustment difficulties and their service needs. In a review of the research investigating the problems experienced by this population (Kiselica, Stroud, et al., 1992), my colleagues and I concluded that the teenage father typically is at risk to drop out of school; to be excluded from abortion or adoption decisions; to develop inadequate parenting skills; to experience relationship difficulties with his peers, the mother of the child, the mother's family, and his family; to lose opportunities to bond with his child; and to feel hopeless about his future. Hendricks's (1988) study of teenage fathers suggested that they have diverse needs, requiring information, practical help, and counseling. In two studies of teenage fathers, Elster and Panzarine (1983) and Hendricks (1988) reported that the majority of the fathers expressed an interest in receiving preparation for fatherhood, including training in the responsibilities of being a young father and child-care training.

Although teenage fathers appear to want help, they are often distrustful of service providers because they fear that they will be negatively evaluated (Hendricks, 1988). Consequently, teenage fathers are unlikely to use counseling and educational services unless persistent and varied outreach strategies are undertaken to recruit them (Hendricks, 1988; Robinson, 1988).

There are many outreach tactics that counselors can use to recruit teenage parents for counseling. Some teenage fathers can be identified by tapping into existing services for teenage mothers, such as obstetrical–gynecological clinics, Planned Parenthood, and pediatric services (Robinson, 1988). Formal networks between school counselors and teachers, administrators, and the clergy can lead to many referrals for counseling. Informal networks between counselors and teenagers can lead to other referrals (Kiselica, Stroud, et al., 1992).

The outreach task of identifying teenage parents for counseling is followed by the challenge of keeping them engaged in the counseling process (Kiselica, Stroud, et al., 1992). A strong rapport between the counselor and the teenage parent is necessary to sustain a relationship that can weather the many crises precipitated by the experience of unplanned parenthood (Kiselica & Pfaller, 1993).

Several initiatives taken by professionals can help them establish a solid foundation of trust with teenage fathers. Helping clients with practical concerns, such as finding a job or a means of transportation, can earn the counselor credibility in the eyes of some teenage fathers (Hendricks, 1988). Correcting client misconceptions about counseling (Kiselica, Stroud, et al., 1992) and portraying oneself as an advocate for the teenage parent (Brindis, Barth, & Loomis, 1987) also enhance rapport.

By making these efforts to establish a therapeutic rapport, the counselor is more likely to win the trust of the teenage father. Nevertheless, the teenage father may still be hesitant to participate in group training. The following approach on fatherhood was designed with this issue in mind.

GROUP PSYCHOTHERAPEUTIC PREPARATION FOR FATHERHOOD

Professional counselors are likely to find that teenage fathers are leery of participating in group experiences, because of the strong negative evaluations they have received from others. Teenage fathers are often berated by adults in numerous ways for their part in an out-of-wedlock pregnancy. Specifically, young fathers commonly are the target of angry lectures regarding their irresponsible sexual behavior, are accused of exploiting the adolescent mother, and are warned not to repeat the same "mistake" again. They commonly fear that professional counselors will condemn them in the same manner and, consequently, avoid such service personnel.

For these reasons, group leaders should not get defensive if the teenage father initially appears guarded. In addition, leaders should avoid discussing the issue of sexual responsibility during the early phase of fatherhood training and should always conduct training in such a nonjudgmental manner. A supportive, safe environment is needed to ensure that all group members will be receptive to the training.

To achieve this goal, my colleagues and I (Kiselica, Doms, and Rotzien, 1992) envisioned a three-phase support group to incorporate a movement from exploring personal issues that teenage fathers are ready to face (e.g., sharing reactions to the unplanned pregnancy) to discussing potentially upsetting topics (e.g., parental and sexual responsibility). Specifically, in Phase 1, teenage participants develop group cohesion, share their reactions to the unplanned pregnancy, and clarify their attitudes about fatherhood. During Phase 2, group members learn about child development, child care, and the father–child relationship. Finally, responsible sexual behavior and pertinent coping skills are taught in Phase 3 (Kiselica, Doms, & Rotzien, 1992).

Phase 1: Clarifying Attitudes About Fatherhood

Phase 1 begins with the creation of a therapeutic environment through which group members can explore their reactions to unplanned fatherhood. Phase 1 varies in length from 4 to 6 sessions, the exact number of sessions determined by how much time is necessary for the group to address initial concerns of the participants (Kiselica, Doms, & Rotzien, 1992).

The Role of Recreational Activities

Several authorities on the subject of group counseling and psychotherapy have recommended that structured icebreaker activities be used to create initial cohesion among group members (e.g., Bergin, 1993; M. S. Corey & Corey, 1992; G. Corey, Corey, Callanan, & Russell, 1992; Devencenzi & Pendergast, 1988; Kottler, 1983; Napier & Gershenfeld, 1993). However, both Barber and Munn (1993) and I (Kiselica, 1993) have noted that recreational activities, such as basketball, are more effective than traditional icebreaker activities in helping teenage fathers to interact and feel comfortable with each other. Barber and Munn contended that recreational activities are helpful because the physical exertion involved in those activities helps boys discharge some of their presession anxieties. Elsewhere, I (Kiselica, 1995) have added that athletic activities appeal to teenage fathers and promote group cohesion because adolescent boys commonly relate to one another by physically doing things together.

With others, I have recommended that recreational activities be used not just as icebreakers but as initial activities for subsequent group sessions. The recreation segment should last from about 45 minutes to 1 hour and be followed by a 30- to 40-minute educational section in each session throughout the group (Kiselica, 1995; Kiselica et al., 1994).

Informality and Responding to Immediate Needs

Teenage fathers prefer informal counseling experiences (Barber & Munn, 1993; Hendricks, 1988), especially during the early stages of participation in a program (Kiselica, 1993). Therefore, it is recommended that the group leader create a very informal but caring tone during the first session, through a number of possible strategies. For example, after participants have exchanged introductions and taken part in a recreational activity, it can be helpful to offer a free meal or snack, especially with young fathers from impoverished backgrounds (Barber & Munn, 1993). It also is recommended that the group leader ask about and respond to the fathers' most immediate concerns to help them become invested in the group experience. Expressed concerns commonly involve practical matters, such as finding a job or obtaining legal advice regarding paternity matters (Hendricks, 1988). If group leaders spend the first session or two focusing on these requests in an informal context, then participants are likely to maintain their trust in them and to be receptive to more formal, structured experiences (Kiselica, 1995; Kiselica et al., 1994).

Processing Reactions to Teenage Fatherhood

During the next session the more traditional psychotherapeutic work begins, with a discussion of the rules and the purpose of the group. After the recreation period, the importance of confidentiality, respect, and a commitment to working together are explained. Although the general purpose of the group is to prepare for fatherhood, the group leader should remain flexible and adapt the overriding purpose of the support group to the most pressing needs of each group of fathers (Kiselica, 1995; Kiselica et al., 1994), whose concerns are likely to vary as they attempt to cope with the transition to parenthood. As Hendricks (1988) noted, unless such adaptability is practiced, young fathers are likely to drop out of counseling. This perspective needs to be maintained throughout the course (Kiselica, 1995; Kiselica et al., 1994).

After the rules and purposes of the group have been negotiated, more substantive issues can be addressed. Because the unplanned pregnancy is such a salient issue for most young fathers, participants should be encouraged to share their reactions to the pregnancy (Kiselica, 1995; Kiselica et al., 1994). Several films on teenage fathers are excellent tools for stimulating a discussion of these reactions. *Fathers Too Soon?* (Planned Parenthood Association of Cincinnati, 1987) is a powerful, 9-minute videotape featuring actual teenage fathers talking about their experiences. Each young man featured in the film describes his reaction to the pregnancy, the impact of the pregnancy and parenthood on his family, his relationships with peers and the baby's mother, his educational and career plans, and his view of his future. In addition, the fathers talk about their participation in child rearing. Other, similar films include *Me, A Teen Father?* (Centron Films, 1980), *Wayne's Decision* (Memphis Association for Planned Parenthood, 1980), and *Teenage Father* (Hackford, 1978). As an alternative to these movies, counselors might consider using a filmstrip titled *His Baby Too: Problems of Teenage Pregnancy* (Vanderslice, 1980).

Because these audiovisual aids depict both the joys and sorrows of teenage fatherhood, they typically captivate participants and prompt them to disclose their similar experiences. The group leader can facilitate this process by raising probing questions, such as "How are the fathers in this film like or unlike you?" This rapidly promotes an atmosphere of empathic, group support that solidifies cohesion among group members. Sometimes two sessions are needed to adequately process the reactions of each group member (Kiselica, 1995; Kiselica et al., 1994).

Clarifying Attitudes About Masculinity and Fatherhood

During the next session, other films can be used to help young men clarify their attitudes about masculinity and fatherhood. *Dad and Me* (King Screen Productions, n.d.), is a 9-minute film portraying the loving relationship between a father and his son. *A Man's Place* (Allan Keith Productions, n.d.), depicts the various child-rearing perspectives of five men, as well as alternative models of masculinity and male gender roles. *Fathers* (Steinberg & Jassim, 1980) is a 23-minute film that provides an intimate look at three fathers whose children range in age from preschool to adolescence. *Fathers: Today and Yesterday* (Family Service, n.d.) is a 38-minute videotape of interviews with men and women about the role of fathers, currently and a generation ago; it includes diverse points of view about the ideal father and the barriers that fathers face.

As group members react to any of these productions, the group leader should ask them to express their views on masculinity and their visions of themselves as fathers. Throughout these exchanges, young fathers typically express their attitudes toward their own fathers. This is vital material that should be explored in depth. Two sessions may be necessary to address the many issues that are raised. By discussing his own father's strengths and shortcomings, the teenage father can develop a clearer sense of the type of father he would like to be. In those instances in which his own father has been a positive role model, the participant should be encouraged to think of how he can pass on the love he received from his father to his own child. Boys whose fathers have been caring figures should be prompted to describe specifically how their fathers have been heroes to them. This self-disclosure is particularly helpful to other participants whose fathers are dysfunctional, because it provides them with a clearer sense of the characteristics of a nurturing father. At times, some members may need to be referred for adjunctive, individual counseling to effectively mourn the absence of a loving father in their lives. In processing negative reactions to their fathers, such members should be asked, "How would you do things differently with your child?" and "How can you be a better father for your child?" (Kiselica, 1995; Kiselica et al., 1994).

Wrap-Up Session

Phase 1 concludes with a session in which each participant summarizes his views about fatherhood and masculinity. In addition, the fathers are encouraged to verbalize changes in their thinking, feelings, and behavior that were prompted by group sessions (Kiselica, Doms, & Rotzien, 1992).

Phase 2: Child Development Education and Parenting Skills Training

Phase 2 is designed to include from 5 to 12 sessions, with the precise number of sessions determined by the degree to which pertinent resources are available (Kiselica, Doms, & Rotzien, 1992).

Using Consultants

Because the material covered during this phase is educational, the counselor's role is highly instructional. This phase can be taught directly by the counselor. However, because of the trust that has been developed by this point, the fathers are likely to accept instruction by an outside consultant who is introduced by the counselor. Thus, other professionals can be used as consultants during Phase 2. Potential consultants to consider include the following: home economics teachers; community child-care workers; and university faculty from departments of home economics, nursing, early childhood education, and psychology (Kiselica, Doms, & Rotzien, 1992).

Counselors as Instructors

Counselors who decide to teach the information from Phase 2 themselves can rely on several pertinent resources. The *Guide to Setting Up an Infant Care Course* (Collegiate School, n.d.) provides concrete suggestions for developing a course on child care for young men. *Early Childhood STEP: Systematic Training for Effective Parenting of Children Under Six* (American Guidance Services, 1987a) is a film that provides new parents with information on early childhood development and positive ways to discipline and communicate with young children. The six-part video series *Growing Together* (American Guidance Services, 1987b) was developed specifically for teenage parents. The series covers basic parenting skills, safety tips, and such topics as building the baby's self-esteem, using proper baby-feeding techniques, nutrition, maintaining good health, and promoting the baby's physical, emotional, and social development.

Although these resources give a good introduction to child development and parenting, the father's role in these processes is underemphasized. Elsewhere (Kiselica et al., 1994), I have recommended that the following section regarding the father's role and experiences be included in the training so that young fathers can understand the positive, reciprocal influence that they and their children can have on each other's lives.

Father's Role in Child Development

Fathers tend to differ from mothers in both the quantity and quality of their caretaking activities. Although fathers seldom assume the role as principle caretaker, they nevertheless are highly competent caretakers when called on to do so (Lamb, 1976, 1977). Therefore, teenage fathers should be challenged in a supportive manner to assist in the rearing of their children (Kiselica et al., 1994).

Fathers spend proportionately more time playing with their children than do mothers. Furthermore, when they play with their babies, mothers and fathers play in qualitatively different ways. For example, fathers play more physically active, rough-and-tumble games with infants. Mothers, in contrast, play more low-key conventional games, such as pat-a-cake and toy-mediated games (Lamb, 1976, 1977). Children prefer their fathers as play partners whereas they look to mothers as soothers during periods of fatigue and distress (Lamb, 1976). Thus, teenage fathers need to understand the salient role they take when playing with their children. In addition, they should be encouraged to reflect on the importance of the comforting role and recognize that nurturant fathers can soothe their children during times of distress (Kiselica et al., 1994).

Fathers are important to their children's gender differentiation and intellectual development. Fathers have tended to spend more time with their infant sons than with their infant daughters (Belsky, 1979; Kotel-chuck, 1976; Lamb, 1976, 1977), and by age 2, children tend to exhibit a preference for the same-sexed parent (Belsky, 1979; Kotelchuck, 1976). These findings suggest that the differential responsiveness of fathers to sons versus daughters might play a role in the child's gender-identity develop-ment (Thompson, 1983). Regardless of the child's gender, however, posi-tive involvement by fathers is associated with increased intellectual com-petence in children (Clarke-Stewart, 1978). In addition, fathers who express warmth, closeness, and involvement tend to have competent and achievement-oriented children (Radin, 1981).

In summary, although fathers differ from mothers in their caretaking roles and in how they are perceived by their children, the emotional and physical involvement of fathers as parents can have a positive impact on their children's development.

While sharing this information with the group, it is important for counselors to process fathers' reactions. One common response to antici-pate is a sense of affirmation about the father's role, especially among boys who might have been discouraged or denied involvement with their chil-dren by the mother and her family. Another familiar response is an ex-pressed discomfort with the nontraditional, nurturing role of fathers. The advantage of the group approach is that participants tend to vary in their representation of traditional and nontraditional gender role orientation; teenage fathers who are more comfortable with their nurturing sides can serve as role models for the more traditional, instrumental peers (Kiselica, 1995; Kiselica et al., 1994).

The Experience of Fatherhood

Most men experience a complex series of emotional and physical re-actions to fatherhood, beginning with their reactions to the pregnancy. During the prenatal period, expectant fathers often experience stress that is manifested by physical aches and pains (Bogren, 1986). They may feel acute anticipatory anxiety about their role during labor and childbirth. At the same time, they have empathy for the mother and typically attempt to be sensitive to the expectant mother's needs (Barnhill, Rubenstein, & Rocklin, 1979). This constellation of reactions, sometimes referred to as the "couvade syndrome" (Trethowan & Conlon, 1965), has been found to occur in teenage fathers (Kiselica & Scheckel, 1995). Because it would be beyond the scope of this chapter to provide a thorough discussion of the couvade syndrome and how to help teenage fathers manage it, readers should consult Kiselica and Scheckel's coverage of the subject.

After the birth of the child, men appear to bond with their children immediately, especially if the father is present during the delivery. During the postnatal period, fathers commonly experience a strong emotional involvement with the infant. They enjoy gazing at their babies and delight in having physical contact with their children (Greenberg, 1985).

The postnatal period is also a time of transition, as both fathers and mothers struggle with the changes in their relationship and the reduction of free time prompted by the addition of children to the family. The typical father experiences stress in juggling the demands of being a father, spouse, and worker. Nevertheless, he tends to view his child as a source of joy that can provide a renewed sense of excitement about life (Robinson & Barret, 1986).

In summary, although fatherhood can prompt stress and anxiety, it also can help to define the father's identity and to provide him with a significant source of satisfaction. Providing and discussing this information can prepare teenage fathers for prenatal, delivery, and postnatal experiences. Through this process, participants can identify and share their particular anxieties, expectations, and mechanisms for coping (Kiselica, 1995; Kiselica et al., 1994).

Child-Care Experiences

Didactic training can be enhanced through field trips to child-care centers from which young fathers can acquire hands-on experiences of observing and caring for children. Fathers should be taught how to observe infants and toddlers, prepare bottles and feed preschoolers, comfort children, diaper infants, change toddlers' clothes, prepare children for bed, and play with children in an appropriate manner (Kiselica, Doms, & Rotzien, 1992).

Finally, parent education should conclude with infant first aid training and a review of emergency procedures. This added feature can further bolster fathers' self-efficacy for responding to their children's needs. Counselors might consider enlisting local fire, police, or hospital staff to offer such training to the group (Kiselica, Doms, & Rotzien, 1992).

Wrap-Up Session

During the final session of Phase 2, each group member summarizes and processes what he learned and the changes in thinking, feeling, and behavior that were prompted by this module (Kiselica, Doms, & Rotzien, 1992). In particular, the group leader should encourage fathers to discuss how they are applying new information on parenting in their actual father–child relationships. Moreover, the fathers need to identify how they can use this information to be supportive and considerate of their partner's efforts to be a responsible mother.

Phase 3: Responsible Sexual Behavior and Pertinent Coping Skills Training

Phase 3 is designed to run from 5 to 10 sessions. The number of sessions depends on the length of time that can be devoted to discussions and practice of pertinent skills (Kiselica, Doms, & Rotzien, 1992).

Setting the Stage: Discussing Pressures to Engage in Sexual Relations

As mentioned earlier, the topic of sexual responsibility is a sore subject for teenage fathers and must be introduced delicately. A safe way to broach the subject is to informally ask fathers "What's going on out there?" with regard to the sexual activities of adolescents. This type of probe usually elicits reports on the sexual behaviors of peers and an indication that most teenagers are engaged in sexual relations. Gradually, the group leader can shift the focus away from the sexual experiences of other adolescents to those of the fathers themselves, particularly the pressures they face to engage in sexual intercourse (Kiselica, 1995; Kiselica et al., 1994).

Two films are good tools for stimulating this discussion. *No Time Soon* (Select Media, 1989) is a very realistic, 16-minute video interview with two inner-city adolescent boys, one African American and one Hispanic American. The boys talk frankly about how they learned about sex, their opinions of girls, pressures on guys to engage in sexual relationships, birth control, relationships, and what it means to be a man. The video *It Only Takes Once* (Intermedia, 1987) presents teenagers from a high school human sexuality class discussing the feelings and pressures that accompany adolescent sexual experiences.

Challenging Unsafe Sexual Practices

As the participants react to the films, the group leader should ask members who are comfortable doing so to describe their current involvement in sexual relations. A discussion of such behavior provides the group leader with an opportunity to challenge any participant who is not practicing safe sex and to confront him about the realistic possibility that he might father other children. Elsewhere (Kiselica et al., 1994), I have suggested the following, pertinent confrontations:

- Given your recent experiences as a teenage father, are you ready to become a father again?
- Because of the topics covered in Phase 1, have you thought seriously about your conceptions of fatherhood?
- In light of this thinking, are you acting as a responsible father by engaging in unsafe sex?
- Given your systematic learning of child development in Phase 2, you should now more fully understand the many needs of young children. Are you capable of adequately responding to the needs of another child?

I have also recently added an additional confrontation to raise: Do you really want to risk contracting a serious sexually transmitted disease, such as AIDS, and possibly risk death? (see Kiselica, 1995).

Although the group leader can confront teenage fathers about unsafe sexual practices, it is probably more effective to have the fathers confront one another on this issue. Usually, some teenage fathers recognize that they would be placing themselves in danger of experiencing even more adjustment difficulties by risking repeated paternity. Consequently, they have decided to carefully plan for the next pregnancy. These fathers are typically the ones who confront other participants who are less cautious sexually.

This also is an opportune time to confront any father who demonstrates a cavalier sexual attitude toward the mother of his child. If a father remains sexually involved with the mother of his child, he needs to understand how the added responsibilities associated with the birth of a second child complicates the lives of adolescent mothers (see Horowitz, 1980). To avoid making his partner's life more difficult, both he and his partner will have to practice safe sex until they are sure of their commitment to one another and of their capabilities to raise a child properly. Again, confrontations of this sort are most successful when they originate from teenage fathers in the group who are more responsive to the needs of their child's adolescent mother.

The group leader can capitalize on these confrontations by asking the fathers to describe measures they use to deal with pressures to have sex. The disclosure of their coping tactics can serve as a segue to formal coping skills training.

Coping With Pressures to Engage in Sexual Relations

The final training task combines coping skills training for dealing with sexual pressures with didactic instruction on human sexuality, reproduction, and contraceptive use. Research findings have suggested that this two-phase approach to training maximizes the potential for preventing unplanned, adolescent pregnancies (see Brindis, 1991).

The group leader can use pertinent readings to begin the coping skills phase of the training. For example, the book *Teen Sexuality: Decisions and Choices*, by Rench (1988), provides many ideas that adolescents can use to assert themselves during sexual encounters. These include suggestions for how to respond to sexual pressure, what to say, and how to avoid repeated, uncomfortable situations. An outstanding feature of this book is that it also discusses alternatives to sexual intercourse as a means of expressing affection. Group members can read chapters of this book at home and then discuss their reactions during the group sessions.

As a supplement to this bibliotherapy assignment, the group leader can incorporate the cognitive–behavioral training procedures used by Schinke, Blythe, Gilchrist, and Burt (1989). Such training begins with education about human reproduction and contraception. Coaching in cognitive problem solving follows to assist youths in recognizing problems, deriving a variety of solutions to problems, and anticipating outcomes when solutions are exercised. Nonverbal and verbal communication is taught in such a way that trainees are prepared to broach the topic of sex with a date or spouse and to raise a discussion with the date or spouse about contraceptive use. Finally, group members are taught to planfully transfer rehearsed behavior in real-life situations.

During the sexual education phase of the training, the group leader can again employ the services of a consultant. It is recommended that a male consultant be used so that the teenage fathers and the consultant can have frank, male-to-male discussions about human sexuality and contraception. Potential consultants include a physician, nurse, health educator, or Planned Parenthood counselor (Kiselica, Doms, & Rotzien, 1992).

Wrap-Up Session

Coping skills training concludes with each participant stating his views on responsible sexual behavior, as well as any changes in thinking, feeling, and behavior that were prompted by this module (Kiselica, Doms, & Rotzien, 1992).

Addressing Termination Issues

Once the formal training has been completed, attention is directed toward termination issues. Group members discuss their progress toward becoming caring, responsible fathers. Each member shares his self-evaluation of the progress he has made and solicits feedback from other members. In addition, group members help each other to identify work that still needs to be done. For example, one member may still feel unclear about proper child-care procedures, whereas another might still have a cavalier attitude toward sex. Unfinished business is defined, and plans for addressing it are formulated. The group leader asks participants to describe their anxieties related to termination and explains that some degree of anxiety is normal as groups end their work together. Boys who wish to remain in touch for peer support are encouraged to do so. In addition, the group leader assures participants that they can seek him or her out for more help in the future. It is advisable that the group leader also inform the boys of a date for a follow-up session, at which time the young fathers can receive a "booster shot" of the fatherhood training. Finally, the group leader provides the boys with information regarding other pertinent community resources.

CONCLUSION

In this chapter, I have highlighted a three-phase support group designed to help adolescent fathers clarify their views on masculinity and fatherhood, teach them parenting skills, and promote responsible sexual behavior. Space limitations have prevented a discussion of other important counseling considerations with teenage fathers, but these have been covered in detail elsewhere.[1]

The ideas suggested in this chapter must now be subjected to empirical evaluation. Coordinators of young father programs and academicians are urged to work collaboratively to develop outcome research projects designed to assess the clinical utility of this particular group approach to parenting skills training with teenage fathers. Ideally, such research would consist of randomized control-group, comparative studies designed to assess the relative impact of different experimental conditions on attitudes toward masculinity and fatherhood, parenting skills, and sexual behavior.

In addition to experimental outcome research, practitioners and scholars alike are encouraged to document anecdotal data regarding tactics that enhance this therapeutic group process with adolescent fathers. As documented elsewhere (see Kiselica, 1995; Kiselica, Doms, & Rotzien, 1992; Kiselica et al., 1994), my ongoing work with teenage fathers has led to an evolving approach to fatherhood training that has grown more sensitive to the needs of this population over time. It is my earnest hope that

---

[1]These considerations include developing comprehensive service programs (Achatz & MacAllum, 1994; Brown, 1992; Kiselica, 1995); developmental career and educational counseling (see Kiselica & Murphy, 1994); counseling to address relationship issues (Kiselica, 1995); interprofessional collaboration (see Kiselica & Pfaller, 1993); the couvade syndrome in teenage fathers (see Kiselica & Scheckel, 1995); legal counseling; and multicultural issues (see Kiselica, 1995).

the skillful and perceptive work of other professionals will result in additional refinements of the model described in this chapter.

REFERENCES

Achatz, M., & MacAllum, C. A. (1994). *Young unwed fathers: Report from the field.* Philadelphia: Public/Private Ventures.

Allan Keith Productions. (Producer). (n.d.). *A man's place* [Film]. New York: Producer.

Allen-Meares, P. (1984). Adolescent pregnancy and parenting: The forgotten adolescent father and his parents. *Journal of Social Work and Human Sexuality, 3,* 27–38.

American Guidance Services. (Producer). (1987a). *Early childhood STEP: Systematic training for effective parenting of children under six* [Film]. Circle Pines, MN: Producer.

American Guidance Services. (Producer). (1987b). *Growing together* [Film]. Circle Pines, MN: Producer.

Barber, J., & Munn, A. (1993, March). *Male involvement.* Symposium conducted at the Annual Conference of the Indiana Council on Adolescent Pregnancy, Indianapolis, IN.

Barnhill, L., Rubenstein, G., & Rocklin, N. (1979). From generation to generation: Father-to-be in transition. *The Family Coordinator, 28,* 229–235.

Barth, R. P., Claycomb, M., & Loomis, A. (1988). Services to adolescent fathers. *Health and Social Work, 13,* 277–287.

Belsky, J. (1979). Father–infant interaction: A naturalistic observational study. *Developmental Psychology, 15,* 601–607.

Bergin, J. J. (1993). Small-group counseling. In A. Vernon (Ed.), *Counseling children and adolescents* (pp. 197–234). Denver, CO: Love Publishing.

Bogren, L. Y. (1986). The couvade syndrome. *International Journal of Family Psychiatry, 7,* 123–136.

Brindis, C. D. (1991). *Adolescent pregnancy prevention: A guidebook for communities.* Palo Alto, CA: Health Promotion Resource Center.

Brindis, C., Barth, R. P., & Loomis, A. B. (1987). Continuous counseling: Case management with teenage parents. *Social Casework: The Journal of Contemporary Social Work, 68,* 164–172.

Brown, S. (1992). *If the shoes fit: Final report and program implementation guide of the Maine Young Fathers Project.* Portland: University of Southern Maine, Human Services Development Institute.

Centron Films. (Producer). (1980). *Me, a teen father?* [Film]. Lawrence, KS: Producer.

Children's Defense Fund. (1986). *Adolescent pregnancy: What the states are saying.* Washington, DC: Author.

Clarke-Stewart, K. A. (1978). And daddy makes three: The father's impact on mother and young child. *Child Development, 49,* 466–478.

Collegiate School. (n.d.). Guide to setting up an infant care course. New York: Author.

Corey, G., Corey, M. S., Callanan, P., & Russell, J. M. (1992). *Group techniques* (4th ed.). Pacific Grove, CA: Brooks/Cole.

Corey, M. S., & Corey, G. (1992). *Group process and practice* (4th ed.). Pacific Grove, CA: Brooks/Cole.

Devencenzi, J., & Pendergast, S. (1988). *A guide for group facilitators: Self and social discovery for children of all ages.* San Luis Obispo, CA: Belonging.

Elster, A. B., & Lamb, M. E. (Eds.). (1986). *Adolescent fatherhood.* Hillsdale, NJ: Erlbaum.

Elster, A. B., & Panzarine, S. (1983). Teenage fathers: Stresses during gestation and early parenthood. *Clinical Pediatrics, 22,* 700–703.

Family Service. (Producer). (n.d.). *Fathers: Today and yesterday* [Film]. Charlottesville, VA: Producer.

Furstenberg, F. F. (1976). *Unplanned parenthood: The social consequences of teenage childbearing.* New York: Free Press.

Furstenberg, F. F., Brooks-Gunn, J., & Morgan, S. P. (1987). *Adolescent mothers in later life.* New York: Cambridge University Press.

Greenberg, M. (1985). The birth of a father. New York: Continuum.

Hackford, T. (Producer and Director). (1978). *Teenage father* [Film]. Los Angeles: Children's Home Society of California.

Hendricks, L. E. (1980). Unwed adolescent fathers: Problems they face and their sources of social support. *Adolescence, 15,* 861–869.

Hendricks, L. E. (1981). Black unwed adolescent fathers. In L. E. Gary (Ed.), *Black men* (pp. 131–138). Beverly Hills, CA: Sage.

Hendricks, L. E. (1982). Unmarried Black adolescent fathers' attitudes toward abortion, contraception, and sexuality: A preliminary report. *Journal of Adolescent Health Care, 2,* 199–203.

Hendricks, L. E. (1983). Suggestions for reaching unmarried Black adolescent fathers. *Child Welfare, 62,* 141–146.

Hendricks, L. E. (1988). Outreach with teenage fathers: A preliminary report on three ethnic groups. *Adolescence, 23,* 711–720.

Horowitz, N. (1980). Impact of a second adolescent pregnancy. In J. E. Beger (Ed.), *Teenage pregnancy: Research related to clients and services* (pp. 179–192). Springfield, IL: Charles C Thomas.

Intermedia. (Producer). (1987). *It only takes once* [Film]. Seattle, WA: Producer.

King Screen Productions. (Producer). (n.d.). *Dad and me* [Film]. Saint Louis, MO: Phoenix Films.

Kiselica, M. S. (1992, August). Are we giving teenage fathers a mixed message? In L. Silverstein (Chair), *Transforming fatherhood in a patriarchal society*. Symposium conducted at the Annual Convention of the American Psychological Society, Washington, DC.

Kiselica, M. S. (1993, March). *Male involvement in teenage pregnancy and parenthood*. Symposium conducted at the Annual Conference of the Indiana Council on Adolescent Pregnancy, Indianapolis.

Kiselica, M. S. (1995). *Multicultural counseling with teenage fathers: A practical guide*. Newbury Park, CA: Sage.

Kiselica, M. S., Doms, J., & Rotzien, A. (1992, March). *Promoting parental excellence through courses on fatherhood for adolescent boys*. Paper presented at the Annual Convention of the American Association for Counseling and Development, Baltimore, MD.

Kiselica, M. S., & Murphy, D. K. (1994). Developmental career counseling with teenage parents. *Career Development Quarterly, 42*, 238–243.

Kiselica, M. S., & Pfaller, J. (1993). Helping teenage parents: The independent and collaborative roles of counselor educators and school counselors. *Journal of Counseling and Development, 72*, 42–48.

Kiselica, M. S., Rotzien, A., & Doms, J. (1994). Preparing teenage fathers for parenthood: A group psychoeducational approach. *Journal for Specialists in Group Work, 19*, 83–94.

Kiselica, M. S., & Scheckel, S. (1995). Teenage fathers and the couvade syndrome (sympathetic pregnancy): A brief primer for school counselors. *The School Counselor, 43*, 42–51.

Kiselica, M. S., Stroud, J. C., Stroud, J. E., & Rotzien, A. (1992). Counseling the forgotten client: The teen father. *Journal of Mental Health Counseling, 14*, 338–350.

Kiselica, M. S., & Sturmer, P. (1993a). *Adolescent pregnancy and parenting services: Indiana resource directory*. Indianapolis: Indiana Council on Adolescent Pregnancy.

Kiselica, M. S., & Sturmer, P. (1993b). Is society giving teenage fathers a mixed message? *Youth and Society, 24*, 487–501.

Kotelchuck, M. (1976). The infant's relationship to the father: Experimental evidence. In M. E. Lamb (Ed.), *The role of the father in child development* (pp. 329–344). New York: Wiley.

Kottler, J. A. (1983). *Pragmatic group leadership*. Monterey, CA: Brooks/Cole.

Lamb, M. E. (1976). Interactions between 8-month-old children and their fathers and mothers. In M. E. Lamb (Ed.), *The role of the father in child development* (pp. 307–328). New York: Wiley.

Lamb, M. E. (1977). Father–infant and mother–infant interaction in the first year of life. *Child Development, 48*, 167–181.

Memphis Association for Planned Parenthood. (Producer). (1980). *Wayne's decision* [Film]. Memphis, TN: Producer.

Napier, R. W., & Gershenfeld, M. K. (1993). *Groups: Theory and experience* (5th ed.). Boston: Houghton Mifflin.

Planned Parenthood Association of Cincinnati. (1987). (Producer). *Fathers too soon?* [Film]. Cincinnati, OH: Producer.

Radin, N. (1981). The role of the father in cognitive/academic/intellectual development. In M. E. Lamb (Ed.), *The role of the father in child development* (2nd ed., pp. 379–428). New York: Wiley.

Rench, J. E. (1988). *Teen sexuality: Decisions and choices.* Minneapolis, MN: Lerner Publications.

Robinson, B. E. (1988). *Teenage fathers.* Lexington, MA: Lexington Books.

Robinson, B. E., & Barret, R. L. (1986). *The developing father: Emerging roles in contemporary society.* New York: Guilford Press.

Rotzien, A. (1992). *The development of a scale to assess attitudes toward teenage parents.* Unpublished master's thesis, Ball State University, Muncie, IN.

Sander, J. H., & Rosen, J. L. (1987). Teenage fathers: Working with the neglected partner in adolescent childbearing. *Family Planning Perspectives, 19,* 107–110.

Schinke, S. P., Blythe, B. J., Gilchrist, L. D., & Burt, G. A. (1989). Primary prevention of adolescent pregnancy. In N. Cervera & L. Videka-Sherman (Eds.), *Working with pregnant and parenting teenage clients* (pp. 208–219). Milwaukee: Family Service America.

Select Media. (Producer). (1989). *No time soon* [Film]. New York: Producer.

Smollar, J., & Ooms, T. (1987). *Young unwed fathers: Research review, policy dilemmas, and options: Summary report.* Washington, DC: Department of Health and Human Services.

Steinberg, D., & Jassim, L. (Producers). (1980). *Fathers* [Film]. Los Angeles: Churchill Films.

Thompson, R. A. (1983). The father's case in child custody disputes: The contributions of psychological research. In M. E. Lamb & A. Sagi (Eds.), *Fatherhood and family policy* (pp. 53–100). Hillsdale, NJ: Erlbaum.

Trethowan, W. H., & Conlon, M. F. (1965). The couvade syndrome. *British Journal of Psychiatry, 111,* 57–66.

U.S. Congress, Select Committee on Children, Youth, and Families. (1986). *Teen pregnancy: What is being done?* (1985). Washington, DC: U.S. Government Printing Office.

Vanderslice, C. (Ed.). (1980). *His baby too: Problems of teenage pregnancy* [Filmstrip]. Pleasantville, NY: Sunburst Communications.

IV

ALCOHOLISM, TRAUMA, AND VIOLENCE

INTRODUCTION

ALCOHOLISM, TRAUMA, AND VIOLENCE

Issues of violence and abuse are becoming more prevalent in U.S. society. The increased occurrence of these phenomena has stimulated the development of programs to deal specifically with these issues, along with research to evaluate and help refine interventions. The traumatic effects on both the abused and the abuser are also undergoing study. Chapter authors in the last part of this book discuss a variety of violence and abuse issues, ranging from alcoholism to sexual abuse of both males and females. Some present clinical programs designed to help survivors of such abuse, whereas others cover interventions designed to help the perpetrators of the abuse.

As in previous parts of the book, the value of the group setting—be it group psychotherapy, psychoeducational groups, or workshop groups—is emphasized throughout. The real potential of the group environment and the important ways in which men can positively respond to these settings, especially in the supportive and encouraging presence of other men, is emphasized here.

The first chapter in this part describes group programs for alcoholic men. Calamari, Cox, and Roth provide an impressive array of background literature and insights into their group approach to helping alcoholic men deal with their addictions and their often traumatic reactions to this form of substance abuse.

Moving directly into the subject of trauma, Catherall and Shelton give an overall view of the growing focus on psychological interventions for trauma survivors. First, they inform on the surprisingly large area that this subject covers. They then elaborate on how to deal with men in trauma-focused groups, pointing out the pitfalls that clinicians need to avoid when placing a trauma survivor into a group setting. The importance of dealing with shame and the timing and common stages of men's trauma reactions are appropriately emphasized.

The next chapter in Part IV acquaints the reader with a less known and discussed subject, that of the adult male who was sexually abused as a child. Harrison and Morris describe how male victims differ from female survivors of child sexual abuse. They also provide clinicians with a new group treatment program to help male survivors better understand themselves and feel more confident.

At this point, the focus of the chapters progresses from work with survivors of trauma to interventions for perpetrators of violence and abuse. Harway and Evans give an excellent introduction to the latter area, which continues to gain notoriety and exposure. Providing insights on the male batterer, these authors put forth their group intervention model, the key to which is understanding the dynamics of abuse. In the group setting, batterers learn more about themselves and their behavior from each other and can more actively explore ways of modifying their behavior to reduce and, one hopes, eliminate their abusive behavior.

With her chapter, Becker continues the exploration of the dynamics of the male offender, presenting a group model for eliminating the aberrant behaviors of adolescent males who have sexually abused others. All readers will gain a better understanding of this population, and clinicians can amass valuable ideas for group programs and interventions aimed at adolescent male offenders.

The last chapter of the book concentrates on adult male perpetrators. Specifically, Lazur offers a look at the difficult task of treating the incarcerated adult male sex offender. He examines the many problems inherent to relating to these emotionally detached men and how they best respond in a group setting. Most of all, he details the struggle inherent to moving these men beyond their massive denial and projections.

20

GROUP TREATMENTS FOR MEN WITH ALCOHOL PROBLEMS

JOHN E. CALAMARI, W. MILES COX, and JEFFREY D. ROTH

During the past 2 decades, treatments for substance-abuse disorders in general and alcohol problems in particular have undergone significant changes. Research and clinical experiences with substance abuse, now considered the most prevalent form of psychopathology (cf. Myers et al., 1984), have promoted significant innovations in treatment. Furthermore, because this problem appears to affect males as much as 5 times more than females (American Psychiatric Association, 1994, p. 202), treatment intervention in this area must be structured to address the characteristics of males presenting with this maladaptive method of coping. Although researchers continue to observe that females are much more likely to present clinically with anxiety or major depression, males continue to abuse substances as their primary method of modulating distress.

In this chapter, we review several interventions for men with alcohol problems. First, we briefly discuss self-help groups, the traditional and well-established group intervention for alcohol dependence. Alcoholics Anonymous (AA), the best known of these organizations and the most commonly used self-help group, has a long history and now operates in all 50 U.S. states and 100 different countries (McCrady, 1993). Our primary focus, however, is on psychotherapeutic groups. In these groups, mental health professionals systematically apply psychological principles to bring about changes in behavior. We present two contrasting group treatments, one based on the tenets of psychoanalytic theory and the other based on cognitive–behavioral principles. Before describing these three kinds of interventions, we briefly define alcohol abuse and dependence and review the principles and advantages of group psychotherapy that are most relevant for working with men who have alcohol problems.

ALCOHOL ABUSE AND DEPENDENCE

Alcohol abuse and dependence have been difficult phenomena to define. In the United States, ethyl alcohol in various forms is widely consumed and is generally viewed as a socially acceptable kind of substance use when done in moderation. Therefore, it has proven difficult to make a definitive distinction between socially sanctioned imbibing and behavior that indicates a pathological syndrome that is usually called *alcoholism*. The basis of this distinction has important implications for therapeutic interventions, because many problem drinkers resist the idea that their drinking is detrimental in any sense. In our clinical experience, presenting clients with objective and logical criteria by which to evaluate whether their alcohol consumption is problematic has been quite useful in overcoming such resistance. Accordingly, we briefly describe below current definitions of alcohol abuse and dependence (see Johnson & McCown, 1993, and Nathan, 1991, for more comprehensive discussions).

For many years there was little agreement among researchers or clinicians about how to define the construct of "addiction." Some emphasized tolerance as the defining criterion, such that greater amounts of a drug were required to produce a desired effect, and withdrawal symptoms that occurred when drug use was discontinued. However, an exclusive emphasis on such physiological processes fails to do justice to the recognized behavioral correlates of the substance-abuse disorders. These include preoccupation with obtaining the drug, associated vocational dysfunction, and social behavior changes. Johnson and McCown (1993) suggested that a more useful definition of drug addiction is that proposed by Jaffe (1985):

> Addiction is characterized by a behavioral pattern of compulsive use typified by (a) overwhelming involvement with the use of a drug, and (b) a strong tendency to relapse after cessation of use. Addiction as defined above concerns compulsive behaviors and socially atypical involvement with substances and does not necessarily imply tolerance or physical dependence. (Johnson & McCown, 1993, p. 438)

Debates about the relative importance of the physiological and behavioral dimensions of addiction have helped to precipitate many changes in the definitions of substance abuse and dependence. The most recent criteria for defining these problems are presented in the fourth edition of the *Di-*

agnostic and Statistical Manual of Mental Disorders (*DSM-IV*; American Psychiatric Association, 1994). Substance abuse is defined in the *DSM-IV* as psychoactive drug use to such an extent that the individual is often intoxicated throughout the day, fails to meet important life obligations, and fails in attempts to abstain from use of the substance. Symptoms of physiological dependence are not included in the *DSM-IV* substance abuse syndrome definition. Substance dependence, by contrast, is defined as involving the symptoms of more severe drug abuse and is frequently associated with tolerance and withdrawal symptoms. Substance dependence is also understood to involve a maladaptive pattern of substance use that leads to clinical impairment or distress.

Presenting men in groups with these clearly defined criteria for identifying alcohol abuse and dependence can be a potent catalyst for lengthy and sometimes heated discussion within the groups. Exploring these definitions may also form the basis for group members to identify commonalities in their problematic behavior or may serve as a means for confronting group members who contend that their drinking is not injurious.

GROUP PSYCHOTHERAPY FOR MEN WITH ALCOHOL PROBLEMS

Group psychotherapy has a long history, with some arguing that this treatment method is preferable to individual psychotherapy because it is a cost-effective intervention. More important, group psychotherapy is viewed as producing considerable therapeutic benefits that are not realized in individual therapy. Many forms of psychopathology have their origins in complex social milieus. Thus, the social learning opportunities that group treatments provide may, especially for men, be best suited for addressing problems (Phares, 1992). This is particularly true for problems that are often characteristic of the substance abusing male and that emerge during interactions with the group. We now explore some of the unique therapeutic effects that group psychotherapy can provide and illustrate how these effects can be realized in group treatments for men who have alcohol problems.

Yalom (1985), in the opinion of many psychotherapists, has best articulated the core principles of group psychotherapy. He contended that the therapeutic process in group treatment is driven by 11 primary factors: instillation of hope, universality, imparting of information, altruism, the corrective recapitulation of the primary family group, development of socialization techniques, imitative behavior, interpersonal learning, group cohesiveness, catharsis, and existential factors (see Yalom, 1985, for a complete discussion of these principles). We next illustrate how some of these important principles operate in groups of men who have alcohol problems.

If therapeutic gains are to be made, then hope must be instilled and maintained in men with established alcohol problems. Typically, men with substance abuse problems do not present clinically until their disorder has severely disrupted their lives (e.g., through threatened job loss or marital separation). Often these individuals' extreme sense of hopelessness appears to drive their self-destructive drinking and associated maladaptive behaviors. We have succeeded in promoting hope among our group therapy clients by encouraging salient small improvements in behavior, such as an increase in the number of days of sobriety. Men with alcohol problems often summarily dismiss the importance of such positive changes, but encouragement from group members can help to prevent this reflexive and self-defeating tendency. Furthermore, we have found it beneficial to have more advanced group members (who often have had multiple treatment failures) describe the substantial gains they eventually realized in many life areas through their lengthy and difficult struggle to change. As Yalom (1985) and others have pointed out, AA and similar self-help groups have made use of the testimonies of recovering members, with their stories providing both inspiration and a model for others to emulate.

Possibly the most dysfunctional characteristic of men with chronic alcohol problems is their assumption that their current and past life circumstances are unique. As Yalom (1985) aptly noted, individuals' sense of uniqueness is often intensified by their social isolation. Alcoholic men are frequently isolated because of their damaged or destroyed relationships with significant others. Hearing other group members describe their own problems with family mistreatment, illegal activities, or behaviors that were considered too shameful to talk about can have a profoundly beneficial effect.

The therapy group also provides abundant opportunities for interpersonal learning (Yalom, 1985). For instance, men with alcohol problems learn how to develop and maintain relationships through their experiences in the group, although they may have previously assumed that such meaningful contacts could not again be a part of their life. The group quickly becomes a social microcosm in which interpersonal styles of interacting surface and provide opportunities for corrective feedback (Yalom, 1985). For example, alcoholic men in particular may deny the dysfunctional nature of their interpersonal styles and the impact that this manner of interacting has on others. Yet, interactions within the group quickly provide many opportunities for these detrimental modes of relating to manifest themselves. In our experience, the frank but usually constructive feedback from other recovering men typically prompts clients to become aware of their own interpersonal difficulties and to begin the process of learning new ways of interacting with others.

By the time alcoholic men enter (or reenter) treatment, they usually have experienced severe negative consequences from their drinking. Many report having lost everything of value to them because of their drinking, yet such dire consequences have not caused them to alter their behavior. The treatment group can be the very environment in which to provide restorative social experiences that have a genuine positive effect on the dysfunctional behaviors of men with chronic alcohol problems. The treatment group can be a unique setting in which men are prompted to identify their affective experiences and express these feelings openly. Our clinical experience has suggested that such identification and initial processing of affective experience is a critical function of the group experience for men. This emotional processing functions to counteract characteristically male alexithymia, which may drive men's tendency to abuse substances rather than to openly display anxiety or depressive symptomatology.

The major obstacles for the alcoholic man entering a therapy group are the symptoms of his alcoholism. Hopelessness, social isolation, and shame lead the potential group member to believe that a therapy group cannot help, that other group members cannot understand his unique situation, and that his experience is too terrible to talk about. An honest exploration of these issues in initial individual interviews conducted before the client enters the group may be useful in supporting the new group member. Emphasis on the potential utility of simply showing up for group meetings may help to challenge hopelessness and the alcoholic's inflated assumptions of what is expected by the therapist and other group members. Permission to enter the group gradually, by occasionally remaining silent for a period of time, may allow the substance-abusing man to benefit from the role modeling of more experienced men who share information that the new member has considered too shameful to discuss.

SELF-HELP GROUPS

Although AA was founded in 1934 (Thoreson & Budd, 1987), self-help groups for substance use disorders burgeoned during the 1980s (McCrady, 1993). According to McCrady, during this decade many other self-help organizations in addition to AA became popular, such as Narcotics Anonymous, Cocaine Anonymous, and Pot Smokers Anonymous. Furthermore, a broad range of problems came to be viewed as addictive phenomena; one example is eating disorders, for which the self-help organization Overeaters Anonymous was founded. Also during the 1980s, awareness heightened among individuals who had grown up in alcoholic families, resulting in the Adult Children of Alcoholics movement (McCrady, 1993). As McCrady pointed out, all of these programs were based on disease models of addiction and have been widely influential. Our clinical experience has repeatedly been that, after sometimes experiencing initial resistance, participation in AA groups typically becomes a very important component of the alcoholic male's treatment program.

We now briefly review the group intervention strategies incorporated into the AA program, a program that continues to experience immense popularity. The summary that follows of these strategies is based on DuPont and McGovern's (1994) and Thoreson and Budd's (1987) earlier comprehensive reviews.

AA and the related self-help groups that have developed since its founding share a common structure. The structure of AA includes a fundamental axiom that recovery from alcoholism entails both an alteration in behavior (abstinence from drinking) and an alteration in one's belief system (a spiritual awakening). The central focus in behavior change is initially achieved through attending AA meetings and is reinforced by choosing a *sponsor* (a more experienced member of AA) to help guide the newly recovering alcoholic into sobriety.

Meetings may have widely varying formats. At speaker meetings, one or two individuals with long-term sobriety share with the group their experience of the adverse impact of alcohol in their lives, how they came to AA, and what they have experienced in recovery. Speaker meetings are sometimes open to the interested public. More intimate sharing of experience among a larger group generally occurs at closed meetings, where the group may focus on a topic, on specific AA literature (such as the Big Book, the basic AA text for recovery [Alcoholics Anonymous World Service, 1984]), or on discussion of the 12 steps.

The 12 steps are suggested guidelines for developing the belief system changes recommended by AA as supportive of ongoing sobriety. Steps 1, 2, and 3 lead to the alcoholic's surrendering control over alcohol to a power greater than himself or herself. These steps are abbreviated as "I can't do it, someone else can, and let them." Steps 4 through 7 involve a recommendation for self-reflection, called a *personal inventory*, that helps the alcoholic sort out adaptive from self-defeating behaviors. Steps 8 and 9 involve members practicing their changes in beliefs by making amends in relationships with themselves and significant others. Steps 10 through 12 are maintenance steps designed to facilitate members' deepened ability to accept help and guidance from outside themselves and to offer such help to others.

Many basic structures and mechanisms of group psychotherapy are present in AA groups. Meetings of both psychotherapy groups and AA groups typically last from 1 hour to 1 1/2 hours, and both meet on regular schedules. Psychotherapy groups coalesce around a therapist or institution; AA groups coalesce around the 12 steps, common language, and such common rituals as the Serenity Prayer. In each kind of group, members may become aware of commonalities by identifying with each others' problems. Methods for resolving problems are shared in both contexts, and both kinds of groups offer significant social support. Unlike some therapy groups, AA members are explicitly discouraged from confronting each other during most meetings, however. Such confrontation, known as "cross talk," is understood to produce dissonance and controversy. Also unlike in some therapy groups, AA members are explicitly encouraged to maintain contact with other members outside the group, including choosing a sponsor, as mentioned above.

In short, the major structural feature distinguishing AA from therapy groups is the absence of a mental health professional. The traditions of AA explicitly encourage members to rotate leadership, with the understanding that this leadership role provides important opportunities for personal growth (spiritual awakening). This emphasis on service to the group becomes a model for self-governance that provides opportunities at many levels for the recovering alcoholic to resume a useful existence.

PSYCHOANALYTIC GROUP THERAPY

Historically, alcoholic men have not been considered good candidates for psychoanalytic psychotherapy. Recently, attempts to adapt the psychoanalytic model to the treatment needs of both male and female substance abusers have been reported. Khantzian, Halliday, and McAuliffe (1990) described modified psychodynamic group therapy for substance abusers as a treatment procedure designed specifically for cocaine addicts. Although congruent with the fundamental assumptions of the psychodynamic approach, their model involved many conceptual refinements and procedural innovations. Their treatment procedures involve focusing more on the here and now and using the group as a means of increasing awareness in the individual. Group processes are understood as promoting insight into the individual's psychological vulnerabilities and as an ideal setting for the occurrence of significant curative experiences. In these groups,

> the individual is recognized and affirmed, even after revealing secrets that have caused him or her shame. It is this power of the group to accept the person, even beyond the addiction, which provides the curative force. It is this acceptance that frees the individual from narcissistic isolation; only then is an understanding of self and others really possible. (Khantzian et al., 1990, p. 20)

Next, we describe an extension of psychoanalytic psychotherapy structured for alcoholic men working in groups. We focus on the largely unconscious issues and beliefs that we see as characteristically masculine and as substantial barriers to overcoming alcohol dependence.

The major obstacle to the use of psychoanalytic psychotherapy in the treatment of alcoholism has been that researchers and theorists have insisted on identifying various characteristics of alcoholics as causal to their disease. Among these characteristics are conflicts about dependency, delayed gratification, expression of frustration and tension, exercise of power, and narcissistic needs. These conflicts may be expressed overtly or covertly in a group of male alcoholics in terms of their experience of what it means to be a "real man." In our view, if these characteristics are understood as central to the continued practice of alcoholic behaviors rather than as etiologic, then a model of treatment can emerge that focuses on the examination of these conflicts. Alternative strategies for resolving these issues without attempting to control them with alcohol can then be developed.

The primary issue of membership in a therapeutic group for men recovering from alcoholism is the ability of group members to identify both as men and as recovering alcoholics. Primary obstacles to this are a number of stereotypically masculine beliefs, such as that "real men can hold their liquor." Allied with this belief are several similar convictions that raise concerns about what it means to be a member of such a group: "Real men do not need help," "real men do not ask for help," "real men do not have feelings," and "real men do not expose their feelings." Overt expression of these themes may occur as an articulated consensus of the group or may be presented by a member spokesman. This issue may be expressed as a wish, fear, or statement of reality.

The therapist's role in identifying and interpreting conflicts is central to the psychoanalytic model. Therefore, a group that is enunciating its belief that alcohol solves its problems is supported by the therapist in documenting its experiences with alcohol. These beliefs are not ridiculed, and group members are not blamed or shamed for having these beliefs. Furthermore, the therapist is also not pulled out of his or her role by engaging in speculation about what causes group members to drink. The therapist maintains sensitivity to the group's definition of itself as masculine and supports examination of members' experiences of themselves as men.

If the expression of these primary issues is suppressed, either by group members or the therapist, one result may be a group that uses the defense of compliance against receiving help. Compliance, also called *quasi-group cohesion*, is a covert agreement on the group's part to give an appearance of working together to escape (or be discharged) from treatment. This maladaptive reaction is sometimes precipitated by such underlying beliefs as "real men can tough out any hardship (with the reward of a drink at the end)" and "real men can subvert their individual needs in the service of teamwork (escape and drinking)."

Compliance is also an attempt on the group's part to solve the problem of its conflict with the therapist. In appearing to cooperate with the perceived wishes of the therapist, the group actually covertly takes the position that it does not need the therapist at all. Ideally, the therapist may point out to the group that they are proceeding as if they did not need help and as if they believed that asking for help would be shameful. When the group is able to acknowledge this covert dynamic, it can then return to its primary task.

Quasi-group cohesion or compliance is not the only problematic reaction of the male psychotherapy group. The opposite of compliance, the reenactment of alcoholic behavior—popularly called "acting out"—may also be observed. This behavior may be direct, including a relapse into drinking, or may take such other forms as lateness, absence, suicidal threats, and somatization. These behaviors occur frequently in the alcoholic's relationship with job and family, and the transfer of these behaviors to the relationship with the group may both be a potent obstacle and an opportunity to examine directly the unmanageability of the disease. The emergence of relapses into drinking and other maladaptive behavior should be used to interpret another central belief of these men: "Real men succeed at any task (including controlling their drinking)." The direct expression of the shame relating to the acting-out behavior is facilitated by the therapist and used as a vehicle to unite the group productively. This process may correspond to Vannicelli's (1982) description of "drinking in the service of the group."

Sensitivity to the phenomena of scapegoating, subgrouping, and special relationships is necessary to the therapist's successful use of confrontation as a response to the reenactment of alcoholic behavior. If the group's response to a member's relapse is criticism and contempt, then the group establishes a norm and expectation of punishment, which may lead to the quasi-group cohesion previously described. Alternatively, the group may operate according to the belief that "real men do not become teacher's pet." One or more members may then be covertly chosen to be condemned by the therapist for their alcoholic behavior. Dysfunctional alliances can subsequently be formed around using alcohol or drugs together or even using recovery groups as a way to exclude some group members. The therapist must understand and be able to confront the members about their special relationship with alcohol and the related belief that "a real man holds his liquor and is held by his liquor (and no one else)." Special and exclusive relationships detract from the group's availability to serve all of its members and, therefore, must be resolved in the group process.

Nevertheless, as in the case of the reenactment of alcoholic behaviors, the phenomena of scapegoating and special relationships can be used to a therapeutic advantage. An important function of these phenomena is to limit tensions and frustrations that result from differences among individual group members' feelings and needs. From a systems point of view, the group in effect uses its members to contain feelings and tensions on behalf of the whole group. In addition to using members to enact alcoholic behaviors, the group may use member relationships to enact racial, ethnic, or sexual conflicts. When the therapist is able to identify this process and alert the group to issues among individual members that relate to group-level conflicts, the group can return to its task of examining its feelings and beliefs about getting help. The therapist should also use this opportunity to examine the belief that real men do not express or expose their feelings. Fantasies about the result of expressing anger, hurt, or loneliness in the face of exclusive relationships and interpersonal conflicts can then be examined directly.

The therapist also uses the opportunity presented by exclusive relationships to work with the group's exercise of power and gratification of narcissistic needs. Beyond the group, members may become friends, engage in financial transactions, or even have sexual contact. To the extent that these relationships are withheld from the group and are conducted secretively, they function as reenactments of the alcoholic behavior. If the therapist participates in condemning or attempting to control these behaviors, the group returns to quasi-cohesive activity or compliance. The therapist can most usefully view these relationships as covert requests from the group for help with its relationship with the therapist. Group members may have difficulty examining feelings of affection—including feelings of sexual attraction—as well as feelings about financial arrangements with the therapist (i.e., payment of therapy fees) that may be difficult to acknowledge and process. The group can exercise power covertly by enacting these types of feelings between group members, thereby excluding the therapist. Of great importance is the ultimate frustration of group members' need for affection or approval from the therapist whom they have excluded. The task of the therapist remains that of naming the feelings, identifying the covert expression of power, and alerting the group to the loss of narcissistic gratification.

What is necessary for a therapist to function effectively in leading this type of group intervention with alcoholic men is complex. Psychoanalysts call therapists' reactions and responses to a patient's disease *countertransference*. The literature on alcoholism labels the effect of the disease on family members *codependence*. Thus, to the extent that the therapist becomes part of the alcoholic's "psychological family," the therapist's countertransference may be related to the codependence of the alcoholic's family members. The therapist's compulsion to identify an etiology to the disease may occur as a primary manifestation of countertransference. Just as clearly, any of the following may contribute to the ability of the male leader of a group of male alcoholics to function in the group therapist role: the therapist's conflicts about his own drinking, his identification as a man, and his comfort in experiencing his own feelings and the feelings of others. Other potential sources of difficulty for the therapist include any existing compulsions in the areas of sex, money, work, or food that might selectively blind him to the emergence of these behaviors in the group, with this behavior occurring as a substitute for alcoholic behavior. Similarly, any ambivalence the therapist may experience about homosexual feelings can color his response to the group's fears and fantasies. If, for example, the therapist cannot accept his own homosexual feelings and impulses, then he may experience difficulty identifying with the group's experience of the therapist being seductive. A therapist who is phobic about receiving homosexual impulses may participate in condemning any affectionate impulses that are directed toward him by an individual or by the group. Finally, the presence of alcoholism in the current family or family of origin of the therapist may elicit counterproductive strategies on his part that fall in the category of enabling or codependent behavior.

COGNITIVE–BEHAVIORAL INTERVENTIONS

In sharp contrast to proponents of the disease model of alcoholism, cognitive–behavioral therapists view alcohol problems as ranging along a continuum of alcohol use, from abstinence to nonproblematic use, to different degrees and types of problematic use (McCrady, 1993). Furthermore, adherents of cognitive–behavioral models view alcohol problems as having multiple causes, including biological, psychological, and environmental ones (Cox & Klinger, 1988, 1990; Donovan, 1988; McCrady, 1993). Additionally, the goals of cognitive–behavioral interventions may be significantly different from those of other treatments, allowing for the possibility that controlled drinking rather than total abstinence may be an appropriate goal for at least some kinds of problem drinkers (e.g., Marlatt, Larimer, Baer, & Quigley, 1993). Finally, cognitive–behavioral interventions for substance-abuse disorders have most often been used in individual therapy, although they have recently also been applied with marital partners (e.g., McCrady, 1993; O'Farrell, 1987) and the family unit (e.g., O'Farrell, 1987). We next describe Systematic Motivational Counseling (SMC; Cox, Klinger, & Blount, 1995) as an example of a cognitive–behavioral intervention for alcohol problems that can be used in a group therapy format for men who have alcohol problems. Although the model has broad applicability, we judge it to be highly useful in addressing characteristically male motivational patterns associated with alcohol dependence.

SMC was derived from the motivational model of alcohol use (Cox & Klinger, 1988; Cox et al., 1995). This model is integrative, taking into account the biological, psychological, and environmental variables that contribute to alcohol use but showing how etiologic variables interact with one another to lead to a final motivational pathway to alcohol use. According to the model, excessive drinking is governed by the same variables that affect people's motivational patterns generally. Individuals are motivated to acquire positive incentives that they expect will bring them pleasure and to eliminate or avoid negative incentives that cause discomfort.

The motivational model explains how drinking alcohol acquires high incentive value for particular individuals and how it does so within the context of the other incentives in people's lives.

SMC begins with administration of the Motivational Structure Questionnaire (MSQ; Klinger, Cox, & Blount, in press). It asks people to name and describe their current concerns (Klinger, 1975, 1977) in 16 major life areas, using open-ended questions. In addition, each respondent characterizes the goal striving corresponding to each concern along various dimensions. Dimensions of goal striving include (a) the desired action, (b) the role that is being played, (c) the degree of commitment, (d) expected affect on successful or unsuccessful goal attainment, (e) expected chances of success regarding goal attainment, (f) temporal dimensions (e.g., when each goal is expected to be reached), and (g) the effects that continued alcohol use will have on goal attainments.

Quantitative indexes of responses are calculated, from which a profile is drawn to depict a respondent's motivational structure. The profile shows the degree to which the respondent's overall motivational patterns are adaptive or maladaptive. Specifically, it illustrates the extent to which the person (a) has few or many goals, (b) is appetitive or aversively motivated, (c) plays an active or spectator role in goal strivings, (d) puts forth much or little effort to achieve goals, (e) displays effort that is fruitful or fruitless, (f) expects little or great joy from goal attainments, (g) is ambivalent or lacks ambivalence regarding goal pursuits, (h) expects little or great sorrow upon failure to attain goals, (i) is optimistic or pessimistic about goal attainments, and (j) feels that goals are easily accessible or distant, as well as (k) the degree to which continued alcohol use will interfere with or facilitate goal attainments.

The motivational model depicts a close interplay between people's motivational structure (which the MSQ reveals), the level of people's life satisfaction, and people's motivation to drink or not drink alcohol. Specifically, to the extent that people have adaptive motivational patterns that increase their likelihood of successful and satisfying goal pursuits, their motivation to obtain emotional satisfaction by drinking alcohol will be reduced. If people have maladaptive motivational patterns that decrease their likelihood of successful and satisfying goal pursuits, then their motivation to try to obtain emotional satisfaction by drinking alcohol will be enhanced.

The overriding aim of SMC, therefore, is to change problem drinkers' maladaptive motivational structure so that, as a consequence, they get greater emotional satisfaction from life and feel less propelled to try to get that emotional satisfaction by drinking alcohol. SMC involves two kinds of components: core counseling components and motivational restructuring components. The core counseling components primarily involve administration and interpretation of the MSQ, explaining the rationale for SMC, and setting treatment goals. There are eight major restructuring components:

1. constructing goal ladders, consisting of subgoals underlying the achievement of long-range goals;
2. setting between-session goals, particularly homework assignments to be completed;
3. shifting from an aversive lifestyle (being motivated to escape from or prevent negative emotion-arousing events) to an appetitive lifestyle (being motivated to preserve or acquire positive emotion-arousing events);
4. improving the ability to meet goals (e.g., by acquiring the skills necessary for the achievement of appropriate and realistic goals;
5. bolstering self-esteem (e.g., by teaching the client to be more self-forgiving);
6. resolving conflicts among goals whose achievement interferes with each other;
7. disengaging from goals that are likely to be unreachable or emotionally unsatisfying; and
8. identifying new sources of enjoyment (both immediately gratifying activities and long-range goals that will be sources of emotional satisfaction).

In contrast to the core counseling components that are much the same for all clients, motivational restructuring components are tailored to meet the needs of each client. Particular restructuring components are chosen to be used on the basis of each client's particular motivational difficulties, as revealed by his or her motivational profile. For this very reason, special benefits could accrue from using SMC in a group setting, although, to date, the technique has been used only with patients undergoing individual counseling.

If SMC were used in the group setting, clients exhibiting particular adaptive motivational patterns could serve as role models for clients with corresponding maladaptive motivational patterns. Likewise, clients with particular kinds of maladaptive motivational patterns could have the opportunity to observe other clients with the same kinds of patterns, thus making the dynamics of their own motivation more salient for them. As motivational issues become the focus of group discussions, clients could help each other devise strategies for overcoming common difficulties. In short, the very same advantages that Yalom (1985) described for group therapy in general could be realized from using SMC in a group psychotherapeutic context. Cox et al. (1995) have provided a number of examples of how the components of SMC have been applied in individual counseling. Below, we suggest how some of the cases that they described could have been dealt with even more effectively in group therapy specifically for men with alcohol problems.

Cox et al. (1995) described a client whose MSQ revealed that his goals related to acquiring material possessions, such as acquiring a new car and expensive clothes. Many people might desire such things, and rightly so, but probing revealed that this particular client's desire to have these material possessions was driven by his belief that people would rebuff him if he did not have them. Because this client could not afford such expensive items, he avoided social contact, which in turn interfered with his obtaining other important goals that he had identified, such as "obtain true and honest friends," "keep friendly toward people," and "obtain a healthy and caring relationship." The conflicts among his various life goals left this client feeling lonely and isolated and inclined to drink alcohol to counteract his feelings of discomfort. Individual counseling sessions involved the therapist challenging the client's perception that he must have material possessions and helping him to find alternative ways to make social contacts. However, we speculate that, had this patient been treated with SMC in a group with other men with alcohol problems, even greater and more rapid benefits would have accrued, not only for this particular patient but also for others in the group with similar motivational conflicts.

As described previously, one salient component of SMC is the construction of goal ladders. Doing this involves assisting the client in breaking down major long-range goals into a series of short-term goals that are specific, realistic, and easily obtainable. Such an approach to obtaining major life goals contrasts sharply with typical patterns that we have observed in many men with alcohol problems. That is, such men often name grandiose and clearly unrealistic goals that they want to obtain, but they then experience considerable distress when these goals are not readily achieved. The negative affect that results can precipitate bouts of excessive drinking. Cox et al. (1995) described another client who indicated that one of his major goals was to buy a house. Because such a goal was financially unfeasible for this client at this particular time, he was encouraged to postpone trying to achieve this goal and, in its place, to strive to accumulate a small savings in the bank, with which he might later make a down payment on a house or reward himself in some other manner. Again, we can easily hypothesize greater and more immediate benefits for this client had SMC been applied in a group setting.

Finally, we can explore how the SMC component of identifying new healthy incentives to pursue and enjoy life instead of drinking alcohol might be usefully applied in a group context. Seen in individual counseling, one individual, after giving up alcohol, decided to find new pleasures by indulging in nonalcoholic beverages. This goal translated into his going to a grocery store each week to select special coffee beans to brew. Another client who was seen individually was an avid reader; he was encouraged to volunteer his time to help others in a library. The altruistic pleasures that he derived from doing so helped to reduce his boredom and his associated urges to drink alcohol. Although these two examples are taken from clients seen in individual SMC, we can imagine how the benefits could be multiplied through modeling effects that would occur in a group context.

In general, cognitive–behavioral approaches to the treatment of alcoholism are proliferating. Group cognitive–behavioral interventions have evolved from the community reinforcement approach of Azrin (e.g., Azrin, Sisson, Meyers, & Godley, 1982)—in which patients were encouraged to meet in job clubs to enhance employment-seeking skills and to create a social support system not tied to drinking—to interventions based on complex theoretical formulations, such as SMC. We expect to see further refinements in the cognitive–behavioral approach to the treatment of couples with one partner as a problem drinker (e.g., McCrady, 1993). Further modifications will likely be made in group interventions for high-risk populations such as adolescents (e.g., Goldstein, Reagles, & Amann, 1990), and effective cognitive–behavioral individual treatment procedures (e.g., Sobell & Sobell, 1993) should be extended to group therapy work, in particular work with the male alcoholic.

CONCLUSIONS

In this chapter, we have described difficulties that professionals have encountered in their attempts to precisely operationalize definitions of alcohol and other substance-abuse problems. We also described the latest attempts to formulate satisfactory definitions, namely, the criteria for alcohol and substance abuse and dependence that are specified in the recently published fourth edition of the *DSM-IV*. Finally, we discussed how exploring agreed-upon definitions of alcohol problems in a group context can serve as an impetus for group members to recognize that their drinking is problematic, which they might otherwise be reluctant to do.

We have also described three different group treatments for men with alcohol problems. The first was self-help groups, specifically AA, which is a very widely used intervention for men with alcohol problems. Its treatment philosophy centers around the disease model of alcoholism. Although AA groups involve only recovering alcoholics helping other alcoholics, many of the group dynamics that operate in professionally led groups are clearly recognizable in such self-help groups. Second, we described a model of psychoanalytic group psychotherapy that is consistent with the disease model of alcoholism. This model uses a here-and-now focus to examine maladaptive patterns in group members' relationships with each other and the therapist. Conflicts and beliefs can subsequently be exposed, examined, shared, confronted, and interpreted in terms of their role in maintaining alcoholic behavior. Third, we discussed SMC as one example of a cognitive–behavioral intervention that should be implemented as a group treatment for men with alcohol problems. SMC involves systematically analyzing and attempting to correct problem drinkers' maladaptive motivational patterns that have previously interfered with their emotional satisfaction and propelled them to try to find that satisfaction by drinking alcohol.

REFERENCES

Alcoholics Anonymous World Service. (1984). *Alcoholics Anonymous* (3rd ed.). New York: Author.

American Psychiatric Association. (1994). *Diagnostic and statistical manual of mental disorders* (4th ed.). Washington, DC: Author.

Azrin, N. H., Sisson, R. W., Meyers, R., & Godley, M. (1982). Alcoholism treatment by disulfiram and community reinforcement therapy. *Journal of Behavior Therapy and Experimental Psychiatry, 13,* 105–112.

Cox, W. M., & Klinger, E. (1988). A motivational model of alcohol use. *Journal of Abnormal Psychology, 97,* 168–180.

Cox, W. M., & Klinger, E. (1990). Incentive motivation, affective change, and alcohol use: A model. In W. M. Cox (Ed.), *Why people drink: Parameters of alcohol as a reinforcer* (pp. 291–314). New York: Gardner Press.

Cox, W. M., Klinger, E., & Blount, J. P. (1995). *Systematic motivational counseling: A treatment manual.* Unpublished manuscript.

Donovan, D. M. (1988). Assessment of addictive behaviors: Implications of an emerging biopsychosocial model. In D. M. Donovan & G. A. Marlatt (Eds.), *Assessment of addictive behaviors* (pp. 3–50). New York: Guilford Press.

DuPont, R. L., & McGovern, J. P. (1994). *A bridge to recovery: An introduction to 12-step programs.* Washington, DC: American Psychiatric Press.

Goldstein, A. P., Reagles, K. W., & Amann, L. L. (1990). *Refusal skills: Preventing drug use in adolescents.* Champaign, IL: Research Press.

Jaffe, J. (1985). Drug addiction and drug abuse. In A. Gilman, L. Goodman, T. Rall, & F. Murad (Eds.), *The pharmacological basis of therapeutics* (7th ed., pp. 522–573). New York: Macmillan.

Johnson, J. L., & McCown, W. G. (1993). Addictive behaviors and substance use: An overview. In P. B. Sutker & H. E. Adams (Eds.), *Comprehensive handbook of psychopathology* (2nd ed., pp. 437–450). New York: Plenum Press.

Khantzian, E. J., Halliday, K. S., & McAuliffe, W. E. (1990). *Addiction and the vulnerable self: Modified dynamic group therapy for substance abusers.* New York: Guilford Press.

Klinger, E. (1975). Consequences of commitment to and disengagement from incentives. *Psychological Review, 82,* 1–25.

Klinger, E. (1977). *Meaning and void: Inner experience and the incentives in people's lives.* Minneapolis: University of Minnesota Press.

Klinger, E., Cox, W. M., & Blount, J. P. (in press). Motivational Structure Questionnaire for Alcoholics (full version). In *NIAAA Handbook of Alcoholism Treatment Assessment.* Washington, DC: U.S. Government Printing Office.

Marlatt, G. A., Larimer, M. E., Baer, J. S., & Quigley, L. A. (1993). Harm reduction for alcohol problems: Moving beyond the controlled drinking controversy. *Behavior Therapy, 24,* 461–504.

McCrady, B. S. (1993). Alcoholism. In D. H. Barlow (Ed.), *Clinical handbook of psychological disorders* (2nd ed., pp. 362–395). New York: Guilford Press.

Myers, J. K., Weissman, M. M., Tischler, G. L., Holzer, C. E., Leaf, P. J., Orvaschel, H. A., Anthony, J. C., Boyd, J. H., Burke, J. E., Kramer, M., & Stoltzman, R. (1984). Six-month prevalence of psychiatric disorders in three communities: 1980–1982. *Archives of General Psychiatry, 41,* 959–967.

Nathan, P. E. (1991). Substance use disorders in the *DSM-IV. Journal of Abnormal Psychology, 100,* 356–361.

O'Farrell, T. J. (1987). Marital and family therapy for alcohol problems. In W. M. Cox (Ed.), *Treatment and prevention of alcohol problems: A resource manual* (pp. 205–233). San Diego, CA: Academic Press.

Phares, E. J. (1992). *Clinical psychology: Concepts, methods, and profession* (4th ed.). Pacific Grove, CA: Brooks/Cole.

Sobell, M. B., & Sobell, L. C. (1993). *Problem drinkers: Guided self-change treatment.* New York: Guilford Press.

Thoreson, R. W., & Budd, F. C. (1987). Self-help groups and other group procedures for treating alcohol problems. In W. M. Cox (Ed.), *Treatment and prevention of alcohol problems: A resource manual* (pp. 157–181). San Diego, CA: Academic Press.

Vannicelli, M. (1982). Group psychotherapy with alcoholics: Special techniques. *Journal of Studies on Alcohol, 43,* 17–37.

Yalom, I. D. (1985). *The theory and practice of group psychotherapy* (3rd ed.). New York: Basic Books.

21

MEN'S GROUPS FOR POSTTRAUMATIC STRESS DISORDER AND THE ROLE OF SHAME

DON R. CATHERALL and ROBERT B. SHELTON

Over the past decade, group therapy has become an increasingly prominent modality of treatment for Posttraumatic Stress Disorder (PTSD). Once the disorder of PTSD was recognized in the *Diagnostic and Statistical Manual of Mental Disorders* (3rd ed.; American Psychiatric Association, 1980), clinicians quickly found that having survivors discuss their experiences with other survivors was a particularly beneficial experience. The largest trauma population to use psychotherapy groups has been male war veterans, but there is also a significant number of women who have participated in psychotherapeutic incest survivor groups. Thus, most clinical experience in this area has been with same-gender groups.

In this chapter, we focus on some of the special dynamics that tend to characterize psychotherapy groups for men who have PTSD. We begin by taking a closer look at the disorder of PTSD and at the role that natural groups play in helping people cope with traumatic experiences. We review current knowledge about the group treatment of PTSD and summarize the guidelines that we recommend. We then highlight those PTSD issues that we have found to have a specific impact on therapy groups. Finally, we focus on those issues that bear most directly on PTSD groups designed specifically for men. In particular, we stress the role of shame in those groups and suggest how it can be managed.

323

THE NATURE OF PTSD

PTSD differs from most other psychiatric disorders in that the presence of a specified precipitating event is required in order to make the diagnosis. That event is a trauma that lies outside the usual range of human experience. Following the trauma, three clusters of symptoms develop, with either delayed or acute onset: (a) reexperiencing of the trauma through dreams, flashbacks, or intrusive memories or thoughts; (b) avoidance of reminders of the trauma and a numbing of general responsiveness; and (c) a state of heightened arousal as evidenced by such symptoms as irritability, sleep problems, and exaggerated startle response (American Psychiatric Association, 1994).

The Subjective Experience

Subjectively, the individual with PTSD feels very alienated from others and is no longer able to maintain many of the underlying assumptions that provide individuals with feelings of safety and security (Janoff-Bulman, 1992). In its more severe or chronic form, the disorder is extremely disabling. Individuals with chronic PTSD develop dysfunctional lifestyles that revolve around the ongoing management of their symptoms. Chronic PTSD is usually accompanied by a constellation of other problems, including chemical dependency, job instability, and interpersonal difficulties with intimacy and authority. The PTSD patient does not feel in control of his or her ongoing stream of consciousness; he or she is vulnerable to disruptions by intrusive thoughts, by heightened sensitivity to external stimuli, and by affective swings (Kroll, 1993).

The Social Dimension

Perhaps the most painful aspect of the PTSD experience is the feeling of being different or damaged. Because PTSD patients are inevitably preoccupied with their trauma and symptoms, they are shunned by others. People do not want to really listen closely to their experiences because they are disturbing to others as well. Relating closely to a trauma survivor can produce secondary traumatization in the listener, and the listener can develop PTSD symptoms (Haley, 1974, 1978). In effect, the listener's own cognitive map of the world can be altered by hearing traumatic material (McCann & Pearlman, 1990). Hence, many listeners do not allow themselves to truly relate to the survivor's experience; instead, they imply that they would not react similarly if they were in the survivor's situation (Catherall, 1991). This failure by others to respond appropriately constitutes an additional trauma for survivors (Catherall, 1989; Symonds, 1980). The result is that survivors end up feeling that there is something wrong with them rather than feeling that something terrible has happened to them. Subjectively, this is an intense experience of shame for survivors.

Healing From Traumatization

The overall process of recovery from traumatization takes place within meaningful relationships, as survivors examine their experience in the safety of another's caring and nonjudgmental acceptance (Catherall, 1992; Herman, 1992). Inherent in this context is the understanding that there is not something wrong with them and that their experiences are a normal response to an abnormal situation (Frank, 1961; Ochberg, 1991). This normalizing process helps survivors to overcome some of the feelings of alienation and damage to their self-esteem. As survivors feel stronger, they are more able to find the discipline and courage to make lifestyle changes, to examine the terrible thoughts and feelings associated with their trauma, and to accept a more benign and realistic perspective on themselves and their experience (Figley, 1989).

THE ROLE OF THE GROUP IN SURVIVING TRAUMATIC SITUATIONS

The preceding paragraph describes the importance of relationships in helping people to recover from traumatization. But it is also well known that relationships—as experienced in natural groups—can be very important in helping individuals to survive traumatic situations in the first place. When a trauma is experienced in a group situation, each individual relies on the group to sustain him or her and give him or her hope. When the group fails to sustain individuals, there is a significantly higher rate of PTSD among its members (Quarentelli, 1985), and the overall sense of community breaks down for everyone (Erikson, 1976).

Freud (1921/1955) was one of the first to note the human proclivity to bond into groups in the face of threatening situations. This phenomenon is most pronounced in situations involving extreme stress, such as among soldiers, prisoners of war, and concentration camp prisoners (Davidson, 1984; Klein, 1974; Luchterhand, 1971). Experiencing a trauma as a member of a group appears to provide the individual with a strength that goes beyond his or her own capacities. On the other hand, losing other members of the group can be particularly devastating to the individual in these situations of extreme interdependency (van der Kolk, 1987). Fox (1974) has suggested that young Marines in combat are narcissistically identified with one another and experience such losses as a loss of part of themselves. In a sense, the individual's experience of self can expand to include the entire group when individual survival depends on group survival.

In addition to the proclivity to bond with others when experiencing trauma, individuals seek to connect with others when recovering from traumatic stress. This may be particularly true when the original stress was experienced in a group context. Being able to discuss their traumatic experience with others provides a normalizing influence, emotional support, help with current problems, and an opportunity to adjust their perspective on themselves and their experience (Figley, 1989). From the earliest stages of recognition of PTSD, the group setting has been a favored modality of treatment. Particularly for men, engaging in a trauma-related group form of treatment is often easier than engaging in other forms of treatment because of the credibility established by the participation of other men.

History

In the past decade and a half, groups for trauma survivors have flourished. These have included large numbers of both self-help groups and professionally run psychotherapy groups. The incest survivor movement has developed a strong base of self-help groups, in addition to numerous professionally run groups. The combat veterans' movement began with self-help peer groups, but most of those groups have fallen aside in favor of the professionally run groups available through the Department of Veterans Affairs. Groups that have been composed primarily of men are combat veterans' groups and the debriefing groups used by both the military and private industry.

Combat Veterans' Groups

The largest number of trauma survivors treated in groups has been combat veterans. In the United States, this work has occurred through the Department of Veterans Affairs, in Veterans Administration hospitals, outpatient clinics, and through the Readjustment Counseling Service Vet Centers. Israel has also been a leader in the treatment—including the group treatment—of combat veterans. These many thousands of groups constitute an impressive experience base for the group treatment of men suffering from PTSD. There is also a considerable literature describing this treatment. Unfortunately, there is little in the way of research on the process and outcome of such interventions. The entire area of PTSD treatment is still quite new, and it is difficult to isolate the effects of group treatment from those of the many other modalities (e.g., individual therapy, milieu therapy, pharmacotherapy, and family therapy) used with this population.

Critical Incident Stress Debriefings

An area of group treatment in which widespread usage has developed is the debriefing of an intact group following an acute trauma (Mitchell, 1983). This form of group treatment is most effective when an entire group has been exposed to traumatic stress. Generally, the process consists of no more than a few sessions and is initiated within 72 hours of the traumatic exposure. The group is structured around each individual telling his or her story, that is, his or her particular experience during the traumatic episode and thoughts and feelings related to that experience. The idea of a "debriefing" evolved from the military, referring to a process of discussing and evaluating an action immediately after it occurs to learn the most from the participants. Anecdotal experience suggested that the process of the discussion itself had a beneficial effect on the participants. Research has supported this observation; that is, effectiveness of the debriefing process derives primarily from the experience of talking, particularly from talking with others who experienced the same event (Robinson & Mitchell, 1993).

Types of Groups for PTSD Treatment

Clinicians working in this area use many types of groups, including psychoeducational groups, process groups, and support groups. The type of group used is influenced by the overall treatment approach. For example, inpatient units often use groups to process issues arising in the milieu and journal groups to process the inpatient experience itself. Groups are frequently used to provide support for outpatients who live isolated lives. Psychoeducational groups that teach living skills are often used with more chronic populations whose lives have stagnated because of their PTSD symptoms. And groups that teach meditation and relaxation training are useful with PTSD patients who are struggling with their arousal symptoms. All of these kinds of groups are used with non-PTSD populations as well, although the content of psychoeducational materials may differ. There is one kind of group that is unique to trauma survivor populations, however: the trauma-focused group.

The Trauma-Focused Group

The trauma-focused group was developed specifically for individuals who had been traumatized and had not integrated the experience (Herman, 1992; Rozynko & Dondershine, 1991; Walker & Nash, 1981). The trauma-focused group differs from the more traditional process-oriented group in several important ways (Yalom, 1985). This type of group is almost always time-limited, is highly structured, and possesses rigid boundaries (Herman,

1992; Herman & Schatzow, 1984). The focus of the group is on the past experience of the members' traumas, and current interpersonal issues between members are not explored. Instead, empathic listening and expressions of support are encouraged. The primary task is for each individual to tell his or her story. Often, as members tell their stories and listen to one another, additional thoughts and feelings surface that had been suppressed, repressed, dissociated, denied, disavowed, or otherwise avoided. The desired result is that members of the group achieve a greater integration of their trauma-related thoughts and feelings.

The leader is usually very active in trauma-focused groups and often intervenes to block conflict. The leader's job is to keep the group focused on its task and to maintain an atmosphere of safety so that members can concentrate on the intensive work of uncovering their past trauma. There is a tendency for all trauma-focused group members to relate more to the leader than in process groups, where the leader's role is minimized and interaction between group members is facilitated (Brende, 1981). The leader protects the group from excessive anxieties about having to relate to one another and helps the group members contain their anxiety about being overwhelmed by their own and each other's trauma stories. The leader must set an example of being able to listen to a great deal of very disturbing material, which facilitates the group's ability to approach each member's traumatic memories (Herman, 1992).

Guidelines Concerning Group Treatment for PTSD

Clinicians have consistently reported the value of group treatment for PTSD. They have observed the normalizing influence, the support from other group members, and the fact that trauma survivors will often allow themselves to be influenced by their fellow trauma survivors in a manner different from how clinicians are allowed to influence them. Although there is not much research on the actual process and outcome of group treatment independent of other forms of treatment, experience has taught us some guidelines:

1. Trauma survivors do not fare as well when mixed into groups of people with other disorders, particularly personality disorders. They are generally looking to relate to people who have been through something very similar to their own experience.
2. Quick debriefing of an exposure to traumatic stress is most useful with an intact group. Putting together a group of strangers is less helpful for the immediate debriefing process (Quarentelli, 1985).

3. Putting together a group of strangers will work when the format is for longer term group treatment. They can become more useful to one another as they come to develop relationships with one another.

4. As in other forms of group treatment, the leader's role as gatekeeper is crucial. As gatekeeper, the leader controls the membership of the group and determines when new members will be added. The coming and going of members must be attended to or the atmosphere of safety in the group will crumble. It is the leader's responsibility to help the group anticipate and process the loss of members. Similarly, the leader must help the group deal with the interruption of adding new members and, ultimately, help the group integrate the new members.

5. The telling of an individual trauma story can be a form of joining the group and does not always mean that the experience is being processed or integrated as it is spoken. Sometimes individuals deal with their anxiety about being in the group by revealing too much of their story prematurely and, afterward, feel excessively vulnerable and overexposed. Group leaders sometimes have to protect individuals from premature overexposure.

6. Groups of trauma survivors begin by looking for similarities among members. As the group develops, it moves toward accepting the differences between members.

7. A danger in composing a group of alienated people that are all struggling with the same problem is that they may come to feel related to one another but may still be unable to relate to people who do not share their problem. Some clinicians use cotherapy teams that include at least one therapist without a background of exposure to trauma as a way of confronting the group members' belief that no one else can relate to them. For example, the Veterans Administration often uses male–female leader teams with combat veterans. Another mechanism used to deal with this problem is to keep the group time-limited so that members remain aware that they will soon be expected to relate to those outside the group again (Herman, 1992).

8. Safety is a paramount concern. People who have been traumatized continue to feel vulnerable to similar, future trauma, even after the primary symptoms of PTSD have remitted (Greening & Dollinger, 1992). People who are still symptomatic are obviously in a continuing state of concern for their

safety. Herman's (1992) first stage of recovery is labeled "safety." But the need for safety does not disappear as one recovers; rather, it remains as an ongoing requirement for all further progress.

9. There must be particular attention to creating an atmosphere of honesty in the group. Rozynko and Dondershine (1991) have emphasized the importance of honesty in their trauma-focused groups for Vietnam combat veterans. They noted the prevalence of distortions and fabrications among the combat veterans and suggested that, when honesty is an avowed goal, the peer-group format allows correction of many distortions and often a reduction of the associated guilt. In that regard, they distinguished between the reporting of traumatic events and the telling of war stories, and they prohibit the latter.

The Impact of Issues Specific to PTSD

There are several issues specific to PTSD that affect the group process.

Stages of Recovery

PTSD differs from many other disorders in that there is a distinct cause to the disorder and an observable process of recovery from it. The recovery process follows some kind of order and is usually described in terms of stages. The stages of recovery are generally viewed as beginning with intensive focus on the primary symptoms, and, as those symptoms improve, the individual gradually moves toward an increased connection with others. Herman (1992) outlined three primary stages of recovery: (a) safety, (b) remembrance and mourning, and (c) reconnecting. The implication for group work is that individual members may be at different stages of recovery, with different needs and different areas of vulnerability.

Group Composition

The composition of the group is determined first by similarity of trauma experience and, second, by the stages of recovery among the various members. As a general rule, individuals should be placed in a group with other survivors who are at the same stage of recovery. It is a mistake to place someone who has not yet achieved a basic feeling of safety into a group that is working hard at the process of uncovering the trauma (i.e., a trauma-focused group). Herman (1992, p. 224) noted that individuals are ready for uncovering trauma when (a) their safety and self-care are securely established, (b) their symptoms are under reasonable control, (c) their social supports are reliable, and (d) their life circumstances permit engagement in a demanding endeavor.

It is also a mistake to place someone who is profoundly isolated into a group in which the other members are actively working on their connections to one another. Such isolated individuals often respond better to an individual therapy relationship in the early stages of recovery. This is not an absolute rule, however; some individuals prefer the less intensive focus on themselves that is possible in many groups.

Traumatic Reenactment

One element of the PTSD syndrome that can affect the group process is the tendency for traumatized individuals to reenact their trauma—that is, to have transference reactions to other group members and experience group events as recurrences of their trauma. It helps to understand these reenactments in terms of the specific traumatic experiences of the individual. A group member may, for example, begin to experience another member as the innocent bystander, perpetrator, or lost comrade associated with his or her particular trauma. This issue can become even more complicated in the group setting, because different members can be involved in the same interaction, with each experiencing his own particular reenactment and, at the same time, playing a role in other members' reenactments.

Negative Affectivity

Negative affectivity refers to the tendency to experience normal, everyday events as catastrophic (Eysenck & Eysenck, 1968; Watson & Clark, 1984). Individuals who manifest this state tend to overreact to situations and live their lives in a constant crisis. Needless to say, this can create considerable stress in a group setting. A rise in an individual's level of negative affectivity has been described as "a fundamental mechanism of adaptation to the traumatic environment" and common among survivors of extreme trauma, such as former prisoners of war (Eberly, Harkness, & Engdahl, 1991, p. 369). Trauma survivor groups frequently encounter individuals with elevated levels of negative affectivity; their presence constitutes a challenge for the group, which must tolerate those individuals without scapegoating them or chasing them out of the group.

Secondary Traumatization and Retraumatization

The act of relating to a trauma survivor and hearing about his or her traumatic experience can create posttraumatic stress symptoms in the listener (Figley, 1995; Haley, 1974). Likewise, discussing one's own trauma in a nonsupportive environment can be retraumatizing (Rozynko & Dondershine, 1991). The implication is that participation in a group that is focused on trauma can affect everyone, including therapists who do not have trauma in their own pasts. The possibility of the group experience itself being traumatic is thus quite real. It is obviously the leaders' job to ensure that this does not happen. But the anxiety that the group experience itself might be traumatic should be acknowledged and taken seriously. It is important that therapists not deny their own anxiety about this possibility and receive supervision if they need help in containing that anxiety.

ISSUES SPECIFIC TO PTSD GROUPS FOR MEN

Several aspects of the experience of having PTSD are especially difficult for men acculturated to the Western definition of the male role. That role is often interpreted to mean that men should lead adventurous, even violent, lives without being negatively affected by such experiences (Catherall & Lane, 1992; Thompson, Grisanti, & Plick, 1985). Being traumatized by a life event is viewed as a source of shame by men who have been inculcated with such attitudes. Seeking help with the effects of the traumatization is not consistent with the emphasis on autonomy and independence that characterizes the Western ideal of masculinity (Good, Dell, & Mintz, 1989; Pollock, 1990). Thus, the actions of both acknowledging the traumatization and seeking help with it are potentially shame producing for many Western men.

Experience and Expression of Affect and Emotion

Men with PTSD are frequently unable to moderate the intensity of their affect—it feels out of control; consequently, they avoid interpersonal situations that will be affectively stimulating. A central factor in the social disconnection of trauma survivors is the disturbing impact on others of the survivor's experience and expression of raw displays of emotion. Indeed, innate displays of affect are so influential that the only time people typically get social sanction for these raw displays is when they are small children. In virtually every culture, being an adult means having the capacity to moderate innate affective display.

Because there is a cultural prohibition against excessive expression of certain affects, many men unconsciously shift their experience of those unacceptable affects into more culturally sanctioned affects that they can express. Patients with PTSD rank high on measures of shame and depression and low on measures of self-esteem (Wong & Cook, 1992). In Western culture, the open acknowledgment and direct expression of feelings of shame, depression, and low self-esteem are viewed as weak and unmasculine, and the expression of such affects is actively avoided by many men (Brannon, 1985; Thompson et al., 1985).

Because men with PTSD have an impaired ability to moderate their affective experience and displays, they tend to manifest either (a) an overly moderated display that is experienced as a numbness or (b) an unmoderated display that can be intensely disturbing to others. Even the most loving spouse may have great difficulty enduring these raw affective displays. People are typically repelled by the trauma victim's displays of raw, unmodulated affect. The male trauma victim senses that others are repelled by something about him and, hence, finds another reason to feel shame.

The Survivor's Sense of Shame

All of the affects except one, that of shame, focus the individual's attention on a stimulus. For example, when they are afraid, people focus on the stimulus that caused the fear. But shame causes them to defocus from a previously positive stimulus (Nathanson, 1992). When they feel shame in a relationship, they turn away from the relationship. Shame has been perhaps best defined as "a felt sense of unworthiness to be in connection" (Jordan, 1989). Male trauma survivors in a group are extremely sensitive to the possibility of feeling a shameful unworthiness to be part of the group.

One way to modify affective display is to prevent awareness of the affect by unconsciously changing it into another affect that is more culturally sanctioned. Many men act angry when they feel shame. When feeling angry, they have a greater feeling of control and little, if any, sense of shame. To deal with the shame of men with PTSD in groups, group leaders should watch the sequences of behavior. The affect of "shame–humiliation" is shown by the turning away of the head, blushing, and an experience of cognitive dysfunction that is often seen as a form of confusion (Tomkins, 1963). If an outburst of anger in a group was preceded by hanging of the head, facial flushing, and cognitive confusion, then the leader may hypothesize that something stimulated the individual's feelings that he was not worthy to be part of the group.

SHAME IN MEN'S PTSD GROUPS

In group psychotherapy, shame may be involved in a variety of behaviors. Defensiveness, particularly defensiveness with anger, often covers shame. Nathanson (1992) has asserted that individuals have predictable response styles to shame. He listed those characteristic styles as withdrawal, attack self, avoidance, and attack others. The therapist sensitive to shame will look for these aspects in group members and in subgroups. Sometimes the whole group will adopt one of these styles.

The therapist should thus watch for eyes to avert from the person speaking, for the hanging head, for facial flushing, and for confusion. When the therapist gets confused by members' reactions, shame may have just entered the interaction. When group members make statements implying psychological pain, such as "I feel hurt" or "that was painful," shame may have been evoked. Statements such as "I don't know what to think" may be made either in anticipation of or as a reaction to shame. Statements suggesting that the person just wants to disappear or not be noticed generally are usually about shame.

The Healing Property of the Group

The treatment of shame associated with trauma may be best accomplished in group psychotherapy. Shame is the affect that makes people want to disappear, to not be noticed, and to feel that if they were known, they would be shunned. Group psychotherapy provides a natural treatment for inordinate shame. Most men avoid shame by immediately turning to some strategy to avoid feeling the shame. All of their mechanisms for avoiding affective experience come into play. But the shame-sensitive group will help its members be aware of the shameful feeling evoked before the defenses gather too much momentum. Being able to identify and have a name for the feeling of shame brings power to most PTSD patients.

Further support is provided when the group helps its members to focus on the shame—what evoked it and what it is about. When group members become curious rather than defensive about the origins of their own shame and the shame of others, the group will be working well. Group psychotherapy provides an opportunity for members to openly admit their sense of shame and reveal their unworthiness to be a part of the group. If others listen in an accepting fashion, then the affect can no longer be shame, because the connection with others is not severed. The person and the shame itself are exposed to scrutiny, and abandonment does not follow. In group therapy, exposing oneself to the possibility of shame and humiliation is one of the prices for membership. Paying that price begins to change members' sense of themselves.

The Shame-Sensitive Group Therapist

The shame-sensitive group therapist is sensitized to people's defenses against shame. When these defenses are activated, shame-sensitive therapists look for the shame experience, seeking to understand what provoked the shame and what this experience may say about the group. When therapists increase their curiosity about their own sense of shame, the group will prosper. When therapists make mistakes in male PTSD groups, they are often trying to either restore pride after a shaming event or to avoid a deeper exploration of the shame affect available to the group. When the therapist makes the mistake of being too helpful, not sitting with the group, talking too much, or not speaking the unspoken, it is often a reaction to shame or to its anticipation. When the leader stays curious about his own experience of shame, however, the male PTSD patient gets a strong model for his own recovery.

CONCLUSION

Groups composed of men who share similar traumas and are at similar points in their recovery are a powerful form of treatment for PTSD. Inevitably, these groups must confront issues with which men commonly have difficulty—that is, experiencing and expressing powerful feelings of fear, vulnerability, and shame. The power of the raw affect experienced by the traumatized person may feel overwhelming, both to the individual and to the members of the group. It is only human to try to avoid that which we find overwhelming. But, in a group context, that avoidance can lead to further feelings of isolation, shame, and being damaged on the part of the victim.

A psychotherapy group for men with PTSD must confront those raw affects rather than avoid them. The group leader must set an example in that regard. The leader's role in these groups is vital in terms of gatekeeping, establishing and maintaining an atmosphere of safety, and keeping the group sensitive to issues of shame. But, as in many other forms of group psychotherapy, it is the connection with the other group members that provides the healing experience for men in PTSD groups.

REFERENCES

American Psychiatric Association. (1980). *Diagnostic and statistical manual of mental disorders* (3rd ed.). Washington, DC: Author.

American Psychiatric Association. (1994). *Diagnostic and statistical manual of mental disorders* (4th ed.). Washington, DC: Author.

Brannon, R. (1985). A scale for measuring attitudes about masculinity. In A. Sargent (Ed.), *Beyond sex roles* (pp. 110–116). St. Paul, MN: West.

Brende, J. O. (1981). Combined individual and group therapy for Vietnam veterans. *International Journal of Group Psychotherapy, 31*, 367–378.

Catherall, D. R. (1989). Differentiating intervention strategies for primary and secondary trauma in posttraumatic stress disorder: The example of Vietnam veterans. *Journal of Traumatic Stress, 2*, 289–304.

Catherall, D. R. (1991). Aggression and projective identification in the treatment of victims [Special issue]. *Psychotherapy, 28*, 145–149.

Catherall, D. R. (1992). *Back from the brink: A family guide to overcoming traumatic stress*. New York: Bantam.

Catherall, D. R., & Lane, C. (1992). Warrior therapist: Vets treating vets. *Journal of Traumatic Stress, 5*, 19–36.

Davidson, S. (1984). Human reciprocity among the Jewish prisoners of the Nazi concentration camps. In *Proceedings of the Fourth Yad Vashem International Historical Conference* (pp. 555–572). Jerusalem, Israel: Yad Vashem.

Eberly, R. A., Harkness, A. R., & Engdahl, B. E. (1991). An adaptational view of trauma response as illustrated by the prisoner of war experience. *Journal of Traumatic Stress, 4,* 363–380.

Erikson, K. T. (1976). *Everything in its path: Destruction of community in the Buffalo Creek Flood.* New York: Simon & Schuster.

Eysenck, H. J., & Eysenck, S. B. G. (1968). *Manual for the Eysenck Personality Inventory.* San Diego, CA: Educational and Industrial Testing Service.

Figley, C. R. (1989). *Helping traumatized families.* San Francisco: Jossey-Bass.

Figley, C. R. (1995). *Compassion fatigue: Coping with secondary traumatic stress disorder in those who treat the traumatized.* New York: Brunner/Mazel.

Fox, R. P. (1974). Narcissistic rage and the problem of combat aggression. *Archives of General Psychiatry, 31,* 807–811.

Frank, J. (1961). *Persuasion and healing.* Baltimore: Johns Hopkins University Press.

Freud, S. (1955). Group psychology and analysis of the ego. In J. Strachey (Trans. and Ed.), *Complete psychological works, standard edition* (Vol. 18). London: Hogarth Press. (Original work published 1921.)

Good, G. E., Dell, D. M., & Mintz, L. B. (1989). Male role and gender role conflict: Relations to help seeking in men. *Journal of Counseling Psychology, 36,* 295–300.

Greening, L., & Dollinger, S. J. (1992). Illusions (and shattered illusions) of invulnerability: Adolescents in natural disaster. *Journal of Traumatic Stress, 5,* 63–76.

Haley, S. A. (1974). When the patient reports atrocities: Specific treatment considerations of the Vietnam veteran. *Archives of General Psychiatry, 30,* 191–196.

Haley, S. A. (1978). Treatment implications of post-combat stress response syndromes for mental health professionals. In C. R. Figley (Ed.), *Stress disorders among Vietnam veterans* (pp. 254–267). New York: Brunner/Mazel.

Herman, J. L. (1992). *Trauma and recovery.* New York: Basic Books.

Herman, J. L., & Schatzow, E. (1984). Time-limited group therapy for women with a history of incest. *International Journal of Group Psychotherapy, 34,* 605–616.

Janoff-Bulman, R. (1992). *Shattered assumptions: Toward a new psychology of trauma.* New York: Free Press.

Jordan, J. V. (1989). Relational development: Therapeutic implications of empathy and shame (Working Paper No. 39). *Writings from the Stone Center,* 1–13.

Klein, H. (1974). Delayed affects and aftereffects of severe traumatization. *Israel Annals of Psychiatry, 12,* 293–303.

Kroll, J. (1993). *PTSD/borderlines in therapy: Finding the balance.* New York: Norton.

Luchterhand, E. G. (1971). Sociological approaches to massive stress in natural and man-made disasters. In H. Krystal & W. Niederland (Eds.), *Psychic traumatization* (pp. 29–54). Boston: Little, Brown.

McCann, I. L., & Pearlman, L. A. (1990). Vicarious traumatization: A framework for understanding the psychological effects of working with victims. *Journal of Traumatic Stress, 3*, 131–150.

Mitchell, J. M. (1983). When disaster strikes: The critical incident stress debriefing process. *Journal of Emergency Medical Services, 8*, 36–39.

Nathanson, D. L. (1992). *Shame and pride: Affect, sex, and the birth of the self.* New York: Norton.

Ochberg, F. M. (1991). Post-traumatic therapy. *Psychotherapy, 28*, 5–15.

Pollock, W. S. (1990). Men's development and psychotherapy: A psychoanalytic perspective. *Psychotherapy, 27*, 316–321.

Quarentelli, E. L. (1985). An assessment of conflicting views on mental health: The consequences of traumatic events. In C. R. Figley (Ed.), *Trauma and its wake, Vol. 1* (pp. 173–215). New York: Brunner/Mazel.

Robinson, R. C., & Mitchell, J. (1993). Evaluation of psychological debriefings. *Journal of Traumatic Stress, 6*, 367–382.

Rozynko, V., & Dondershine, H. E. (1991). Trauma focus group therapy for Vietnam veterans with PTSD. *Psychotherapy, 28*, 157–161.

Symonds, M. (1980). The "second injury" to victims [Special issue]. *Evaluation and Change*, 36–38.

Thompson, E. H., Grisanti, C., & Plick, J. H. (1985). Attitudes toward the male role and their correlates. *Sex Roles, 13*, 413–427.

Tomkins, S. S. (1963). *Affect/imagery/consciousness, Vol. 2. The negative affects.* New York: Springer.

van der Kolk, B. A. (1987). The role of the group in the origin and resolution of the trauma response. In B. A. van der Kolk (Ed.), *Psychological trauma* (pp. 153–171). Washington, DC: American Psychiatric Press.

Walker, J. I., & Nash, J. L. (1981). Group therapy in the treatment of Vietnam combat veterans. *International Journal of Group Therapy, 31*, 379–389.

Watson, D., & Clark, L. A. (1984). Negative affectivity: The disposition to experience aversive emotional states. *Psychological Bulletin, 96*, 465–490.

Wong, M. R., & Cook, D. (1992). Shame and its contribution to PTSD. *Journal of Traumatic Stress, 5*, 557–562.

Yalom, I. D. (1985). *The theory and practice of group psychotherapy* (3rd ed.). New York: Basic Books.

22

GROUP THERAPY FOR ADULT MALE SURVIVORS OF CHILD SEXUAL ABUSE

JEFFREY B. HARRISON and LARRY A. MORRIS

Adult–child sexual behavior has its roots in antiquity. Young castrated boys were prized as sexual partners by wealthy Romans, and the use of child courtesans was once an acceptable part of life in China and Russia. Even the ancient Greeks condoned sexual activities with children. And sexual contact of children by adults, as well as incest taboos, can be found in most cultures.

Child sexual abuse in modern times has been thought to exist, but its frequency has been judged to be rare. An early study by Hamilton (1929), suggesting that about 22% of male children and 20% of female children had been exposed to some form of inappropriate sexual behavior by an adult, was largely ignored by a nation insulated by a state of denial and protective misinformation. Likewise, few took notice in 1937, when Bender and Blau warned that child seductions were more frequent than court and social agency reports had indicated. Although some progress was made in educating the public about the possibility of child sexual abuse with the publication of Alfred Kinsey's landmark reports of male sexual behavior in the 1940s (Kinsey, Pomeroy, & Martin, 1948) and female sexual behavior in the 1950s (Kinsey, Pomeroy, Martin, & Gebhard, 1953), accurate incidence and prevalence rates remained elusive. For example, Weinberg (1955) estimated only 1 case of incest per million persons in 1930, whereas research by Landis (1956) suggested that 35% of women and 30% of men had experienced some form of inappropriate sexual contact during childhood. In the 1960s, DeFrancis (1969) estimated 40 cases of child sexual abuse per million persons, and Helfer and Kempe (1968) discovered that 14% of California's child maltreatment cases involved sexual abuse. However, in the absence of well-controlled studies and reliable figures, the public, as well as professionals, remained skeptical about the prevalence of child sexual abuse.

This all began to change in the 1970s, when Sgroi (1975) challenged therapists to admit to the presence of child sexual abuse. Also at this time, a number of female sexual abuse victims began to break the silence by coming forward and telling their stories. Scholarly works on the subject by Finkelhor (1979), Justice and Justice (1979), Herman (1981), and Russell (1984) soon followed. These and other researchers (e.g., Fritz, Stoll, & Wagner, 1981; Lewis, 1985) began to report that sexual child abuse was as real as physical abuse, and perhaps even more common.

Fortunately for all victims of personal trauma, women challenged the status quo that kept issues like sexual abuse hidden in society. As women began to disclose their histories of abuse and challenge gender roles in American culture, men were provided more opportunities to acknowledge their histories of abuse and examine their gender roles as well. Even so, research on victims of child sexual abuse over the past 2 decades has clearly had a female focus (Faller, 1989; Finkelhor, 1984; Swift, 1980). For years, researchers and clinicians could find few reliable resources specifically addressing male sexual abuse issues. But something important happened in the late 1980s and early 1990s: Male survivors of child sexual abuse finally began to break the silence about their victimizations. Porter (1986); Lew (1988); Bolton, Morris, and MacEachron (1989); and Hunter (1990) soon provided the first comprehensive look at male survivors of child sexual abuse.

A review of the research literature that has developed regarding male child sexual abuse reveals a wide range of findings. For example, surveys of the general population in the United States (Cameron et al., 1986; Finkelhor, 1984; Kercher & McShane, 1984; Murphy, 1987, 1989), in Canada (Badgley et al., 1984), and in Great Britain (Baker, 1985) have suggested a prevalence rate ranging from 8% to 13%. Among studies of male college students, the rate has ranged from about 5% to 33% (Condy, Templer, Brown, & Veaco, 1987; Finkelhor, 1979; Fritz et al., 1981; Fromuth & Burkhart, 1987; Landis, 1956; Lisak, 1993; Risin & Koss, 1987; Seidner & Calhoun, 1984; Urquiza, 1988). Finally, clinical studies have suggested male sexual abuse rates ranging from 9% to 50% (American Humane Association, 1981; DeFrancis, 1969; DeJong, Kemmett, & Hervada, 1982; Ellerstein & Canavan, 1980; Farber, Showers, Johnson, Joseph, & Oshins, 1984; Grayson, 1990; Neilsen, 1983; Ramsey-Klawsnik, 1990; Reinhart,

1987; Rogers & Terry, 1984; Showers, Farber, Joseph, Oshins, & Johnson, 1983; Spencer & Dunklee, 1986; Swett, Surrey, & Cohen, 1990).

The child sexual abuse literature of today is questioned by even some of its principal contributors. This is especially true for studies that purport to assess the prevalence of child sexual victimization. But even with all the research quandaries, data still suggest an astounding rate of child sexual abuse: from 3% to 50% of male children and from 6% to 62% of female children. Neilsen (1983) has noted that male victims comprise 25% to 35% of the caseloads of therapists working in the area of child sexual abuse. Clearly, clinicians no longer require Sgroi's (1975) challenge to admit to the presence of this abuse. The challenge now is to meet the therapeutic needs of child victims and adult survivors of childhood maltreatment, regardless of their gender. In this chapter, we present one approach to providing effective treatment strategies to adult male survivors of child sexual abuse.

MALE DISCLOSURE OF CHILD SEXUAL ABUSE

Even though an increasing number of males appear to be disclosing their child sexual abuse experiences, many remain silent. Traditionally, men have been identified as a group that rarely seeks psychological treatment. Research also shows that males are much more reluctant to disclose sexual victimization experiences than females (Finkelhor, 1984, 1986; Fritz et al., 1981; Johnson & Shrier, 1985; Landis, 1956; Myers, 1989; Nasjleti, 1980; Neilsen, 1983; Porter, 1986; Rogers & Terry, 1984; Swift, 1980). When males do disclose, they often wait until many years after the sexual abuse occurred. When Perry (1993) surveyed a large sample of male survivors currently in therapy, he discovered that 91% waited until adulthood before making their initial disclosure. It is interesting to note that 55% disclosed at intake and 20% disclosed within 5 sessions, but 25% disclosed at various stages in therapy, with some waiting until after 26 sessions.

Most researchers and clinicians (e.g., Dimock, 1988; Finkelhor, 1986; Hunter, 1993; Lew, 1988; Morris, 1993; Nasjleti, 1980; Struve, 1990; Van-der Mey, 1988) have pointed to male socialization experiences as the most influential factors in developing a disdain for revealing perceived personal weaknesses. For example, traditional concepts of masculinity provide very few models for men to incorporate victimization, especially sexual victimization, as part of their masculine identity. Essentially, males are told to deal with trauma by "taking it like a man." Stereotypical concepts of masculinity and victimization seem mutually exclusive. The heroic stereotype of the male is that he fights, resists, and even dies before he will succumb to any form of victimization. Most men who have been victimized feel that they must conceal or minimize their history of trauma to avoid being exposed as unmasculine and risking ridicule. These cultural stereotypes are often internalized by men, producing shame and making it difficult for them to reveal themselves to others in society as well as to themselves. As one of our clients stated, "There was not only a silence with others about my being abused, there was also a silence within myself."

If trauma is unacknowledged or minimized by the client, he may be at greater risk of additional victimization experiences. Similarly, if trauma is inaccurately interpreted by the client, then he may internalize a sense of shame and self-doubt. In an effort to cope with this damaged sense of self, the individual is more prone to repressive and self-destructive coping styles, such as isolation, denial, or emotional numbing or acting out. This points to the need for men to be given the encouragement and support to seek treatment for the trauma they have experienced and to develop the ability to disclose and resolve issues integral to their abuse experiences.

Unfortunately, the influence of cultural stereotypes is not limited to clients. Sometimes clinicians expect strength and self-reliance from their male clients and are surprised and even unprepared for clients' vulnerability when they ask for help or disclose feeling traumatized. Clinicians sometimes unwittingly collude with the silence and shame that their male clients have concerning issues of abuse. It is often surprising how protective and reluctant some clinicians are to refer their male survivors to group treatment, even after they have participated in a substantial amount of individual treatment. For this reason, it is important that clinical colleagues support and encourage one another to refer male survivors to appropriate treatment resources.

Although this need for specific treatment is not unique to men, the modalities for facilitating this treatment may vary from methods of working with women and from more traditional "talk therapy." Historically, men have participated in psychotherapy less frequently than women. This is not because men have fewer problems than women. It is more likely that the cultural pressures for men to be strong and self-sufficient often prevent men from seeing psychotherapy as a viable option.

Additionally, traditional psychotherapy has relied on the client to have the ability to verbally express his or her emotional experience. When men come to therapy, they often present their problems differently than women. Men tend to describe their poor level of functioning and give examples of what they perceive as failed performance as their primary reasons for seeking treatment, whereas women often present a description of their affective experiences. In the early phases of treatment, when men are encouraged to define their emotions, they often use words that are not adequate for describing their beliefs or emotions. This inability among men to identify and describe their feelings in words, known as *alexithymia*, has been observed by other therapists (e.g., Krystal, 1982). Levant (1992) proposed that alexithymia is "a result of being socialized to be emotionally stoic. Not only were boys not encouraged to learn to identify and express emotions, but more pointedly they were told not to" (p. 383). This may unintentionally mislead the therapist as well as create interpersonal difficulties in men's lives. Therefore, the development of constructs, symbols, and language for self-expression provides a valuable foundation for men's treatment.

When men enter treatment, they often report not self-disclosing for fear that they will lose control of the degree to which they share information about themselves. This concern is often greatest regarding information related to the topic of child sexual abuse. Many men report that they disclose very little about themselves in general, for fear that the information they share with others will somehow create a situation beyond their control that will eventually require a disclosure of their most intimate secret: sexual abuse. Therefore, it appears that many adult survivors treat the issue of self-disclosure as a digital phenomenon rather than as an analog phenomenon. That is, male trauma survivors conceptualize information about themselves and their histories of abuse as being either completely divulged or completely withheld, rather than conceptualizing self-disclosure as a process involving varying degrees of intensity or intimacy.

The process of avoiding self-disclosure affects both the quality of relationships that survivors develop with others and the contextual settings that survivors choose for interactions with others. Three factors—the relationship to the other person, the setting in which the self-disclosure will take place, and the intensity of self-disclosure—can be viewed as operating in interaction with one another. The intensity and intimacy of these factors tend to complement one another. For example, when a trauma survivor attempts to withhold information about himself, he may, consciously or unconsciously, choose to interact with others in less intimate settings and likewise limit vulnerability and the development of intimacy with people. Through treatment, survivors can develop greater ability in assessing the level of intimacy in a relationship and the appropriateness of an environment for the level of self-disclosure in which they wish to engage. Thus, they calibrate their level of self-disclosure with the levels of intimacy in the relationship and appropriateness of the environmental context. Therapists can create a graph that reflects the theoretical relationship of the intensity between these three factors for each of their clients (see Appendix A). This graph can be used as a model to enhance the client's understanding of how these factors relate to one another and, ultimately, to the client's ability to self-disclose more intentionally. By using examples that the client presents, the therapist can plot the client's perceived intensities (with ratings from 1 to 10, where 10 is the highest level of intensity) of each factor and how he might make adjustments, in any or all of the factors, to make the process of self-disclosure safer and purposeful.

THE TREATMENT MODEL

With the treatment model we present here for male survivors we have several intentions: (a) to help men develop a language to describe their experiences and emotions, (b) to help men develop healthier masculine identities, (c) to help men develop healthier coping strategies, (d) to help them gain mastery over the degree of self-disclosure they make about themselves and child sexual abuse, and (e) to help integrate this history into their identities. We propose three basic stages of treatment: the individual phase, the group phase, and the prevailing phase. Whereas the group phase of treatment is typically the stage in which clients report making the most progress, the individual phase provides a better opportunity to assess and prepare the client for the ensuing therapeutic process. The prevailing phase is a healing experience outside of the formal treatment process, through which some positive meaning can emerge out of the trauma experience. Graduating through the various phases of treatment encourages men to move from victims, to survivors, to an even higher level of functioning beyond survivorship. Therapy for trauma clients can thus help them not only to survive but to prevail (N. V. Hickey, personal communication, September 15, 1991).

Individual Phase

Assessment

Early in treatment, therapists should assess the following for clients: how the abuse has affected them, how they have coped, why they have broken their silence at that time, what self-perceptions they entertain, what goals they have for treatment, and the extent to which they make disclosures appropriately. Because many men have withheld the experience of being sexually abused for many years, there are often other complications in their lives that have arisen due, in part, to the sexual abuse, silence around the issue, and a lack of treatment. Before men participate in group treatment, it is important that they have begun an individual treatment process that focuses not only on issues directly related to sexual abuse, but also on the complications that survivors' silence and coping styles may have supported. Furthermore, clients should have the opportunity to assess the safety of the therapeutic relationship before disclosing details about sexual abuse. Often in the early phases of treatment, the process of disclosure about child sexual abuse becomes the focus of treatment, and this may be approached by male clients as a performance expectation rather than a therapeutic procedure. Perceiving treatment as a task to be completed, some male clients may attempt to demonstrate their ability to function more effectively by disclosing a great deal of material rapidly, instead of developing skills for making purposeful and safe self-disclosures.

Development of Symbols and Language

Much of the individual work with men focuses on the development of new symbols and language that can be used to represent their emotional experiences with accuracy. When men are able to develop symbols or words for their experiences, they are able to find their "voice" and to organize and understand their thoughts and feelings. Once the client is guided and supported in using his own skills and symbols to express himself, he is often better prepared to participate in group treatment.

Group Phase

Transition to Group Treatment

The individual therapy phase, having helped men build symbols and language for their emotional experiences, prepares them to more adequately participate in group psychotherapy. As men become clearer about their sexual abuse experience, they often begin to question whether or not other men have had similar experiences. This curiosity about other survivors is an indication that men might be interested in expanding the community within which they self-disclose about sexual abuse and, so, might be ready for group treatment. Group therapy should be explained as a forum for men to help decrease their isolation and expand their healing community by including other men who share their concerns about child sexual abuse.

Structure of the Group

Time-limited groups reinforce safety and consistency of therapy. Twelve-week sets of group therapy allow men to be reassured that, during that time, the group population will remain fairly consistent. Members can terminate at the end of a set, and new members can join at the beginning of a set. During the first few groups of each set, a great deal of structure is provided. The men introduce themselves, and the facilitator makes it clear that all participants have a history of having been sexually abused as children. Group members are given a treatment contract with guidelines for their participation in the group (see Appendix B). The treatment agreement we use was adopted from rules that Lew (1988, p. 222) recommended to help establish a foundation for building a safe and respectful environment for healing.

The concept of disclosure is discussed in group so that men become familiar with viewing disclosure of sexual abuse as part of a larger issue of self-disclosure. Disclosure of a sexual abuse history is not considered as a single event but as a process that may take place over and over again in a man's life, with varying degrees of detail depending on the purpose for the disclosure, the relationship, and the setting in which the disclosure might take place. Later in the group process, men are encouraged to use this model to make decisions about self-disclosure of their sexual abuse experiences to the group.

Structured Tasks

After providing group guidelines and a model for thinking about disclosures, the facilitator asks group members to share their understanding of how having been sexually abused has affected them and how they have coped. All responses are recorded on a large easel pad, and photocopies of responses are provided for each member at the next group session. The originals are hung on the walls for several weeks, as room permits. This visual stimulus provides men with an alternative means of learning, retaining, and processing what they and other members have said aloud in the group. Many issues related to the abuse are discussed and worked with during the early phase of the group.

Physical Enactments

Psychomotor interventions, similar to the work conceptualized by Albert Pesso (1990), are used to aid male abuse survivors in working through important issues. Some common issues include asking for help, expressing oneself, setting limits, confronting perpetrators, experiencing a feeling of being protected, trusting others, and accepting care or protection from other men. Physical interaction or enactments in group require permission from group members and a brief explanation of the task. An example of such an intervention might be helpful in describing the importance of this kind of group work.

Early in the group process it is not uncommon for men to identify isolation, lack of trust, total self-sufficiency, or macho self-presentation as either effects of the abuse or coping styles related to having been abused. Being able to ask for help is thus particularly important for sexually abused males because many have lost their ability to trust others. Their isolation is often further compounded by stoic stereotypes of masculinity, which many have internalized. When questioned about their ability to ask others for help, men sometimes report having difficulties with this issue. More often, they report an adequate capability to ask for help, but a lack of necessity. An "asking for help" exercise often assists men in forming a clearer understanding of their abilities and emotional experiences of help seeking.

The exercise might include having the member who will ask for help stand on one side of the group room while the facilitator and the rest of the group stand on the other side of the room. The group is instructed to simply invite the man asking for help to come over to their side of the room, once he asks for help, and to ask about his needs once he arrives. Then, the help seeker is instructed to think about what he would like to be helped with and, when he is ready, to say "I need help." The group responds by inviting him to "come over." If the man is then able to walk across the room to the group, then the group members ask how they can help. The exercise appears simple, yet many men report having very difficult experiences related to this task. Many find themselves unable to speak up initially. Sometimes their voices crack, or they speak in a very soft whisper. For others, approaching the group once they have been invited to move across the room represents an obstacle.

In processing this task, men are usually able to describe their emotional experiences in greater detail, and they can subsequently begin to work through material that has been difficult and identify patterns in the way they relate to others around their need for help. Many men discover that asking for help is more difficult for them than they had originally believed. Facilitating interpretations of experiences of requesting help often assists them in developing insight into their interpersonal functioning both within and outside of the group. Metaphors and literal translations of what clients say can often be used to choreograph an exercise.

Similar exercises can be designed to create physical enactments of a variety of issues. The difficult issue of confronting the perpetrator of one's abuse is particularly well suited for a physical enactment exercise. An exercise for this topic might be stimulated when a group member describes avoiding a perpetrator, because the survivor does not know what to say or fears losing control, yet expresses a need to confront. For example, the group member might be asked to talk to an empty chair as if the perpetrator were sitting in it. If the client is unable to confront while sitting, because he feels intimidated, the therapist could suggest standing up to talk to the imagined perpetrator. Sometimes this is enough to allow self-expression; some men report feeling as if they are "more grown up" when they stand. As one of our clients stated, "standing up for myself feels better than just sitting there." Often the client still needs some intervention for finding his voice and expressing himself. If this is the case, then the man having difficulty with self-expression might request that another group member be his "voice." With both participants' expressed permission, the man selected to serve as the "voice" might be placed standing in front of the man requesting assistance. Both would be facing the imagined perpetrator. The man who has had difficulty speaking up would then be asked to whisper what he would like to say (if he could) and the man functioning as his "voice" can speak to the chair that represents the perpetrator. Several trials in this manner can be made until the first client can speak for himself, following the model his peer has set, or until he becomes frustrated with his peer's attempts to speak for him and decides to express his thoughts himself. Sometimes it is helpful for a man who is having a difficult time expressing himself to have other group members literally stand behind him to "back him up." With permission, the man confronting the perpetrator may want a few group members standing behind him to place their hands on his shoulders to provide additional symbolic support as he attempts to express himself.

Other group members or therapists should never be used to play the role of the imagined perpetrator in exercises of this nature, because it would not be safe for any of them to be symbolically identified as an offender. Inappropriate expressions of anger, such as kicking or damaging furniture, should be prohibited in this type of exercise because this might be threatening to group members, including the member acting out the anger. Throughout this type of exercise, it is important to monitor group members with respect to their personal feelings of safety. The pace of the exercise should be adjusted to the needs of all the group members.

These and other, similar interventions are often more emotionally evocative than a group discussion alone. They provide a nonverbal alternative, or supplement to, the process of working through important material. Our clients have reported that the active work in group helps them avoid the tendency to overintellectualize. Enactments can be used throughout the group phase of treatment.

Formal Disclosure Exercise

When members are ready to make more detailed disclosures to the group about their sexual abuse experiences, the Structure for Disclosure Story (see Appendix C, adapted from Porter, 1986) is presented as a way of helping them contain and organize any disclosure they are thinking about making. This format allows men to begin the process by simply answering each successive question to whatever degree they choose. The responses to the questions can be recorded on a large easel pad. By writing down what is said in the process of making a disclosure, men can go back and review their statements after they have gone through all the questions. They are given the opportunity to modify their responses and provide a greater level of detail if they desire or to present more of a narrative style of disclosure on the basis of the facts they already provided. Many men report some anxiety before making a complete disclosure of their history of abuse in group therapy but report relief and a sense of freedom and mastery once they have completed the task.

Men often report feeling more capable of intentionally making disclosures with varying degrees of detail once they have gone through the process of disclosing to varying degrees in the group. Members often discuss ways that they have been making more intentional self-disclosures in their lives. An example of this would be the progress that one of our clients made, who had always kept silent about having been abused, and how he used this model to make a self-disclosure that helped decrease his feelings of isolation. After several months of treatment, he reported that he had been to a birthday party where his 8-year-old child was a guest. Another parent asked him, "Don't you wish you were a kid again?" Using the model, the man responded, "No, I didn't have a very pleasant childhood, but I'm glad these kids seem to be happy." The self-disclosure he made about his history of child sexual abuse was appropriate for the setting and for the relationship he had with this other parent, whom he had never met before. Before treatment he claimed that he would have depicted his childhood as fine. With a closer friend, in a more private setting, he might have made a more detailed self-disclosure of his abuse history. This is usually not limited to self-disclosure of the trauma these men have experienced; instead, it usually involves other aspects of themselves and their lives that they were reluctant to discuss in the past for fear that any disclosure would reveal information about their trauma experiences that might leave them feeling vulnerable or manifest feelings of shame.

Termination and Referral

Toward the end of 12 weeks, group members make decisions about whether to participate in another set of 12 weekly sessions. Many men complete between two and five sets of the weekly group sessions. Each new set begins with men discussing how they believe they have been affected by having been sexually abused as children and how they have coped with this in their lives. With the introduction of new group members, the dynamics of the group change. Men that have been in several 12-week sets often begin to take a mentoring role with newer members. Some of these more senior group members request referrals for more general psychotherapy groups, in which group membership is not limited to survivors of child sexual abuse or to men. We have interpreted this as an indication of a survivor's healing, because he seeks to expand his identity to include himself in a treatment community that is not defined solely by a history of child sexual abuse.

Prevailing Phase

As noted above, some men are interested in graduating from survivors' group treatment to more nonspecific treatment groups, whereas others are interested in doing something more for other survivors or child victims. This is the juncture in treatment where men might be ready to participate in some type of activity that aids the healing of others and allows them to feel that, through their own healing, something positive has been created out of their traumatic experiences. Simply put, this may indicate that a client has graduated from surviving to prevailing. Activities associated with prevailing may involve participating in education, advocacy around issues of abuse, or a structured intervention such as a "Survivors' Talk" (Hickey, Harrison, & Morgan, 1992), in which men can provide information, role modeling, and hope to young boys more recently abused. Although the therapists involved ensure that the process being planned is ethical and clinically appropriate, this phase of treatment really represents the collaborative and creative efforts of both clients and therapists. Sometimes this stage of prevailing may also focus on preventive activities, that is, providing enrichment and healthy experiences to boys who have not necessarily been identified as victims of sexual abuse.

SUMMARY

The purpose of this chapter was to foster a better understanding of the specific clinical issues presented by male survivors of child sexual abuse and to offer a group treatment approach sensitive to those issues. The challenge to therapists now is to use these ideas to develop additional treatment strategies that will enhance the healing process for male survivors.

REFERENCES

American Humane Association. (1981). *National study on child neglect and abuse reporting*. Denver, CO: Author.

Badgley, R., Alfred, H., McCormick, N., Proudfoot, P., Fortin, D., Ogilivie, D., Rae-Grant, Q., Gelinas, P., Pepin, L., & Southerland, S. (1984). *Sexual offenses against children* (Vol. 1). Ottawa: Canadian Government Publishing Centre.

Baker, A. W. (1985). Child sexual abuse: A study of prevalence in Great Britain. *Child Abuse and Neglect, 9*, 457–467.

Bender, L., & Blau, A. (1937). The reaction of children to sexual relations with adults. *American Journal of Orthopsychiatry, 7*, 500–518.

Bolton, F., Morris, L. A., & MacEachron, A. (1989). *Males at risk: The other side of child sexual abuse*. Newbury Park, CA: Sage.

Cameron, P., Proctor, K., Coburn, W. J., Forde, N., Larson, H., & Cameron, K. (1986). Child molestation and homosexuality. *Psychological Reports, 58*, 327–337.

Condy, S., Templer, D. I., Brown, R., & Veaco, L. (1987). Parameters of sexual contact of boys with women. *Archives of Sexual Behavior, 16*, 379–394.

DeFrancis, V. (1969). *Protecting the child victims of sex crimes committed by adults*. Denver, CO: American Humane Association.

DeJong, A. R., Kemmett, G. A., & Hervada, A. A. (1982). Epidemiologic factors in sexual abuse of boys. *American Journal of Diseases of Children, 136,* 990–993.

Dimock, P. (1988). Adult males sexually abused as children. *Journal of Interpersonal Violence, 3,* 203–221.

Ellerstein, N., & Canavan, W. (1980). Sexual abuse of boys. *American Journal of Diseases of Children, 134,* 255–257.

Faller, K. C. (1989). Characteristic of a clinical sample of sexually abused children: How boy and girl victims differ. *Child Abuse and Neglect, 13,* 281–291.

Farber, E. D., Showers, J. C., Johnson, C. G., Joseph, J. A., & Oshins, L. (1984). The sexual abuse of children: A comparison of male and female victims. *Journal of Clinical Child Psychology, 13,* 294–297.

Finkelhor, D. (1979). *Sexually victimized children*. New York: Free Press.

Finkelhor, D. (1984). *Child sexual abuse: New theory and research*. New York: Free Press.

Finkelhor, D. (1986). *A sourcebook on child sexual abuse*. Newbury Park, CA: Sage.

Fritz, G. S., Stoll, K., & Wagner, N. A. (1981). A comparison of males and females who were sexually molested as children. *Journal of Sex and Marital Therapy, 7,* 54–59.

Fromuth, M. E., & Burkhart, B. R. (1987). Long-term psychological correlates of childhood sexual abuse in two samples of college men: Definitional and methodological issues. *Violence and Victims, 2,* 241–253.

Grayson, J. (Ed.). (1990). Male survivors of childhood sexual abuse. *Virginia Child Protection Newsletter, 31*. Harrisonburg, VA: James Madison University.

Hamilton, G. V. (1929). *A research in marriage*. New York: Albert & Charles Boni.

Helfer, R. E., & Kempe, C. H. (1968). *The battered child* (3rd ed.). Chicago: University of Chicago Press.

Herman, J. (1981). *Father–daughter incest*. Cambridge, MA: Harvard University Press.

Hickey, N. V., Harrison, J. B., & Morgan, T. (1992, May). *Survivors talk: An integrated treatment approach for adult and child male survivors of sexual child abuse*. Paper presented at the 1992 National Symposium on Child Victimization, Washington, DC.

Hunter, M. (1990). *Abused boys: The neglected victims of sexual abuse*. Lexington, MA: Lexington Books.

Hunter, M. (1993, August). Males who have experienced childhood sexual abuse: Recovery issues. In L. A. Morris (Chair), *Wounded warriors: Male survivors of childhood sexual abuse*. Symposium conducted at the 101st Annual Convention of the American Psychological Association, Toronto, Ontario, Canada.

Johnson, R. L., & Shrier, D. K. (1985). Sexual victimization of boys: Experience at an adolescent medicine clinic. *Journal of Adolescent Health Care, 6,* 372–376.

Justice, B., & Justice, R. (1979). *The broken taboo: Sex in the family*. New York: Human Sciences Press.

Kercher, G., & McShane, M. (1984). The prevalence of child sexual abuse victimization in an adult sample of Texas residents. *Child Abuse and Neglect, 8,* 485–502.

Kinsey, A. C., Pomeroy, W. B., & Martin, C. E. (1948). *Sexual behavior in the human male*. Philadelphia: W. B. Saunders.

Kinsey, A. C., Pomeroy, W. B., Martin, C. E., & Gebhard, P. H. (1953). *Sexual behavior in the human female*. Philadelphia: W. B. Saunders.

Krystal, H. (1982). Alexithymia and the effectiveness of psychoanalytic treatment. *International Journal of Psychoanalytic Psychotherapy, 9,* 353–378.

Landis, J. (1956). Experience of 500 children with adult sexual deviants. *Psychiatric Quarterly Supplement, 30,* 91–109.

Levant, R. F. (1992). Toward the reconstruction of masculinity. *Journal of Family Psychology, 5,* 379–402.

Lew, M. (1988). *Victims no longer: Men recovering from incest and other sexual child abuse*. New York: Nevraumont.

Lewis, I. A. (1985). [*Los Angeles Times* Poll #98.] Unpublished raw data. Los Angeles, CA: Author.

Lisak, D. (1993, September). *Research on male victims of childhood abuse: What do we know and what do we need to know?* Paper presented at the Fifth Annual National Conference on Male Survivors, Washington, DC.

Myers, M. F. (1989). Men sexually assaulted as adults and sexually abused as boys. *Archives of Sexual Behavior, 18,* 203–215.

Morris, L. A. (1993, September). *Socialization of male sex role and the male survivor: Clinical issues*. Workshop presented at the Fifth Annual National Conference on Male Survivors, Washington, DC.

Murphy, J. E. (1987, July). *Prevalence of child sexual abuse and consequent victimization in the general population*. Paper presented at the Third National Family Violence Conference, Durham, NH.

Murphy, J. E. (1989, January). *Telephone surveys and family violence: Data from Minnesota*. Paper presented at the Responses to Family Violence Conference, West Lafayette, IN.

Nasjleti, M. (1980). Suffering in silence: The male incest victim. *Child Welfare, 59,* 203–215.

Neilsen, T. (1983). Sexual abuse of boys: Current perspectives. *Personnel and Guidance Journal, 62,* 139–142.

Perry, A. P. (1993). *The disclosure experience of the male victim of sexual abuse: Findings from a phenomenological study*. Paper presented at the Fifth Annual National Conference on Male Survivors, Washington, DC.

Pesso, A. (1990). *Moving psychotherapy: The Pesso system*. Cambridge, MA: Brookline.

Porter, E. (1986). *Treating the young male victims of sexual assault: Issues and intervention strategies*. Syracuse, NY: Safer Society Press.

Ramsey-Klawsnik, H. (1990, November). *Sexually abused boys: Indicators, abusers and impact of trauma*. Paper presented at the Third National Conference on the Male Survivor, Tucson, AZ.

Reinhart, M. A. (1987). Sexually abused boys. *Child Abuse and Neglect, 11*, 229–235.

Risin, L. I., & Koss, M. P. (1987). The sexual abuse of boys: Prevalence and descriptive characteristics of childhood victimizations. *Journal of Interpersonal Violence, 2*, 309–323.

Rogers, C. M., & Terry, T. (1984). Clinical interventions with boy victims of sexual abuse. In I. Stewart & J. Greer (Eds.), *Victims of sexual aggression* (pp. 91–104). New York: Van Nostrand Reinhold.

Russell, D. E. H. (1984). *Sexual exploitation: Rape, child sexual abuse, and workplace harassment*. Beverly Hills, CA: Sage.

Seidner, A. L., & Calhoun, D. S. (1984, August). *Childhood sexual abuse: Factors related to differential adult adjustment*. Paper presented at the Second National Conference for Family Violence Researchers, Durham, NH.

Sgroi, S. M. (1975). Child sexual molestation: The last frontier in child abuse. *Children Today, 44*, 18–28.

Showers, J., Farber, E. D., Joseph, J. A., Oshins, L., & Johnson, C. F. (1983). The sexual victimization of boys: A three-year survey. *Health Values, 7*, 15–18.

Spencer, M. J., & Dunklee, P. (1986). Sexual abuse of boys. *Pediatrics, 78*, 133–137.

Struve, J. (1990). Dancing with the patriarchy: The politics of sexual abuse. In M. Hunter (Ed.), *The sexually abused male, Vol. 1. Prevalence, impact, and treatment* (pp. 3–46). Lexington, MA: Lexington Books.

Swett, C., Jr., Surrey, J., & Cohen, C. (1990). Sexual and physical abuse histories and psychiatric symptoms among male psychiatric outpatients. *American Journal of Psychiatry, 147*, 632–636.

Swift, C. (1980). Sexual victimization of children: An urban mental health survey. In L. Schultz (Ed.), *The sexual victimology of youth* (pp. 18–24). Springfield, IL: Charles C Thomas.

Urquiza, A. J. (1988). *The effects of childhood sexual abuse in an adult male population*. Unpublished doctoral dissertation, University of Washington, Seattle.

Vander Mey, B. J. (1988). The sexual victimization of male children: A review of previous research. *Child Abuse and Neglect, 12*, 61–72.

Weinberg, S. K. (1955). *Incest behavior*. New York: Citadel Press.

APPENDIX A
HYPOTHETICAL RELATIONSHIP BETWEEN RELATIONSHIP, SETTING, AND SELF-DISCLOSURE

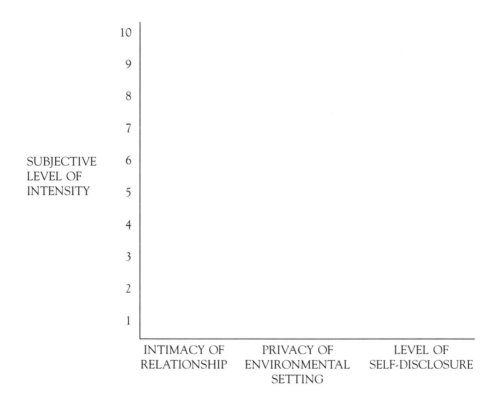

APPENDIX B
TREATMENT AGREEMENT

I, _____, am interested in being a participant in the treatment group for men who are survivors of childhood sexual abuse with _____ [treatment provider]. As a member, I agree to the following guidelines established for the welfare of myself and other group members:

1. I agree to be in an appropriate relationship with an individual therapist actively working on the issues of abuse.
2. I agree to sign releases for my individual and group therapists to exchange information so that we are all working to facilitate my recovery.
3. I agree to keep complete confidentiality about other group members. I understand that I may share my own experiences with anyone I choose, but only in a manner that *completely* protects the identity of all other participants.
4. I agree to attend each session on time, sober and drug-free. If I am unable to attend any session, I will give ample notice and call in case of emergency.
5. I agree that any contact with other group members, even by phone, must be mentioned in the following group session.
6. I agree to have no sexual contacts with group members.
7. I agree not to have any physical contact with other group members without their expressed permission.
8. I agree not to be living in an abusive environment or abusing another person.
9. Because this is a group for *nonoffending* survivors, I understand that I would no longer be able to participate if I recall memories of being sexually abusive in the past for which I have not received appropriate treatment.
10. Because my recovery is a major event in my life, I agree to care for myself to the best of my ability (i.e., proper sleep, proper diet, exercise, and remaining drug- and alcohol-free).

Client Signature _____

Witness Signature _____

Date _____

APPENDIX C
STRUCTURE FOR DISCLOSURE STORY

1. Who molested you?
2. How old were you?
3. How old were they?
4. Was it a single incident or repeated over time?
5. How many times or over what period of time?
6. Where did it happen?
7. What did he or she do to you?
8. What did they say to you about the molestation?
9. How did you feel at the time?
10. Who else knew about the molestation?
11. Why do you think you were molested?
12. When did it stop?
13. How did it stop?
14. When did you first disclose this to anyone? Why?
15. Were you believed?
16. Why had you remained silent as long as you did?
17. What was it like to disclose this information the first time?
18. What was it like to tell this story now?

Note. From *Treating the Young Male Victim of Sexual Assault: Issues and Intervention Strategies* (p. 51), by E. Porter, 1986, Syracuse, NY: Safer Society Press. Copyright 1986 by Safer Society Press. Adapted with permission.

23

WORKING IN GROUPS WITH MEN WHO BATTER

MICHELE HARWAY and KENDALL EVANS

Male aggression is a well-documented fact in society (Roth, 1994). The National Academy of Science's Panel on the Understanding and Control of Violent Behavior in the United States has reported that violence in the United States exceeds that in other Westernized countries (National Research Council, 1993). That this aggression is particularly pronounced in the family and against domestic partners has also been extensively described by Gelles and Straus (1989), as well as by others. For example, Straus, Gelles, and Steinmetz (1980) have indicated that "Americans run the greatest risk of assault, physical injury and even murder in their own homes by members of their own families" (p. 4). Those individuals most likely to hurt others in the home are usually men, and men are also the most likely initiators of violence in the home (Barnett, Keyson, & Thelen, 1992; Jacobson, 1993; Kurz, 1993).

We begin this chapter with an overview of battering—providing definitions, prevalence statistics (especially among those presenting for therapy), and descriptions of those who batter. In the sections that follow, we present a conceptual model for understanding the dynamics of batterers. This includes a critique of Walker's (1984) cycle of violence model as limited in explaining the phenomenological experience of batterers. In its place, we propose a model of the cycle of violence from an abuser's viewpoint that focuses on feeling avoidance. Treatment approaches to battering are then reviewed and critiqued with this model in mind. In the rest of the chapter, we present a group treatment model for batterers based on our proposed feeling avoidance model. This discussion includes information regarding composition of groups and length of treatment, a detailed description of the contents of treatment, a rationale for why this approach is more effective than others, and a description of the necessary qualifications of therapists attempting this approach.

WHAT IS BATTERING?

Battering is an act of control by one intimate partner over another. It may involve physical violence—that is, using one's physical strength or presence to control another—or it may involve verbal and emotional abuse, such as using one's words or voice to control another. Men who make use of verbal or emotional abuse often graduate to using physical violence to control their partners. Even when verbal abuse does not end in physical abuse, the psychological mechanisms that stimulate and maintain these two forms of control are the same. We describe these psychological mechanisms and their contribution to abuse later in the chapter.

Battering may include a variety of behaviors. These behaviors range from those appearing moderate (e.g., holding down a partner or unplugging the phone) to the more extreme (e.g., trying to run over someone with a car or using guns and knives). However, it is extremely important from a treatment perspective to recognize that batterers use a spectrum of violent behaviors. Consequently, battering should be recognized not as a response to anger, but as a strategy for maintaining power in a relationship, which the man sees as his entitlement. It is this faulty belief system and the maintenance of the sense of entitlement—through self-pity, denial, rationalization, manipulation, and general disregard for the partner—that need to be challenged in treatment. Because the core of battering is abuse, the terms *batterer* and *abuser* are used interchangeably in this chapter.

Battering Statistics

How common is battering? Prevalence statistics include only physical abuse and vary widely. Browne (1993) indicated that from 24% to 34% of American women will be physically assaulted by an intimate partner at some time. Gelles and Straus (1989) reported that one out of six wives they studied indicated that her husband had hit her during their marriage, with the attack taking the form of a severe beating in 6 cases out of 1,000 and involving the use of guns or knives in 2 cases out of 1,000. Likewise, Koss (1990) has reported that 50% of dating couples experience violence during courtship. Many agree, however, that the reported figures are likely to actually underestimate the true incidence of battering, because most studies are self-reports and typically exclude those who are very poor, do not speak English well, have chaotic lives, or are not at home when researchers contact them (in some cases, because they are in jail or other institutions or on military bases). In addition, some women are unwilling to speak to researchers even when promised anonymity, because they fear repercussions from their domestic partners. And none of the studies of the prevalence of battering include figures on emotional or psychological abuse.

Incidence of Battering Among Psychotherapy Clients

Whatever the actual prevalence of battering, it is high enough that all therapists are likely to find in their waiting rooms a battered spouse, a batterer, a child of these couples, or someone else affected by spousal violence. There is some indication that among psychotherapy clients the prevalence is even higher. Holtzworth-Munroe et al. (1992), in searching for a nonviolent control group for their study of spousal violence, had great difficulty finding nonviolent couples who were in marital therapy. In five different samples of maritally distressed but supposedly nonviolent couples being treated at psychological and family therapy clinics, 55%–56% of the men (depending on the sample) reported having at some time engaged in violent behavior toward their wives. From 43% to 46% of these men had been violent toward their wives in the preceding year. Although most of the violent behaviors were not severe (e.g., pushing, slapping, and throwing things), some severe violent behaviors (such as choking or using a knife or gun) were involved. Holtzworth-Munroe et al.'s study suggests that the incidence of battering among maritally distressed couples is likely to be substantially higher than among the general population, especially given that openly violent men had already been identified and excluded from the couples proposed for the control groups they examined.

Therapists' Knowledge About Battering

Holtzworth-Munroe et al.'s (1992) study also calls into question the competence of therapists to assess for and treat battering: If so many therapists were fooled into thinking that the couples they were treating were nonviolent, when clearly by their own admissions the men had physically assaulted their wives, then how adequate was the treatment that their clients received? Two other studies (Hansen, Harway, & Cervantes, 1991; Harway & Hansen, 1990, 1993) have suggested that therapists from certain backgrounds (e.g., psychologists, psychiatrists, and marriage and family therapists) may be ill-prepared to treat male batterers and their wives. These suggest that, when presented with cases in which instances of battering were clearly delineated, a majority of therapists did not identify violence as an issue and that the interventions that ensued were inappropriate and, in many cases, dangerous to the clients.

WHO BATTERS?

Batterers have been described in the literature in a variety of ways. Reviewing 400 studies, Hotaling and Sugarman (1986) found common traits associated with batterers. These included sexual aggressiveness, alcohol abuse, and lack of assertiveness. Bernard and Bernard (1984) described profiles of batterers from the Minnesota Multiphasic Personality Inventory as corresponding to the borderline personality type. Hamberger and Hastings (1986) described batterers as frequently having antisocial or compulsive personality disorders. Finally, Walker (1984) has described a violence-prone personality for batterers.

Jacobson (1993) reported that 20% of the batterers he studied in the laboratory were "vagal reactors"; that is, the men showed decreases in heart rate and other physiological measures during altercations, suggesting a dissociation between behavior and physiological reaction. He also reported that 45% of the men met criteria for antisocial personality disorder, showing a failure to increase physiological responsiveness during arguments.

In his review, Gondolf (1993) concluded that there is "increasing speculation that no conclusive 'batterer profile' exists" (p. 107). He based this on the fact that most of the current research was conducted on small clinical samples and showed much contradiction and overlap. He cited Hamberger and Hastings's (1991) study—comparing batterers to a control group—as suggesting that when properly conducted, studies show that batterers as a group do not differ much from the general population.

Thus, although studies have suggested that there may indeed be identifiable subgroups of men who batter, it is likely that batterers can be found in any group of men, from those who are socially prominent and accomplished to those who are socially disenfranchised.

THE CONCEPTUAL MODEL: UNDERSTANDING BATTERER DYNAMICS

Instead of focusing on the batterer as the phenomenon needing explanation, it may be more useful to look at the dynamics of battering. There may be no common profile of personality traits or characteristic pathology of batterers, but there is a common pattern of behavior.

In understanding batterer dynamics, it is important to know about the cycle of violence described by Walker (1984). Walker began by assuming that all couples experience tension. When one member of the couple is a batterer, however, the tension eventually results in an explosion of violence, which quickly leads to remorse and to what she has described as the "honeymoon" period, with the batterer openly courting the battered partner. However, because nothing is solved, additional and renewed tension continues to rise in the relationship.

Walker's (1984) model has been extremely useful in understanding some characteristic behavior patterns of abusive relationships. For example, the world external to the relationship tends to see the couple during the honeymoon period, when the man looks loving and rational. However, the woman has the symptoms of traumatic stress disorder, which make her look emotionally unstable, angry, vacillating, hysterical, and so on. Moreover, potential helpers expect the woman to take action against someone upon whom she has depended in the past, who has just terrified her but is now acting like the loving man with whom she wanted to be originally. However, taking action can appear (and, in fact, may be) more dangerous than letting it go and "forgiving." Both man and woman are motivated to minimize and deny the violence and the abuse in support of the loving relationship that the honeymoon period seems to prove that they have.

Usually, the tension and violence continue if not interrupted. Episodes often get worse and more frequent. Eventually the honeymoon period may disappear, because neither partner can pretend that it will not happen again, after it happens so often. The cycle of violence model thus predicts that the cycle will continue: The relief from tension that follows the explosive violence is sufficient to reinforce the cycle. The cycle also reflects a kind of predictability—a dynamic homeostasis—that enables it to self-regenerate.

The main use of this cycle model clinically has been to help battered women. Survivors can use the model to see past the honeymoon period and past their own excessive guilt and to understand that the abuse and violence will continue, no matter what they do within the relationship. They learn that they cannot ever change themselves enough to affect the cycle.

The key to understanding battering is to know that the cycle of violence is controlled by the abuser's behavior. Until and unless the survivor steps outside the cycle, she will be enmeshed in it. The batterer's pattern of behavior is independent of the behavior of his immediate partner. This has been evidenced by Jacobson's (1993) research, which showed that in the course of an argument between a batterer and his wife, her behavior had no effect on the outcome or the process of the argument. It did not matter if she was nice or mean; her behavior was irrelevant to whether the batterer escalated and the argument got worse.

Unlike other family problems, violence controls the family system; it is not the other way around. Moreover, to a much greater degree than with other problems, the roots of violence lie in cultural rules and social functioning, and in individual coping styles and histories, as opposed to in family systems or patterns.

POWER AND CONTROL

The concept of the cycle of violence has been updated with the Duluth Minnesota Domestic Violence Project's Power and Control Wheel (Pence & Paymar, 1990). The wheel illustrates the idea that the core issue in an abusive relationship is not the cycle of violence—not the violence at all—but the pervasive issue of control. The wheel describes how using one's words or voice to control someone are common behaviors of abusive men (Harway & Hansen, 1994). It has taken time to identify this as the most crucial issue because the drama of violence has been so compelling. However, it is crucial to effective intervention to understand that violence is the enforcer for the control that a male batterer tries to have in many contexts.

Battered women in support groups often find the power and control wheel model to be very liberating and empowering. It makes sense out of their phenomenological experience, when they may have felt "crazy" in the past because the pattern of behavior their partners exhibited made no sense to them. Many battered women have the experience of being blamed, directly and indirectly, for the abuse and violence they suffer. The power and control wheel helps support their experience of being controlled and abused.

THE PHENOMENOLOGICAL EXPERIENCE OF BATTERERS

Although battered women find the power and control wheel and an explanation of the cycle of violence to be helpful, abusers do not find them as useful. Abusers often do not believe that these models fit their phenomenological experience. Admittedly this is partly because men are in denial of the effects and the reality of their own behavior. In addition, men often do not experience themselves as particularly powerful in the world or in their relationships. Thus, when accused of trying to control relationships, they feel misunderstood. Several men with whom we have worked have said that at the moments that they were the most abusive, they were terrified by feelings of being "out of control."

The model we propose here focuses on the batterer's phenomenological experience: his feelings, his behavior, and the consequences of his behavior, from his viewpoint. Although this volume focuses on working with men, the model is equally applicable to women. These factors are examined simultaneously in the contexts of the batterer's history, his culture, his current situation, his relationships in general, and the relationship under question in particular. The model has largely been developed out of the work of Kendall Evans.

THE CYCLE OF VIOLENCE FROM AN ABUSER'S VIEWPOINT: FEELING AVOIDANCE

The feeling avoidance model, outlined in Figure 1, examines the cycle of violence with a focus on how the abuser experiences it. Most abusers in relationships experience tension and other unacceptable feelings. This tension may or may not be about events within the relationship. It also may be a distant or unclear experience. Eventually the tension becomes too much for the abuser's usual coping mechanisms, and there is a crisis. This crisis is about feelings overwhelming the person—feelings such as hurt, shame, helplessness, fear, guilt, inadequacy, and loneliness that the person has been taught are bad or are felt only by "weaklings." The person therefore feels a need to use defenses. It is important for the therapist to realize

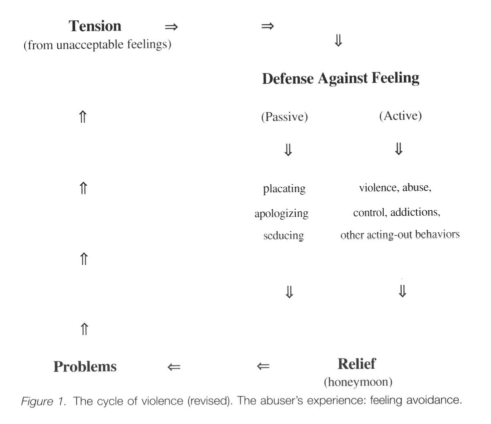

Figure 1. The cycle of violence (revised). The abuser's experience: feeling avoidance.

that these defenses are used against feelings. They are not a solution to the problems that led to the feelings. Such defenses against feelings can include (a) placing blame and denying responsibility, making the other the enemy who must be attacked (i.e., partner abuse); (b) controlling everyone and everything around (also abuse); (c) using alcohol or drugs to temporarily take away the pain (leading to addictions); or (d) seeking negative excitement, such as one-night stands, to distract (i.e., acting out).

All of these defenses can lead to relief in the short run, which reinforce their use, despite the fact that they also lead to increased problems. At the point in the cycle where problems occur, the abuser may be apologetic and placating—exhibiting honeymoon behavior—to defend against blame, guilt, and loss. Such behavior is just another way of protecting against feelings by controlling his partner.

Honeymoon behavior may drop off after a while, when repeated abuse makes it impossible for either partner to believe the abuser's apologies. At this point, temporary relief still keeps the cycle going. The consequences of the abuser's defenses actually cause increased bad feelings and continued rising tensions. This cycle of behavior regularly repeats, and it can get more frequent, more abusive, and more dangerous over time unless interrupted or controlled by external factors.

In the cycle, the survivor's behavior is irrelevant: Whether she is passive or placating does not matter. This cycle is of the individual abuser's making. Moreover, an abuser lives within his cycle in many if not all of his relationships; that is, an abuser may only be violent in intimate relationships, but will be controlling and abusive in most of his relationships. One might not label this behavior as abusive, because it is within the ordinary range of what is expected of men (e.g., a man might be extremely controlling of his secretary). Noticed or not, it is the controlling behavior that men exhibit and the coercion that abusers use to enforce control that lie at the core of partner abuse experienced by the survivor. It is the cycle of avoidance in dealing with one's central issues by being abusive that is the core issue for batterers themselves. If this behavior pattern is not changed, abuse will continue.

The feeling avoidance model is consistent with the work being done in the fields of alcohol and addiction treatment and sex offender treatment, especially with regard to relapse-prevention work. This is no accident. Alcohol and drug abuse are related to domestic violence, as many correlational studies have shown (e.g., Dutton, 1988; Edleson & Tolman, 1992). But the relationship between the factors remains elusive unless one assumes alcohol and drug abuse as well as domestic violence are defenses against feelings. Therefore, an abuser who is actively abusing substances will rarely stop abusing his partner, because he is still avoiding feelings. Likewise, a sober abuser will generally still be abusive toward his partner unless he gets specific treatment to stop abusive behavior and confront his feelings.

TREATMENT APPROACHES TO BATTERING

The spectrum of violence described above and the mechanisms that the batterer uses to maintain control over his partner while allowing him to deny responsibility for the violence suggest that confronting the violence and underlying psychological mechanisms will be difficult (if not impossible) to accomplish effectively in individual therapy. Thus, group participation is usually recommended for effective treatment. However, as Gondolf (1993) has pointed out, not all interventions are of equal value. With this in mind, we next review common group treatment programs and their effectiveness rates. Ultimately, we present one model for group treatment of batterers that has been remarkably effective.

The three major approaches to group treatment of batterers include programs (a) focusing on anger management; (b) addressing skill building in a psychoeducational setting; and (c) confronting men's tendencies toward power and control, with a view toward making men accountable for their behavior. Some treatment programs include several of the above components.

Anger-management programs are based on the belief that battering is caused by a man's inability to control his temper. Intervention consists of teaching the batterer to avoid outbursts by identifying the cues that precede them and the behaviors of the partner that provoke them. As Gondolf (1993) suggested, however, anger-control programs by themselves are ineffective, partly because they give the batterer, whose problem is wanting to control his environment, yet one more thing to learn to control. Moreover, Gondolf also suggested that anger-management programs do not properly identify that men's sense of entitlement and privilege is one cause of battering. Consequently, anger-control modifications to batterers' behaviors seem to be of the "quick fix" variety (Gondolf, 1993, p. 110) rather than to lead to long-lasting and deep change.

Similarly, skill-building programs lead to rather superficial change as well. Instead of attempting to modify underlying psychological processes, skill-building programs focus on teaching more effective communication skills, stress reduction, gender roles, conflict management, and the like. Cognitive restructuring is also often a component. Although skills building can be an effective component of batterer treatment programs, by itself it often leads to batterers who learn to be more effective at controlling others through abuse.

A third type of intervention involves confronting men's tendency toward power and control and teaching batterers to take responsibility for the abuse. However, as we describe later, this type of intervention, although critical to include in a broader program of intervention, has only limited effectiveness on its own because it tends to shame and guilt men and lead to large dropout rates among already defensive clients.

Newer approaches, such as Jenkins's (1990) social constructionist approach, assume that men will "relate respectfully, sensitively and nonabusively with others unless restrained from doing so" (p. 32). Treatment hinges on finding out what is stopping the man from taking responsibility to relate respectfully and equitably with his partner and what is stopping him from taking responsibility for his abusive behavior. Focusing on restraints, Jenkins (1990) believes, "promotes an active consideration of alternatives to abuse and what has been stopping the male from engaging in them. He is invited to become preoccupied with his own competence in challenging restraining habits and ideas and discovering and practicing alternatives to abuse" (p. 32).

Research on the effectiveness of batterer treatment programs has been equivocal. There is some evidence that these programs effectively curb physical violence (60% of men who completed the programs were not physically violent 6 months after completion; Tolman & Bennett, 1990), but nothing to indicate that the cycle of violence and abuse has been removed from these men's repertoire (60% of men continued to be verbally abusive; Tolman & Bennett, 1990; Edleson & Syers, 1990). Recall that previously described types of batterer treatment programs have also failed to deal with the underlying dynamics of the abuse. Unless and until this aspect is included in treatment, the patterns of abuse in families can be expected to continue.

GROUP INTERVENTION IN THE CYCLE OF FEELING AVOIDANCE

Most of the materials produced on the treatment of batterers emphasize the necessity for the core intervention to be group work. There are a variety of explanations given for this, such as the idea that men are socialized together into the culture of women blaming and violence and that they can best be resocialized in groups of men. One practical reason for group work is that the more experienced participants can, more effectively than the therapist, confront the denial and abusive beliefs of the newer group members, while reinforcing their own changes.

The best reason for group work may be that it facilitates working with men in the area of their interpersonal functioning. Some men are so filled with shame that it takes hearing that other men have the same problems and have found a way to be different to give them the courage to examine themselves. For example, clients may espouse feminist convictions and a conscious commitment to nonviolence but, in fact, may be controlling and attacking in their interactions with others. In the group, the contradiction between their politics and their behavior is addressed and provides the focus for change.

The intervention process that works best with batterers is a mixture of therapy and education—a blend of cognitive–behavioral techniques, traumatology, feminist analysis, and psychodynamic approaches. Like therapy with other resistant clients, the work with batterers cannot depart too far from looking at behavior change as the most important goal and the most common topic of group conversation.

However, in group work as well as in other areas of life, "a man convinced against his will is of the same mind, still." Durable personality change depends on building an effective group process and involving each man in personal relationships that support frequently painful self-awareness and difficult self-confrontation. Shaming a client by forcefully confronting him without a supportive relationship rarely enables positive change and often results in disaster. In addition, men rarely listen to alternatives to their own beliefs unless they feel heard and understood. In particular, they need to know that their pain and feelings of powerlessness are validated before they are ready to deal with the extent to which they create their own problems by their abusive behavior.

Most of the earlier theories and treatment approaches are limited in effect because they are limited in scope. Yet each is important and necessary in the treatment of domestic violence. It is important to focus on the behavior of violence and control; however, it is also important to work with the abusers' feelings of pain. Treatment must emphasize the effects and consequences of the abuser's behavior, and there must be social consequences, such as arrest and jail, for batterers' treatment to succeed. But it is also important to acknowledge that the abuser is not just his abuse. He is many other human things as well—a total person.

Batterers' treatment must address sexism as a major part of the subject matter of group work. It is also important to work with the individual circumstances of each person's life. Anger-control techniques are important, but they are only another tool to a man who still wants control. Therefore, although communication and other relationship skills have to be taught, attitude change, and, more important, personality change also have to be goals. Understanding how a batterer is repeating family-of-origin behaviors may also help one plan appropriate interventions.

In general, batterers do not seem to be significantly different from other men psychologically. There have been indications that batterers are somewhat more angry at women, somewhat more impulsive, and somewhat more uncomfortable with societal rules than other men. Few batterers are severely disturbed, however (Hamberger & Hastings, 1991). A clear majority of batterers are survivors of childhood abuse or have experience in watching abuse. Their abusive behavior is often patterned on the abuse they suffered (Straus, Gelles, & Steinmetz, 1980), in addition to being the way they cope with the abuse they suffered. Therefore, education and retraining are simply inadequate to significantly change most batterers. Batterers need healing and recovery, like any other victim, before they can stop using the coping patterns caused by their own victimization.

The group sessions that we describe in detail below do not always focus solely on domestic violence. Group members talk about work, friendships, childhood, and many other topics. This is important because talking about the cycle of defense against feelings in any area of their life will lead to personal change and to a reduction in violence and abuse. Therapists must understand that abuse is a symptom of a human being living a dysfunctional pattern of behavior, as a result of dysfunctional life experiences within a dysfunctional society.

THE TREATMENT MODEL: GROUP TREATMENT OF BATTERERS

The following is a description of the batterer's treatment program directed by Kendall Evans. Another Way is a project of a private nonprofit counseling agency in Los Angeles, California, and has been in existence for 7 years. Services are offered on a sliding-scale fee basis to male and female clients, who are similar in demographic composition to the surrounding mixed-ethnicity community, except that non-English-speaking clients are referred out.

Group Composition

About two thirds of the male clients are referred by the courts to the program, through diversion or probation. These involuntary clients frequently come in convinced that they are the real victims, either of a vindictive wife or an insensitive, "male-bashing" court system. Clients who admit to violent behavior usually either minimize it or rationalize that the woman provoked their behavior. Many clients try to claim innocence in spite of a guilty plea, saying that they agreed to a plea to avoid jail or on (reportedly bad) advice from a public defender.

In general, these clients attribute responsibility for the events and consequences of their acts to other people and things. However, there are a few who come in taking full responsibility for their behavior, motivated by their own awareness that their lives are not working. The violence perpetrated by the court-referred men varies in seriousness, with injuries requiring hospital treatment being the minority. Men causing more serious injury apparently are more frequently sentenced to jail time and so are not referred for therapy as frequently.

The male clients who are not court referred are usually referred by their partners, meaning that they are trying to keep a partner or get her back by coming to therapy. These clients have a higher dropout rate and frequently are less motivated than court-referred clients, although a few enter therapy motivated to change.

The women referred by the court seem to have some of the same dynamics as the men, yet they are also significantly different. They seem more likely to be battered women fighting back or to be more emotionally disturbed than male referrals. There is also the fact that being violent is not generally accepted behavior for women in the same way that it is for men. Some programs include women in coed groups and report good results (Richardson, 1990). However, because the state of California requires court referrals to go to same-gender groups, women and men join different groups in the Another Way program. Given the focus of this book, we discuss only the male groups here.

Time Frame

If a client stays with the group for more than four sessions, he usually finishes his 1-year contract. Most men who stay for 1 year seem, on the basis of clinical assessment and interviews with their partners, to change significantly. Most have completely stopped being violent and are significantly less emotionally abusive. Some men actually stay beyond their 1-year commitment for 2–3 years, and these tend to be the men who change the most. After the first year, clients also often participate in individual and couples counseling with generally excellent results.

At the same time, there are also some clients, maybe as many as 20%, who do not change significantly. They may maintain an awareness of legal consequences, which will reduce their acts of violence, but they are just as emotionally abusive as when they started. A small number of men drop out within the first four sessions when they realize that they will be confronted and pushed to participate. Voluntary clients also have a high probability of dropping out if their initial attendance immediately resulted in reunification with their partner.

Group Functioning

In the group, treatment generally focuses on emotional violence more often than physical abuse, because emotional abuse recurs frequently. Nevertheless, there is often the threat of serious injury in the situations described by clients, and safety is the first priority issue. Safety for clients, their partners, and group participants is emphasized at all times. In addition, there does not seem to be a reliable way to discriminate in a few assessment sessions between men who have a low or high risk of becoming violent.

Group work with batterers seems to follow a loose pattern or progression, partially dictated by the treatment priorities inherent in the situation. For example, one way of clarifying seemingly competing priorities is to make safety the clear number one priority. One way of ordering the phases of treatment is represented by the acronym SAFER, which stands for safety, awareness, focus (on commitment to change), education, and recovery.

A typical session starts with clients doing a "check in." Clients reporting more serious events in the past week or more serious emotional states are encouraged to begin to work first. Each client reviews the relevant parts of his week, usually having to do with coping with some part of his life. There is usually feedback from group members and facilitators, which involves giving support for feelings and new behaviors, exploring possible alternative behaviors, examining coping behaviors, and examining past traumas triggered by present events. Clients are encouraged to take responsibility for their feelings, behavior, and lives and are confronted for being abusive, blaming, denying, rationalizing, avoidant, aggressive, passive, and so on.

Blocks to Change

In general, the men that end up in these groups tend to be appropriately labeled *resistant* (Edelwich & Brodsky, 1992). They tend to feel powerless, to avoid self-awareness, to insist on being right, and to hang on to cultural supports for their behavior, such as stereotypes about men being dominant and unemotional.

Some batterers have invested major parts of their identity in their "maleness," as this is defined by being different from and dominant over women. Talking about feelings, cooperating, walking away from an aggressive challenge, and being considerate can all be seen as being "not male" and therefore threatening to such clients' sense of identity. Some clients were raised in emotionally abusive environments that left them filled with shame, so that questioning any aspect of their behavior becomes very painful. For them, the need to be right is experienced as a survival issue. For almost all clients, a confrontation that shames the client does not lead to significant or useful change. Shame is toxic, counterproductive, and easily stimulated.

For other men, the work revolves around the difficulty of giving up the power they feel when they use coercion successfully to control another person. Men who are generally doing well and use intellectual defenses are frequently too proud to let themselves learn anything different from another person. Many men feel relatively powerless in their lives and fear giving up any power they may have attained. Others feel powerful, enjoy the power, identify with it, and fear having nothing if they give up misusing power. Many clients feel unable to change or appear unable to even conceive of changing. Surprisingly, high proportions of men in these batterers groups appear to be quite passive generally and resist change indirectly, by simply not acting.

Overcoming the Blocks

The key to overcoming the blocks of batterers is the use of the group process with this specialized clientele. In this setting, what is examined includes the relationship of the group to the wider society. The fact that the group cooperates with the courts and focuses on safety is important. The partners of clients who are willing are interviewed, and the client is reminded that safety (especially that of the partner) is the first priority. The fact that battering is against the law and negatively sanctioned by society is the frame within which clients' behavior is challenged.

Nevertheless, the client's own needs are not neglected. The client has to feel heard, understood, and accepted. As stated above, shaming a client does not work and is usually destructive. Batterers use abuse to cope with the traumas they themselves have suffered and have not healed from. They cannot heal if they continue their abuse, because abuse covers the pain that needs healing. They cannot stop the abuse without learning other ways to cope with their pain, and, ultimately, they cannot reliably stop abusing without healing from their own pain. Behavior change alone is simply not enough.

The group process provides both the support and the examples that are needed for change to occur. The newer or more resistant clients learn from the examples, support, and confrontations of the more experienced men. Conversely, the more experienced men learn from seeing themselves in others' stories. Educational material, such as facts about the consequences of violence, is presented to clients as situations come up in their lives, so that they are more emotionally ready and desirous of learning new ideas and behaviors than they would be with a simple didactic approach.

The power of the group process is sometimes very surprising. Passive–avoidant men often learn to become more assertive, whereas inconsiderate, aggressive men learn to soften and show nurturing. It is not possible to predict in an individual client's case how successful he will be in group. However, it is possible to maximize each person's chance of success by observing his group process and using the group to draw him out or confront his controlling or aggressive behavior.

Clients identify with and use the cycle of feeling avoidance that we have described above. It makes sense of their experience, offers them a way out of feeling trapped, and explains their behavior without blaming and shaming them. Too often, such clients' therapy experience involves simply being told that they are "bad" and should stop being bad. But this does not really help clients change. Understanding clients' violent behavior within the context of their past history makes sense of their behavior and helps them understand how to meet their own needs better through change.

Clients from ethnic minority groups sometimes have a hard time feeling comfortable enough to open up to the group experience. It is important to make sure that each client has at least one other person with whom he can identify in the group. Learning to understand the lives of men different from oneself is part of the value of the group for many batterers, who can be racist as well as sexist. Learning self-respect is also a powerful gain from effective group process.

Group, Individual, and Couples Therapies

One of the controversies in the domestic violence treatment field is over which form of treatment is most effective. Although much research needs to be done before anything definite can be stated, the experience from cases going through the Another Way program has tended to support the clinical experience of most battered women's advocates—namely, that couples therapy is both more dangerous and not as effective as group therapy (Jacobson, 1994; Segel-Evans, 1991). The dynamics of the cycle of feeling avoidance support the idea that violence is a choice made by an individual, independent of the immediate environment, including his partner. It may take two to cooperate or communicate, but it only takes one to abuse.

In practice, when clients can look exclusively at their own behavior, they change. When a client is in a situation such as couples counseling, where he can either continue to blame his partner or include her in the discussion, he does not change his behavior. Similarly, individual therapy can be effective in helping batterers heal, but it is generally less effective in helping resistant clients change their behavior than is group therapy.

Therapist Qualifications

Not every therapist can work effectively with this population. Therapists working with batterers need to be comfortable with the parts of themselves that can be aggressive and abusive. Otherwise they are more likely to shame clients for abusive and aggressive behavior that they feel ashamed of themselves. Therapists in this work also need to be flexible and somewhat streetwise to avoid losing credibility with clients and being easily misled.

Understanding how women experience male violence and oppression is also essential, and sometimes easily overlooked, when one is trying to understand the male client's experience. It is essential to be able to maintain multiple foci or awarenesses. For example, one must be able to understand how a man can feel controlled by his wife, who in turn is being terrorized by him, without losing a sense of objectivity about what is real and what dangers exist in the situation.

Every therapist has a consistent tendency to attract a particular range of transference reactions—what could be called their *transference value*. Many therapists would like to be a "good parent" to most of their clients, but they are reluctant to encourage that much dependency and so settle for being a good aunt or good uncle. Unfortunately, certain therapists attract critical parent reactions. Therapists working with batterers need to have good parent transference value; that is, they need to be experienced as nurturing, nonjudgmental, wise, and firmly in control. The gender of the therapist is less important than one's ability to be a good parent. Female therapists with sexualized or critical interactions or male therapists with critical or competitive interactions will be equally ineffective.

SUMMARY

Prevalence statistics make it clear that battering is much more common than has heretofore been believed. In particular, the incidence is likely to be particularly high among couples who seek out therapy. At the same time, some evidence exists that therapists are not properly prepared to assess for and intervene in cases of domestic violence (e.g., Hansen, Harway, & Cervantes, 1991; Holtzworth-Munroe et al., 1992). Evaluations of treatment modalities used in working with batterers have shown that group intervention is most effective (Gondolf, 1993), although one should realize that not all group treatment is the same.

We have proposed a group intervention model for working with men who batter. The key to working effectively with male batterers is understanding the dynamics of abuse. The core component of this dynamic is described as the cycle of feeling avoidance—a modification of Lenore Walker's (1984) cycle of violence—as described from the phenomenological experience of batterers. The feeling avoidance model posits that when tension experienced by the batterer overwhelms his usual coping mechanisms, a crisis is precipitated. The crisis is generated because feelings threaten to overwhelm the man, who was taught that such feelings are bad. He defends against his feelings by blaming his partner (making her the enemy who must be attacked), by controlling those around him, by using substances to numb his feelings, or by acting out. Use of such defenses leads to relief, which in turn reinforces the usefulness of these defenses. Remorse or honeymoon behavior are themselves defenses against feelings of guilt or blame. Because the cycle is the batterer's cycle, his partner's behavior is irrelevant to the continuation or exacerbation of the cycle. Batterer treatment groups that focus on describing the cycle of feeling avoidance use group process to confront the batterer while providing support for change, include trauma recovery approaches, and combine cognitive–behavioral techniques, psychodynamic approaches, education, and feminist analysis—all with an emphasis on safety.

REFERENCES

Barnett, O. W., Keyson, M., & Thelen, R. E. (1992, August). Women's violence as a response to male abuse. Paper presented at the 100th Annual Convention of the American Psychological Association, Washington, DC.

Bernard, J. L., & Bernard, M. L. (1984). The abusive male seeking treatment: Jekyll and Hyde. *Family Relations, 33,* 543–547.

Browne, A. (1993). Violence against women by male partners: Prevalence, outcomes, and policy implications. *American Psychologist, 48,* 1077 1087.

Dutton, D. (1988). *The domestic assault of women.* Boston: Allyn & Bacon.

Edelwich, J., & Brodsky, A. (1992). *Group counseling for the resistant client.* Lexington, MA: Lexington Books.

Edleson, J., & Syers, M. (1990). The relative effectiveness of group treatments for men who batter. *Social Work Research and Abstracts, 26,* 10–17.

Edleson, J., & Tolman, R. (1992). *Interventions for men who batter: An ecological approach.* Newbury Park, CA: Sage.

Gelles, R. J., & Straus, M. (1989). *Intimate violence: The causes and consequences of abuse in the American family.* New York: Simon & Schuster.

Gondolf, E. W. (1993). Treating the batterer. In M. Hansen & M. Harway (Eds.), *Battering and family therapy: A feminist perspective* (pp. 105–118). Newbury Park, CA: Sage.

Hamberger, L. K., & Hastings, J. E. (1986). Personality correlates of men who abuse their partners: A cross-validation study. *Journal of Family Violence, 1,* 37–49.

Hamberger, L. K., & Hastings, J. E. (1991). Personality correlates of men who batter and nonviolent men: Some continuities and discontinuities. *Journal of Family Violence, 6,* 131–148.

Hansen, M., Harway, M., & Cervantes, N. (1991). Therapists' perceptions of severity in cases of family violence. *Violence and Victims, 6,* 225–235.

Harway, M., & Hansen, M. (1990). Therapists' recognition of wife battering: Some empirical evidence. *Family Violence Bulletin, 6*(3), 16–18.

Harway, M., & Hansen, M. (1993). Therapist perceptions of family violence. In M. Hansen & M. Harway (Eds.), *Battering and family therapy: A feminist perspective* (pp. 42–53). Newbury Park, CA: Sage.

Harway, M., & Hansen, M. (1994). *Spouse abuse: Assessing and treating battered women, batterers and their children.* Sarasota, FL: Professional Resource Press.

Holtzworth-Munroe, A., Waltz, J., Jacobson, N. S., Monaco, V., Fehrenbach, P. A., & Gottman, J. M. (1992). Recruiting nonviolent men as control subjects for research on marital violence: How easily can it be done? *Violence and Victims, 7,* 79–88.

Hotaling, G. T., & Sugarman, D. B. (1986). An analysis of risk markers in husband to wife violence: The current state of knowledge. *Violence and Victims, 1,* 101–124.

Jacobson, N. (1993, October). *Domestic violence: What the couples look like.* Paper presented at the Annual Convention of the American Association for Marriage and Family Therapy.

Jacobson, N. S. (1994). Rewards and changes in researching domestic violence. *Family Process, 33,* 81–85.

Jenkins, A. (1990). *Invitations to responsibility.* Adelaide, Australia: Dulwich Centre Publications.

Koss, M. P. (1990). The women's mental health agenda: Violence against women. *American Psychologist, 45,* 374–380.

Kurz, D. (1993). Physical assaults by husbands: A major social problem. In R. J. Gelles & D. R. Loseke (Eds.), *Current controversies on family violence* (pp. 88–103). Newbury Park, CA: Sage.

National Research Council. (1993). *Understanding and preventing violence.* Washington, DC: National Academy of Sciences.

Pence, E., & Paymar, M. (1990). *Power and control, tactics of men who batter: An educational curriculum.* Duluth, MN: Minnesota Program Development.

Richardson, A. (1990). *The effects of the presence of female batterers on male batterers.* Unpublished master's thesis, California Family Study Center, North Hollywood.

Roth, J. A. (1994, February). *Understanding and preventing violence: Research in brief* (p. 4). Washington, DC: National Institute of Justice.

Segel-Evans, K. (1991). The dangers of traditional family therapy when intervening in domestic violence. *The California Therapist, 3,* 45–48.

Straus, M. A., Gelles, R. J., & Steinmetz, S. K. (1980). *Behind closed doors: Violence in the American family.* Garden City, NY: Anchor/Doubleday.

Tolman, R. M., & Bennett, L. W. (1990). A review of quantitative research on men who batter. *Journal of Interpersonal Violence, 5,* 87–118.

Walker, L. E. (1984). *The battered woman syndrome.* New York: Springer.

24

OUTPATIENT TREATMENT OF ADOLESCENT MALE SEXUAL OFFENDERS

JUDITH V. BECKER

Children, adolescents, and adults in U.S. society continue to fall prey to individuals who commit sexual offenses against them to satisfy sexual and psychological needs. To decrease sexual offending, interventions must be developed and implemented in three areas. Primary prevention would focus on identifying the biological, psychological, sociological, and cultural factors that predispose individuals to engage in coercive sexual behaviors or to engage in sexual activity with individuals who are unable to give their consent. A second level of intervention would be to identify those individuals who are at risk for becoming sexual perpetrators and to treat them before they commit an offense. The third level of intervention would be to provide services to those children and adolescents who have already engaged in sexually offending behavior or who have sexual behavior problems.

Over the past 20 years, the knowledge base has increased tremendously concerning the systematic evaluation of individuals who have committed sexual offenses. Until recently, most of the information that was known about sexual offenders had come from incarcerated offenders. Although these data have increased understanding of sexual offenders who are apprehended and convicted, clearly not all offenders are arrested and incarcerated. Also, data on incarcerated offenders are not altogether reliable; incarcerated offenders who disclose sex offenses that they have committed beyond those for which they were convicted would risk further prosecution or affecting their parole.

Abel, Becker, Cunningham-Rathner, Mittelman, and Rouleau (1988), in an attempt to learn more about the psychopathology of adult male sexual offenders, interviewed 411 nonincarcerated men with paraphilias under a certificate of confidentiality. Among the findings were (a) that most sex offenders had multiple paraphilias, (b) that most had committed more offenses than they had been arrested for, and (c) that 58% of the adult offenders reported the onset of deviant sexual interests in adolescence.

ADOLESCENT MALE SEXUAL OFFENDERS

During the past decade, American society has become increasingly aware of the problems of adolescents engaging in sexual misconduct, including the abuse of children and the sexual assault of peers and adults. Although the exact prevalence of sexual offenses committed by adolescent males is unknown, it has been estimated that they account for 20% of the rapes committed in the United States as well as about 40% of the cases of child molestation.

Over the past 10 years, there has been a tremendous response on the part of mental health professionals to the problem of youthful sexual offenders. In the 1980s, a National Adolescent Perpetrator Network was founded, and a national task force was appointed as part of that network. The network published its preliminary report in 1988 (National Adolescent Perpetrator Network, 1988), and a revised report was published in 1993 (National Adolescent Perpetrator Network, 1993). These reports are highly recommended for any psychologist who is considering working with juvenile sex offenders.

Prior to the 1980s, there were only 19 published articles in the psychological literature regarding juvenile offenders. Authors conducting a recent literature review (Becker, Harris, & Sales, 1993) found 73 citations in the psychological literature. As greater attention is given by the media and professionals to youthful offenders, there should be an increase in clinical research regarding etiology, characteristics, and treatment outcomes. Two edited books on juvenile sexual offending were published in the 1990s (Barbaree, Marshall, & Hudson, 1993; Ryan & Lane, 1991), and both are recommended reading.

In general, male adolescent sexual offenders are a heterogeneous group. No single profile has emerged to define them. Two typologies for classifying male adolescent offenders have been proposed, however (Knight & Prentky, 1993; O'Brien & Bera, 1986), and both await empirical validation. The treatment of adolescent sexual offenders, as with the etiology of offending, has received little empirical investigation, and only one controlled therapy-outcome study currently appears in the scientific literature (Borduin, Henggeler, Blaske, & Stein, 1990).

Assessment

Because the majority of adolescent sexual offenders are not self-referred for treatment but are usually referred by the juvenile court system or child protective services, it is quite common for the adolescent (and, on occasion, the parents) to deny or minimize that the adolescent has committed a sexual offense or may have a sexual behavior problem. Therefore, it is crucial that the psychologist obtain and review police reports, victim statements, and any other records related to the offense. It is also important to interview the adolescent's parent or parents. Typically, this assessment consists of a clinical interview, psychometric testing, and, in some cases, psychophysiologic assessment (e.g., for males, penile plethysmography). The following information should be obtained during the clinical interview: demographic information; family history; developmental history; criminal history; social history; drug and alcohol history; prior psychiatric and medical history; details of academic performance; history of maltreatment; and in-depth sexual history, including fantasies, urges, and behaviors. It is important to query adolescents about all types of paraphiliac behavior in addition to the sexual offense or offenses they committed. It is rare for an adolescent to volunteer other instances of inappropriate behavior engaged in or fantasies that he or she is having unless directly asked.

Unfortunately, to date there has been no psychometric test or combination of psychological tests that can definitely determine whether a person has committed a sexual offense or whether they are at risk for reoffending. Given the high incidence of comorbidity in this population, a comprehensive battery of tests should be conducted, including intelligence and personality measures. When deemed appropriate, penile plethysmography may be used with male adolescents. The Association for the Treatment of Sexual Abusers has established guidelines for the use of the plethysmograph (Association for the Treatment of Sexual Abusers, 1993). The National Juvenile Sexual Offending Task Force (National Adolescent Perpetrator Network, 1993) has also addressed the use of this procedure, which should only be undertaken with the consent of the adolescent and his parents or guardian.

Following a comprehensive assessment, the therapist should develop an individualized treatment plan. The adolescent may need individual, group, and family therapy as well as adjunctive therapies (e.g., for substance abuse problems). Although some adolescents can remain with their families and receive outpatient therapy, others may be in need of day treatment, placement with a therapeutic foster home or group home, or residential treatment. Those youth remanded to a juvenile corrections facility should receive treatment while incarcerated and follow-up care with appropriate monitoring and supervision provided.

Models of Treatment

Models for treatment of sexual offenders include biological, relapse prevention, cognitive–behavioral, and family therapy. Those clinicians who adhere to a biological model for paraphilias have discussed the use of biological treatment, including the use of antiandrogens (cyproterone acetate and medroxyprogesterone acetate), which reduce circulating serum testosterone levels by different physiological mechanisms. Other pharmacological agents that have been used include thioridazine and clompiramine (Bradford, 1993).

Behavioral and cognitive–behavioral theorists have used varying aspects of classical conditioning and operant conditioning to modify deviant sexual behaviors. Because clinical experience has indicated that sex offenders routinely use cognitive distortions to justify or rationalize their behavior, part of the intervention also focuses on the cognitive-remediated processes. More recently, these cognitive–behavioral techniques have been included as part of a model of relapse prevention (Laws, 1989). The relapse prevention model is a theory-based model whose basic premise is that precursors to sexual abuse with sexual aggression can be identified and that offenders can learn self-management techniques in conjunction with supervision to help them control their own inappropriate sexual behaviors. Offenders are taught techniques to enhance their self-control, and external control is provided through supervision by community members as well as professionals who monitor the offender's behavior. Gray and Pithers (1993) presented a modification of the relapse prevention model for sexually aggressive adolescents and children.

Motivating the Adolescent Sex Offender for Treatment

Sex offenders are in general not usually self-motivated to receive treatment. Instead, their motivation comes from the criminal justice system, a probation officer, defense attorneys, or family members. Consequently, it falls on therapists to educate the adolescent about the importance of treatment and to teach him or her the potential benefits of being involved in treatment.

Along with a lack of motivation for treatment, adolescents are frequently in denial or minimization relative to their offenses. The following methods have been useful in confronting or breaking down denial with male adolescents:

1. Let the client know that you have reviewed the victim's statement and you have familiarized yourself with all available material relative to his past records (juvenile, family court, and psychological, if applicable).
2. Be supportive during the initial interview and appeal to his desire to "get it off his chest" by discussing the offense.
3. Do not judge the client. Clients, particularly sex offenders, watch very closely for signs of being judged either verbally or nonverbally.
4. Let the client know that continued denial and minimization may prolong the treatment process or may prolong the time until he can be reunited with his family (e.g., in sibling incest cases).
5. Describe in detail what the intervention consists of and what the client will gain from the intervention.
6. Let the client know that he is not alone and that other juveniles also have sexual behavior problems.

At times, it is helpful to place the adolescent who is denying or minimizing in an ongoing group with adolescents who have made full disclosures. Frequently, the "admitters" serve as positive role models for those who are in denial. They can confront those in denial and also explain that at one point in time they were "in the same place." When working with adolescent sex offenders, it is critical to address the family's denial or minimization of the problem. Frequently, parents will feel embarrassed, ashamed, or guilty and will defend against these feelings by denying or minimizing. The therapist needs the family as an ally to assist in ensuring that the adolescent participates in and remains in therapy. If the parents are not educated to their child's problem and do not work collaboratively with the therapist, then they may not be able to provide the supervision the adolescent needs.

Therapist Issues

It is recommended that each group be facilitated by male and female cotherapists when possible. Therapists need the support of one another and can also assist each other in understanding and processing the group. They also serve as good role models for male and female interactions.

A GROUP TREATMENT MODEL FOR ADOLESCENT MALE OFFENDERS

A group treatment model is appropriate for male adolescent offenders for several reasons. First, the adolescent learns that he is not the only one who has misused his sexuality. Second, he has the opportunity to receive feedback from his peers about how they perceive his behavior. This is particularly interesting when one has a "mixed" group—composed of boys who have engaged in incest, in extrafamilial abuse, or who had male victims versus female victims. Third, because some group members have admitted to their offenses, they can serve as models for appropriate disclosure to those boys who are minimizing or are still in denial. Finally, not all group members are deficient in social interaction skills, so some can serve as models for those boys who are lacking in that area.

Several orientation sessions are advised when undertaking a group intervention. This gives therapists and adolescents an opportunity to feel comfortable with one another before beginning the therapy work. Although there are no research data available addressing effects of the therapists' gender, clinical experience has shown that it is beneficial to have a male and female cotherapy team. It is critical that group cohesiveness be built and that a fostering of mutual acceptance and understanding of group members occurs.

The therapists should first inform adolescents that they have been referred for therapy because they have misused their sexuality and that therapy sessions will help them learn what caused them to misuse their sexuality. They should also be told that they will learn appropriate techniques and skills for dealing with inappropriate sexual fantasies, urges, and behaviors. In addition, the therapists should explain that therapy will assist adolescents in developing an appreciation for the impact that their behavior had on their victims and on victims' families. Other therapeutic goals include learning to relate to peers in a healthy, functional manner and learning to be responsible for their sexuality.

The multicomponent program based on a cognitive–behavioral model that I have used in treating adolescent male sexual offenders is a modification of a program initially developed and evaluated for adult male offenders. It was important to modify the adult program to make the intervention more developmentally appropriate. What follows is a brief description of our treatment model. For a more detailed discussion, please see Becker and Kaplan (1994).

Because the majority of male adolescents in treatment are typically under the jurisdiction of the juvenile court and on probation, the limits of confidentiality should be explained. The court or the probation officer will, in all probability, request periodic reports on the adolescent client's treatment progress and attendance. The client should be made aware of this.

The treatment components include verbal satiation in individual therapy, a technique that teaches the adolescent to use inappropriate sexual fantasies in a repetitive manner to the point of boring or fatiguing themselves with their inappropriate fantasies. A preliminary evaluation of the efficacy of this technique with male adolescent offenders indicated that the adolescents who benefited the most from it were those who had abused females younger than 3 years of age (Kaplan, Morales, & Becker, 1993). Consequently, this treatment might not be appropriate for all male adolescent offenders, and therapists are advised to use it on an individual basis. On successful mastery of this technique, the adolescent can be entered into group therapy.

Cognitive Restructuring

On completion of the satiation sessions, adolescents enter closed-group treatment. Our experience has been that seven male adolescents constitute an optimal group; however, because adolescents may drop out, the initial group size should be more than seven.

During this component of treatment, each adolescent is asked to state the age and gender of his victim, whether the victim was related to him, and the frequency of the offending behavior. Clients are then asked to explain to the group how they gave themselves permission to engage in a sexual behavior that is proscribed by society. Their permission-giving statements are termed *cognitive distortions*; these distortions are confronted and modified through cognitive restructuring. Role-plays are used in which the therapists adopt the maladaptive beliefs of the adolescents. The adolescents are assigned different roles (e.g., victim or judge), and they have to educate the therapists as to what is inappropriate about adhering to their beliefs. This role reversal provides the adolescent an opportunity to look at his own inappropriate beliefs in a less threatening setting.

Covert Sensitization

The next component focuses on developing covert sensitization scripts. The adolescents learn that this component of treatment will facilitate their recognizing how risky emotional and environmental states may serve as precursors for their inappropriate sexual behavior. They also learn what the consequences will be to themselves and their victim if they reoffend. Each adolescent has the opportunity to learn the "chain" of precursors that lead to his committing a sexual offense. All are then taught how to interrupt the chain by considering consequences that will occur if they continue on the path to inappropriate sexual behavior. To assist in recognizing their particular precursors and practicing the techniques, clients are asked to make a minimum of eight 15-minute audio tapes in which they describe the chain and interrupt it by describing its usual consequences.

Skills Building

Another component focuses on social skills training and anger control. Many adolescent offenders have difficulty recognizing and controlling their angry impulses and use physical aggression as a means of problem solving. Through this component, they learn how to discriminate "feeling states" and to appropriately direct their feelings. The videotape *Rethink Workout for Teens: Learning to Manage Anger* (Research Press, n.d.) is shown in the group to initiate such changes. Role-plays are then initiated in which the adolescents have the opportunity to learn and practice alternatives to anger. Many of them are undersocialized and have difficulty establishing peer relationships. Some have adequate social skills but use these skills to manipulate their peers. Role-playing, discussion, and didactics are used to facilitate appropriate peer social interactions.

Sexual Education and Communication

Another component of group therapy focuses on social, sexual, and health issues that the adolescents may be confronting. Therapists address such issues in the following ways:

1. They teach members about puberty and adolescent development, sexual anatomy, and physiology.
2. They correct sexual myths and discuss pregnancy prevention and sexually transmitted diseases (including HIV and AIDS).
3. They raise awareness of adolescents' own attitudes and feelings concerning sexuality, helping to clarify their values about sexuality.

Victim Empathy

Most often the adolescent offender does not appreciate the impact that his behavior has had on the victim, either psychologically or physically. In some cases, the behavior is "hit and run"; that is, the adolescent abuser assaults or molests, leaves the scene, and does not have the opportunity to see how the behavior has affected the victim. In cases where offenders live with their victims (e.g., incest), they usually do not sense or attend to victim impact. Various activities are therefore used in group therapy in an attempt to engender empathy in the adolescent offenders. Adolescents are required at the beginning of their component of treatment to write an apology letter to their victims. Those letters are not mailed but are used by the therapists to assess the victim's empathetic level. Attention during this component of treatment is focused on teaching clients and helping them understand the nature of the problems that victims experience when they are abused. Most groups contain members who have been molested themselves—physically, sexually, or psychologically—and so therapists attempt to process with them how they felt and how their own maltreatment has affected them, to the benefit of the other members. Finally, adolescents role-play reading their empathy letters to the victim and his or her family. When clinically appropriate, such as in cases of intrafamilial abuse, these empathy letters may actually be used in family therapy sessions.

Relapse Prevention

A final component of group therapy involves having each adolescent write his own plan for avoiding relapse. The plan includes what situations to avoid (e.g., for those adolescents who molest children, refraining from baby-sitting); what techniques and interventions to use when stressed or when inappropriate sexual fantasies occur; and, ultimately, who to contact when they feel their "controls" are breaking down.

Elsewhere (Becker, 1990), I have reported 1-year posttreatment follow-up data indicating that this multicomponent treatment is effective. According to self-reports and reports from parents and criminal justice agencies, only 9% of youthful offenders recommitted sexual crimes following this treatment.

ADJUNCTIVE THERAPIES

A number of adolescents may also receive individual therapy to address their own victimization issues. Alternatively, some might receive treatment for substance abuse or conduct disorders. Pharmacotherapy can be used for those adolescents with attention deficit/hyperactivity disorder or mood disorders.

OTHER TREATMENT ISSUES

Working With Parents

It is imperative that parents be informed and involved from the onset of adolescent therapy. Without their support, intervention can be difficult. Therapists must realize that parents may also need support as they experience the shame and embarrassment associated with their son's behavior. Parent support groups (facilitated by a mental health professional) can offer parents the opportunity to meet other parents of youthful offenders and decrease their feelings of isolation. Frequently, families need therapy to assist in identifying how family dynamics may have contributed to or re-inforced the adolescent's problem. Finally, parents will need to learn parenting skills to provide proper supervision and monitoring for their child in the future.

Confidentiality Issues

Adolescents in group therapy are informed that material disclosed in the group is to "stay in the group." Because the possibility exists that an adolescent may attend the same school as another group member or live on the same street or in the same town, it is important that each member state whether he wants to be recognized if he meets another group member in the community. In my groups, I only use first names, and I do encourage members to maintain contact with one another outside of group.

Adolescents are aware of the limits of confidentiality relative to danger to themselves and others. They are also made aware that because they have signed releases to the probation department, attendance and progress reports will be shared with probation officers.

Constituting Groups

Adolescents should be placed in groups that are appropriate to their age and developmental levels. For example, it would be inappropriate to place an immature, learning-disabled 13-year-old in a group with mature non-learning-disabled 17-year-olds. Clinical experience has shown that mixing incest offenders with nonincest offenders has not created any problems. Nor has it posed a problem to mix adolescents who have victimized males with those who have victimized females.

Homework Assignments

It is important that the adolescent feel that therapy does not occur just 1 day a week for 75 or 90 minutes. Also, he needs to assume some responsibility for his therapy. Consequently, homework should be assigned for a time outside of therapy. Assignments can include journaling, practicing covert sensitization, practicing social skills, or doing community work as part of restitution.

Noncompliance

Therapists should inform adolescents from the first session that the therapy process is a collaboration. It should be clear that, if they do not attend sessions or do their homework assignments, there ultimately will be consequences for them to deal with. By making members a part of the process, exploring noncompliance, and holding them responsible, therapists can hold noncompliance to a minimum. Because most adolescent offenders have been referred by the juvenile court, they can also be informed that noncompliance will be reported to their probation officers when updates are requested.

Aftercare

Adolescents need to learn that they can return for therapy "booster sessions" when needed and that a responsible adult or adults will be supervising their behavior and remain available to them for support while they are in the community. It is critical that they understand that, if they are stressed and they experience an inappropriate sexual urge, this does not mean that their therapy has not worked; it only means that they need to further explore with their therapist why the urge or fantasy has returned.

CONCLUSION

Over the past 20 years, the fund of knowledge about individuals who have sexual behavior problems has greatly increased. Society now acknowledges that juveniles may also have sexual behavior problems and that some commit sex offenses. There has been an increase in treatment programs for these youth and their family members.

However, the field still lacks an empirically based model to explain why some individuals misuse their sexuality. Although treatment-outcome data look promising, further research is needed to identify which interventions work best for which category of offender. To date, little research has been done on primary and secondary prevention. I hope to see efforts in those directions in the next decade.

REFERENCES

Abel, G. G., Becker, J. V., Cunningham-Rathner, J., Mittelman, M., & Rouleau, J. (1988). Multiple paraphiliac diagnoses among sex offenders. *Bulletin of the American Academy of Psychiatry and Law, 16,* 153–168.

Association for the Treatment of Sexual Abusers. (1993). *The ATSA practitioner's handbook.* Lake Oswego, OR: Author.

Barbaree, H. R., Marshall, W. L., & Hudson, S. H. (1993). *The juvenile sex offender.* New York: Guilford Press.

Becker, J. V. (1990). Treating adolescent sexual offenders. *Professional Psychology: Research and Practice, 21,* 362–365.

Becker, J. V., Harris, C. D., & Sales, B. D. (1993). Juveniles who commit sexual offenses: A critical review of research. In G. C. N. Hall & R. Hirschman (Eds.), *Sexual aggression: Issues in etiology and assessment, treatment and policy* (pp. 215–228). Washington, DC: Taylor and Francis.

Becker, J. V., & Kaplan, M. S. (1994). Sexual disorders. In V. B. Van Hasselt & M. Hersen (Eds.), *Advanced abnormal psychology* (pp. 359–372). New York: Plenum Press.

Borduin, C. H., Henggeler, S. W., Blaske, D. M., & Stein, R. J. (1990). Multi-systemic treatment of adolescent sexual offenders. *International Journal of Offender Therapy and Comparative Criminology, 34,* 105–114.

Bradford, J. H. W. (1993). Antiandrogen and hormonal agents. In H. E. Barbaree, W. L. Marshall, & S. E. Hudson (Eds.), *The juvenile sex offender* (pp. 278–288). New York: Guilford Press.

Gray, A. S., & Pithers, W. D. (1993). Relapse prevention with sexually aggressive adolescents and children: Expanding treatment and supervision. In H. E. Barbaree, W. L. Marshall, & S. E. Hudson (Eds.), *The juvenile sex offender* (pp. 290–319). New York: Guilford Press.

Kaplan, J. S., Morales, M., & Becker, J. V. (1993). The impact of verbal satiation on adolescent sex offenders: A preliminary report. *Journal of Child Sexual Abuse, 2,* 81–88.

Knight, R. A., & Prentky, R. (1993). Exploring characteristics for classifying juvenile sex offenders. In H. E. Barbaree, W. L. Marshall, & S. E. Hudson (Eds.), *The juvenile sex offender* (pp. 45–83). New York: Guilford Press.

Laws, R. D. (1989). *Relapse prevention with sex offenders.* New York: Guilford Press.

National Adolescent Perpetrator Network. (1988). Preliminary report from the National Task Force on Juvenile Sex Offending. *Juvenile and Family Court Journal, 39*(Whole No. 2).

National Adolescent Perpetrator Network. (1993). The revised report from the National Task Force on Juvenile Sexual Offending. *Juvenile and Family Court Journal, 44*(Whole No. 4).

O'Brien, M., & Bera, W. (1986). Adolescent sexual offenders: A descriptive typology. *A Newsletter of the National Family Life Education Network, 1,* 1–5.

Research Press. (n.d.). *Learning to manage anger: The rethink workout for teens* [Videotape]. Champaign, IL: Author.

Ryan, G. D., & Lane, S. L. (1991). *Juvenile sexual offending: Causes, consequences and correction.* Lexington, MA: Lexington Books.

25

MANAGING BOUNDARIES: GROUP THERAPY WITH INCARCERATED ADULT MALE SEXUAL OFFENDERS

RICHARD F. LAZUR

Within the past 20 years men have attempted to redefine the male gender role (Levant, 1992; Levant & Pollock, 1995; Pleck, 1981), in part in reaction to the damaging effects of traditional male socialization (Piel Cook, 1990; Pleck, 1976; Scher, 1979). Nowhere else are the effects of traditional male gender role socialization more evident than in a sexual offense.[1] Traditionally defined in terms of power (Pleck, 1975), competition (Pleck, 1975, 1980), domination (Kaufman, 1987), invulnerability (O'Neil, 1981), alexithymia (Silverberg, 1986), and homophobia (David & Brannon, 1976), the traditional male gender role has suggested that men take control, use other people, show no feelings, and get what they want without regard to the cost to self or others.

This is what happens in a sexual assault. A man takes control of another person, dominates, and seeks his own gratification without regard to others. Sex becomes an act of violence (Kaufman, 1987). In committing such an act, a man distorts and exaggerates characteristics of traditional male gender role socialization. An individual's gender role is integrated into personality dynamics as he or she matures and develops. If there are failures along the developmental continuum, distortions in perception or

---

[1] I recognize that women also commit sex offenses, but for the purposes of this chapter and in keeping with the focus of this book, I focus only on treatment for the male sex offender.

exaggerations in behavior are folded in the person's development. This results in an aberration of perception, behavior, or both, which, if occurring in the traditional male gender role, can result in acts of sexual violence. The sex offense thus becomes the symptom of distortions in traditional male gender role socialization.

This chapter addresses the personality dynamics of the sex offender and the distortions that take place in male gender role socialization. I focus on boundary management in group psychotherapy with incarcerated rapists and child molesters, providing excerpts from my own clinical experience with this population to illustrate important aspects of this treatment.

THE SEX OFFENDER

Although sex offenses range along a continuum from nonassaultive to assaultive behaviors (Abel, Becker, Cunningham-Rathner, Mittelman, & Rouleau, 1988; Abel & Osborn, 1992; Bradford, Boulet, & Pawlak, 1992), all involve the violation of boundaries (Lazur, 1992; O'Connell, Leberg, & Donaldson, 1990). A sex offender sees the world differently than most people. He uses people as objects for his pleasure. As an individual, he may lack appropriate social skills (Overholser & Beck, 1986; Stermac, Segal, & Gillis, 1990). Often, he does not know how to interact genuinely with another person, especially someone of the opposite sex; alternatively, he may be socially adept and able to finesse his way. He is either unable to start a conversation and is withdrawn or is glib and sociable, capable of winning the trust of others. Whatever his personal style, strengths, and weaknesses, the sex offender manipulates people to give him what he wants. Using people, he is isolated and unable to form an attachment. Consequently, he is unable to gratify his dependency and nurturance needs in a healthy manner.

Personality Dynamics

Although there is no definite sex offender personality type (Maletzky & McGovern, 1990), a significant number of sex offenders do experience a personality disorder (Abel, Mittelman, & Becker, 1985; Berner, Berger, Guitierrez, & Jordan, 1992; Mander, 1994; McGrath, 1991; Prendergast, 1991). Externalizers who shift the blame to others and avoid responsibility for their actions, sex offenders sidestep anxiety at every possible turn. Significant distortions in thinking, known as *thinking errors*, persist. Thinking errors are the "mental processes required by the criminal to live his kind of life" (Yochelson & Samenow, 1976, p. 359). They are habitual patterns acted out in daily life that go unrecognized by the individual himself, but propel him to act in a self-serving way that violates the rights of others.

Thinking errors include, but are not limited to, a refusal to disclose, to self-evaluate, to be receptive, to take responsibility, and to put oneself in another's position. They involve the quest for power and domination through put-downs and attacks, ownership, and lack of trust. In the distortions in the sex offender's thinking, "he [fluidly] moves from an undervalued conception of himself to an overvalued one . . .[where] in his thrusts for power, . . . [he] views himself as an extraordinary and prestigious figure" (Yochelson & Samenow, 1976, p. 276).

The belief that he is "an extraordinary and prestigious figure" is important in the criminal's offense and treatment. It is what motivates him to act in a way that violates the boundaries of another person. He believes he is impenetrable; nothing can beat him, not even the law. This faulty cognition drives the offender. He sees no wrong in his behavior, and, consequently, he sees no need to change. As Herman (1990) has explained, "the fact that victims loathe being assaulted should not obscure the fact that offenders enjoy assaulting them" (p. 182). The following example from one group session demonstrates the offender's uniqueness.

> Despite reading to the group his presentence report, which described in vivid detail how Jared would prey on the trust and innocence of the fourth-grade girls he taught, he denied that his actions were criminal. He was a teacher, a respected member of the community, not some perpetrator. He never understood why some parents reported him to the police. He was just trying to give the girls attention they didn't get at home when his hand slipped under their dresses or when he would have them fondle him while seated at his desk. The authorities must have had the wrong guy; they couldn't want *him*. After all, *he* was a teacher.

Thinking errors impede the sex offender's ability to change. Embedded in them, he uses them automatically and without awareness; they are simply a part of who he is. They are as integral a part of his psyche as the color of his eyes are to his body. The therapist needs to be aware of these errors and be able to identify when they occur if change is to take place.[2]

Ownership is when the offender thinks he should have what he wants when he wants it. Put-downs are a way to jockey for power by intimidating or verbally attacking someone. Not learning from past experience, he avoids obligations and does not consider another person's position. Lack of trust is simply not trusting anyone because it would make him vulnerable. The hallmark of criminal thinking is seeing oneself as the victim, especially once the offender is held accountable for his actions.

Primary emotions for the sex offender are anger and fear: anger at not being able to do what he wants, and fear of the loss of control, of being caught, of being put down, of being a nothing, and, ultimately, fear of

[2]For a more detailed description of *thinking errors*, refer to the works of Yochelson and Samenow.

death. Whereas most people experience anger as a transient emotional experience, it is much more to the sex offender:

> An anger reaction in the criminal "metastasizes." It begins with an isolated episode, but spreads and spreads until the criminal has lost all perspective. Eventually, he decides that everything is worthless. His thinking is illogical. (Yochelson & Samenow, 1976, p. 268)

A black-or-white thinker, the sex offender sees himself as either being able to do anything or as being a nothing. Most people experience occasional feelings of inferiority, but their feelings are not pervasive; nor do they believe that everyone sees their inferiority and that it will not go away. The sex offender, however, fears being reduced to what Yochelson and Samenow (1976) have called a "zero state": His view of himself is that he is nothing, everyone else sees that he is nothing, he will never be anything else, and this state will never end. He will do anything to avoid this state.

Characterized as being egocentric, untrusting, unable to form attachments or a transference, and refusing to take responsibility for his actions (Stein & Brown, 1991), the sex offender lacks the basic ingredients necessary for interpersonal interaction. Unable to empathize, he has little understanding or compassion for the effects of his actions. Group therapy is a place where he can learn how he comes across to other people, the effects of his behaviors, and how his actions affect other human beings. Although he may recite psychological jargon learned along the way and mouth his understanding of another person's feelings, his actions often belie his words. His lack of interpersonal relationships becomes evident in the psychotherapy group. If left unchecked, however, a group of sex offenders will develop collusion rather than cohesion and will seek individual ends rather than group objectives. Without monitoring of their boundaries, they can easily become a gang and not a group.

Differences Between Rapists and Pedophiles

Personality patterns suggest that, psychologically and behaviorally, the profiles of the rapist and the child molester are different. The rapist tends to be much more aggressive–narcissistic (Hall, 1988), domineering, macho, and more likely to be involved in a criminal lifestyle such as drug dealing at the time of the offense (Miner, Day, & Nafpaktitis, 1989). The pedophile appears more docile—even passive (Jenkins-Hall & Marlatt, 1989)—seems cooperative, tends to violate a household member, has positive feelings toward his victims, and is more likely to perceive them as willing participants (Miner et al., 1989). Consider the following description of a rapist.

> With his powerful gait and chiseled features on his strong, sculpted body, 34-year-old Gary would seize control of his environment and

emit an attitude of "don't mess with me." His steel-blue eyes penetrated like a fox which, when confronted, took on a glaze of a wild animal ready to attack. He denies doing anything wrong: he was celebrating his 32nd birthday, drinking in a bar where he met a woman, they drank together, and he took her home. He refutes the victim's account and those of the two people who found her nude, lying among the bushes in the early morning of a winter day. When Gary finally did admit to raping her, he rationalized, "It was my birthday! I was only getting what any man wants. It was my gift."

And compare with this description of a child molester:

Sheepishly compliant, 32-year-old Dale could steal into a room without being noticed. His delft-blue eyes look longingly, wistfully, fearful of being berated for something he did or did not do. In his soft voice, he denies touching his three- and five-year-old daughters despite their vivid descriptions and drawings of "how daddy would play while mommy was at work." When Dale admitted to the molestations, he explained, "I didn't do it as often as they said."

Whatever the outward appearance, both rapists and child molesters seek to control their environments, to garner power, and to manipulate to get what they want. Although they may look different in attitude, demeanor, and vocalizations, both suffer the same psychological afflictions, which propel them to violate the physical and emotional boundaries of others and to act out sexually to achieve their own desired goals.

SEX OFFENDER TREATMENT

Sex offender treatment is an arduous, time-consuming, and, at times, emotionally draining undertaking for the treatment provider. Treatment is often met with resistance, disparagement, and failure on the part of the sex offender. Because the sex offender frequently experiences a personality disorder (Abel et al., 1985; Berner et al., 1992; Mander, 1994; McGrath, 1991; Prendergast, 1991), causing blame to be externalized and maintained, his behaviors—fantasies, planning, grooming, and assaulting   comfortably fit with his self-concept and personal identity. In his eyes, he is a good person who has done nothing wrong.

If treatment is to be successful, it is important that the sex offender see how his behavior is self-directed and self-maintained and not an impulsive act. It is critical that he recognize his violation of another person's physical, emotional, and psychological boundaries. It is useful if he can see how the distortions in his personality have led him to act in unacceptable ways against members of his family or community. If he can determine how he has exaggerated the worst elements of the traditional male gender role, then he can perhaps modify his behaviors, adopt a different attitude, and change.

The goal of sex offender treatment is to ensure the safety of the community—to ensure that there are no more victims. Successful treatment involves a multimodal approach including cognitive restructuring (Becker, chap. 24, this volume; Jenkins-Hall & Marlatt, 1989; Pithers, Martin, & Cummings, 1989; Yochelson & Samenow, 1976), modification of sexual arousal (Day, Miner, Sturgeon, & Murphy, 1989; Laws, 1989; Maletzky & McGovern, 1990; Quinsey & Earls, 1990), identification of risk factors (MacDonald & Pithers, 1989; Pithers, Beal, Armstrong, & Petty, 1989; Pithers, Kashima, Cummings, Beal, & Buell, 1988), social skills training (McFall, 1990), and possibly antiandrogen and hormonal treatment (Bradford, 1990). Treatment should be based on the belief that sex offenders are responsible for their own behavior. Irresponsible sexual behaviors are learned; thus, they can be unlearned (Mander, 1994; Marshall, Laws, & Barbaree, 1990; Pithers et al., 1988; Yochelson & Samenow, 1976). Appropriate partner choice and activities can be acquired in their place. Treatment involves examining the offender's pattern of maladaptive interpersonal interactions, challenging his thinking, and offering him alternative, healthy choices. Sexually assaultive behavior can be controlled (Mander, 1994).

Within the context of a multimodal treatment program, specialized group psychotherapy is the treatment of choice for use with sex offenders[3] (Lazur, 1992; Pithers, Martin, & Cummings, 1989). The group setting provides the opportunity for the offender to actively challenge his belief systems, examine his pattern of choices, learn new behaviors, and receive support for adapting his behaviors. Treatment focuses on having the offender take responsibility for his behaviors. Witness the following interaction from one therapy group:

> Clem has just finished describing to the group how he would send his 10-year-old stepdaughter to the store for potato chips and candy and then have her sit close to him on the couch while he watched a pornographic video. Her mother would be at work, and this would be their time together. He detailed how he would take her hand, place it on his thigh, and slowly move it to his crotch. Then he would kiss her. He described his fantasy—himself a participant in the film, his stepdaughter the seductive film star—until his behaviors would become increasingly aggressive and he engaged in intercourse with her. Group

---

[3]Although individual therapy may be used in addition to group therapy, the personality dynamics of the sex offender involve an attempt to manipulate and convince the therapist of improvement, so that even the most experienced clinicians can be duped in one-on-one situations. Family treatment may be used as an adjunct in treatment, but only with careful preparation, timing, and clear definition of goals. If the offense occurred within the family, then individual members must deal with that crisis. To reunite them as a family, especially in the early stages, is countertherapeutic and possibly more damaging than useful.

members are silent. Even though they have committed similar acts, they are riveted by the scenes Clem has just detailed; a few find it arousing. Then they start to ask questions: "Did he think about his stepdaughter?" "Did he plan it?" "What was he thinking?" "How did he get away with it?" The questions come throughout the next week as Clem's assault pattern is examined by the group. Each member is assigned to write a personal reaction to Clem's offense and to determine similarities to their own. They are charged to look for thinking errors, to identify the assault cycle, to have one-on-one conversations with Clem about their reactions to what he did, and to follow those conversations with written reports for their group counselor.

In group treatment, each member identifies his reaction to the speaker's offense, compares both the attack and his reaction to it with his own crime, determines the pattern of assault, and challenges the offender's thinking. All along, he looks for where those same thinking errors occur in his own reasoning. By having members confront one another, each offender is forced to examine the pattern of thinking that led him to make his choices and act the way he did. The experience is contained within the group, and each individual has an opportunity to make alternative choices and to change his pattern of interaction.

Confrontation and changing behaviors is hard work. It is especially difficult if the offender does not believe that what he has done is wrong. He may see himself as a good person who should not be punished (O'Connell et al., 1990; Yochelson & Samenow, 1976). The incarcerated offender usually seeks some self-serving goal from entering a treatment program; that is, he wants a "carrot," in the form of a tangible goal (such as the promise of early release or parole), to sustain his interest in treatment. Therefore, in sentencing, judges must send the message of the value of treatment completion. As guardians of society's boundaries, judicial authorities must make it clear that the sex offender's acts have violated those boundaries, that this will not be tolerated, and that he needs to not just learn about his pattern of behaviors but change them.

MANAGING THE BOUNDARIES

Management of boundaries is the group leader's primary function in intervention for sex offenders (Kernberg, 1973; Rice & Rutan, 1981; Singer, Astrachan, Gould, & Klein, 1975). Boundaries define the group's task, its composition and construction, its relationship to the external environment in which it exists, the psychological and emotional needs of individual members, and the relationship among members. As Singer et al. (1975) explained, "the management function involves regulating who comes in, what is done, and in what format" (p. 139).

External Boundaries

In managing an incarcerated group, a contract is negotiated at an administrative level between the therapist–provider and the correctional system that clearly details the goals and means of treatment. Management of this boundary is the work of the treatment administrator. The value of treatment needs to be clearly stated by those in authority in the correctional system lest local correctional staff attempt to interfere, often in a passive–aggressive manner. The purpose of jail is to protect society. Treatment often is a significant way to reach this same goal; however, it is not a way that many correctional officers may understand.

Correctional staff may, quite unintentionally, undermine treatment by having an industrious group member "excused" from group to perform a "necessary task," such as baking bread, unclogging the sewer, or performing other inmate job functions. When this kind of interference has an impact on a group session, the therapist needs a clear line of authority with which to ensure the primacy of the treatment group. Managing these external boundaries is as important as managing the internal group dynamics, because the external determines the practical understanding of the group's importance. If the correctional system does not view treatment as critical, then the implicit message to group members will be that treatment is insignificant. This message will be reflected in members' attitudes and approaches to the goals of sex offender treatment.

The value of sex offender treatment within a correctional system will vary according to the individual beliefs of the members of the system involved in treatment. Frequently, correctional staff will overtly endorse an administrative policy as part of their jobs, yet personally disagree with the policy and relay that disagreement in their behaviors and attitudes toward the treatment program. Because they spend significantly more time with inmates than do clinical staff, treatment may be subtly sabotaged. Thus, although the management of personnel boundaries is the task of the correctional administration, for effective treatment of inmates such management must be done in conjunction with the treatment administrator. If a correctional department commits to sex offender treatment, then it is incumbent on the department to staff the facility with personnel who are also committed to the treatment process and goals.

Effects of Male Gender Role Socialization on Boundary Management

Tolerance of sexual behaviors, minimizing the gravity of sexual assault, and blaming the victim (Stermac et al., 1990) infiltrate the fiber of society's attitudes toward sexual behaviors. Sexual assault is rewarding to the offender (Herman, 1990). Treatment staff need to be alert to the nuances and effects of traditional male gender role socialization on their own as well as the offenders' thinking. Male and female correctional staff as well as therapists have their own biases, beliefs, and tolerances for prescribed gender role behaviors. All too often, traditional male gender role socialization condones assaultive behaviors as masculine. Likewise, one upmanship, not expressing feelings, taking charge, and being in control are considered manly traits.

Treatment staff's lack of awareness of gender role socialization may interfere with their ability to be objective. For men, this may mean identifying with another man, whereas women may run the gamut from being Pollyannaish to punitive. Although most people overtly acknowledge the horrific nature of a sexual offense, it requires an examination of personal belief systems to get beyond the offense's sexual properties. In the case of child molestation, staff may despise the offender, only minimally veiling their animosity and disgust. With the rapist, a man may secretly fantasize about the offender's act and project subtle forms of consent, whereas a woman may act out her own issues of revenge for victimization or fear of being abused. These behaviors are covert, and often unconscious, but they reflect personal and societal biases about sexual acts. It is important that the group therapist be aware of personal and gender biases in working with sex offenders, so that such biases are not played out in the group. The goal is to manage the group so that successful completion of the task occurs. Consider the following scenario of a new male correctional officer in a sexual treatment unit.

> A correctional officer for 15 years, Ted wanted to work the treatment unit "to do something different." Defining himself as "a man's man," he "couldn't imagine" some of the crime details he heard. "How could a man do those things?" he asked, reflecting on his own daughter, now an adult. During his first 6 months, Ted's clinical supervisor noticed subtleties in Ted's interactions with the inmates: He was harsh to the child molesters, giving them more assignments, being curt when they sought direction, and making offhanded comments about their behaviors. Ted liked to talk with the rapists, who often visited his office; it was even rumored that he brought them back issues of *Playboy*. When confronted by the supervisor, Ted denied any wrongdoing. But his group didn't appear to be gaining any ground. Confrontations were flat; the language was used but it didn't seem to have significance. No one was changing. Ted's supervisor consulted with other treatment staff, who also noticed the same things. The administrator consulted with corrections, who discovered that Ted would make offhanded comments about treatment methods and the staff. In effect, his attitude was countertherapeutic. When Ted did not respond to his supervisor's coaching, he was transferred to a security detail in another part of the prison.

Internal Boundaries

If the group is an essential component of sex offender treatment, then admitting an inmate to the treatment program is admission into the group. The inmate must be willing to participate in a treatment program, in which he will need to identify attitudes, beliefs, behaviors, and feelings that motivate him to act sexually against another person. As mentioned before, sex offenders are not without motivation, but strive for goals that are typically self-serving and destructive to others (Mander, 1994). As Mander explained, "there is little or no intrinsic motivation to alter the patterns which lead them to offend. Typically motivation for these individuals must begin as various forms of external control, incentive and structure" (1994, p. 9).

Sex offender treatment is designed to instill strategies in the offender through which he will recognize his propensity to reoffend; identify risk factors; recognize his assault cycle; examine psychological factors influencing and affecting his behaviors; be aware of arousal patterns; and, ultimately, take responsibility for his behaviors and refrain from further sexual assault. These goals need to be clearly articulated in the treatment contract.

Because an offender's attitudes, beliefs, and behaviors are an integral part of his personality, they are usually played out in the group process, either with the leader or other group members. When a violation of boundaries is inherent in the sex offender's character, it will be acted out in the group process, as illustrated below.

> Ralph said he wanted to change, but he would offer only the minimal amount of information about his assault on his two latency-age daughters. In group, his temper would flare whenever a group member challenged something he said or didn't say. He barely did the assignments. He didn't get along with other guys in the unit; he would change the TV channel or take the newspaper without asking. His manner was gruff. Although Ralph said he wanted treatment, he was not willing to do the work spelled out in the treatment contract. After he had been confronted numerous times by group members and treatment staff, Ralph was removed from treatment for failure to comply.

The differences between rapists and pedophiles, discussed earlier, become evident in group. Rapists are usually more assertive and, at times, may even be aggressive. They "tend to be more confrontational than pedophiles, energizing the group [whereas] pedophiles tend to be more empathetic than rapists, lending the group some compassion" (Pithers, Martin, & Cummings, 1989, p. 300). A mix between the two in group therapy is beneficial to both: The rapist can learn empathy and the child molester assertiveness. The boundary of group composition needs to be managed, however; 3 or more rapists in a 10-member group seems to be disruptive. Similarly, a combination of new members with more seasoned members who understand treatment goals can keep the group moving toward its goal. Consider the varying effects of a rapist and a child molester, respectively, illustrated in the cases below.

> Articulate and likable, 26-year-old Mark would linger after group and ask questions about the assignments or comment about how useful treatment was and how he was changing. In group, he would confront others on their sexual fantasies, patterns of behavior, and thinking. He was well-liked by other group members, who would tolerate his inquisitions and rarely challenge his position in group or his reason for being there. When discussing his offense, a date rape, he gave the impression that the charges were an accident: He simply was enjoying his female companion that evening. Although he professed to be changing, in actuality he was becoming more skilled at manipulations. He controlled the group through his questioning and subtle posturing and sought to make a favorable impression on the therapist, all the while continuing his familiar pattern of assault. He continued the patterns of rape, only in a more subtle, less forceful manner.

> Maintaining a cooperative, polite demeanor, 38-year-old Thad appeared passive and compliant during his first year of treatment. He was convicted of anal and vaginal penetration of his 10- and 12-year-old daughters over a 4-year period. He ran heavy equipment and was in demand by the prison grounds crew to work on an excavation project. He posed no security risk, and group members as well as staff liked him. It was only when he made a request that was denied that his dark side became evident. He stiffened, turned beet red, scowled, shouted, and threw a temper tantrum. One female correctional officer who denied a request of his observed that these probably were the behaviors that his victimized daughters saw and that if she were not in authority in a controlled setting, he most certainly would be terrifying.

THE SEX OFFENDER IN GROUP THERAPY

The most important act to perform as group facilitator is to manage the group's boundaries (Bader, 1981). Boundary management is crucial and time-consuming. Well-defended and skilled in getting his way, the sex offender will attempt to manipulate the group environment like he has manipulated other people in his life. Because he will act in a way that he believes others will want him to act, he will say what he believes others want to hear. He thus loses contact with himself and, in so doing, casts off responsibility.

Group members bring personal needs, anxieties, and fears with them to the group (Singer et al., 1975). It is incumbent on the group leader to be aware of the sex offender's particular needs, recognizing that he operates under cognitive distortions that justify and rationalize his behaviors (Long, Wuesthoff, & Pithers, 1989). Denial, projection, and rationalization are prominent psychological defenses used by offenders. Scorning external reality and consequent internal anxiety, this denial blocks "accurate appraisal of the severity of the deviant behaviors, its impact on the victims, and its potential consequences to the offender" (Jenkins-Hall & Marlatt, 1989, pp. 48, 49).

The offender's defensive structure is so pervasive and ingrained that he is unaware of distortions in his thinking or repercussions of his behaviors. As O'Connell et al. (1990) explained,

> offenders usually do not see themselves as callous and hurtful because they maintain many of the trappings of prosocial concern and respectability. They fool themselves and those around them: They do not see themselves as sex offenders. (p. 14)

Offenders may see themselves as "nice guys"; often, even their victims' families hold the same view. Thus, their denial persists. Sidestepping behaviors by recounting the injuries that were done to them as children, members may try to distract treatment from the goal that they take responsibility for their sexual assaults. Although members' hardships may be true and worthy of empathy, the therapist must maintain the boundaries of treatment so that the focused goal is sex offenders' acceptance of responsibility for the violations and pain that they have caused other human beings.

The sex offender uses specific tactics to avoid change (Yochelson & Samenow, 1976). He may selectively attend, hearing only what agrees with his thinking. Although he may look like he understands, if "uninterested in what is being said, he allows his physical presence and a few nods of his head to serve as indicators that he is receptive. Meanwhile, he turns his attention to more exciting ideas and simply serves his time" (Yochelson & Samenow, 1976, p. 507). Should anyone question his inattention, the offender may shift the burden to the other person. He may claim that the point is not being made clearly, agree when he does not mean it, or mutter something vague—all in an attempt to get the questioner off his back (Yochelson & Samenow, 1976). Agreeing is very effective; it stops the conversation. The untrained participant may believe that the sex offender understands, but that may not be the case. It may be that he could not be bothered any longer.

Minimizing, making excuses, and claiming to have made a mistake (but not taking responsibility for it) are other ways the sex offender avoids change and continues to deceive. Silence is also a very effective and potent way to control the group. Passive–aggressive behaviors, such as being late, writing long, tedious assignments that go into minute detail but avoid the main issue, not doing assignments, not completing work on time, and taking whatever other possible means to delay change will occur during treatment. The offender may also adopt a macho stance (e.g., swagger or show tattoos). He may bully, intimidate, and flex his muscles. One of my group members would sit in group and ripple his pectorals when anyone said anything he did not like. Such behaviors are all part of a game to gain power, to guard against being intimidated, and to garner status. They are also effective ways of preventing change.

The sex offender's thinking is concrete. His interpretations may be idiosyncratic and focus on literal meaning while overlooking the true concept. For example, one inmate in my group insisted that his 4-year-old niece was seducing him when her dress would lift, revealing her underpants, as she climbed into a chair. Another refused to discuss the three little girls whose parents did not press charges against him; he was not charged, so he was not going to examine how those behaviors fit his assault pattern. The sex offender may also try to confuse, by being very concrete and not able to think abstractly. He may talk fast or so low that it's difficult to hear. He may become circumstantial, change the subject, or talk about other things—all in avoidance of changing. He may avoid describing events: "Two months of manipulation may be depicted in one or two sentences" (Hildebran & Pithers, 1989, p. 239). Or he may go into such minute detail about irrelevant information that he neglects the main issue. If the truth is going to work against him, he may lie. He may also find God, with the attitude of "you can't tell me what to do because I have God." But finding religion may simply be another tactic for avoiding change.

Boundary Violations Within Group

The sex offender's violation of group boundaries becomes evident in group when he comes late or returns late from a break, takes ownership of a preferred seat, or interrupts group to use the facilities, among many other behaviors. In addition to lying outright, he may commit lies of omission; that is, he minimizes so that he will look good. "What others do not know will not hurt them and will help him" (Yochelson & Samenow, 1976, p. 351). This again, is part of his not taking responsibility for his actions or for himself.

Group Cohesion

Unlike members of postoedipal-issue groups—who develop bonds and have feelings of support, commitment, and a sense of belonging (Singer et al., 1975)—sex offenders remain isolated entities focused on their own goals, avoiding those of treatment and the group. Using people to get what he wants, the sex offender has difficulty taking another's perspective. Consequently, the bonds he develops in group tend to be self-serving.

Like most people, upon initial entry into the group, the sex offender seeks acceptance. However, rather than engaging others through social skills, he runs through his repertoire of behaviors to see which will provide him with the security and safety he seeks. Anxious, he may try to power thrust to guard against possible intruders. A macho stance, indifference, or a hostile attitude are defenses used to keep others at bay and provide him with the time he needs to scout out his new environment (again, rapists are more likely to adopt this stance than pedophiles). Established group members may strut their defenses to ward off possible threats to the security they have already established within the group. With the introduction of a new member, the interpersonal dynamics shift as everyone jockeys for position.

> New to the group, Ken positioned his muscular body with a manner that seemed to broadcast to others to not get close. This was reinforced by his belligerent tone, the strident intensity of his voice, and the clipped monosyllabic phrases he used to respond to questions. Cliff had been in treatment over a year, and he called Ken on his attitude. Cliff said all the things he thought the therapist would want to hear. But on closer examination, Cliff appeared to be threatened by Ken and attempting to mark his territory, a fact that became evident the next day, when they got in a spat over a bar of soap. It was an issue of safety and a power play within the dynamics of the group.

After his safety is established, the sex offender may try to use others to advance his personal agenda. Although this may give the appearance of compliance with treatment, it more often has to do with the offender seeking his desired goals, whatever they may be. If it meets his needs, he will form a connection with others; however, he does not form attachments. Although he may talk with others, he does not share information about himself beyond the superficial. He thus does not invest himself in others. Once his needs are no longer being met in a relationship, he ends it abruptly. Whereas cohesion fosters self-disclosure, the sex offender prefers to remain unknown; he avoids finding out about himself. He fears that he is nothing; that if he reveals himself to others, they will discover he is nothing; and that the state will never end. The following case illustrates this pattern of thought.

> Chad got other inmates in the group to like him; he confronted staff, appeared "helpful," and performed small favors. He disclosed his sexual abuse of his infant daughter, but avoided describing the details. He offered excuse after excuse to not read the court document that detailed his crime, until finally he could delay no longer. He was nervous,

but his "buddies" were kind to him. With appropriate regret and self-disgust, he read how he beat the infant lying in the crib with the buckle of his belt. One group member asked, "Why? Why did you do that, Chad?" Chad casually replied, "Ah, I couldn't take the sound of the kid crying anymore." A ripple of horror went around the room, and Chad's buddies didn't speak with him anymore.

One of the therapist's goals is to have the group reach the point where individual members make self-discoveries. Interpersonal interaction provides a means to this goal. Group cohesion is integral to change: It provides a safe environment for self-disclosure and fosters the willingness to integrate feedback and examine behaviors (Vinogradov & Yalom, 1989). By keeping members on task, the therapist helps them reach the point where they slowly start to disclose information about themselves and, layer by layer, shed the defenses that shield their authentic selves. In this process, members sink into the state of nothingness known as the zero state (Yochelson & Samenow, 1976). Here is where change can occur.

Once a vulnerability is exposed, the individual must be respected and the vulnerability not used against him. Otherwise, the safety of the group is destroyed; it would no longer be safe for anyone to disclose. In a group where members can be self-serving, such protections cannot be guaranteed. The group therapist must make it clear that transgressions affecting safety will not be tolerated and can result in dismissal from the group (and treatment). However, such warnings may be too late if precautions are not taken beforehand. As much as the therapist would like, it is impossible to control every aspect of treatment. As in any therapy, life events should be used to maximize therapeutic impact.

For the therapist, managing the interpersonal boundary means ensuring safety, fostering interpersonal awareness, breaking up coalitions, and using relationships and everyday life events as therapeutic events. This is not an easy task, and the group leader needs to be ever-mindful of the group process and its boundaries.

Transference

There are intrapersonal, interpersonal, and group processes at play in this type of therapy (Singer et al., 1975). The function of the group leader is to manage all three to keep the group on task so that the desired goals are achieved.

Within any group, strong feelings and fantasies about the leader will be active; competitiveness, rivalry, and attractions along a variety of dimensions will be operant; there will be a tendency for the group to act, albeit unwittingly, so as to maintain a minimum of experienced anxiety, and a tendency to punish any who threaten to raise the anxiety level of the group. (Singer et al., 1975, p. 169)

This is particularly true in groups of sex offenders. There is a significant level of hostility directed toward the therapist. A therapist who maintains boundaries and focuses on changing thinking and behaviors can expect to be viewed as mean, cruel, vindictive, and nonfeeling. Female therapists may be seen as man haters or lesbians, and male therapists may be accused of homosexuality. While outwardly appearing to defer to the authority of the treating clinician, the sex offender will wage a war for control. He will go through the motions without awareness of their content and utility. Whether the leader is male or female, there will be competition and one-upmanship. Female leaders are often sexualized, devalued, and perceived as inappropriate envoys of authority. Male leaders are viewed as competition, and their authority is diminished through subtle put-downs, passive resistance, or some other form of devaluation.

> In group and individual meetings, compliant Tom deferred to the male–female treatment staff; he would talk about how much he was learning about himself and how useful the program was. In a routine inspection of his room, however, a correctional officer found Tom's drawings of dismembered body parts of the team members in various sexual poses. When asked how this related to his program, he replied, "they're just drawings. They don't have anything to do with the program."

Change in the Sex Offender

Change involves recognition of a behavior and dissatisfaction with its results or consequences, examination of what drives the behavior, a decision, a willingness to do something different, and the fortitude and perseverance to act differently in face of similar circumstances. As Wheelis (1969) noted, "we create ourselves. The sequence is suffering, insight, will, action, change" (p. 63). For the sex offender, change is not easy. It certainly is not as automatic as he believes it is, nor is it as painless as he would like.

Although the sex offender may say he understands the damage his behavior has done to others, until he acts differently, such understanding is of little value. Words are easy for this type of client, but actions are difficult. Constantly informing the therapist about how much change he is making is often the only thing a group member talks about. If he is really making change, he will not talk about it, because it is too painful. If he sees the damage he has caused, he will act differently; he will feel like nothing.

Reaching the feeling of nothingness, the zero state, is critical if the sex offender is to change. "It is difficult for the noncriminal to imagine how disabling (although transient) this sense of worthlessness, hopelessness, and futility is" (Yochelson & Samenow, 1976, p. 265). Hopelessness—even though the matter may not appear so momentous to an objective observer—is the hallmark of the zero state. Derived from the criminal's self-descriptions, the zero state may appear like depression but "rather than appearing flat, inert, and despairing, he is blazing with anger (often unexpressed)" (Yochelson & Samenow, 1976, p. 266). Psychomotor retardation or poverty of thought are absent, although there may be vegetative signs as the offender obsessively ruminates about his current state. He is agitated, and there is plenty of physical and mental activity. He seeks to dispel the mood as quickly as possible. In this state, the sex offender is willing to listen to ways of changing his thoughts, feelings, and behaviors. It is thus only at this point that therapeutic interventions can be useful.[4]

This is a critical time in the group process. Other members who are not in the zero state may become alarmed and anxious. They may fear that the same feelings of nothingness will permeate them; some may even leave treatment. But this is a time for change to occur. The goal is to keep the focus on the thinking, feeling, and behavior patterns that lead to sexual assaults. The sex offender in the zero state is primed to identify and disclose his patterns of arousal, distortions, risk, and desires. It is as if he were momentarily stripped of his defenses, and he is experiencing his authentic self. He does not know who he is. He does not know what he is feeling. He does not know how to act. He only knows that it is uncomfortable, that his familiar defenses are not working, and that he fears this state will last forever.

The therapist must capitalize on the sex offender's negative feeling state and on his anxiety. This is the "crack in the door" that allows the therapist in—really for the first time—to offer alternative ways of thinking, acting, and feeling to the offender. Once in, the therapist can offer hope for a different set of behaviors—behaviors that assume personal responsibility, awareness of consequences, and logical thinking. It is the only hope the offender has; the alternative is his former way of life. For most, although the future appears daunting, the prospect is good. The offender will discover that he can think differently and, most important, can act differently. He need no longer offend.

In managing boundaries, the leader must acknowledge this anxiety as necessary for change, offer hope without being overly optimistic, and always attend to the group task. With the offender in zero state, the therapist must acknowledge the authentic self and focus on accountability for assaultive sexual behaviors and injuries caused to innocent others. This is critical if members of the sex offender treatment group are to identify

---

[4]For a more detailed description of how change can be effected, see chap. 24, by Becker, in this book.

patterns of arousal, identify circumstances of risk, and develop strategies to refrain from sexual assaults.

EFFECTS ON THE THERAPIST

Effectively managing the boundaries of a sex offender group requires being clear about one's own issues around sexuality and assaultive behaviors. The therapist must have a clear sense of values that will guide the therapy without overshadowing it. It helps to have a stomach for unpleasantness. In all likelihood, the group therapist will hear more grizzly tales of human suffering than were ever thought imaginable. Awareness of male gender role socialization and of its impact on social mores, attitudes, and behaviors is also critical.

Therapists of sex offender groups must focus on the process of therapy in boundary management, because sex offenders violate boundaries. Content may be useful, but therapeutic intervention occurs in the process.

Working with sex offenders is not an easy task. It is high impact, low reward, and leads to easy fatigue, feelings of uselessness, despair, and burnout. Therapy with this population is often devoid of the inherent gratification enjoyed by those who enter the healing professions; the gratification is in the hope that there will be no more victims. It is important to keep the work in perspective, to take it in stride, and above all, to keep the responsibility on the offender. In order to do this work, the most important boundary one must remember to manage is taking care of oneself.

SUMMARY

A sex offense violates the boundaries of another person. The male sex offender who commits such an act tends to encounter difficulties in interpersonal relationships, does not believe his behaviors are offensive, renounces responsibility for them, and usually suffers a personality disorder. His thinking is distorted. He believes he is impenetrable and that nothing can beat him, not even the law. This faulty cognition is what drives him to violate the boundaries of others.

Within a context of multimodality treatments—each addressing a specific component of the offender's maladaptive behaviors—group therapy provides a place where the sex offender can learn how his behaviors affect others. In group, the offender is able to examine the pattern of thinking that motivates his choices and behaviors; he can then make alternative choices and change.

Behavioral differences appear to exist between rapists and pedophiles, and these become evident in group situations. A combination of both is useful for group balance, just like a combination of new and more seasoned members who understand treatment goals can keep the group moving toward its goal.

Well-defended and skilled in getting his way, the sex offender will use every available defense to avoid change, which only occurs when he reaches the zero state (Yochelson & Samenow, 1976). Change involves the recognition of his behavior, dissatisfaction with its consequences, awareness of motivation, a decision, a willingness to act differently, identification of contributing circumstances, and the fortitude and perseverance to act differently in the face of these circumstances. Once members reach a zero state, it is a critical time in the group process. Through it all, the therapist must keep the focus on the thinking, feeling, and behavior patterns that led to the sexual assaults.

Both external and internal boundaries must be managed for effective sex offender treatment. The therapist must have a clear sense of values, awareness of male gender role socialization, knowledge of the effects of sexuality and assaultive behaviors, and a willingness to work to ensure the safety of children, women, and men. The rewards of this work are limited; they rarely come from the offenders themselves, but lie in the knowledge and hope that there will be no more victims.

REFERENCES

Abel, G. G., Becker, J. V., Cunningham-Rathner, J., Mittelman, M., & Rouleau, J. L. (1988). Multiple paraphiliac diagnoses among sex offenders. *Bulletin of the American Academy of Psychiatry and the Law, 16*, 153–168.

Abel, G. G., Mittelman, M. S., & Becker, J. V. (1985). Sex offenders: Results of assessment and recommendations for treatment. In M. H. Ben-Aron, S. J. Hucker, & C. D. Webster (Eds.), *Clinical criminology: The assessment and treatment of criminal behavior* (pp. 191–205). Toronto, Ontario, Canada: M & M Graphics.

Abel, G. G., & Osborn, C. (1992). The paraphilias: The extent and nature of sexually deviant and criminal behavior. *Clinical Forensic Psychiatry, 15*, 675–687.

Bader, L. (1981). [Boundaries in group therapy]. Unpublished class notes. Newton: Massachusetts School of Professional Psychology.

Berner, W., Berger, P., Guitierrez, K., & Jordan, B. (1992). The role of personality disorders in the treatment of sex offenders. *Journal of Offender Rehabilitation, 18*, 25–37.

Bradford, J. M. (1990). The antiandrogen and hormonal treatment of sex offenders. In W. L. Marshall, D. R. Laws, & H. E. Barbaree (Eds.), *Handbook of sexual assault: Issues, theories, and treatment of the offender* (pp. 297–310). New York: Plenum.

Bradford, J. M., Boulet, J., & Pawlak, M. A. (1992). The paraphilias: A multiplicity of deviant behaviors. *Canadian Journal of Psychiatry, 37,* 104–108.

David, D. S., & Brannon, R. (Eds.). (1976). *The forty-nine percent majority: The male sex role.* Reading, MA: Addison-Wesley.

Day, D. M., Miner, M. H., Sturgeon, V. H., & Murphy, J. (1989). Assessment of sexual arousal by means of physiological and self-report measures. In D. R. Laws (Ed.), *Relapse prevention with sex offenders* (pp. 115–123). New York: Guilford Press.

Hall, R. L. (1988). Assessment and diagnosis. In G. W. Barnard, A. K. Fuller, L. Robbins, & T. Shaw (Eds.), *The child molester: An integrative approach to evaluation and treatment* (pp. 48–56). New York: Brunner/Mazel.

Herman, J. (1990). Sex offenders: A feminist perspective. In W. L. Marshall, D. R. Laws, & H. E. Barbaree (Eds.), *Handbook of sexual assault: Issues, theories, and treatment of the offender* (pp. 177–194). New York: Plenum Press.

Hildebran, D., & Pithers, W. D. (1989). Enhancing offender empathy for sexual abuse victims. In D. R. Laws (Ed.), *Relapse prevention with sex offenders* (pp. 236–244). New York: Guilford Press.

Jenkins-Hall, K. D., & Marlatt, G. A. (1989). Apparently irrelevant decision in the relapse process. In D. R. Laws (Ed.), *Relapse prevention with sex offenders* (pp. 47–55). New York: Guilford Press.

Kaufman, M. (Ed.). (1987). *Beyond patriarchy: Essays on pleasure, power, and change.* New York: Oxford University Press.

Kernberg, O. (1973). Psychoanalytic object-relations theory, group processes and administration. *Annuals Psychoanalysis, 1,* 363–386.

Laws, D. R. (Ed.). (1989). *Relapse prevention with sex offenders.* New York: Guilford Press.

Lazur, R. F. (1992, August). Boundaries and power: The male sex offender in group. Paper presented at the 100th Annual Convention of the American Psychological Association, Washington, DC.

Levant, R. F. (1992). Towards the reconstruction of masculinity. *Journal of Family Psychology, 5,* 379–402.

Levant, R. F., & Pollock, W. S. (Eds.). (1995). *A new psychology of men.* New York: Basic Books.

Long, J. D., Wuesthoff, A., & Pithers, W. D. (1989). Use of autobiographies in the assessment and treatment of sex offenders. In D. R. Laws (Ed.), *Relapse prevention with sex offenders* (pp. 88–95). New York: Guilford Press.

MacDonald, R. K., & Pithers, W. D. (1989). Self-monitoring to identify high-risk situations. In D. R. Laws (Ed.), *Relapse prevention with sex offenders* (pp. 88–95). New York: Guilford Press.

Maletzky, B. M., & McGovern, K. B. (1990). *Treating the sexual offender.* Newbury Park, CA: Sage.

Mander, A. (1994). *Sex offender treatment programs standards of care.* Juneau: State of Alaska Department of Corrections.

Marshall, W. L., Laws, D. R., & Barbaree, H. E. (1990). *Handbook of sexual assault.* New York: Plenum.

McFall, R. M. (1990). The enhancement of social skills: An information-processing analysis. In W. L. Marshall, D. R. Laws, & H. E. Barbaree (Eds.), *Handbook of sexual assault: Issues, theories, and treatment of the offender* (pp. 311–330). New York: Plenum Press.

McGrath, R. J. (1991). Sex offender risk assessment and disposition planning: A review of empirical and clinical findings. *International Journal of Offender Therapy and Comparative Criminology, 35,* 328–350.

Miner, M. H., Day, D. M., & Nafpaktitis, M. K. (1989). Assessment of coping skills: Development of a situational competency test. In D. R. Laws (Ed.), *Relapse prevention with sex offenders* (pp. 127–136). New York: Guilford Press.

O'Connell, M. A., Leberg, E., & Donaldson, C. R. (1990). *Working with sex offenders.* Newbury Park, CA: Sage.

O'Neil, J. M. (1981). Patterns of gender role conflict and strain: Sexism and fear of femininity in men's lives. *Personnel and Guidance Journal, 60,* 203–209.

Overholser, J. C., & Beck, S. (1986). Multimethod assessment of rapists, child molesters, and three control groups on behavioral and psychological measures. *Journal of Consulting and Clinical Psychology, 54,* 682–687.

Piel Cook, E. (1990). Gender and psychological distress. *Journal of Counseling and Development, 68,* 371–375.

Pithers, W. D., Beal, L. S., Armstrong, J., & Petty, J. (1989). Identification of risk factors through clinical interviews and analysis of records. In D. R. Laws (Ed.), *Relapse prevention with sex offenders* (pp. 88–95). New York: Guilford Press.

Pithers, W. D., Kashima, K. M., Cummings, G. F., Beal, L. S., & Buell, M. M. (1988). Relapse prevention of sexual aggression. In R. Prentky & V. Quinsey (Eds.), *Annals of the New York Academy of Sciences: Vol. 528* (pp. 244–260). New York: New York Academy of Sciences.

Pithers, W. D., Martin, G. R., & Cummings, G. F. (1989). Vermont treatment program for sexual aggressors. In D. R. Laws (Ed.), *Relapse prevention with sex offenders* (pp. 127–136). New York: Guilford Press.

Pleck, J. H. (1975). Man to man: Is brotherhood possible? In N. G. Mablin (Ed.), *Old family/new family: Interpersonal relationships.* New York: Van Nostrand Reinhold.

Pleck, J. H. (1976). The male sex role: Problems, definitions, and sources of change. *Journal of Social Issues, 32,* 155–164.

Pleck, J. H. (1980). Men's power with women, other men, and society. In E. H. Pleck & J. H. Pleck (Eds.), *The American man* (pp. 417–433). Englewood Cliffs, NJ: Prentice Hall.

Pleck, J. H. (1981). *The myth of masculinity.* Cambridge, MA: MIT Press.

Prendergast, W. E. (1991). *Treating sex offenders in correctional institutions and outpatient clinics: A guide to practice.* Binghamton, NY: Haworth Press.

Quinsey, V. L., & Earls, C. M. (1990). The modification of sexual preferences. In W. L. Marshall, D. R. Laws, & H. E. Barbaree (Eds.), *Handbook of sexual assault: Issues, theories, and treatment of the offender* (pp. 279–295). New York: Plenum Press.

Rice, C. A., & Rutan, J. S. (1981). Boundary maintenance in inpatient therapy groups. *International Journal of Group Psychotherapy, 31,* 297–309.

Scher, M. (1979). On counseling men. *Personnel and Guidance Journal, 57,* 252–254.

Silverberg, R. A. (1986). *Psychotherapy for men: Transcending the male mystique.* Springfield, IL: Charles C Thomas.

Singer, D. L., Astrachan, B. M., Gould, L. J., & Klein, E. B. (1975). Boundary management in psychological work with groups. *Journal of Applied Behavioral Sciences, 11,* 137–176.

Stein, E., & Brown, J. D. (1991). Group therapy in a forensic setting. *Canadian Journal of Psychiatry, 36,* 718–722.

Stermac, L. E., Segal, Z. V., & Gillis, R. (1990). Social and cultural factors in sexual assault. In W. L. Marshall, D. R. Laws, & H. E. Barbaree (Eds.), *Handbook of sexual assault: Issues, theories, and treatment of the offender* (pp. 143–159). New York: Plenum Press.

Vinogradov, S., & Yalom, I. (1989). *Group psychotherapy.* Washington, DC: American Psychiatric Press.

Wheelis, A. (1969, May). How people change. *Commentary,* pp. 56–66.

Yochelson, S., & Samenow, S. E. (1976). *The criminal personality* (Vols. 1–2). New York: Jason Aronson.

AUTHOR INDEX

Numbers in italics refer to listings in reference sections.

411

Bitter, J. R., 67
Blakeslee, S., 247, 250, 256
Blaske, D. M., 379, 388
Blau, A., 339, 350
Bloom, B., 247, 255
Blount, J. P., 315, 316, 320, 321
Blumenfeld, W. J., 169, 177
Bly, R., 31, 92, 114, 126
Blythe, B. J., 295, 300
Bograd, M., 7, 17, 18
Bogren, L. Y., 291, 297
Bolton, F., 340, 350
Bonds-White, F., 186, 190
Borduin, C. H., 379, 388
Borg, M. J., 105, 111
Boulet, J., 390, 408
Bourne, P. G., 72, 79
Bowlby, J., 271
Bowman, P., 185, 190
Bowman, T., 272, 280
Boyd, J. H., 321
Boyd-Franklin, N., 131, 149
Bozett, F., 258, 260, 261, 267
Bradford, J. H. W., 380, 388
Bradford, J. M., 390, 394, 407, 408
Brannon, R., 21, 22, 32, 229, 230, 232,
       233, 239, 239, 332, 335, 389, 408
Breakey, W., 49
Brehm, S., 13, 18
Brende, J. O., 328, 335
Breunlin, D. C., 149
Briere, J., 45, 48
Brindis, C. D., 285, 295, 297
Brock, G. W., 274, 280
Brod, H. A., 18, 21, 31, 33
Brodsky, A., 370, 374
Bromberg, W., 165, 177
Brooks, G., 220, 227
Brooks, G. R., 7, 11, 18
Brooks-Gunn, J., 283, 298
Brown, J. D., 392, 410
Brown, R., 340, 350
Brown, R. D., 104, 111
Brown, S., 296n1, 297
Browne, A., 48, 358, 374
Budd, F. C., 309, 310, 321
Buell, M. M., 394, 409
Burke, J. E., 321
Burkhart, B. R., 340, 351
Burnam, A., 37, 39, 48
Burnett, D. J., 272, 273, 280
Burt, G. A., 295, 300

Calhoun, D. S., 340, 353
Callanan, P., 287, 298
Cameron, K., 350
Cameron, P., 340, 350
Campbell, J. L., 270, 280
Canavan, W., 340, 351
Cancian, F. M., 250, 254
Carden, A., 98, 111
Carlson, T. A., 81, 95
Cass, V. C., 170, 177
Cath, S., 220, 227
Catherall, D. R., 324, 325, 332, 335
Caton, C. L. M., 39, 48
Celentano, E., 240
Centron Films, 288, 297
Cerhan, J. U., 71, 73, 79
Cervantes, N., 359, 373, 374
Chao, G. T., 98, 111
Chapman, R. B., 22, 31
Charng, H., 250, 255
Charnon, E., 282
Chen, C., 73, 79
Children's Defense Fund, 283, 298
Chodorow, N., 220, 227
Christenson, C., 262, 267
Clark, L. A., 331, 337
Clarke-Stewart, K. A., 291, 298
Clatterbaugh, K. C., 21, 31
Claycomb, M., 284, 297
Coburn, W. J., 350
Cochran, S. D., 83, 94, 95, 165, 177
Cohen, C., 341, 353
Cohen, C. I., 39, 48
Cohen, M., 49
Cohen, N. L., 45, 49
Coleman, A., 186, 190
Coleman, E., 170, 177
Collegiate School, 290, 298
Collins, J. D., 273, 280
Condon, S. M., 271, 280
Condy, S., 340, 350
Conlon, I., 182, 186, 191
Conlon, M. F., 292, 300
Connell, R. W., 219, 227
Conover, S., 39, 49
Cook, D., 332, 337
Cooper, C. R., 270, 271, 280–282
Cope, N., 49
Corey, G., 70, 79, 287, 298
Corey, M. S., 287, 298
Corley, R., 260, 267
Corneau, G., 23, 31

Vessey, J. T., 7, *19*
Vinogradov, S., 403, *410*
Vogelsong, E., 279, *281*

Wagner, N. A., 340, *351*
Wainrib, B., 197
Waldron, I., 231, *241*
Walker, J. I., 327, *337*
Walker, L. E., 357, 360, 361, 373, *375*
Wallach, M. A., 39, *48*
Wallach, T., 182, *191*
Wallerstein, J. S., 247, 250, *256*
Walsh, F., *149*
Waltz, J., *374*
Washington, C., 134, *149*
Washington, C. S., 81, 83, 94, 96
Watson, D., 331, *337*
Watts, D., 184, *191*
Weinberg, G., 169, *179*
Weinberg, M., 258, *267*
Weinberg, S. K., 339, *353*
Weinstein, S. F., 235, *240*
Weiss, R., 245, *256*
Weiss, R. S., 103, *112*
Weissman, M. M., *321*
Werdinger, I. F., 272, *282*
Werrbach, G. B., 270, *282*
Werrbach, J., 22, *34*
Wheelis, A., 404, *410*
White, G. M., 71, *80*

Wiehe, V. R., 43, *48*
Wieman, R. J., 274, *282*
Wilinsky, H., 54, *68*
Wilson, W. J., *37, 49*
Winarski, J., *49*
Winnicott, D. W., 102, *112*
Wolleat, P., 23, *34*
Wong, M. R., 332, *337*
Woodley, T., 182, 189, *191*
Woods, W. J., 165, *179*
Wright, J. D., 36, 38, *49*
Wright, P., 13, *19*
Wright, R., 147, *149*
Wuesthoff, A., 400, *408*
Wyatt, R. J., 39, *48*
Wyer, T., 152, *161*

Yalom, I., 403, *410*
Yalom, I. D., 14, 15, *19*, 237, *241*, 245, 246, *256*, 307, 308, 317, *321*, 327, *337*
Yang, D., 73, *79*
Yankelovich, D., 100, *112*
Yochelson, S., 390–392, 394, 395, 400, 401, 403, 405, 407, *410*

Zaidi, L. Y., 45, *48*
Zane, N., 73, *80*
Zey, M., *112*

SUBJECT INDEX

Alcohol abuse and alcoholism (*continued*)
among homeless men, 39
as discussion topic in homeless men's group, 46
and fatherhood, 221n1
group treatment for men suffering from, 305–320
cognitive–behavioral interventions, 315–319
and identification of abuse or dependence, 306–307
interpersonal learning in, 308
obstacles to joining, 309
psychoanalytic therapy, 311–315
self-help groups, 309–311
therapeutic process in, 307–308
Alcoholics Anonymous (AA), 305, 310–311
Alexithymia, 232, 342–343
Alienation, in noncustodial fathers, 247–248
Alternative wisdom, 105
Anger, 58, 62–63. *See also* Rage
in African American men's groups, 136, 141–142
control of, in group of adolescent male sexual offenders, 384
homeless men's group, expressed in, 41
management of, with groups of batterers, 365
Another Way program, 368
Anxiety, pregroup, 220
Asian American men, 69–79
and academic achievement, 73
and acculturation into American society, 73–74
and demographics, 69
in groups, 74–79
assertiveness-training groups, 77
final meeting, 78
goals, group, 76–77
homework assignments, 78
initial meeting, 76
mixed-group work, 78
pregroup screening, 76
process, group, 77
recruitment, 75
worldview of, 70–73
emotional expression, 71
individualism versus collectivism, 72

power distribution, 72–73
Assertiveness-training groups, 77
Assessment
of adolescent male sexual offenders, 379–380
of male survivors of sexual abuse, 344–345
Audiovisual aids
in gender role journey workshop, 198, 204
in group of adolescent male sexual offenders, 384
in teenage-father groups, 288–290, 293
Avoidance
by batterers, 363–364
by sexual offenders, 400–401

Batterers and battering, 357–374
among homeless, 45–46
and avoidance, 363–364
behavioral dynamics of, 360–362
and control, 362
definition of battering, 358
group intervention, 366–373
composition of group, 368–369
functioning of group, 369–372
versus individual and couples counseling, 372
and therapist qualifications, 372–373
time frame for, 369
phenomenological experience of batterers, 362–363
psychotherapy clients, incidence of battering among, 359
statistics on, 358–359
and therapists' knowledge, 359–360
traits associated with batterers, 360
treatment approaches, 365–366
Behavior rehearsal, 28
Bibliotherapy, 64. *See also* Readings
Biological fathering, 244–245
Blacks. *See* African Americans
Boundary management, in intervention with sexual offenders, 395–399, 401
external boundaries, 396
internal boundaries, 398–399
and male gender role socialization, 396–397

Protégés, 98, 99
Psychoanalytic group therapy, 311–315
Psychological fathering, 244–245
PTSD. *See* Posttraumatic stress disorder

Quasi-group cohesion, 312–313

Racism, as topic in African American men's group, 141, 146
Rage, 62–63, 136, 141–142. *See also* Anger
Rapists, pedophiles versus, 392–393, 398
Rapport, establishment of therapeutic, 285–286
Readings
in gender role journey workshop, 198
for teenage-father groups, 295
Recognitions, 29
Recollections, processing of early, 61–62
Recording, of university-based group, 86–87
Recreational activities, in teenage-father groups, 287
Recruitment. *See also* Initial meeting and contact
Asian American men's group, 75
university-based group, 84–85
Relationship enhancement therapy, 273–275
Relationships, as theme of university-based group, 90–91
Resistance to therapy. *See also* Therapy-resistant men
among African American men, 134–136
among Hispanic men, 155–157
and male code, 231–233
in men with alcohol problems, 309
by teenage fathers, 285
Ritualized male groups, 12–13
Rituals
in African American men's groups, 146–147
in Somerset Institute's Modern Men's Weekend, 116–117
Robert Wood Johnson Foundation, 38
Role-playing, 28, 64. *See also* Modeling
in group of adolescent male sexual offenders, 384
in PARD, 277

Rotations, therapist, 87–89
Rules, group, 25

Safety, atmosphere of
in all-gay-male groups, 172
in middle-class men's groups, 57–58
Safety concerns
and female therapists, 182–183
in group treatments for PTSD, 329–330
Sages, 105
Screenings, pregroup
Asian men's groups, 76
gay-father groups, 264–265
Self-disclosure
by adult male victims of sexual abuse, 343, 348–349
encouraging, in therapy-resistant men, 14–15
by therapist, 28
Self-help groups, for men with alcohol problems, 309–311
Setting. *See* Physical setting
Sexism, 14, 169
as focus of batterers' groups, 367
as topic of discussion, in gender role journey workshop, 209–210
Sexual abuse. *See also* Sexual offenders
among homeless men, 39
by gay fathers, 262–263
male disclosure of child, 341–343
research on child, 339–341
as topic in African American men's group, 140–141
treatment model for male survivors of, 344–350
assessment, 344–345
formal disclosure exercise, 348–349
group phase, 345–349
individual phase, 344–345
physical enactments, 346–348
prevailing phase, 349–350
referral, 349
structure of group, 345–346
symbols and language, development of, 345
termination, 349
Sexual behavior, as focus of teenage-father groups, 293–295

in Somerset Institute's Modern Men's
Weekend, 117–124
storytelling, 60
support and trust work, 63
talking stick, 60–61
therapist, self-disclosure by, 28
touching, 26, 28
Teenage fathers, 283–297
adjustment difficulties facing, 285
establishment of rapport with,
285–286
resistance to therapy by, 285
stereotypical views of, 284
therapeutic groups for, 286–297
attitudes, clarification of, 286–289
child development education and
parenting skills training in,
289–293
sexual behavior as focus of,
293–295
termination issues, 295–296
Tension, and battering, 360–361
Terminations
African American men's groups,
136–138, 145
Asian men's groups, 78
giving notice, rule for, 25
male abuse survivors, group of, 349
plan for living, submission of, 28
teenage-father groups, 295–296
university-based group, 89
Therapist. *See also* Female therapists
African American men's groups,
145–147
batterers' groups, 359–360, 372–373
and gay-affirmative psychotherapy,
176
in homeless men's group, 42
modeling and self disclosure by, 28
in PARD, 276–278
rotations of, in university-based
group, 87–89
Therapy-resistant men, 7–17
all-male therapy groups for, advantages of, 12–17
communication skills, potential to
improve, 16
emotional isolation, potential to
overcome, 13–14
emotions, potential to uncover
suppressed, 15–16
familiarity, 12–13

hope, instillation of, 15
overdependence on women, potential to overcome, 14
participative self-disclosure, encouragement of, 14–15
engagement of, 9–11
hard-sell approach, 10
soft-sell approach, 10–11
individual therapy for, problems with,
12
marital and family therapy for, disadvantages of, 11
steps in therapeutic process, 9
successful outcomes with, 8–9
Touching, 26, 28
Traditional fathers, 244
Transference. *See also* Countertransference
and female therapists, 186–189
in groups of adult male sexual offenders, 403–404
Trust
in African American men's group,
142
in all-gay-male groups, 174
exercises for development of, 63

Universality, 245
University-based groups, 81–94
class and classism in, 84
confidentiality in, 87
description of group, 82–83
formats, 82–83, 85–86
future directions for, 93–94
intergenerational issues affecting,
83–84
limitations of, 94
new members, ritual for, 87
obstacles to starting, 84–86
open-group format, disadvantages of,
85–86
recording sessions of, 86–87
recruitment for, 85
setting of, 86, 93–94
terminations, 89
themes of, 89–93
codependency, 90–91
fathering, 91–92
mothers, 92–93
relationships, 90
therapist rotations in, 87–89

Videotapes, in group of adolescent male sexual offenders, 384
Violence against women. *See* Batterers and battering
Virginia, 259
Vision quest, 115–116

Wisdom, 105
Women. *See also* Batterers and battering; Female therapists
   in gender role journey workshop, 209–210

overcoming overdependence on, in therapy-resistant men, 14
physical and emotional illness, susceptibility to, 231
relative openness to therapy, 11
Women in Transition group, 85
Work, and struggle for self-determination, 54–55
Writing, creative, 64

Zero state, 405

ABOUT THE EDITOR

Michael P. Andronico's interest in groups began before he received his PhD from Rutgers University in 1963. He has been leading groups, including men's groups, for over 35 years. He is a Fellow of the American Psychological Association (APA) and is presently President of APA's Division of Group Psychology and Group Psychotherapy. He is past president of the Group Psychotherapy Section of APA's Division of Psychotherapy.

Michael Andronico is also a Fellow of the American Group Psychotherapy Association and a past president of the New Jersey Group Psychotherapy Society. He is currently Clinical Professor of Psychiatry at the University of Medicine and Dentistry of New Jersey, Robert Wood Johnson Medical School.

Throughout his career, Michael Andronico has taught and supervised clinicians, focusing on group settings. He has conducted workshops on group psychotherapy and men's groups at local, state, national, and international professional meetings. He has many years of experience consulting with agencies and institutions, using the group format to develop group programs and group supervision. He has published extensively on these subjects, in both journals and books. He has also been interviewed on network television about men's issues. Michael Andronico currently practices in Somerset, New Jersey, and is the Clinical Director of the Somerset Institute for Psychotherapy, Education, and Research.